# The
# Mystic
# Fable

Hieronymus Bosch, detail of central panel of *The Garden of Earthly Delights,*
Prado, Madrid. Photograph: Giraudon/Art Resource, New York.

Michel de Certeau

# ✠ The ✠
# ✠ Mystic
# ✠ Fable ✠

Volume One

*The Sixteenth and
Seventeenth Centuries*

Translated by Michael B. Smith

The University of Chicago Press
*Chicago & London*

# RELIGION AND POSTMODERNISM
*A series edited by Mark C. Taylor*

The University of Chicago Press, Chicago 60637
The University of Chicago Press, Ltd., London
© 1992 by The University of Chicago
All rights reserved. Published 1992
Paperback edition 1995
Printed in the United States of America
01 00 99 98 97 96 95    5 4 3 2

ISBN (cloth): 0-226-10036-7
ISBN (paper): 0-226-10037-5

Originally published as *La Fable Mystique, XVIe–XVIIe Siècle,* by
Michel de Certeau. © Éditions Gallimard, 1982.

Library of Congress Cataloging-in-Publication Data

Certeau, Michel de.
  [Fable Mystique. English]
  The mystic fable / Michel de Certeau ; translated by Michael B.
Smith.
     p.   cm. — (Religion and postmodernism)
  Translation of : La fable mystique.
  Includes bibliographical references.
  Contents: v. 1. The sixteenth and seventeenth centuries.
  1. Mysticism—Europe—History—16th century.   2. Mysticism—
Europe—History—17th century.   I. Title.   II. Series.
BV5077.E85c4713   1992
248.2'2'09409031—dc20                                    91-4827
                                                          CIP

# CONTENTS

# II

# *A Topics*

# III

# *The Circumstances of the Mystic Utterance*

# IV

# *Figures of the Wildman*

# Translator's Note

The present text is neither a paraphrase nor an adaptation but a translation. The concomitant restrictions have led to some stylistic strangeness at times. A refusal on the author's part to choose between a connotative and a denotative mode of expression has prohibited my opting neatly for a conceptual or a literary approach in translation. Resolutely middle-of-the-road, my ambition has been the salvaging of main meanings, and as much of the co-meant as I could. What the French reader finds, stylistically, in the original is a firm, probing movement that does not give way to striking approximations or the attraction of its own reverberations: an elegant, unhurried accuracy in which historical hypotheses have time to assess and assimilate the significance of "resistances" encountered en route. Long paragraphs induce the emergence of historical configurations at the intersection of several planes of analysis.

One of the major difficulties for the translator of this volume has been the relative paucity of terms, in post-Reformation English, to match the rich store of ecclesiastical and theological vocabulary still current and available within the tradition of French Catholicism. More serious still, the theme of Michel de Certeau's *Mystic Fable* is *la mystique*. This term cannot be rendered accurately by the English word "mysticism," which would correspond rather to the French *le mysticisme,* and be far too generic and essentialist a term to convey the historical specificity of the subject of this study. There is no need here to retrace the steps by which *la mystique,* the noun, emerged from the prior adjective, *mystique,* as that process is carefully reconstructed in chapter 3. But it may be of some interest to note that this grammatical promotion has its parallel in English, in the development of such terms as "mathematics" or "physics," fields of inquiry of increasing autonomy, also taking their names from an adjectival forerunner. I have, therefore, *in extremis,* adopted the bold solution of introducing a made-up English term, *mystics* (always in italics, to distinguish it from the plural of "a mystic"), to render *la mystique,* a field that might have won (but never did, in English) a name alongside metaphysics, say, or optics.

My heartfelt thanks to Luce Giard, who has checked the entire translation against the original, enhancing the accuracy of the former in a great many instances; and to Ellen R. Feldman, for her painstaking editorial help during the final stages of this project. I gratefully acknowledge the support of Berry College and Kathy Gann's professional assistance with manuscript preparation. For checking my rendering of de Certeau's translation of Palladios against the Greek original, thanks are due my colleague Marc-André Wiesmann, and for her patience with my abstraction over the last few years, to my wife Helen.

# Introduction

This book does not lay claim to any special jurisdiction over its domain. It stands exiled from its subject matter. It is devoted to mystic
discourse of (or about) presence (of God), but its own discourse does
not share that status. It emerges from a mourning, an unaccepted
mourning that has become the malady of bereavement, perhaps akin
to the ailment melancholia, which was already a hidden force in sixteenth-century thought. One who is missing moves it to be written.
This story continues to be written during travels through a country
from which I'm away. In explicating the conditions of production of
this text, I desire from the outset to strip this log of my textual
peregrinations of the prestige (in this case they would be brazenly
immodest, even obscene) of being taken for a discourse accredited by
a presence, authorized to speak in its name, or presumed privy to an
insider's knowledge.

What should be there is missing. Quietly, almost painlessly, this
discovery takes effect. It afflicts us in a region we cannot identify, as if
we had been stricken by the separation long before realizing it. When
this situation finds expression, it may still borrow the words of the
ancient Christian prayer: "May I not be separated from Thee." Not
without Thee. *Nicht ohne.*[1] But the necessary, having become the
improbable, is in fact the impossible. Such is the figure of desire. It is
obviously a part of the long history of that *One*, the origin and meta-

1

morphoses of which so intrigued Freud. One sole being is lacking, and all is lacking. This new beginning orders a sequel of wanderings and pursuits. One suffers the pangs of absence because one suffers the pangs of the One.

The One is no longer to be found. "They have taken him away," say so many chants of the mystics who inaugurate, with the story of his loss, the history of his returns elsewhere and otherwise, in ways that are the effect rather than the refutation of his absence. While no longer "living," this "dead" one still does not leave the city—which was formed without him—in peace. He haunts our environs. A theology of phantoms would doubtless be capable of analyzing how he reappears on another stage than the one from which he vanished. Such a theology would be the theory of this new status. Hamlet's father's ghost once became the law of the castle in which he was no longer present. Similarly, the absent one who is no longer in heaven nor on earth inhabits a strange third region (neither one nor the other). His "death" has placed him in that limbo. Speaking in approximate terms, this is the region the mystic authors designate for us today.

These ancient authors introduce into our present-day world the language of a "nostalgia" in relation to that other country. There they create and maintain a place for something like the Brazilian *saudade*, a homesickness—if it is true that this other country also remains our own, but we are separated from it. What these authors bring into play is therefore not reducible to an interest in the past, nor even to a voyage into the recesses of our memory. They are like statues erected to mark the boundaries of an "elsewhere" that is not remote, a place they both produce and guard. They form, with their bodies and their texts, a frontier that divides space and transforms their reader into an inhabitant of the country, or the suburbs, far from the nowhere where they house the essential. They articulate in this way the foreignness of our own place, and therefore a desire to return to our native land. I, like Kafka's "man from the country," asked them to let me enter. At first, the doorkeeper would answer, "It is possible, but not at the moment." After twenty years of waiting "near the door," I have come to know, "by examining him," the appointed keeper of the threshold down to the least details, "even the fleas in his fur collar." So it has been with my guardian Jean-Joseph Surin and many others—more than a match for my most patient erudition—whose texts never ceased peering down upon my search. Again, Kafka's doorkeeper says, "I am only the least of the doorkeepers. From hall to hall there is one doorkeeper after another, each more powerful than the last. The third doorkeeper is already so terrible that even I cannot bear to look at him."[2] He, too, is foreign to the soil he delimits in marking the threshold. Should the same be said of these mystics?

Does the laborious waiting in front of these night watchmen allow one at last to behold "a radiance that streams inextinguishably from the gateway of the Law?" That brightness, Kafka's allusion to the *Shekinah* of God in the Jewish tradition, may be the very radiance of a desire that has come from "elsewhere."[3] But it gives itself up neither to work nor to age. It is testamentary: a kiss of death. It appears only at the moment when the door closes before the dying man, that is to say, at the moment when the demand is extinguished, not of itself, but from lack of vital forces to sustain it. At that point, the separation is accomplished. The guard leans over to shout to the dying man the true nature of his wait: "This gate was made only for you. Now I am leaving, and I am closing the door."[4] Until that final hour, the task of writing remains. Its labor in the interval draws on the unacceptable and insurmountable division. It lasts (and will last) for as many years as there are between the first request the man from the country addressed to the keeper of his desire and the moment when the angel withdraws, leaving the word that puts an end to patience. Why, indeed, does one write, near the threshold, sitting on the stool mentioned in Kafka's story, unless it is to struggle against the inevitable?

## SQUARING THE MYSTIC CIRCLE

The color overflows its designated space. In Uccello, there is a flow of red across the frames that break up *The Profanation of the Host* into scenes—the blood of the painting crossing the compartments of the narrative. In Miró, too, the throbbing of color pierces with its arrows the space created for its thrusts. There is hemorrhage of these fluxes beyond their bodies. An analogous overflow mocks my efforts to delineate, in the thicket of our data and analytic apparatus, the sequence of a narrative account whose subject is Christian *mystics* in the sixteenth and seventeenth centuries. Nevertheless, a demarcation is necessary, if only so that what overflows its borders may become visible. Here are the areas of inquiry on the basis of which the advancing lines of four approaches, like four sides of a frame, will gradually appear: the link between this "modern" *mystics* and a new eroticism, a psychoanalytic theory, historiography itself, and the "fable" (which relates simultaneously to orality and fiction). These four discursive practices establish a framework. The organization of a space, though necessary, will be seen to be unable to "stop" the subject matter. It places mystic speech within a set of codifications that cannot contain it. It is a form whose matter overflows. At least this explanation of my "interests," in circumscribing the framework within which a representation is to be produced, will allow us to see the way the subject crosses the stage, escapes and flows beyond.

## An Eroticism of the Body/God

As a certain *mystics* was developing and then declining in modern Europe, a form of eroticism appeared. This was no mere coincidence. Both sprang from a "nostalgia" connected with the progressive decline of God as One, the object of love. Both are equally the effects of a separation. Despite all the inventions and the conquests that have marked that Occident of the One (the fall of the ancient Sun of the universe inaugurated the modern Western world), despite the proliferation of arts that made possible the maintaining of some kind of relationship with presences that are now all vanishing, despite the replacement of the Missing One by an indefinite series of ephemeral productions, the ghost of the One always returns. Possessions themselves are structured around something *lost.* Thus Don Juan, anxiously pursuing his *mille e tre* conquests, knows they repeat the absence of the unique, inaccessible "woman." He goes running toward the specter of disappearance, the statue of the commander, with a gesture of defiance that has the value of a suicide and that confronts, at last, the non-place of the other. Not without thee, Death.

Since the thirteenth century (courtly love, etc.), a gradual religious demythification seems to be accompanied by a progressive mythification of love. The One has changed its site. It is no longer God but the other, and in a masculine literature, woman. In place of the divine word (which also had a physical nature and value), the loved body (which is no less spiritual and symbolic, in erotic practice) is substituted. But the adored body is as elusive as the vanishing God. It haunts writing, which sings its loss without being able to accept it—a process that is itself erotic. Despite the changes of scene, the One does not cease organizing by its absence a "Western" productivity that develops in two directions: now proliferating conquests destined to fill an original lack, now returning to the principle of these conquests and wondering about the "vacancy" of which they are the effects.

Into this latter category falls the mystic configuration that extends from the thirteenth to the seventeenth century, and that was both bound and hostile to a technicalizing of society. It carries to the point of radicalism the confrontation with the vanishing entity of the cosmos. It refuses to mourn it, at a time when this seems acceptable to others who think they could come to terms with that loss. It accepts the challenge of the unique. Its literature, therefore, has all the traits of what it both opposes and posits: it is the trial, by language, of the ambiguous passage from presence to absence. It bears witness to the slow transformation of the religious setting into an amorous one, or of faith into eroticism. It tells how a body "touched" by desire and engraved, wounded, written by the other, replaced the revelatory, didactic word. Thus, the mystics struggled with mourning, that angel of the night; but the medieval propaedeutics of an assimilation to truth became, with them, hand-to-hand combat.

Of course their procedures are sometimes contradictory, since in multiplying the mental and physical techniques that fixed the conditions of possibility of an encounter or dialogue with the Other (method of prayer, meditation, concentration, etc.), they end up, in spite of having laid down the principle of an absolute gratuitousness, producing an ersatz presence. That preoccupation with technique is already the effect of what it opposes. Unbeknownst even to some of its promoters, the creation of mental constructs (imaginary compositions, mental void, etc.) takes the place of attention to the advent of the Unpredictable. That is why the "true" mystics are particularly suspicious and critical of what passes for "presence." They defend the inaccessibility they confront.

The essential question concerns the possibility of hearing and of making oneself heard: the question of prayer or of contemplation. No messenger could possibly be a substitute for the Unique:

> *Acaba de entregarte ya de vero;*
> *no quieras enviarme*
> *de hoy más ya mensajero,*
> *que no saben decirme lo que quiero.*

> Surrender thou thyself completely.
> From today do thou send me
> Now no other messenger,
> For they cannot tell me what I wish.[5]

The Word itself had to be born in the void that awaited it. That had been the theology of the Rhenish in the thirteenth and fourteenth centuries. It survived still in the works of John of the Cross, an intellectual who remained very scholastic. But already in his works, or in those of Teresa of Avila (more "modern" than he) and after him, the approach took physical forms, more concerned with a symbolic capacity of the body than with an incarnation of the Verb. It was an approach that caressed, wounded, ascended the scale of perceptions, attained the ultimate point, which it transcended. It "spoke" less and less. It was written in unreadable messages on the body transformed into an emblem or a memorial engraved with the sufferings of love. The spoken word [*parole*] remained outside of this body, written but indecipherable, for which an erotic discourse would henceforth be in search of words [*mots*] and images. While the Eucharist (a central locus of this displacement) made of the body an effectuation of the spoken word, the mystic body ceased being transparent of meaning; it became opaque, the mute setting for a "je ne sais quoi" that altered it, a lost land equally alien to speaking subjects and to the texts of a truth.

Besides, despite the difference between the types of experience, the word appeared less and less certain with the passing of generations. In the middle of the seventeenth century, Angelus Silesius, whose poems aspired to the paternal word that would call him "son," used the conditional whenever he referred to that founding nomination, as if, by that suspensive modality, he were admitting that he already knew that what he awaited could no longer come and that he had nothing but the substitute "consolation" of musical strophes repeating an aspiration while lulling a mourning to sleep. No doubt it is true that, for reasons that need clarifying, the woman's experience held up better against the cluttered ruins of symbolic systems, which were theological and masculine, and which thought of presence as the coming of a Logos. But precisely the presence to which these Mothers and Ladies bore witness disengaged itself from the Word. It was, the "pure love" of Madame Guyon included, the echo of a voice in a "sleep" of the spirit, a diffuse, wakeful awareness of nameless rumors, an infinity of the Other, the certainties of which, nights of the body, no longer had any points of reference on the level of signifiers.

## TRANSITIONAL FORMS: *MYSTICS* AND PSYCHOANALYSIS

Through the mutations of the spoken word, these mystics explored all possible modes (both theoretical and practical) of communication, which they viewed as an issue formally separable from the hierarchical organization of knowledge and the validity of statements. In isolating a way of inquiring we can recognize today as being that of the speech act, and which at that time took the form of a dichotomy between love and knowledge, and the privilege of the relation over the proposition, and so on, they took leave of the medieval universe.[6] They moved into the modern period. That transformation, however, took place within the world that was "passing away." It respected, by and large, the religious language that had been passed on to it, but used it differently. It still addressed, generally, the members and producers of that universe (clerics, the faithful) in the terms of their tradition, but it deconstructed from within the values they held to be essential. From the certainty of the divine Interlocutor whose language is the cosmos to the verifiability of the propositions that made up the content of revelation, from the priority of the Book over the body to the (ontological) supremacy of an order of beings over a law of desire, there was not one postulate of this medieval world that was not touched or undermined by the radicalism of these mystics.[7]

Their "experimental science" thus introduced a series of new problems that, though still elaborated within the framework of the field they were transforming, were nonetheless bound up with one another. The question of the subject, the strategies of interlocution, a new "pathology" of bodies and societies, a conception of historicity founded on the present instant, theories of absence, of desire or of love, and so on, formed, by their intertwining, a coherent whole. But their application within a field epistemologically foreign to them was unstable and limited. It would give way, together with its presupposed world. Of course, the directions of inquiry thus opened up would occasion important movements, but they would lead away from the mystic constellation and undergo other evolutions depending on new configurations. Many a mystic "motif" would reappear, but changed, in turn, into another discipline (psychological, philosophical, psychiatric, novelistic, etc.). It is as if the negative process of scrutinizing and auditing the accounts of the era, which was conducted by that *mystics*, were completed, by the end of the seventeenth century, with the downfall of the system that had maintained the process—but it was that very process that carried the system's contradictions to the extreme. Hundreds of brilliant fragments remain, products of the innovations permitted or required by a period of transition.

It would not be farfetched to compare the current history of psychoanalysis with the fate of the epistemological configuration of *mystics*. Psychoanalysis, too, was intended for the producers and clients of the "bourgeois" system, which even now supports it, and is bound to their "values" and to the nostalgic longings of an age that is replacing the bourgeois with the technician or the technocrat. Yet psychoanalysis at the same time undermines the presuppositions of the bourgeois system: the a priori of individual units (upon which a liberal economy and a democratic society rest), the privileged status of consciousness (the principle of the "enlightened" society), the myth of progress (a conception of time) and its corollary, the myth of "education" (which makes the transformation of a society and of its members the ethical duty of the elite), and so on. But that erosion takes place within the field it destroys by questioning the conditions of its possibility. Psychoanalysis, moreover, only maintains itself thanks to the "resistances" it encounters within the bourgeois society and thanks to a "presumed knowledge," further defined by the ideology of a culture, a knowledge with which it accredits itself in order to ply and make use of the faith it inspires.

That analogy of functioning between *mystics* and psychoanalysis may appear strengthened by the role played by the religious and Jewish frame of reference in Freud, or, in Lacan, by the entity of *mystics*, which comes in at strategic moments of discourse. But rather than an affinity of sources, which is always questionable, it is the characteristic procedures common to both that present a strange similarity. In both fields, the steps consist in (1) launching a radical attack against the founding principles of the historical system within which these procedures are carried out; (2) authorizing a critical analysis by establishing a space (be it "mystical" or "unconscious") posited as different but not distant from the configuration organized by those founding principles of the historical system; (3) specifying theory and practice through a central attention given to enunciation ("prayer" or "transference"), the interrogation of which eludes the logic of statements and is supposed to make possible the transformation of social "contracts" by setting out from the subjects' structuring relations; (4) supposing that the body, far from being ruled by discourse, is itself a symbolic language and that it is the body that is responsible for a truth (of which it is unaware); (5) seeking in representations the traces of the affects ("intentions" and "desires," etc., or motive and drives) that produce them, and perceiving the "tricks" (the rhetorical "devices") that produce the quid pro quos between the hidden and the shown.

One could adduce many other examples. They could be further explicated by the recurrence of "concepts" that, in both domains, organize the lexicon that is used: "the Other" or "otherness," "desire," the "splitting" of the subject, "strange familiarity," the duplicity of "ownness," the narcissistic mirror, the vocabulary of sexuality and difference, and so on. The elements that are thus repeated, in practices and in words, from the sixteenth to the twentieth century, could not be pure coincidence.

These homologies at least authorize comparisons between the two fields. The interest analysts have taken in mystical phenomena or texts, which falls within a long psychiatric tradition, has made possible the elaboration of theoretical instruments appropriate to that confrontation. But in attempting, for my own part, this dual practice, I do not take for granted that there is, within the present-day Freudian and Lacanian tradition, a body of concepts capable of accounting for a past "object." Seventeen years of experience at the École freudienne de Paris have not produced a competency that it would suffice merely to "apply" to historical cases, but rather an awareness of theoretical procedures (Freudian and Lacanian) capable of bringing into play what the language of the mystics had already articulated and capable of displacing and amplifying its effects. These theoretical procedures can become caught up in the very reversals they bring to light. This mutual seizure threatens to make us "forget" ("I don't want to know about it") the fundamental distinctions that must be maintained; but it occasions, by a movement of frontiers, what we call a *reading*, that is, innumerable ways of deciphering, in the texts, what has already written us.

SAYING THE OTHER: HISTORIES OF ABSENCES

The mystic groups and books nevertheless constitute a specific *historical* reality. Although, from that point of view, they appear in the formal guise of absence—a past—they are amenable to an analysis that sets them within a multiplicity of correlations among economic, social, cultural, epistemological, and other data. To establish these coherences (correlation is the instrument of the historian) is to preserve the difference of the past from the seduction of partial resemblances, from generalizations suggested by philosophical impatience, or from continuities postulated by genealogical piety. My work on mystic writings—which began with years of peregrination in French or foreign archives, caverns in which the tenacity of research masks the solitary pleasure of the lucky find—wended its way through the labyrinthian (and how very full of ruse after all) detours of establishing critical editions.[8] It comes from many a sojourn in these remote corners of the past that reveal to the historian the infinitude of a local singularity.

These paths cannot be forgotten. They initiate us into a strangeness that never stops surprising us and dominating our expectation. They also have their rules. The patient application of technical scholarship is the price of preserving historical difference. In this process, a "negative work" is carried out within the double "fiction" of images of the past and of scientific models. The historian delves within that space, sculpturing a historiography. The accumulated, correlated documents must acquire the capacity to alter, by their resistance, the body of hypotheses and codifications on the basis of which we try to interpret them.

The mystics, too, lead us back to these particularities that block the demonstrations of meaning. Interspersed in their writings are the "almost nothing" of sensations, of meetings or daily tasks. What is of fundamental importance is inseparable from the insignificant. This is what makes the anodyne stand out in bold relief. Something stirs within the everyday. The mystic discourse transforms the detail into myth; it catches hold of it, blows it out of proportion, multiplies it, divinizes it. It makes it into its own kind of historicity. This pathos of the detail (which is reminiscent of the delights and the torments of the lover and the erudite scholar) is manifested first in the way the minute detail suspends meaning in the continuum of interpretation. A play of light arrests the reader's attention: ecstatic instant, a spark of insignificance, this fragment of the unknown introduces a silence into the hermeneutic medley. Thus, little by little, common everyday life begins to seethe with a disturbing familiarity—a frequentation of the Other.

Perhaps a historiography devoted to a few of these mystics should espouse their own practice of time—should lose itself, for example, in erudite detail. But this would be little more than seeming similarity or mimicry. It does seem possible, at least, to place at the center of a study of these mystic accounts the madness of Surin (1600–1655), which is disseminated in a thousand and one fragments throughout the depths of the archives and which was brought on by the disintegration of the cosmological architecture on which John of the Cross could still rely. It is a radicalism induced by a disintegration. It tells its story in the form of an "experimental science" of singularities in which something essential is at stake. It furnishes the blind spot, the heart of darkness within the period from Teresa of Avila to Johannes Scheffler the Silesian (Angelus Silesius). Of course, in retrospect, other reasons can justify this choice. The region of Bordeaux (where Surin was born and died) is the area of transition (and translation) from sixteenth-century mystic Spain to seventeenth-century mystic France. The milieu, the period, and Surin's writings manifest, moreover, the tensions and innovations that, like a barrier reef, raise the mystic wave as it nears the land upon which it will break. From this moment onward, we can move backward toward the horizon from which it came, and finally, analyze the decisive points where the movement dispersed, violently or evenly, on the shores of another figure of history.[9]

None of this, however, constitutes a reconstruction. Something has been lost that will not return. Historiography is a contemporary form of mourning. Its writing is based on an absence and produces nothing but simulacra, however scientific. It offers representation in the place of bereavement. Doubtless it is not certain that we know the present any better than the past nor that equivocalness is any less prevalent in present-day communication. At least in the present we can nourish the illusion of overcoming what the past has rendered insurmountable. Thus it is that the historian of the mystics, summoned, as they are, to *say the other*, repeats their experience in studying it: an exercise of absence defines at once the operation by which he produces his text and that which constructed theirs. A mirrorlike structure: like Narcissus, the historian-actor observes his reflection, which the movement of another element makes it impossible for him to grasp. He seeks one who has vanished, who in turn sought one who had vanished, and so on.

But in fact the symmetry is partially the effect of an optical illusion. Of course, there is an obvious continuity from religion (or *mystics*) to historiography, since both have taken in hand the relationship that a society maintains with its dead and the repairs that meaningful discourse, torn by the violence of conflicts and chance, constantly requires. But the historian "calms" the dead and struggles against violence by producing a reason for things (an "explanation") that overcomes their disorder and assures permanence; the mystic does it by founding existence on his very relationship with what escapes him. The former is interested in difference as an instrument to make distinctions in his material; the latter, as a split inaugurating the question of the subject.

Their practices of time diverge as well. The historian makes time, via chronology, a way of classifying data. He takes the further precaution of relegating all problems of birth to the past. A historiography can never truly think a beginning: it "reduces" it technically to the crossings of series, or simply notes it as a gap in the explanation. Historiography deals only with regularities and their modifications. That avoidance, a limitation imposed by a scientific intent, has as its corollary a parallel avoidance, concerning the knowing subject and the locus of the production of the text, that is, the present beginning and underlying postulate of the work. The establishment of historiography claims answerability for these questions: they are taken care of by its manner of selection and its "discipline."

On the contrary, the mystic is seized by time as by that which erupts and transforms, which is why time is for him the question of the subject seized by his or her other, in a present that is the ongoing surprise of a birth and a death. The endlessness of instants that are beginnings create, therefore, a historicity in which continuities lose their pertinence, just as institutions do. These events, which must be nothing but arrivals from an (impossible?) eternity or a (postponed) end, continually contradict the time produced by historiography. But to what degree can they insinuate another type of duration into historiographical time?

## WHAT REMAINS OF THE FABLE

This intertwining of similarities and differences defines, perhaps, a space. This book, born of the seductive (at times deceptive, at other times creative) intersections between historiography and *mystics*, is situated within this space.[10] It is the product of tensions that have no resolution. It is animated by a final inquiry, which is related to the preceding ones, if it is in fact true that historiography begins at the point where the mourning of the *voice* begins, where work is done on written (engraved, penned, printed) documents. Since a slow revolution has endowed writing with the new power of re-forming the world and remaking history, in short, of producing a different society, oral culture has gradually been abandoned, like so many pockets of "resistance" and "superstition" (that is, of excesses) along the wayside of progress, when it has not in fact become the object of a scriptural *conquista*. Historiography has followed the path of that evolution. Today, even though the transformations introduced by the methods of ethnology and oral history are changing that determination somewhat, historiography remains dominant, a symptom of societies having become dominated by writing.

The spoken word [*parole*] in particular, so closely bound to religious traditions, has evolved, since the sixteenth century, into what its scientific "examiners" and "observers" have for three centuries been designating as the "fable." This term originally referred to the stories whose task it was to symbolize a society, stories that were therefore in competition with historiographic discourse. For the *Aufklärung*, although the "fable" speaks [*fari*], it does not know what it is saying, and one must rely on the writer-interpreter to obtain the knowledge it expresses without knowing it. It is therefore discarded, classed with "fiction," and like all fiction, it is presumed to mask or to have mislaid the meaning it contains. Whatever the precise details may be of the progressive formation of what, beginning in the eighteenth century, took the form of an anthropology of ancient or contemporary "fables," the transformation that weakened the epistemological and cultural status of the spoken word also relates what had taken place in the religious domain, and marked it profoundly. From the Reformation on, the Scriptures opened up the road to writing and literacy. The primacy of the book was established.[11] The cosmos spoken by God and by church institutions is replaced by the production and methodical learning of an elementary or theological knowledge, a "clericalization" of religious authority, an administrative technicalization of the Churches, and so on.[12] A question emerges at the same time: What *remains* of the spoken word, without which there is no faith? Where does the spoken word subsist? Reformed Christians thought that if the institutions, having become corrupt, were destined to be mute, it was nevertheless possible to hear the teaching spoken Word in the Scriptures. Exegesis, from the seventeenth century on, undermined that confidence. Therefore, the spirituals sought elsewhere and otherwise what could, what *should* speak. They took stock in the promise that had been made: the Spirit would speak. But they found themselves in an analogous situation to the one described in the Bible itself, when after the Babylonian exile, the feeling spread that the prophetic voices no longer spoke.

As early as the thirteenth century, that is, since the time when theology became professionalized, spirituals and mystics took up the challenge of the spoken word. In doing so, they were displaced toward the area of the "fable." They formed a solidarity with all the tongues that continued speaking, marked in their discourse by the assimilation to the child, the woman, the illiterate, madness, angels, or the body. Everywhere they insinuate an "extraordinary": they are voices quoted—voices grown more and more separate from the field of meaning that writing had conquered, ever closer to the song or the cry. Therefore, their movements traverse an economy of the written work and die out, it seems, with the triumph of writing. So it is that the passing figure of *mystics* continues to ask us what remains of the spoken word. That question, moreover, is not unrelated to what, in its own area, psychoanalysis restores.[13]

My analysis of the history of *mystics* revolves, then, around that *mystic fable*. It is only the story of a journey, fragmented by its recourse to diverse methods (historical, semiotic, psychoanalytic), whose techniques make possible the successive definition of definable "objects" within an undefinable reality. Like the painting by Bosch that introduces it, that reality ultimately defies investigation: it overpowers the inquiry with something resembling a laugh. Such would be the "meaning" of this history: the secret that a book, like Kafka's doorkeeper, keeps without possessing it.

## A HISTORIC FORMATION

Sixteenth- and seventeenth-century *mystics* proliferated about a loss. It is the historical figure of that loss, making readable an absence that has multiplied the productions of desire. At the threshold of modernity, an end and a beginning are thus marked—a departure. That literature offers routes to whomever "asks directions to get lost" and seeks "a way not to come back."[14] Down the paths or ways of which so many mystic texts speak goes the itinerant walker, *Wandersmann.*[15]

That *mystics* refers to the collective history of a passage as much as it does to inaugural "wanderings." It appears at sunset to announce a day it will not see; it disappears before morning, the "rout of the mystics" coinciding, as it does, with the rise of the Enlightenment. It is the ambition of a Christian radicalism traced on a background of decadence or "corruption," within a universe that is falling apart and must be repaired. It reiterates at the level of biographical experience all the vocabulary of the Church Reformation: division, wounds, sickness, lying, desolation, and so on. Individual bodies tell the story of the institutions of meaning. The end of a world is postulated in all of the spiritual poetics. Their bright and daring trajectories streak the night sky, from which they have been removed by pious collectors of mystic traces. They are written on that black page from which we must relearn to read them.

## A WAY OF PROCEEDING

In speaking of "nights," then, the texts refer to a general historical situation, but also to a way of living that situation as a question of existence. They are accounts of "passions" *of* and *in* history. The various strains of *mystics,* in their reaction to the vanishing of truths, the increasing opaqueness of the authorities and divided or diseased institutions, define not so much a complementary or substitutive knowledge, topography, or entity, but rather a different treatment of the Christian tradition. Accused (with good reason) of being "new," caught up in and "bound to" circumstances, yet founded on faith in a Beginning that must come about in the present, they institute a "style" that articulates itself into *practices* defining a *modus loquendi* and/or a *modus agendi* (two central expressions that organized such a production). What is essential, therefore, is not a body of doctrines (which is the effect of these practices and above all the product of later theological interpretation), but the foundation of a field in which specific procedures will be developed: a *space* and an *apparatus.* The theoreticians of this mystical literature placed at the heart of the debates that at that time opposed them to "theologians" or "examiners" either the "mystic phrase" ("manners of expression," "turns of phrase," ways of "turning" words)[16] or "maxims" (rules of thought or action for "saints," that is, mystics). The reinterpretation of the tradition is characterized by an ensemble of processes that allow language to be treated differently—the entire contemporary language, not just the separate domain concerning theological knowledge or a patristical and scriptural corpus. Ways of acting organize the invention of a mystic body.

On one hand, a labor of transcending limits takes shape upon a tradition that time has deteriorated and opacified. On the other, from a cosmos of messages (or "mysteries") to be heard, there is a move to mediate practices that trace in language the indefinite transition of writings. These two traits already suffice to single out the modernity of the formations that, for two centuries, have been produced and theorized as "mystic." They also show us how to understand those early texts in our own time, how to recapture the movement their writings brought about within the specific setting of new questions.

Finally, there is a preliminary question. Behind the documents that have come down to us, can one suppose a stable referent (an "experience" or a fundamental "reality") that would make possible a sorting of the texts in function of whether or not they concern that referent? All of these discourses do, indeed, tell of a passion of what *is*,[17] of the world such as it "goes on," or of the thing itself [*das Ding*]—in short, a passion of what is self-authorized and depends on no exogenous guarantee. They are shores exposed to the oncoming sea. They aspire to lose themselves in what they show, like those landscapes by Turner that disappear into air and light. Modulated by pain, enjoyment, or "letting be" (the Eckhartian *Gelâzenheit*), an ab-solute (unfettered) inhabits the torture, the ecstasy, or the sacri-fice of the language that can only *say* it by effacing itself. That absolute owes nothing to the language it haunts; it is absolved from it. But what name or what identity should be ascribed to that "thing," taken independently of the work—in each case local—of letting it appear? The Other that organizes the text is not an outside of the text. It is not the (imaginary) object that one might distinguish from the movement by which it [*Es*] is sketched. To locate it apart, to isolate it from the texts that exhaust themselves trying to express it, would be tantamount to exorcising it by providing it with its own place and name, to identifying it with a remnant not assimilated by constituted rationalities, or to transforming the question that appears in the guise of a limit[18] into a particular religious representation (in turn excluded from the scientific fields and fetishized as the substitute for what is lacking). It is to postulate behind the documents a something or other, a malleable ineffable that could be fashioned to fit any end, a "night in which all cows are black."

It is preferable, therefore, to keep provisionally to what takes place in these texts whose status is indicated by the word "mystic," without forming in advance a definition (ideological or imaginary) of what a scriptural elaboration may have inscribed there. The first thing to consider is the formality of discourse and a trace (a walking, *Wandern*) of the writing: the former circumscribing a locus, the second showing a "style" or "walk," in the sense in which, according to Vergil, "the goddess is recognized by her walk."[19]

A new epistemological "form" appears at the threshold of the modern era with the texts that call themselves "mystic"; they are thereby distinguished from other texts, contemporary or prior (theological treatises, biblical commentaries, etc.). From this angle, the problem is not to find out if an exegetic treatise by Gregory of Nyssa is based on the same experience as a discourse later called "mystic" [adjective *mystique*], nor if they are both constructed upon partially analogous rhetorical devices, but to determine what occurs in a field delimited by a *name* (*"mystics"*) [noun *mystique*] and within which work is being done in obedience to a relevant set of *rules*. A corpus can be considered as being the effect of the relationship between a name (which symbolizes the circumscription of a space) and rules (which specify a production), even if, as in many other cases, the name is also used to enlist earlier or different formations in the unit it isolates (in the sixteenth or seventeenth century, the term "mystic" will be applied to former discourses and a mystic tradition will be formed in that way), and even if the rules of "mystic" composition organize some texts well before they give rise to their own specific combination of elements. (It can be observed that procedures called "mystic" in the modern era are found under other headings in earlier or contemporary documents.) At the beginning of my analysis, therefore, there is the isolation of a "mystic" unit in the system of differentiation of the discourses that articulates a new area of knowledge.[20] A manner of using received language *differently* becomes objectified in a set of delimitations and processes.

One might well wonder what interminglings of disciplines, from the thirteenth century on, made possible the configuration in which *mystics* receives a form proper to it, and what shifts, beginning at the end of the seventeenth century, caused the redistribution of *mystics* into other units. One would have to go back to the founders, Meister Eckhart (1260–1327) and, half a century earlier, Hadewijch of Anvers,[21] to grasp the progressive constitution of a mystic formality; or follow, starting with Madame Guyon (1648–1717), Fénelon (1651–1715), Gichtel (1638–1710), or Arnold (1666–1714), the stages of a transition toward other (philosophical, psychological, or pietistic) genres. It seemed preferable to situate myself first at the center of this field of shifting historical boundaries and to observe it at the moment of its greatest formalization and its end—from Teresa of Avila to

Angelus Silesius. Modes of functioning are more clearly legible at that time, as is, consequently, the determination of a locus; this in turn makes possible a regressive history of its formation and a study of its later embodiments.

To look at processes in this way, to "interpret," in the musical sense of the term, this mystical writing as one would a different speech act, is to consider it a past from which we are cut off and not to presume ourselves to be in the same place it was; it is the attempt to execute its movement for ourselves, to retrace the steps of a labor but from afar, without taking as an object of knowledge that thing which, in passing, changed the written word into a hieroglyphic. To do this is to remain within a scriptural experience and to retain that sense of modesty that respects distances. These trips taken in the textual suburbs of *mystics* already point out pathways to get lost (even if only to lose a kind of knowledge). Perhaps we will be led, by its confused murmurings, toward the city become sea. Thus a literature might render manifest what formed it: a power of prompting departure.

## A REDISTRIBUTION OF SPACE: FROM HERESY TO "THE REFUGE"

For several years, heresy held a strategic place in the analysis of Christianity,[22] until very recently when this socio-ideological theme was gradually replaced by the study of the family and kinship structures, showing the influence of ethnology and psychoanalysis in the field of economic and social history.

The fact that heresy was and still is such a decisive point is not wholly ascribable to the effect of the privilege that has for a long time been granted to religious antidogmatism (or to progressivist and revolutionary political movements) or to historical positions more in keeping with the role that a certain academic intelligentsia thought of itself as playing. It is for reasons more intrinsic to the nature of historical work. Heresy presents the *doctrinal legibility of a social conflict* and the *binary form* of the modality by which a society defines itself, excluding that which it casts in the role of its other (a form from which *mystics* first received its binary structure, opposing an "interior" to an "exterior"). It shows how ideological and social structures mesh, and makes visible the process by which a societal body is formed. It is clear that, from this twin perspective, two other corollary but major issues come into play: the modality of progress (to be classed on the "heretical" side?) in relation to an established system and the role of the intellectual (that is, of heresiarchs and of theological or philosophical innovations) in a functioning societal whole.

Research has not made heresy into an isolable and stable object through the ages. On the contrary, sweeping through the eras and regions in which these manifestations occur—heresies, of course, but also sects,[23] spiritual marginalities,[24] and even collective exclusions directed against paupers and drifters, madmen,[25] cultural or ethnic minorities[26]—the analysis shatters the image that originally brought it about.[27] But it reveals, in the overwhelming intellectual and societal *diversity* of heresies, the repetition of the gesture of exclusion. The "same" is a historical *form*, a practice of dichotomy, and not a homogeneous *content* (which may be religious—a doctrine; social—a deviance; or economic—idleness). The excluded element is always relative to that which it serves, or obliges, to redefine. The *conflict* is articulated upon the contour of a societal *representation* that it makes possible and organizes. This historical process shows how a societal division and an ideological production are codetermined. It leads one to speculate on the functioning of the act of division that permits the foundation of the orthodoxy (or representation) peculiar to a group, or on the knowledge of a particular society afforded us by consideration of the location, manner, and subject of the split—be it passive (to be cut off) or active (to cut oneself off)—that divides it.

The history of the sixteenth and seventeenth centuries presents an incredible proliferation of these divisions in the field of religious expression. Heresy abounded. Three main rifts may serve as points of reference: one, beginning in the fifteenth century, that separated ever more widely the urban "clerics" from the rural masses, and thereby separated intellectual or theological practices from those of the common folk; another, in the sixteenth century, splitting the Catholic world along the age-old line of North against South, and creating the thousand and one varieties of opposition between the Reformed Churches and the Tridentine Reform; and last, one that shattered the unity of the universe into an "old" and a "new" world and brought into play, at one moment, the *spatial* privilege of the American "savage" in relation to aging Christendom, and, at another moment, the *temporal* privilege of the Western present, productive enough to change, little by little, the tradition into a bygone "past." Actually, these divisions overlapped, and their combinations redefined the "nations," parties, sects, and disciplines. The aggressivity between menacing or menaced positions grew in proportion to the overall reclassification they underwent.

This polymorphous "work" appears to obey a common postulate: the *schism* replaces *heresy*, which has become impossible. "Heresy" may be said to exist when a majority position has the power of naming *in its own discourse* a dissident formation and of excluding it as marginal. An authority serves as a frame of reference to the very group that breaks away from it or that it rejects. The "schism," on the contrary, presupposes two positions, neither of which can impose on the other the law of its reason or of its force. It is no longer the case of an orthodoxy confronting a heresy, but of different Churches. Such was the seventeenth-century situation. The conflict pitted heteronomous formations against one another. That "fatal shattering of the ancient religion of unity" progressively shifted over to the State the capacity for being our referential unity: a unity that developed by the principle of inclusion, by a subtle play of hierarchizations and arbitration, and whose structure is of the tertiary type (the three "orders," etc.).

Beliefs and practices would confront one another henceforth within a *political space*, still ordered, to be sure, according to a religious model, around the king, that "outer bishop" whose task was to ensure "a certain police for the exercise of different religions."[28] Each Church took on the appearance of a "party." Its ambition remained totalizing, in keeping with the model of universal and conquering truth, but in fact it was dependent on relations with a State that favored, controlled, or excommunicated. That structure was repeated in the "parties" internal to the Churches. The "universal" claim of each religious group, exacerbated by division, tended to have recourse to the royal power as the sole overall power, to make it into the criterion of or obstacle to truth, to think of itself in terms of being for or against that authority, the very terms gradually imposed upon it by an absolutist politics—thereby granting the state the role (positive or negative) that had formerly been played by the orthodoxy. Le Père Daniel, an extreme case to be sure, would soon declare that "the history of a Kingdom or of a Nation has for its object the Prince and the State; they are, as it were, the center toward which all must tend and refer."[29] But Pascal, for his part, would have "gladly sacrificed his life" to the education of the prince, a task which consisted in inscribing knowledge and wisdom at the center of the political order.[30] Religious faithfulness and deviance are everywhere politicized.

"Stability" and/or "explosion"? The analysis of Alphonse Dupront was conducted in the area between these two polarities.[31] What actually took place was an "explosion" in the arrangement and use of "stable" elements, a phenomenon of social reinterpretation. While religious behavior and symbols still obtained, their functioning was changing. The *content* remained, but it underwent a new *treatment* that, already noticeable in the segmentation brought about by the divisions, would soon be expressed as a political management of differences.[32] The inherited furnishings were redistributed within a new space, ordered by a new way of arranging them and using them. In reworking its data, the schism ushered in the political or scientific move of reclassifying and manipulating. It was a work done on social form—different from and complementary to the evolution that, in other cases, changed the content without modifying the social form into which a variety of ideological fillings passed.[33]

The divisions became classificatory and manipulative operations that redistributed the traditional elements that would later give rise to theoretical "figures" making their principles explicit.[34] Behind the various religious conducts or convictions, the possibility was created of *making* these figures into something else and of *using* them to serve different strategies—a possibility whose equivalent can be seen during the same era, in the more flexible fields of writing or aesthetics, with the art (baroque or rhetorical) of treating and rearranging inherited images or ideas in order to obtain new effects from them. Difficult and violent, the reapportionment of the religious space into Churches or "parties" not only goes hand in hand with a political management of these differences, but also each one of these new groups manipulates customs and beliefs, carries out for its own benefit a practical reinterpretation of situations previously organized according to other determinations, *produces* its unity on the basis of traditional data, and procures for itself the intellectual and political means that will ensure a reemployment or a "correction" of thoughts and conduct. By catechetical control, unification, and diffusion, doctrine becomes an *instrument* that makes possible the fabrication of social bodies, their defense and their extension. The task of *educating* and the concern with *methods* characterize the activity of the religious "parties" and of all the new congregations, which were in this respect becoming more and more similar to the model of the State. To "reform" is to remake the forms. This work, in calling for the elaboration of transformational techniques, doubtless also had the effect of hiding the continuities that resisted these reforming operations and, after a time of massive demonstrations and brutal repression (witchcraft, peasant uprisings, etc.), the effect of making these continuities less and less perceptible beneath the ever-tightening network of pedagogical institutions.

Last, the place formerly occupied by heresy vis-à-vis a *religious* orthodoxy would henceforth be that of a religious orthodoxy as opposed to a *political* one. A prophetic faith organized itself into a minority within the secularized state. It made itself into a "Refuge."[35] The post-Tridentine ambition of reconstituting a political and spiritual "world" of grace reappeared with Pierre de Bérulle in the form of a utopian ecclesiastical hierarchy that would articulate the secrets of mystical life,[36] but that *theoretical* reconciliation of a social order and spiritual inner life was broken off by *actual* history. It was to function only in secret groups (such as the Company of the Saint Sacrament), in the "Refuge" of Port Royal or, later, following a model that was systematized at first by the Calvinistic desire to begin a reformed society (a history and a localization of truth) on the basis of the Scriptures, within Saint-Sulpice Seminaries.[37] The definition of that Scripture varied, but Christian microcosms proliferated: "retreats" in France, "reductions" in the New World.[38] Port-Royal is but the most famous instance.

The gesture of "going on retreat," or of "withdrawing," is the universal indication of the tendency that countered the necessary "docility" or "compliance" of State-connected religious institutions with the *segregation of a place*. Among the reformers, that closure was at once the consequence of the triumph of politicization from 1640 on and the condition of the possibility of an "establishment" of the faith. It defined a "policy" of meaning. The regular life, the religious congregations, the lay associations, the administering of the sacraments and their pastoral regulations, and the popular missions were all responses to the prime necessity of a rupture that organized (after the manner of a "departure," a wall, a social selectivity, a secret, etc.) the circumscription of a field for specific practices.[39] The "mystic" groups and kinds of discourse offer a variant of these social redistributions of space by and for new practices, a variant that at once calls into question the *autonomizing* of a new historical figure and the *passage* from one sociocultural economy to another.

## A Proud Tradition Humbled

Mystic literature corresponds, first of all, to a topography. In modern Europe, it has its locale: regions, social categories, types of groups, forms of work; further, it favors concrete modes of relations to money (begging, communal property, commerce, etc.), to sexuality (celibacy, widowhood, etc.), and to power (allegiances to benefactors, ecclesiastical responsibilities, familial and political ties, etc.). First we must ask ourselves what constants emerge from the data provided by the studies now waking from an "ahistorical" slumber.[40] I will retain a few of these elements, concerning the place of the mystics, or more precisely their social origins and situations.

In the sixteenth and seventeenth centuries, the mystics most often belonged to the regions and social categories that were going into a socioeconomic recession, were disfavored by change, pushed aside by progress, or financially ruined by the wars. That impoverishment developed the memory of a lost past; it clung to models deprived of efficacy and available for an "other world." It redirected toward the spaces of utopia, of dreamy imaginings or writings, aspirations before which the doors of social responsibilities were closed. Apropos of Port-Royal, Lucien Goldmann tried to explain Jansenist spirituality by the situation of the authors, members of the robe, gradually deprived of their former powers.[41] That fact (which is no explanation) can also be observed during the same period in the case of many French mystics, tied through their families to the decadence of the lesser, provincial nobility of the Southwest (such as Surin or Jean de Labadie in Guyenne), to the misery of the country squires, to the devaluation of the parliamentary "offices," and, above all, to "a whole milieu of middle aristocracy, rich in vitality and spiritual needs but of diminished usefulness or social function"[42] or, earlier in the century, to the reversals of the compromised Leaguers (such as the Acaries) or émigrés (like the Englishman Benoit de Canfield). The same connections, except for the parliamentary ones, existed among the hermits.[43] Leaving aside a few mystics who were on the road to promotion (such as the superintendent René d'Argenson),[44] the majority, until the days of Margaret Mary Alacoque, were from the receding milieus or parties.[45] The ebb appears to have uncovered the beaches upon which *mystics* appeared.

In sixteenth-century Spain, Teresa of Avila belonged to a *hidalguía* deprived of functions and of goods;[46] John of the Cross, ministering to the sick in the hospital of Salamanca, belonged to a bankrupt and déclassé aristocracy, and so on. But more important than social ranking were the ethnic discriminations based on the *raza*. Now, close to the marrano tradition—that is, the *gespaltete Seelen* (J. A. Van Praag), divided souls, lives split in two by the necessity of a hidden inner self—the "nuevos cristianos," whose "converted" face was, for their contemporaries, the mask of the excluded Jew, were extremely numerous among the "illuminated" devotees, or *alumbrados*; they were the most eminent figures among them: Melchior, the Cazallas, the Ortizes, Bernardino Tovar, Pedro Ruiz de Alcaraz, San Pedro Regalado, and many *beatas*. They participated in this "*converso* style" (J. H. Silverman) that, after the manner of the picaresque novel, of poetry, or of spirituality, disturbed the literature of the Golden Age with the critical irony or the insatiable lyricism that Américo Castro has associated with a "tortured Semitism" [*semitismo atormentado*]. In Christianity, they articulated the experience of an *elsewhere*, but *within* the tradition they adopted. Neophytes, distant from the age-old way of thinking and acting of Spanish Catholicism, often inclined to free themselves from the formalism of the Synagogue and unwilling to fall into that of the Church, members of a scriptural intelligentsia that was seduced by the Erasmian conception of an evangelical "body" and repelled by the doctrinal racism subjacent to the ranking according to the *limpieza de sangre*, readers of a Bible that they approached independently of its scholastic or established preambles—they introduced into the "letter" the technical and/or mystical play of a different "spirit."[47]

Forbidden in certain orders (first the Hieronymites, the Benedictines, and others), suspect among the Dominicans, these "scorned ones" became the great Franciscans (Francisco de Osuna, Diego de Estella), Augustinian friars (Luis de León), Jesuits (Lainez, Polance, Ripalda, and others), Carmelite friars or nuns. Had not Teresa of Avila's grandfather, having gone back to the Judaism of his ancestors, been subjected, with his three sons (among them Alonso, Teresa's cherished father), to the humiliating public ceremony of abjuration required of the "renegades"(1485)?[48] A family memory, decisive but "unspeakable," as in many other cases. From John of Avila (who makes the University of Baeza the asylum for the "new Christians") to Molinos, a strange alliance joins the "mystic" spoken word to the "impure" blood. The meeting of the two religious traditions, one removed to an inner retreat, the other triumphant but "corrupted," allowed the new Christians to become, to a great extent, the creators of a new discourse, freed from dogmatic repetition, and, like a spiritual Marranism, structured by the opposition between the purity of the "inside" and the lie of the "outside." Just as the massive adoption of German culture by the Jews in the nineteenth century made possible theoretic innovations and an exceptional intellectual productivity, the upsurge of *mystics* in the sixteenth and seventeenth centuries was often the effect of the Jewish difference in the usage of a Catholic idiom.

In Germany, seventeenth-century *mystics* was also the product of men born of an impoverished rural nobility (Theodor von Tschech, Abraham von Franckenberg, Friedrich von Spee, Catharina von Greiffenberg, Johannes Scheffler alias Angelus Silesius, and even Daniel Czepko by his place of work) or of the urban class of lower craftsmen (Jakob Böhme, Quirinus Kuhlmann, Johann Georg Gichtel, Friedrich Ludwig Gifftheil, etc.), that is, the two groups most disfavored by the progress of other categories (the urban bourgeoisie in particular).[49] The decadence of the country nobility and urban craftsmen was accompanied by a growing independence with respect to the religious authorities and a denial of the new order.

What is more, Silesia, Austrian since 1526, a privileged land for mystics (Böhme, Franckenberg, Czepko, Silesius), a haven for the heretics expelled from Saxony, was, being in the eastern part of the Empire, the province that the Thirty Years' War afflicted most heavily (60 to 70 percent losses). With the war came the social deterioration of the condition of the peasantry, the economic competition with Poland and Kurland, and the political alienation of its rights under Charles VI. Sects, theosophies, and *mystics* proliferated in this country disinherited by history.

This topography, which should not be systematized or generalized,[50] already indicates some points of particular instability and forms of disappropriation. In a society in which one must, as Philippe Hurault de Cheverny writes, "give advancement to one's relatives in every way one can,"[51] in which the preservation of the family patrimony demanded the mastery of the passions just as much as it did good management of assets, to lose rank and live beneath one's station was considered morally degrading. Social and family decline damaged an order in which life was a battle against the steady falling off from origins. It was powerless to protect its heritage from the erosion of time.

A tradition was fading away, transforming itself into a past. That is what these groups, imbued with the certainty that the end was approaching, were experiencing more vividly than others. At the extremes, they wavered between ecstasy and revolt—*Mysticism and Dissent*.[52] The guarantees they "held," received from preceding generations, were crumbling, leaving them alone, with neither inherited goods nor assurances for the future, reduced to a present that was henceforth wedded to death.[53] The present was not, therefore, a dangerous pass that reassurances on the future and past acquisitions would allow them to forget. On the contrary, it was the narrow stage upon which their end was being played, written in the facts (a law of history), and to which the possibility of a new beginning (a faith in a different world) was reduced. The only present left to them was an exile.

The fact that the mystics enclosed themselves in the circle of a "nothingness" capable of being an "origin" is to be explained, first of all, by their having been caught up in a *radical* situation they took seriously. They have translated that situation into their texts, not only in the relation an innovative truth bears throughout with the pain of a loss, but, more explicitly, in the social figures that dominate their discourse, those of the madman, the child, the illiterate. It is as if, in our own day, the eponymous heroes of knowledge were the fallen members of our society—old people, immigrants, or the "village idiot," who, says Simone Weil, "truly loves truth," because instead of "talents" favored by education, he has this "genius" that "is nothing but the supernatural virtue of humility in the realm of thought."[54] For the "devotees" of the sixteenth and seventeenth centuries, birth had humility for its site.

That situation was intensified by another, which was, for the believers of the period, indissolubly bound to the first: the humiliation of the Christian tradition. Within that tattered Christendom they experienced a fundamental defection, that of the institutions of meaning. They lived the decomposition of a cosmos and were exiled from it. They were driven out of their country by a history that degraded them. *Super flumina Babylonis*: a theme repeated indefinitely. They were filled with a mourning unmitigated by the rapture of new ambitions. A referential permanence was lacking. With the institution, that opaque reserve for believing and making others believe, their tacit assurances sank beneath them. They sought a firm footing, but in the end the Scriptures appeared as "corrupt" as the Churches. They were equally deteriorated by time. They obscured the spoken Word, the presence of which they were to have prolonged. To be sure, they still marked the spot, but in the form of "ruins"—a word that haunted the discourse of those who called for reform. They still showed the spots in which one was *now* to await the birth of a God who had to be distinguished from all of his signs—which were destined to deteriorate—and who could not be harmed by time's attrition because he was dead. Birth and death, such were then the two poles of evangelical meditation.

Hence the mystics do not reject the ruins that surround them. They remain there. They go there. A symbolic gesture: Ignatius of Loyola, Teresa of Avila, and many others wished to enter a "corrupt" Order. Not that they sympathized with decadence, but these disorderly, quasi-disinherited places—places of abjection, of trial (like the "deserts" where monks once went to battle against evil spirits) and not places guaranteeing an identity or a salvation—represented the actual situation of contemporary Christianity. They were the theaters of the present struggles. Like the Crypt of the Nativity in Bethlehem, like Jerusalem destroyed by the centuries, they marked the very spot where a present foundation that would also be a restoration was to be awaited, where the metamorphoses and revivals of history could be "suffered." Besides, imposed by the circumstances yet desired, sought after as the trial of truth, a certain solidarity with an age-old and collective suffering marked the locus of a "wound" inseparable from a societal misfortune. At this point, an understanding is born by being touched by affliction. "The deciphering of history," as Albert Béguin was wont to say, "is reserved for certain beings of pain and suffering."[55]

One must connect with this religious and social experience the movement that led "spiritual" learned men and theologians toward witnesses who humbled their competency: maids, cowherds, villagers, and so on. These characters, real or fictitious, were like pilgrimages to an alternative "illumination." While the "erudite" made up little scientific oases intended to serve as foundations for rebuilding a world, these intellectual converts to "barbarism" testify to the disarray of their knowledge confronted with the misfortune that had stricken a system of reference. They also testify, perhaps, to a treason on the part of the learned clerics. They participate in the thought that consoled Ockham: *promissum Christi per parvolus baptizatos posse salvari*.[56] Like Bérulle climbing the stairs to a maid's garret, these magi came to the "little ones" to listen to something that still spoke. Their knowledge took leave of its textual "authorities" to become the gloss of "wild" voices, producing the countless biographies of poor "girls" or "inspired illiterates" that made up a prolific stock of spiritual literature of the day. In particular, learned clerics became exegetes of female bodies, speaking bodies, living Bibles spread here and there in the countryside or in the little shops, ephemeral outbursts of the "Word" erstwhile uttered by a whole world. A humbled theology, after having long exercised its magistracy, expected and obtained from its other the certainties that eluded it.

✳   I   ✳

# A Place
# To Lose
# Oneself

Mystic literature did not begin in the sixteenth century, although it found its own name and formal features during the second half of that century. It would be ridiculous, however, to trace the preliminary elements that, after the fact, after that space had been defined, permitted a "tradition" to be constituted for it. It seemed preferable to suggest two of the motifs that organized it—madness and delight—by two fragments. Bits of a tradition, they burst with light like bits of broken glass. Two citations, one of which comes from the very fringes of Christianity, the other from the fringe of the sixteenth century.

Through them, I will also try to show two practices of which that literature is the effect: a withdrawal (ecstatic) brought about by the seduction of the Other, and a virtuosity (technical) in making words confess what they are unable to say. Rapture and rhetoric: these two apparently contradictory practices are related to what language became at the threshold of the Renaissance. Ockhamism—and this is a symbol of a larger evolution—stripped discourse of its ultimate verification, allowing for the progressive separation that took place between an unknown absolute of the divine will and a technician's freedom, capable of manipulating words that are no longer anchored in being. At this point the older tradition, to which the "madness for Christ" testifies, found a linguistic instrument, suitable to mediating a "modern" theory, *mystics.*

*Chapter One*

✠   ✠
✠

# The Monastery
# and the Public Square:
# Madness in the Crowd

The beggar remains invisible in *India Song*. Nameless, faceless. Only
her shadow crosses the picture, while her chant of Savannakhet, far
away from the other voices, comes and goes, innocent, interminable.
She is the passerby who wanders through the texts of Marguerite
Duras. She does not speak. She makes others speak. Carrying hunger
within her, she comes to the doorway of the kitchens. "Throughout
this night of plenty, she, symbol of emaciated Calcutta, squats
. . . amongst the mad beggars. . . . With vacant mind and withered
heart, she waits, as always, for food." She remains there, with the
leftovers. Forgetful, absolved, that is to say, absolute.[1]

Enraptured, she is seductive. And frightening. I begin to follow
her, through stories that are (almost) ageless, in a part of my memory
that has become the foreign territory, once familiar to me, of the
origins of Christianity. I seek her in her Orient, when for the first time
in the Egyptian desert there passes the woman called *salē*, the idiot. At
the beginning of the tradition that figures a form of madness on the
fringes of Christianity, there is that woman. Her appearance dates
from the fourth century, told in the *Lausiac History* by Palladios. The
madwoman wanders about in a kitchen within a veritable republic of
women (there are four hundred of them), an Egyptian convent that
Pachomius established at Mēne or Tismēnai, near Panopolis. This is
the first form of what would become "madness for Christ." A name-

31

less woman, who is no sooner recognized than she disappears, followed by other figures, men called Mark the Mad [*salos*], in the city of Alexandria (sixth century); Simeon the Mad, of Emesa in Syria (sixth century); Andrew Salos, in Constantinople (ninth century); and so on.[2] With the passing of the centuries, that madness moved toward the north and multiplied.

Of these ancient and widely dispersed witnesses from whom would come the groups of "madmen of Christ" [*yourodivyj*] who circulated on the public squares of Moscow in the fourteenth to sixteenth centuries, I ask: What change of direction did they bring about? Not to capture the secret of their seduction (is there any other besides their own rapture?), but to try to circumscribe the vanishing point through which they turn us toward an absolute. We have here a turning aside toward another country, in which the madwoman (the woman who loses herself) and the madman (the man who laughs) create the challenge of the unbound.[3]

## THE IDIOT WOMAN (FOURTH CENTURY)

The passage in *Lausiac History* that introduces the first idiot woman [*salē*] was later entitled: "She who simulated madness [*mōrian*]." The title, and the first sentence from which it was taken, dispose too quickly of an unresolvable question: Is that madness real or affected? Or real because affected? Or made up of several kinds of madness? The tale will end without answering these questions. Here it is, first, in its entirety.

> In this monastery there was a virgin who pretended to be mad, possessed by a demon. The others became so disgusted with her that no one ate with her, which she preferred. Wandering through the kitchen, she would render any service. She was, as they say, the sponge of the monastery. In reality, she was accomplishing what is written: "If someone intends to be wise among us in this life, let him become a fool to become wise." She had tied a rag around her head—all the others are shaven and wear hoods—and it is in that attire that she performed her duties. Of the four hundred [sisters], not one ever saw her chew anything during the years of her life; she never sat at table; she never broke bread with the others. She was happy with the crumbs she wiped up and the water from the pots and pans she scoured, without offending anyone, without murmuring, without speaking little or much, though she was beaten with blows, insulted, laden with curses, and treated with disgust.
>
> Behold an angel appeared to the saintly man Piteroum, an anchoret who had proven himself and resided at [Mount] Porphyrite. The angel

said to him: "Why do you have a good opinion of yourself? Because of your religious life and the place where you live? Do you want to see a woman more religious than yourself? Go to the monastery of the Tabennesiot women and there you will find one with a scarf wrapped around her head. She is better than you. Contending with that crowd, she has never turned her heart from God, whereas you, who stay here, in thought you wander in through the cities."

He who had never gone out set forth. He asked the superiors to let him into the monastery of women. Since he was famous and already old, they did not hesitate to let him enter. Once he had entered, he asked to see them all. But she did not show herself. At last he said to them: "Bring me all of them. One is missing." They told him: "We have an idiot [*salē*] within, in the kitchen"it is thus that one referred to the sick. He told them: "Have her come also, that I may see her." They went to call her. She refused, perhaps because she realized what was happening, or even because she had had a revelation of it. They dragged her away by force and told her: "The saintly man Piteroum wants to see you." He was greatly renowned.

When she was there, he saw the rag on her head and, falling at her feet, said to her: "Bless me [Mother (Amma)]." Like him, she also fell at his feet saying: "You bless me, Lord [*Kurie*]." At this point, all the women were enraptured. They said to the saintly man: "Father [*Abba*] do not take this as an insult: she is an idiot [*salē*]." Piteroum said to them all: "You are the ones who are the idiots [salai], for she is for me and for you our mother [*Ammas*]"—that is how spiritual guides were referred to— "and I pray that I may be found worthy of her on the day of judgment." At these words they fell at the feet of the monk, confessing all manner of things: one had sprinkled her with dishwater, another had pummeled her, another had made her nose swell up. . . . In a word, they all had many abuses to confess. Having prayed for them, he went away.

A few days later, unable to bear her sisters' esteem and admiration, overwhelmed by their demands for pardon, she left the convent. Where she went, where she hid herself, how she ended her days, no one has found out.[4]

A woman, then. She doesn't leave the kitchen. She doesn't leave off *being* something that has to do with the crumbs and leftovers of food. She makes her body from them. She maintains herself by being nothing but this abject point, the "nothing" that puts people off. This is what she "prefers": to be the sponge. Around her hair, a dishrag. No discontinuity between her and this refuse: she doesn't "chew"; nothing separates her body from the offal. She is what is left over, without end, infinite. The opposite of the imagery that idealized the Virgin Mother, who is unified by the Name of the Other, without any connection with the reality of the body—the idiot is totally within the unsymbolizable thing that resists meaning. She takes upon herself the body's most humble functions; she loses herself in the unassertable, below the level of all language. But this "disgusting" castaway makes possible for the other women the sharing of meals, the community of vestiary and corporeal signs indicating that they have been chosen, the communication of words. The excluded one renders possible an entire circulation.

## A CHALLENGE

The story organizes a space, constructed between two extremities: the high place, Mount Porphyrite, symbol and institution of hermetic heroism, "residence" of a man who is a "father" and has "great renown"; and on the other hand, the kitchen, an "inside" and a below, in which that nameless girl wanders, the idiot. Between these two poles, the intermediate zone, a "crowd" (four hundred women) who make up the theater of the verbal exchange, and who are both its condition and a stage, delimited by a female chorus. With the Father above and a woman below, we have a little cosmos, capable of being inverted by the transformation of the woman into Mother [*Ammas*] who would take the place of the Father [*Abbas*]. In the majority of later stories belonging to the same series, the crowd is masculine (it is a male collectivity in a monastery or on the public squares of a city) and the lower pole is then occupied by a man (the madman), but there remains the defiance of a carnivalesque reversal, placing what was lowly at the highest point.

Here, the exchange, *unbelievable* according to the order of things, is introduced into the *possible* by the angel who can cross borders. His spoken word (the spoken word) transcends the spatial arrangement that opposes top and bottom, man and woman, renown and disgust, mastery and aimless wandering, and so on. It is a spoken word that, first of all, reaches across barriers. It gives a "mystical" foundation to the coming together of two solitudes that were foreign to one another. A speech act must "authorize" the action in order for it to take place. Thus, formerly, "before any action by Rome toward a foreign people," certain officials, the *fetiales*, proceeded to put in motion a verbal circuit that "opened a space" of legitimacy for all military or diplomatic operations. This "turn" of spoken words preceded combats and contracts; it made them possible.[5] Similarly, the messenger angel, *shifter* cutting through the hierarchal order, authorizes in advance the transgression that will bring contraries together. Already his speech act inverts high and low. At the threshold of an operation destined to transform positional distribution, it is at the same time both a *challenging word* in relation to the present (there is "more than you") and *theoretic fiction* in relation to a story that is to come. It "repeats" the event that is to happen, like the *repetitio rerum* of the Roman *fetiales*. The speech act itself has the role here, in relation to the rest of the story, that stories have in general: that of opening other spaces in a historical system of facts.

That spoken word, which is detached (analogous to the poet's or the analyst's word), transitive (it crosses over), coming from beyond its speaker (it is a message), and the only word that allows itself to name "God" (there is no other mention in the text)that word represents, for the woman marked by a "scarf wrapped around her head" (not by her idiocy), the possibility that her abjection, the result of scandal, might be expressed as the result of truth ("she is better") and of love ("she has never turned her heart from God"). But the angelic language remains in this realm of the possible.

All the facts related in the story are either exits or entrances. Beginning with the first exit of Piteroum ("he who had never gone out"), they end with the definitive exit of the madwoman ("she left the convent," forever). These acts take place at once upon a geographical surface and its semantic equivalent. That second-level topography is recognizable by a constellation of key words: the madman [*mōros*] and the idiot [*salos*], of course, but also *hubris* (which traditionally meant excess, before designating verbal abuse), the act of "going out of oneself" (like the sisters, who were "beside themselves," stunned), or the status of the two characters, who are out of the ordinary. The spatial practices (entrances and exits) modulate the act of *exceeding the limits* and appear against a background of competition or *defiance*.

This is traditional, in the old monastic setting: all the forms of excess are represented there, from the outrageous fervor of the beginner [*thermotēs*], or the exaltation that would "overstep the bounds of nature" and "take a stance" against them [*eparsis*], to dereliction [*enkataleipsis*], which is the price of temerity. There are thus to be found among them a goodly number of "distorted" ones [*strebloumenoi*], twisted and strained "to excess." On that stage is enacted or "produced" the wavering of the soul between two "contrary passions" or two immoderations [*démesures*] as Theodoret said—that of desire [*epithumia*] and that of the "irascible" [*thumos*], which the mind [*nous*] tries to control, the one by the other.[6] It is in terms of borders to stay within or to cross, that is, in terms of excess, that the story from the *Lausiac History* seems to seek the point in which, coming in and going out—or progressing in wisdom and losing meaning—coincide. The proposition announced at the outset with the quotation from Saint Paul defines the program of the text: "To become mad in order to become wise."[7]

## SEDUCTION

Upon the stage thus divided, two modes of conduct stand opposed though both the actors are constrained, one by the angel and the other by the monk, to relinquish the spot they had chosen for themselves. The opposition between them can be put in two words: Piteroum *advances*; the idiot *retreats*. The first leaves his high place, crosses thresholds, orders, questions, falls to his knees, blames or praises, blesses, and so on. He has the initiative (except for the first one, which comes from the angel). He does not cease "going out" of himself in a multiplicity of acts. "She," on the contrary, withdraws. She stays away from communal meals, from the signs that would identify her with the community, from language itself. She hides, holds her peace, is lost within herself, lost to others. While he goes off to "see" one who is better than himself (his thoughts were already wandering through the cities, she does not yield to the name, she has nothing to see on the outside; she is, on the inside, in an excess from which nothing can distract her. She does not function according to that ideal of the self from which the subject perceives itself "as if seen by the other."[8]

Then comes the moment of the spoken word. The monk marks it by kneeling. Like a ritual, his gesture delineates the space of a different speech act between them. He marks off the bounds, as if tracing a chalk circle, within which the dual act of an exchange will take place. "Bless me [Mother]."[9] His role was to bless. He comes away, off balance, to confess the exteriority (the superiority) of the other. In this way, he brings her out of the indistinction in which she was immersed. He detaches her from her infinite. He puts her in the place he formerly occupied, that of blessing and of being "father" (first and foremost in the order). By the very act that is essential to all exorcism, he names the unnameable. He wants to extract her from the indeterminate, that is, from herself, so that she may be in the place of the father.

She withdraws once again. "You bless me, Lord." She is content to repeat the gestures and words of the other. She has none of her own. She only speaks, therefore, echoing him, herself remaining silent in his words which she repeats, like Memling's mute Sibyl. A variant is introduced, however. She does not answer "*abbas*" [father], as she should in addressing a monk. Nor does she deny him this title (opposites are of the same kind). She is to one side, different. She says: *kurie*, lord. Ambiguous term.[10] The use of the word already tends at that date to make it the equivalent of "Sir." In this case, the idiot uses it to designate the master-man: it is for "you," man, to "bless"; for you, the institutional, virile, paternal power of articulating, by a signifier (benediction), the divine exteriority onto the exteriority of the faithful. Stay in your place, which is the ministerial power of the signifier, linguistic objectification. From this point of view, she "refuses" to take the place that he occupies in the symbolic institution. Thus he will continue his ministry, chide, speak, bless, return to his position. She remains in the other, in the infinite of an abjection without language.

But by *kurie*, "Lord," it may be that she is designating the God from which "she has never turned her heart aside." In that case, she answers Piteroum even less. *She is not addressing him*, but the Other. It is probably impossible for her to speak to a man as to her father, to participate in the circulation of the signifier. With words not her own, that she reorients, she addresses God. Also, in that way, she remains in her world, in the absolute (unbound) infinity of the other. As if "in a sleep," within a boundless nothingness: withdrawn there, into something that has no verbal form, that is deviation and distraction with regard to dialogue. Perhaps she is truly "mad," being lost there in the Other.

### THE EFFECTS OF DEVIATION

The sisters are not wrong about that (and what of him?). Already when questioned about the "lack" around which the representation of the convent was organized, they used the significant formulation: "We have an idiot within [*endon*]." This could also mean: it is our innermost secret, a madness within ourselves. The object of "disgust" allows the institution, as a family, to form and manifest itself according to a law, the wording of which might be "all but one," yet "one" who maintains the abjection or inner madness of "all." The monk addresses that mute "thing" among them. He wants to make it into an "object" to be seen, thereby transforming the underlying principle that makes their communication possible into *one more* element. Between the sisters and him, the status of the "missing one" is equivocal.

When, brought out from the kitchen, the inner secret is expressed, the sisters "go out of themselves" [*exestēsan*]. A difficult term to translate. But here, the degree of that "going out" (are they ecstatic, excited, exhausted, exasperated?) is of less import to the story than the movement itself of being "outside of oneself." They understand. The idiot's fictive response does injury [*hubris*] to the monastic institution.

She withdraws from, does not fall within this institution. That is excess [*hubris*] par excellence. The sisters must get rid of the injury, mend the father. A gesture of nurses, lucid and repairing, toward the symbolic position: it is nothing, she is only an idiot! Rising, he plays the role they recognize as being his, and which they support. He chides them, like a "father," responding to their unspoken demand. They give him satisfaction by confessing to their routine practices of community life. He blesses them. All settles back into place. Has he changed? He leaves. There is nothing else he can do. He returns to his position, with what knowledge the text does not say.

In fact, something has happened. You are, we are, says he, the children of that idiot. We have, you and I, not only madness, but *that* madwoman as our mother. This *particular* and *blinding* point is, in a genealogy of sages, its perpetual *beginning*: singular and unknowable, here is our "spiritual mother." Wisdom is born from there, without our being able to say anything more about it, unless it be in relation to that which finally outdoes all wisdom, in relation to the sudden "flash" or "dawning" of the day of judgment, a something that is beyond language and corresponds to the non-place of the madwoman. Then each one of these women takes upon herself a little of the madness the idiot had borne. They bring their little bits—their crumbs—of madness: me too, me too. . . . Each one is "beside herself." They share dishwater and leavings from the table.. What was previously an object of disgust is no longer rejected: the women take it upon themselves.

The madness of the idiot does not enter into the communication any more than death does. It is not symbolizable. The castaway cannot be made into a "saint." The monastic operation fails. The madness of the madwoman consists in not participating (not being able to participate) in the circulation of the signifier; in being, in relation to madness itself, nothing but its "simulation"; in having experienced with language [*verbe*] nothing but a betrayal; in abstaining from the constitutive power of the spoken word; in denying that "it be done according to Thy word."[11] That woman could not be *there*—there where the discourse of the community places her. Lost in the other, "no one knows" where, she disappears. A "fallen thing," and "enraptured." To know her is to know nothing, "to know even less about her, less and less."[12] Thus it is with the story: it remains in suspense, it does not know. With "her," there is nothing to say or do. Go home with the secret that throws you off the track without your knowing toward what. Wisdom is still "not that."

Will the reader, seduced by this "nothing," in turn become mad also, or, when he has gone home, will he try to forget, if he can, what has been taken away from him? The madwoman, because she is never *there* where it could be spoken, has falsified the contract that the institution guarantees[13] and that protects one against the "vertigo" of not knowing "what to think about the other's desire, what I am to him."[14] Ultimately no contract, not even the first and last of all contracts, language itself, is honored by her. In repeating our words and our stories, she insinuates into them their deceitfulness. Perhaps while the *sym-bolos* is a union-producing fiction, she is a *dia-bolos*, a dissuasion from the symbolic through the unnameability of that thing.[15]

## LAUGHTERS OF MADMEN (SIXTH CENTURY)

Then come the madmen [*mōroi*], idiots [*saloi*], and maniacs [*exēch-euomenoi*]. Of the Mēne idiot woman, they seem to have retained only what has an air of Christlike heraldry and provocation: the dishrag halo about the head, the blows and oaths, the final transformation of derision into "ascension." Leaving aside an anonymous woman who, in a convent near Hermopolis in Thebaid (sixth century) "simulates" drunkenness near the latrines and, recognized as a saint by the monk Daniel, disappears one morning,[16] they are men: Mark, Simeon, Andrew, and so on.

After the madwomen of the convent come the madmen of the city. For the latter as for the former, madness is a means of achieving isolation in a crowd. It is the form hermitism takes when its setting is no longer the desert but a collectivity: whereas the *women* make of madness the way "to retain, in the very thick of the monastic community, the solitude of the anachoret,"[17] the *men* extend that experience to the city, where idiocy isolates them more than a cell. For both groups, *madness* goes together with the *crowd*. The men change it into an urban phenomenon, but one that has close parallels in the figures of the women beggars, prostitutes, and *belles de jour* whose stories have been excommunicated from this literature.

Of these madmen, a particularly picturesque one stands out in the sixth century, Simeon of Emesa (in Syria), who comes down from his lonely hermitage to challenge the city: "I am setting out to play the world along," he said. According to the *Ecclesiastical History* of Evagrius, he had subjected himself to enough trials in the desert to have attained *apatheia* (impassibility) and to be allowed to do anything in Emesa, where he plays the "idiot" [*salos*]. Still wearing his monastic habit, he does not hesitate to raise its skirts or even to take it off in front of everyone. He gets into a women's bath completely naked; he kisses little boys and girls in the street; he pretends to rape a married woman in her room; he accepts without protest the accusation of having seduced a maidservant. He even has his visits to the bordello, and can be seen dancing arm in arm with prostitutes, or climbing on the back of one while having himself flogged by another. He goes so far as to let himself be handled by them. . . . He tries to give the impression of being a bad Christian as well as a man with no morals. Monk though he is, he displays a total disdain for the teachings of the Church. If he sets foot in a church, it can only be to disrupt the liturgy. He chooses Holy Thursday to stuff himself publicly at the pastry shop, and he "eats meat like a godless man."[18]

Eccentric, bare-chested and brazen, jovial and brutal, this provoker wants to "overturn edification" according to the narrator. He boldly carries transgression into the camp of the self-righteous. He irritates, amuses, wins admiration or blows, but he does not divert language toward that which is without place. He is not seductive. Still less so is his later, moralizing counterpart at Constantinople (ninth tenth centuries), Andrew the Mad, such as he is depicted in his *Life*, written by Nicephorus.[19]

## A KIND OF LAUGHTER

Between these two, and the Egyptian idiot woman of the fourth century, Mark the Mad (sixth century) represents an intermediary. In the *Life of Daniel* he is made to emerge suddenly before the *abbas* Daniel in a street in Alexandria, "naked, with a towel wrapped around his buttocks," among madmen.

> He would come and go like an idiot [*salos*] and a maniac [*exēcheuomenos*],[20] stealing food from the marketplace which he would then distribute among the other idiots [*saloi*]. He was called Mark of the Horse. *The Horse* is a public bath: that is where Mark the idiot worked . . . and slept on the benches. . . . He was known to the entire city for his extravagant behavior.[21]

Although popular, the "old man" who had come down from his hermitage in Scete to visit the patriarch on Easter Sunday was unknown in the streets of Alexandria. He was not at home there. The day after his visit to the patriarch:

> The old man found Mark the idiot at the great Tetrapyle. He threw himself upon him and started to shout: "Citizens [*andres*] of Alexandria, help!" The idiot made fun of him. A large crowd gathered around

them. The disciple [Daniel's], frightened, kept at a distance. The people said to the old man: "Don't take this as an insult: he is an idiot." The old man said to them: "You are the ones who are the idiots [*saloi*]. Today I have not found a man [*anthrōpon*] in this city, besides him." Then there also came the church clerics who knew the old man and said to him: "Now what has he gone and done to you, that idiot?" The old man said to them: "Take him to the pope for me."[22] They led him there. The old man said to the pope: "There is at this moment no comparable treasure in this city."[23]

The public square, the public baths, and the market are here the urban equivalent of the kitchen in the female collectivity. Clothed only in his loincloth, the mark of the menial drudge, the remover of filth, rendering any service to the other idiots of the same corporation as his, Mark wanders within a space of bodies to be washed and fed. He is lost in an opaqueness that unites those who have been eliminated from meaning, the filth of the bodies and the madness of the multitude. He is only designated by a nickname, a mockery of a name. Identified with his place, "the Horse," as the idiot woman was with her instrument the "sponge." Below the level of man by distraction and animality, he, too, is situated at that point of abjection that allows the crowd an entire circulation of goods and words. It is upon him that the text hinges, a text that no longer takes up the question of the father [*abbas*] and the mother [*ammas*], thanks to the confrontation between a man and a woman, but rather that of a *man* (who is *anthrōpos*, and what is that?) in the course of a debate between men.

The old man assails the madman: he runs, he grasps on, he shouts. It is a strange intervention. But the story does not give us a psychological portrait; it traces the narrative profile of an enigma. It begins with that "going out." Daniel assails the idiot, as Piteroum did in tearing the idiot woman away from her kitchen. But he goes further than his predecessor: he goes down into the "kitchen"; he ventures into a no-man's-land that is "not safe" between those safe places—his cell at Scete and the patriarch's palace—that is, into a *public* place that is also an insane and material bottom, symbolically undefined, in which his Name is no more valid than the signs of his wisdom. In that amorphous mass of bodies and the crowd, in the night of meaning, he plunges into a gesture that is itself insane. He throws himself into it, outside of his abode and of himself. He, like Piteroum, "falls" on what (he) is lacking, on the secret of that Other. He leaves himself and his role, pretends to be insane, to enter into the indefinite, as if he, in turn, were seized by that sort of universal that overflows meaning. He is seduced, suddenly bewitched, by an absence.

He thus provokes a relation of forces by a hand-to-hand combat that is situated outside the symbolic relation. And in the story there is a proliferation of indications of violence: the frightened disciple, the call for help, the people crowding around the assailed idiot, the intervention of the clerics (that police of the symbol) to come to the aid of one of their own kind, the summons on the idiot brought before the patriarchal tribunal, and so on. It is the old man who has recourse to that violence in places where name and fame do not function. Thus he reveals the relationship that wisdom maintains with a power when it is no longer "at home"—in the monastery or the patriarchate—that is, when it is no longer sustained by an institution. His aggressive precipitation, like that of a monk in a disreputable place, is the slip that reveals, in its cause, what this cause hides from itself or does not know about itself.

The madman is jesting. The crowd, moreover, reflects that fact when it reassures the monk: It is nothing, he's an idiot. But as for the idiot, he has no thought of comforting the sage by being so abject an interlocutor. He does not come to the aid of wisdom by affirming the nullity of the other that wisdom encountered. The idiot *is* that very "other." In this account as elsewhere in the same series of texts, the idiot is a body made for blows and lowly tasks, a body long since dispersed, to be derided and not in need of being defended, no longer having anything to defend. His weakness is the strength of an absence, because already he "is waste." He no more obeys than resists the law of conflict. Fallen into the public domain like a piece of common property, he is delivered from that ownership upon which violence is founded. He neither speaks nor strikes out. He laughs. Thus he resembles one of the madmen presented in these stories,[24] or, later, a madman of the same family, Jean-Joseph Surin: "At every evil all I do now is laugh / I am exempt from fear and from desire."[25] This laugh is a non-place. The idiot *is not there* where Daniel "seeks" him, and he does not "answer." He is not there for Daniel. To whom, then, is this laugh addressed? To something other in him.

In that respect, the crowd is right: It is nothing, it is only an absence, nothing that is addressed to you. But Daniel, from his own perspective, is more lucid than the crowd is, for he gauges the questioning power of this nothing. He answers, therefore, but to those who are speaking to him: "You are the ones who are the idiots." But do his interlocutors really learn this from him? Like the women of Mēne who already expressed, before "confessing" it, the madness they had within, the passersby of Alexandria already know, by their complicity with the idiot, what their "treasure" is and what secret lives with them. On the other hand, discovering what he perhaps did not know, or learning to say it through that exchange with the crowd, the sage who is presumed to know—Daniel or Piteroum—appears to be there only to offer a kind of language to the knowledge of the others (that is, to their madness) and to underscore its altering effects in the privileged places of meaning (the patriarchate, the monastery). This seems to be his "theological" task: to trace, in the symbolic institutions, an otherness already known to the crowd and that they are always "forgetting."

### "THAT MAN"

What then is that "man" discovered by Daniel and found no place else, neither in the city nor in the papal palace? He is the one who has been seduced by the Other. Mark is a "man" by the madness that loses him in the crowd, in the hunger that damages economic and linguistic contracts, in the rapine and squalor that destroy whatever is one's own [*le propre*], in the animality that unsettles and alters the frontiers of humanity. He is man by that which diverts him (but toward what other thing, which is neither bound nor defined, not *there?*). He is the one seduced by an absolute. Is "man" his madness? No, for he is not in his madness either. According to the tale, Mark "simulates" madness as the idiot woman of Mēne did. He cannot be identified, nor does he identify himself, as the rest of the story shows, with the names given him by the crowd: "the idiot," "the Horse," and so on. He is elsewhere. His madness, too, is a semblance, although it does not hide a different truth. It participates in a strategy of appearances that vacillates between appearing wise and appearing crazy. Before the pope, Mark "confesses" that he has been converted to madness and that, just as later Teresa of Avila will want to "enter a corrupt Order," he said to himself: "Come on, let's go into the city and become an idiot [*salos*]." He is disguised. But is it madness or wisdom he disguises?

There is a feminine parallel to this in a contemporary (fourth- to sixth-century) practice. Pelagia, Marina, still others during that period, disguise themselves as men and pass for eunuchs.[26] It is less a question of concealing female identity beneath a male appearance than of abolishing the difference and overcoming the law of being "one *or* the other." An aphorism of the Gospel according to Thomas states the goal: "That the male not be male and the female not be female."[27] Homologous with the Pauline proposition "to become foolish in order to become wise," the injunction of the Gospel beckons toward a third term in which the other two are abolished: the multitude is the universal in which the difference between man and woman, wise men or fools, is to be dissipated. All disguised, men or women, wise men or fools, masks and mockeries of identity, *disappear* into a public, common intermediary zone. The essential is not, therefore, the transgression of an order (which is always there where positions are to be distinguished), but rather the *loss* of distinction in a non-place where there is a play of identities shifting to and fro, like semblances. The crowd, that chasm in which differences disappear, is the eclipsing of sex (male or female) and of *logos* (wise or foolish).

Evagrius notes, speaking of idiots, who were frequent figures at the public baths: "They want to be men with the men and women with the women, and to become as one of either sex without themselves being either."[28] No doubt there will be occasion to inquire more deeply into the body that institutes that absolute non-place, absolved from differences. It is already apparent from these texts that, like the woman disguised as a man, the simulation of madness transcends the order of "one or the other," to waver between "neither one nor the other" and "both the one and the other." While that simulated madness is, with good reason, circumscribed within the realm of the derisive by the multitude, it has as its only sign, in the idiot woman, an effacement and, in the idiot man, a laugh.

Having been declared a saint and called "father" [*abbas*] by Daniel in the presence of the pope, who thereupon puts him up in his palace, Mark will escape. The day after having been identified, he is found dead in his room in the morning. He was at ease when lodged at the Horse, a shady, rejected place. He could not stand the positivity and legitimacy of a patriarchal location. *There* he is but a corpse. The magnificent and pious ceremony organized in honor of the deceased "embalms" a dead man and substitutes a grave in place of "that man." It is "edifying": the place is constructed, reconstructed on the grave of the seducer who led astray the order founded on the making of distinctions. Honor to the dead: they make the palace, the monastery, and any other organization of meaning safe from that *otherness* they had introduced into them while still alive. Unless we have to contemplate something still worse: that their disappearance, covered up by edifying discourse, definitively separates the institution from what it lacks.

## RISKING LIFE AND LIMB

These stories depict relations. They do not treat statements (as would a logic) or facts (as in a historiography). They narrate relational formalities. They are accounts of transfers, or of transformational operations, within enunciative contracts. Thus, for example, there is a missing and seductive otherness of the idiot woman or idiot man only in *relation* to the wise man. The story, a theoretic fiction, sketches enunciative models (challenge, summons, duel, seduction, change of position, etc.) and not content (true statements, meanings, data, etc.). What is essential to it, therefore, is that which, in the form of "coups," transforms the relationships between subjects within the systems of meanings or of facts—as if, in speech, one were to consider only the changes of place among the speakers and not the semantic or economic orders from which these illocutionary exchanges nevertheless receive a field and a vocabulary for their operations.

It is to this problematic that our accounts of madness pertain (to be included in the broader genre of "stories about madmen," a corpus long replete with tricks and turns arising from a different, para-doxical logic). They defy differences, which are transformed into simulations against a background of absence. But here the play is "stabilized," so to speak, thanks to a difference that makes possible the eclipsing of the others: the relation that simulated madness bears to the body. A relation to the body makes possible *practices* of the infinite or, if one prefers, the actual, a spatial bringing into play of the unanalyzable. That relation acts as a limit. It stops the fading away of the Other into simulacra that replace one another indefinitely.

That relation to the body is presented in three modalities: (1) the masculine and the feminine (not to be identified with sexual difference); (2) hole-making orality (food, latrines, etc.) and garbage dissemination (kitchen, baths, etc.), which are correlative to the genesis and loss of all bodies; (3) asceticism, a taking charge of the other by the body. These three modulations all lead back to the absolute point of a "common" life, that is, to the gesture of "losing oneself in the crowd."

1. The eclipsing of sex does not abolish but rather brings into play what differs between a feminine and a masculine practice.[29] First, the accounts draw the idiot woman out of the crowd to declare her spiritual "mother" [*ammas*], thus bestowing upon her a paternal femininity; they draw out the idiot man so that they may find in him the "man" [*anthrōpos*] in making of him a "treasure," a particular sign linked up with meaning, a kind of sacrament. But the two antiheroes avoid that promotion, the idiot woman by her *retreat* to an unknown elsewhere, the idiot man by a *laugh* that his death and burial intensify. *She* faints into an abyss that in point of fact she contains. She disappears into herself, without a trace, "in a space in which no thought remains valid currency."[30] The account lapses into that absence. *He*, by his laughter or his embalmed corpse, produces a mark, but one that transforms the sacrament into a pure signifier, an insane mark, a flash or a scratch of what is going by but is not there: the account lapses

into that derision. In short, the woman turns into the *Other of the signifier*, into that limitless nothingness in which she loses herself. The man becomes the *signifier of the Other* to the point of being that laughter in which meaning no longer resides, and that corpse, a sign in which he no longer subsists. These are two practical experiences of the absolute, but the former brings into play an in-finite body, beyond the reach of faltering language; the latter, a body separated from that in-finite and as if dead, a fragment of language deprived of that toward which it points.

2. In both cases, one has a work dispersed (a thousand things, anything—wanderings) over all things destined to the mouth's gulf and all residual, excess, or dirty things, things eliminated by the body. This work is strewn out over all that goes to the hole, the way in and way out.[31] As it functions here, the body does not serve as a use value (one's own property) or as an exchange value (a communication). It is looked after, a bottomless hole, endless excess, like something that is not there per se, like something that is in a perpetual movement of confection and defection. It is nothing but the interminable exercise of its own appearance and disappearance. The servile activities articulate, in actual, widely distributed tasks—forever feeding, forever washing—the experience of these very real bodies, real and yet elusive between two losses. They lose within what they receive from without, and they lose without what they possess from within—therefore never *there*, like the loved body. It is in actuality a service of love, this service of the body in its physical defection, in its passing mobility, in that element of it that is always missing between the food that prepares its presence and the waste that marks its departures. These servile practices might be seen as the exercise of a sorrow of loving, a physical exercise of the absolute: lost time, dispersed action, and the body broken by the endlessness of preparation and waste.

3. The accounts continually relate madness to an asceticism that would sustain its practices. The word "asceticism" is jarring here. Does it mean that we must pay for our life with our body? That juridical aspect is clearly expressed in the texts considered here. It is part of a debt (to be paid) that, in most cases is associated with a misdeed. But something else is at stake here, something that inverts, by an emptying out and a dispersion, the compactness and uniqueness of the individual usually considered "responsible" for being "ascetic." That different sort of asceticism is hospitality. Not the kind of hospitality that gives out gifts, but that which the host exercises when he or she "receives." In the prodigality of his body and time, lost among the markets or the kitchen, he takes upon himself what the other lacks. He

makes room within himself for that silent voraciousness, like the beggar woman of Bengal who accommodates within her body the insatiable hunger of an *in-fans*. He offers a space within himself to that plural, invading, and silent Other. His body is thus turned inside out and disseminated by the exercise that makes him into a silent *abode* and a transferential *guarantor* for the unanalyzable and insane side of the other. Before the pope, at the hour of judgment, Mark relates that after having been "dominated for fifteen years by the demon of fornication," a prowler in search of prey, he converted his body into a dwelling for the madness of the crowd: "Become a *salos*." In place of the kind of grasp that dominates and counts conquests, there is a physical welcoming of the repressed element of the other. Having expressed this, the idiot man can do no more than die. As for the woman, she remains silent. That hospitable asceticism does not speak.

## THE CROWD

The crowd is thus, by the lost body that "receives" its madness, the paradoxical site of the absolute. It is the beginning and the end of these stories. In evoking the characteristics of this non-place, such as they appear in these stories, one merely retraces, in spatial terms, the functioning of seduction. The crowd is a *neuter* body, which is always the other (the "rest") and "neither one nor the other" in relation to the privileged places where the discourses of wisdom are held. It is a *public* body: anyone, anything, each and every, in contradistinction to the particular identities who are distinguished from this indeterminate background. It is an *originary* body that is looked upon as being an indefinite beginning in relation to the effects produced by the power and the will to "stand out."

But the singular, determinate positions can never totally obliterate their relation to the universal they "come out of." Is this the seduction of the unthinkable origin? The stories of simulated madness relate the leading astray provoked by the antiheroes precisely because these personages are like the rabble, destined to lowly tasks, to a scattered activity, and to an absence of identity. By their bodily relation with the nameless multitude, these fleeting witnesses become the enigmatic indices of the seduction that the crowd (which is diabolical and formless) exerts on the symbolic forms of wisdom. So it is that in their "idiocy" they frighten the wise man while they amuse the public.

One could discern in that crowd a historical homology to "matter" [*hylē*] in which Plotinus recognized the nocturnal fringe and "residue" left out of play by the analytic advance of the intelligence—a shadowy depth of things that would appear to have at once the func-

tion of origin (materia/mater) and of limit (the other) in the work of
distinction, an undetermined area [*aoriston*] that the mind fears as its
own abjection and fall into nonbeing. Plotinus described this formless
something by "sticking" onto the neuter singular article (a category)
the neuter plural of the nominal adjective "other": *to alla*, the (thing
scattered in) others.[32] But here that horizon of others, loosed from
language, is indicated in a *doing* and no longer in a not-knowing. An
ongoing practice shows the seduction exercised by the crowd, whose
madness all wisdom lacks. The absolute is practiced by risking life and
limb in the crowd.

What do we accomplish by commenting on this madness narrated
in remote stories, but whose advance could be traced up to Simone
Weil's notes on "the village idiot?"[33] Is it still the discreet working of
that same seduction that these texts betray? All those discourses could
(would like to?) have the status Socrates already gave to his own: "the
discourse that by my mouth, bewitched by you, you have just pronounced."[34] A break, a drifting, a madness of discourses exiled from
themselves by a lack, by an Other. . . . But they are still texts speaking
about that. They surround with words that absolute that is as disturbing as it is seductive. We are rather at the side of Piteroum and Daniel
(there is absence only for the one who remains *there*). The wise old
man indicates the position of the text—and the position possible for
the reader: the "secret" having been recognized but immediately lost,
each one returns home, to do what with what they have learned?

The work of a silence.

*Chapter Two*

✢ ✢
✢

# The Garden:
# Delirium and Delights of
# Hieronymous Bosch

For months on end, wandering within that closed space named *The Garden of Delights*, getting lost in it. Not that the space vanishes, escapes into those depths, cavities, grottoes, tubes, subterranean haunts, underwater hiding places, and somber sylvan nooks that it portrays. It is all on the surface. It offers itself entirely to the eye, to which it gives, in addition, a totalizing, panoramic view from on high, *a bird's-eye view*. It spreads out "in perspective," as later the different levels do in *The Gardens of Pleasure*. As we go through, we make more and more encounters, exquisite pleasures of the eye in its travels: the rose of a megalith, the silhouette of an orange-picker, lovers in a flower-shaped retreat. But these delights punctuate paths devoid of meaning. Blind enjoyment. What is this place, *locus voluptatis*, and other such gardens of lovers or mystics? What happens there? The painting becomes progressively more opaque as the prolific epiphany of its forms and colors becomes more detailed. The former hides itself in displaying the latter. The painting organizes, aesthetically, a loss of meaning.

## A PARADISE WITHDRAWN

By a historical accident (is it one?), no language comes from without to fill in this lack of meaning. Of the artist, Hieronymous Van Aken, called Bosch, who was for his entire lifetime a painter at Bois-le-Duc,

49

a member of Our Lady Confraternity, and who died in 1516, there remain no more than a few legal papers mentioning debts, contracts, orders, or decease.[1] Not enough to tell his story. No biography can serve as a commentary and/or an alibi for the work (1503–4), this large painted wood panel (220 × 195 cm), immobile in the half-light of the Prado, its paint cracked by five centuries of age. Nor is there any written text by the painter. There is no guide for *The Garden*, which makes up the central panel of this triptych. I lose my way in it.

Despite our knowledge of the iconography of the late Middle Ages, we have here the "pure and simple volatilization of meanings."[2] Wilhelm Fraenger concurs, but, being an acute observer, on the lookout for anything that might "signify," he wants to force the "mute oracle" to speak nonetheless.[3] His dictionary-machine (this "means" that) constrains each signifier to confess to a signified, thus transforming the painting into the transcription of a textual system. For others, and the best of them at that, such as Dirk Bax, the secret of *The Garden* arouses a rapt attention to its details.[4] It is the labor of a Sisyphus, curiosity trapped in the cryptogram-rebus. This painting plays on our need to decipher. It enlists in its service a Western drive to *read*. The meticulous proliferation of its figures calls irresistibly for indefinite narrativizing, whether it be that of a folklorist, a linguist, a historian, or a psychologist. This narrativizing, by countless erudite convolutions, makes each iconographic element tell a meaningful story. Like the discourse that is produced on the basis of dream fragments, the literature on *The Garden* is an endless series of stories elicited by some detail or other of the painting. Using a great many references, works, and *readable* documents, that literature produces its learned stories on the basis of pictorial fragments. Lettered stories seem endlessly generated by *The Garden of Delights*. In point of fact, these scholarly tales (the thousand and one nights of erudition) follow, or postpone, or deny the moment when the pleasure of seeing is the death of meaning. Often as contradictory as peremptory, the texts of knowledge flourish, but only in leaving, if not covering over, the locus of which they speak. Between the painting that brings about enjoyment and the commentaries that make one understand, the difference is first in the contrast between the closed space of the former and the indefinite dissemination of the latter, and in the exteriority of the pleasure of seeing in relation to discursive work.

Could it be, then, that the precondition of discourse is to be expelled from this paradise? One must have lost it in order to be able to make a text of it. In articulating it in a language, we unremittingly prove we are no longer there. It is in vain that I seek a beginning in this painting, in order to construct a linear development of meaning. That space is curved inward upon itself, like the circles and the ellipses Bosch endlessly generates, while at the same time excluding the square.[5] There is no entrance. That is, no doubt, a general problem. "The plastic work presents, for the profane, the inconvenience of not knowing where to begin, but for the connoisseur the advantage of being able to vary abundantly the order of reading, and thus of becoming conscious of the multiplicity of its meanings."[6] *The Garden* cannot be reduced to univocity. It offers a multiplicity of possible itineraries, the traces of which, as in a labyrinth, would constitute so many stories, until one comes to a dead end that marks a forbidden meaning. But there is something more here. The painting seems both to *provoke and frustrate* each one of these interpretative pathways. It not only establishes itself within a *difference* in relation to all meaning; it produces its difference in *making us believe that it contains hidden meaning.*

## THE ILLUSION OF HIDDENNESS

"The art of Bosch," wrote André Chastel on *The Temptation of Saint Anthony*, "proceeds on the basis of a deliberate flight from the object that can be given a name."[7] That "deliberate flight" consists in seducing denomination, all the better to deceive it. The painting routs the nameable (and its stories) by its very familiarity with it, playing the hidden meaning game. Very far from being a code language or a "symbolic cryptography of Nature,"[8] it only gives that illusion; it is separated from them by a distance endlessly created by each of the new interpretations to which it gives rise. This, at any rate, is my hypothesis. So it is no longer enough to say that this paradise is withdrawn, being-there lying behind signs that await a good reader. It does not cease *withdrawing*, thanks to the *secrecy effect* it produces, and that active withdrawal is sustained by the decoding activity that the painting entraps by its simulated secrecy. The "hidden" is the trompe l'oeil by means of which the image constitutes itself in its difference in relation to the sign. *The Garden* leads one to suppose that one is given to *understand* something different from what one is given to *see*. Its "lie," a diabolical temptation (to pretend to conceal is to *seduce* discourse, at once to give rise to it and to lead it astray), is precisely its way of positing the otherness of the painting, of outwitting interpretative colonizations, and of keeping, preserved from meaning, the pleasure of seeing. It produces the unnameable in organizing itself as if the figures were the vocabulary of an unnamed, the ciphers of an unsaid.

The secret of *The Garden* is to *make you believe* that it possesses some sayable secret—or rather to promise one secret (meanings hidden from the understanding) in place of another (the enjoyment given to the eye). It paradoxically engenders its opposite, namely the commentary that turns each form into script and wants to fill that entire colored space with meanings to make it into a page of writing, a discursive analysis. These glosses have the style of President Schreber's *Memoirs*: the *interpretative delirium* that Bosch's challenge unleashes does not tolerate the *Nichtsdenken* ("to think of nothing" or "to think of nothingness"). The production comes from the spectator, captivated by the painting's ruse. Bosch has been called a raving lunatic: quite to the contrary, he *makes others rave.* He turns on our meaning-producing mechanisms. But in withdrawing from the elaborations and works brought on by the false promise of a meaning hidden behind the picture, he becomes a stranger to their places and time, he becomes a non-place and a non-time, differentiating himself more and more from that to which he gave birth. Remote from the tales that tell of him, he functions like the paradise of myths or of delight. A *senseless beginning* causes the discourses of meaning to be produced.

Of course, when I take this beginning to be outside the realm of meaning, I do not thereby avoid the law it initiates; I am no nearer the site it created. On the contrary, my postulate says nothing but what makes me in turn write of (on the subject of: *de*) and exiles me from (far from: *ex*) this painting. My postulate explains nothing other than the relationship that writing maintains with the pictorial space that seduces it, that is, with what gives birth to it yet eludes it, with pleasures shielded from meanings.

Bosch's *Garden of Delights* plays precisely on that relation. In that period of "subtle, savory saying, rhetorical games, laughter and pranks," of *jonglerie* and *fatrasie*, drifting toward a "generalized ambiguity,"[9] at that time when a refined aesthetics also reinforced the doubts that were disarticulating the great dogmatic and symbolic account of the universe, the subject of the painting could be the Edenic life (R. H. Wilenski, 1958), the world before the flood (E. H. Gombrich, 1967), the feast of the senses (H. Rothe, 1955), the *ars amandi* of the Free Spirit Brethren (W. Fraenger, 1947) or an "apothesis of sin" (M. Friedländer, 1941), a *Comoedia Satanica* (F. M. Huebner, 1965), or yet again the satire of vanity by a "Northern Savonarola" (H. Daniel, 1947), and so on. A swarm of hypotheses. To the extent that they seek an ideological referent, they remain secondary, if it is true that this work, "unique in the history of art and religion"—in any case, "without equivalent" in the Flemish production of its day—stages the play of mistaken identity between a garden of pleasurable enjoyment, a delicious nowhere, on the one hand, and on the other the discursivity of history, that is, the autonomy of painting in relation to all the proses of the world.

## THE PAINTING LOOKS BACK

The fact of there being nothing to read in the painting means that there is nothing to look for behind it, that it is all there, marked, including the keeping-at-a-distance of reading. Besides the derision Bosch everywhere attached to readers and talkers (duck-billed preachers, conjurer-braggarts, fish-shaped clerics), several stage directions mark that shielding of painting from discourse: hands off, work of art. I will indicate three of them, one involving its architectonics, the other its emblems, the third its iconic vocabulary.

The *architecture* of each of the three panels focuses on a sort of eye, a pupil repeating the terrestrial globe of the drab outer world, analogous to the pupil in which *The Seven Deadly Sins* (1475–80) was depicted. From that pupil a look, from an inside, comes to rest upon the observer. In the left panel, from out of the round hole dug into the center of the circular fountain—madder-colored like the dawn, an absolute center toward which the entire painting leads us back—an earless tawny owl stares out of the darkness at the observer. Instead of seeing, I am seen. The middle panel also has as its axis and focal point, two-thirds of the way up (the golden number), a fountain of life, a pupil placed between the curves of the woods and repeated by its projection in the form of an ellipse on the lower level (the basin of naked girls), a veined blue globe, both eye and precious stone. At its base, inscribed on the only horizontal line that crosses the painting, there is a cavity in the shadow of which can be seen a man holding a woman's pudenda and looking at the observer.

Acting as a focal point for the panel on the right ("Hell") and placed at the center of gentle curves like eyelashes, the large white oval of a male body—broken egg, tree in ruins—forms an ellipse (and an ellipsis) joined to the disc-shaped plate that serves him for a hat, with, between the two, that head turned toward the observer, with a sidelong look. That looking face is analogous to Dürer's *Melancholia I* (1514), that "genius" of a wisdom that remains serene amidst crises heralding modernity.[10] His body is inhabited, like a cave, by the disorders of the tavern and his head ironically adorned with bagpipes (so much rumor that is but "wind"). But his contemplation escapes, without denying them, the frantic activity and tortures of an infernal environment (this "Hell" is *our* world). This look, an interrogating force born of a "sadness for no reason," sees farther, from out of a retreat unconcerned with all these things. It stops on us, who are moving. It fixes me.

To these three strategic points, "retreats" in the middle of the bursting forth of bodies alternately happy and sad, should be compared the motionless tawny owl and great eagle-owl who, like columns, frame the amorous dances and games in the lower portion of the middle panel. Typically Boschian portrayals of "melancholy," these owls seem to represent within the carnivalesque manifestation the structure that organizes it. Their wide-eyed look traverses the daytime festival as if it were a night. But the important thing is that structure itself that disposes, around the hole from which *another look* protrudes, the multifarious theater of the forms of pleasure or suffering.

As in fairy tales and so many legends, a look emerges from the depths of these gardens. Diabolical or divine, probably neither. In the left panel, Christ uniting Adam and Eve makes up a part of the landscape placed under the dependence of the eye of the owl, who, from the central fountain, a morning bunker, watches the space and "looks for" us. In the same way, Satan only makes up an episode in the left panel, the focus of which is the man-tree. The divine persons (Christ, Satan) are, like the others, subjected to the gaze of another, who organizes the painting and looks at the observer. The gaze of that wisdom is no longer diabolical nor divine; it simultaneously comes from the representation (it is one of its figures) and distances itself from it (it is withdrawn, observing): it is human (superhuman?). It is, *within* the painting, its nucleus of strangeness. It plays that same role in relation to the onlooker, the visitor to this site; it keeps him at a distance. This point, the eye, an object *seen* by the onlookers, begins to *look back* at them.[11] It stops being a sign to be read and looks down on us. It perforates the pictorial sky and judges us.

## Emblems/Enigmas

In the lower right corner of each of the panels, three playlets also involve the relationship of the painting to an explanatory text, that is, to an assigning (written or deictic) of meaning. They are emblematic.[12] To the left, half emerging from the pond in which it swims, a threefold being—having a dolphin's tail, man's torso, and a hooded duck's head—*reads*, in solitude, an open book. In the center, also half emerging from a cave, a man, the only one wearing clothes in the panel, *points* to a nude woman leaning on her elbows behind a sculpted glass crystal, Eve and/or Sibyl, with an apple in her hand and her mouth closed with a seal. Last, to the right, a pig adorned with a nun's headdress holds out a quill pen to a seated man whose face he caresses with his snout and whose leg, an improvised table, supports a document that has already been *written* and (?) ready to be signed. On either side of that odd couple are a lost person with a stoup on his shoulder, carrying more parchments on his head and in his hands, and a gryll[13] in the form of a salamander with a bird's beak, helmeted like a knight, presenting the inkwell and penholder.

To read, to show, to write: these three verbs aim at meaning. But they are turned away from meaning by their iconic representation—ironic on the left, enigmatic in the center, tragicomic on the right. The painting occupies and reverses the place reserved for the writing that is supposed to give to drawing the counterpoint of a "letter" (the "motto") or an explanation (the "gloss"), and therefore trace in script the contracts of language. The picture turns its reference to writing into derision. If writing is an entrance of meaning into the painting by way of the nameable, that door, still marked on the wall of colors, is henceforth blocked. The message remains sybilline, the secret of a woman closed up in the crystal of her monstrance, mouth closed, and shown only by the pointing finger that substitutes a seeing for writing. The contract to be signed seems to be a contract with the devil, a language therefore as deceptive as it is tempting, binding the captives of a meaning destined to deceive. Perhaps the look that the figure pointing to the Sibyl and the reluctant writer turn on the observers of the painting, seconding the one that is directed to those same observers from out of the middle of each panel, indicates what takes the place of writing: reader, *someone* is watching you, without your knowing *who* sees you nor *what* is being shown.

## ENCYCLOPEDIAS THAT CREATE ABSENCES

The *vocabulary* of *The Garden of Delights* also refers to a problematics of meaning, but it does so in order to construct a fiction that plays upon it. Like the traditional *mappa mundi*, like the maps of the time (those of Martin Waldseemüller or Mathias Ringman at Saint-Dié), the garden is a space that makes possible an encyclopedic summation. It is the map of the world, or of a world. It groups forms and signs normally dispersed. Local or exotic produce, flowers, trees, buildings from various countries are brought together in that miniature of the universe that is the vocation of gardens, past and present. In its profusion, Bosch's "paradise" ties in all possible beings. Real or imaginary, it matters little which, they have, as signifiers, equal claim to inclusion in the collection. We have, therefore, lexical series. Mammals: lion, panther, camel, bear, stag, boar, horse, ass, ox, goat, pig, griffin, unicorn, and so on. Birds: stork, heron, spoonbill, rooster, hen, goose, owl, shoveler, jackdaw, parrot, female duck, drake, halcyon, hoopoe, woodpecker, hawfinch, and so on. Fruits: pineapple, cherry, blackberries, gooseberries, strawberry, orange, apple, sloe, melon, and so on. Vegetables: pumpkin, squash, and so on. There are also men and women, blacks and whites, mermaids and *zeeridders* [mermen], winged men, *putti*, fairies, and so. Each species has its mythological variant. It is a museum of natural and imaginary history combined with an anthropological museum.

That collector's competence, always careful of precise detail, extends to shellfish, gems, precious stones (for example, chrysolites, emeralds, "saphistrans," topazes, and so on), various marbles, rare metals (for example, melted gold, wrought copper), and the whole catalogue of crystallomancy so widespread at the time.[14] The same is true of the feasts of that era, reflected in *The Garden* by monumental towers, tiered cakes, sweet dishes displaying unbelievable automata, baroque fountains inhabited by special-effects personnel, baths intended for free love, resembling the masked balls of clerics or the dances of naked youths making provocative gestures during the feast of fools.[15] The four megaliths at the back and the fountain (arranged, by the way, as if in the middle of a town square), the basin with nude girls, the horsemen's carousel, the coral-red tent, the portal arch to the ornate belvedere, the triple pink and blue obelisk next to it, and so on, look like historical documents, as if one were looking at a genre painting of a traveling aristocratic fair. Such a thing had been seen in Lille in 1454, or in Bruges in 1468. This museum is also a journalistic presentation of current events and a plan for a city.

The entomological fervor of this painter of a society also punctuates his collections with the vocabulary of alchemy: the philosophical egg (represented several times and placed in the middle of the carousel, like a "conceptual point" on the medial axis of the painting), the alembic, the retort, the "athanor," the inhabited vase, various cucurbitaceae (the pumpkin, etc.), owls, the hollow tree, crescent moons, the fountain of youth, the lovers in transparent spheres or in baths, and so on.[16]

By the accuracy of its reconstruction, each one of the elements brought together within the space of this museum retains its value of being the recognizable *fragment* of a language. It is present there as one piece of a lacunary system. Thus it, in turn, generates a collector's need to complete it with what the painting does not show, to restore it to its place in the series from which it was extracted and which is outside of the painting. The encyclopedic variety of registers upon which that cartographic composition is based encourages, with each detail, the proliferation of reconstructive undertakings. It moves the viewer to produce a profuse discourse born of the relation that the "fragments" bear to the lacunae to be filled. A strange picture: a plethora of signifiers multiplies the number of lacunae, which leads to the endless account of missing elements.

### THE ALCHEMY OF AN AESTHETICS

This reference to systems evoked by extracts or fragments found on the surface of the painting might be designated under the general heading of alchemical allusions, making up a Boschian metalanguage. Alchemy is, in fact, based on the difference between the visible and the readable. It links esoteric signs (visible but illegible) to "carefully hidden" knowledge.[17] Thus it separates a not-knowing from a knowing how to read. Alchemy will thus be privileged in the commentaries. Indeed, beside the fact that it belongs to the general culture of the period (and not merely to a few isolated groups),[18] arcane discourse corresponds precisely to the situation of the exegetes, who suppose that they have iconic "signs" to decipher on the basis of a knowledge reserved for the "sons of science." This sort of discourse identifies painting with the relationship a number has with the knowledge of the "essences" and their "conversions." It therefore formulates the interpreter's rather than the painter's ideology.

There is alchemy in the painting, but it affects the "conversion" (or, as it was called, the *putrefactio, decoctio,* and *exaltatio*) of this encyclopedic vocabulary, whereas reading first reduces the image to a complex written sign and then makes this sign into the expression of arcane knowledge. Taking up the signs that accommodate all the scientific curiosities of his time in his painting, Bosch makes them function *differently,* just as he does the various fragments of the world that he brings together in the non-place of his painting. He makes them into a garden. Like the steam engine in Turner's painting, the products of contemporary technology are detached from the practice or knowledge of which they were the expression. They are given up to games, to those very games of nude bodies draping them with garlands. Gathered from the trees of knowledge and in the cities at the "autumn of the Middle Ages," they no longer "mean" the work and the messages of a period. This deflection is brought about within the carefully reproduced vocabulary of the cultural or learned discourse of a society. A metamorphosis changes the status of terms without modifying their phenomenal singularity. Another world insinuates itself into the same signs. The painting modifies these signs by assigning them the ambivalent capacity of still being understandable as fragments of meaning systems, even though they are already set within a different space, one that "converts" them into an aesthetics.

˙ Compared to Roman Jakobson's table of linguistic functions,[19] that alchemical "conversion" of the images makes them pass from a "referential" (intending the knowledge of a context) or "conative" (aimed at modifying the receiver of the message) function to a "poetic" one. The iconic vocabulary thus changes not in content but in status. Its value of expression (relative to a referent) or of action (relative to a receiver) fades away before the "palpable" and "sensible" quality of the signifier itself. Thus a sound becomes musical when it ceases to indicate a meaning (the creaking that connotes a door) or an action (the shout that calls for help). This metamorphosis is frequent among the mystics: the criterion of the beautiful replaces that of the true. It carries the sign from one space to another, and it produces the new space. It is by this metamorphosis that a chart of knowledge is transformed into a garden of delights.

## A FANTASY WORLD OF MEANING

Perhaps the golden outline or the colored dotted line with which Bosch often delineates contours and replaces indications of shadow or volume marks this carrying over of objects, their metaphors, into painting. This quasi-signature of his "manner" circumscribes by the trace of a halo what he does with things in detaching them from the world to place them in the painting. On their fringes, the signifiers become iridescent from a different air. Their being changes in a different space.

That foreign luminosity has metonymic value in relation to the metamorphoses that are carried out in the painting, as in one of those retorts dear to Bosch. The procedures that generate a fantasy world can be noted, but they postulate a system of contemporary thought upon which these operations on the signs work. It is this postulate that makes possible the effects of the procedures. But it is a postulate that belongs to a different *episteme* than our own.

From Cazotte to Maupassant, the literary fantastic of the nineteenth century settled in the gap created by the modern split between the "real" and the unreal. That literature presupposed, between *real* and *fictitious*, the break brought about by an epistemology of objectivity. By playing one of these two terms against the other (that noise, that shadow, is it an "illusion" or something "real"?), it progressively muddled the opposition on which the positivist affirmation of reality rests. In place of the localizations that distinguish the objective from the subjective, it substituted the disquieting insecurity of these determinations and therefore of the real itself. This work (novelistic or pictorial) of destabilization attacked the scientistic dichotomy of the nineteenth century from behind the lines. It was synchronic with it, and, since Kafka, has vanished with it.[20]

There is an analogous destabilization in Bosch, but it does not target the border that in the nineteenth century circumscribed an objective knowledge of the real. It is directed over a system of meanings. What it disturbs is the signifiers' status as stable contracts with entities or concepts, their being able, in distinguishing themselves from one another, to denominate the thought (a *ratio*) that organizes beings and to form a system among themselves so as to spell out the great paradigmatic account of the universe and manifest it as a whole conceived by a Logos, to read that whole and have it read by others as the "natural" revelation that a Speaker, through the complex texture of the world, addresses to listeners. That legibility is radically questioned in the fifteenth century, at once by a *critique of the sign*, that is, of the relation (supposedly stable) between signifier and signified, and by the gradual substitution of a *problematics of production* (to create all possible artifacts) for that of deciphering (to internalize by reading—*intus legere*—the mysteries of the world, hidden messages). These two movements intersect, since one insinuates beneath the determination of the ideas an indefinite mobility of the singularities, and the other introduces, thanks to "ways of imagining," the intoxication of creating a multitude of possibilities. Here we have the undoing of the connections of meaning between properties or essences that the act of naming carved out. Ockhamist linguistics, the virtuosity of a new intellectual lability, apocalyptic visions, rhetorics that invent forms and beings sketch out nowhere worlds, within the very text of a cosmos unsure of its postulates. These different languages, artifacts produced by a combinative process detached from the traditional referent, were, moreover, soon to serve as explicative and descriptive ("ethnological") discourses for the New World that Christopher Columbus would discover (1492–1504) at the time when Bosch was to paint his fantastic Peru. Their "artificial" fabrication preceded their experimental use.

The "legend" of the Old World (that which one "must read" of things in their signs) is deconstructed by Bosch, who displaces the units of meaning piece by piece; he disturbs, by his hybrids and changes of proportion, the classifying order that was constituted by linking units of meaning together, the same way a sentence is produced by articulating words together. Everywhere Bosch smuggles in lapsus, disproportion, and inversion.

But he does it with such precision of detail and such methodical art that he imposes at once the verisimilitude of his figures (that is, that which makes us believe in their "realism") and the simulacrum of painting (that is, the real space of fiction). On the one hand, the signifiers give (to our vision) the real (imaginary or not, that is not the question) but without meaning. The verisimilitude of their existing coincides with the impossibility of thinking them. On the other hand, the organization of the forms and colors is so incontestable that its illegibility is thereby increased. There is a sentence and no meaning. That is how the alliance between the *sermo* and the *ratio*, which until then had been foundational, comes to be broken. It is as if one had a grammar but without the corresponding logic. That "different" grammar is no longer linked with the true, the thought, or the named. It is analogous, rather, to the grammar of a glossolalia, the phonemes of which could be taken for words. Built with a "realist" vocabulary, that nonsemantic order troubles the postulates that make one believe in a meaning of things. After all, things may have nothing but a *semblance* of meaning. What has been termed the "intellectual fantastic"[21] of Bosch inquires not so much about the known or the real as about the undecidable part of its meaning, or the surreptitious disappearance of what made intelligibility credible.

THE PRODUCTION OF FORMS:
ONE INSIDE THE OTHER

That disturbance introduced by the "fantastic" is the result of processes. As with the greatest ones, such as Borromini, it is sustained by an intoxication with techniques. In a painting by Bosch, though one may not be able to explain "what it means" (and for the very good reason that it attacks precisely that pretension, which nevertheless reappears endlessly), one can analyze how, according to what rules, it is produced. This replacement, too, is characteristic: the *ratio* of meaning is taken over by a *ratio* of fabrication. In that respect, the *Boschdrollen*,[22] the "drolleries" of Bosch (his "droll stories") do not tell a story past or imaginary, but the story of their production. They put on stage a combinatory mechanism that multiplies the possibilities of relations between the elements and that, in so doing, deconstructs and reconstructs forms. This sort of painting is an art of making (and not an art of saying) in which the artist and the craftsman are one. It harks back, moreover, to the practices of the Van Aken family (the grandfather, the father, three of the uncles, and Bosch's brother are *maelre*, painting professionals, and his nephew is an "engraver of images").[23] That art of making escapes the prestige of the message; rather, it is related to the subtleties and tricks of a trade. It is rooted in the specific circumstances of the working milieu in which aesthetic exercise (in the sense in which one speaks of spiritual exercise) does not conform to the ideologies of schools.

In this genius of formal mutation, one can recognize the ability to produce the fantastic, thanks to processes small in number but carried out with virtuosity. A few examples will suffice to grasp the forms in the very movement of their "formation."

The first process: The form (essentially the circle or the sphere) *opens onto its other* by a transparency, a break, or a hole. The grisaille painted on the closed outer wings of the triptych already shows this movement. In the night of time, the transparent globe of the cosmos, half filled with the dormant water from which the earth emerges like a fermenting swamp, is cut vertically by the interval between these outer panels that will fold back and open the cosmos to the colorful, dancing profusion of *The Garden*. The still, tragic circle of the beginning splits apart to "make room" for the carnival of delight that unfolds upon the three levels of the central panel. The outside is the other of the inside. The circle is exteriority dedicated to difference from its interior. In the *one*, there is the *other*.

That dynamics of metamorphosis, a passage from one form to another, is repeated ten, twenty times in *The Garden*: the couple appearing in the opening of an orange; the figures looking out through the rent in a strawberry as if from the balcony of a belvedere; the three youths enlaced in the volutes of a thistle; the lovers in the half-opened pearl oyster; the partners caressing one another in the bubble (transparent and closed, as in a dream) of a pineapple blossom; others who, carried off on a white horse, hide their amorous play beneath the cupola of a red saddle blanket; others whom a translucent hemisphere encircles with a halo and holds prisoner; or yet again those kissing through the tear in a mottled gourd.

Everywhere, they are obsessive: *enclosure* within the globe, and its opposite, *breaking in*. The latter possesses two iconic variants: either the breaking of the circle if it is opaque, or its transparence if it is closed. The circular island lets the distortion either break its border or take place in the middle of it. The "perfect" form either gets chipped around the edges or scooped out in the center in order to make room for its other. Perhaps the broken egg or crystal ball, that coincidence of the two "moments"—the closing and the hatching—also applies to the terrestrial globe, the garden of delirium-delight, the androgynous embrace and narcissism of the image itself. Its recurrence, in any case, increases the number of ways Bosch stages the deconstruction-recon-struction of the circle, which is the figure of definition (and of the definitive) and the ambivalence of movement (is it opening or clos-ing?). Thus it is with the blackberry from which a heron bursts forth; the urn, a hollow pineapple in which the man lies stretching greedily toward the cherry; the luminous hoop in which a porcupine lies flat; the broken egg into which the crowd, emerging from the sea, rushes as if through the doors of a temple; and many others. These variants orchestrate the formal structure, composed, at the center of the mid-dle fountains, of the round hole out of which emerge the outsider's gaze of the tawny owl or of Eros, and, at the place bearing the signa-ture, the semicircular hollow from which the dark man, unusual be-cause clothed, points to the crystalline nakedness of the close-mouthed Eve-Sibyl.

## PATHS LEADING NOWHERE

To the process that distends the visible in the active contradiction of an interior and exterior must be added the one that produces, in equally varied ways, vagaries of forms. The well-defined loses its out-lines; its edges drift and blend into what is next to them. Rather than a flexibility of transition, we have here forms in transit. They are "metaphors" in process. This slippage, a gentle outflow of figures, is all the more disturbing in that it is carried out with the greatest clarity of detail (nothing hidden, no shading, no blur, no impressionism) and in an absolutely stable, even rigid framework, (the division into three horizontal zones, each equal to one-third the height of the panel; the strict parallelism between the spherical masses at the top and bottom; the pyramidic and cruciform architecture symmetrically located in the lower part; etc.). The forms travel, but within a fixed space. A revolu-tion surreptitiously stirs the elements, but it does not (yet) stir the world or ground, flat as a map, upon which these movements take place.

In a characteristic detail of the lower area of *The Garden*, the slip-page of the descending lines constituted by the position of the figures, on the left and the right, comes to rest on the ground. These driftings stop at *angles of stoppage* (sitting, lying, kneeling, or leaning positions, with hands or feet flat, etc.), the perpendicular base of which is the ground. The flow of forms stops at the edges of a cosmic framework, as if the metamorphoses, an inner mobility, had as their condition of possibility the stability of the outer border. It is the eve of the modern period, which will compromise that circumscription with the experience of an infinite universe. When that time comes, the disappearance of outer limits will bring on, for a long period, the labor of "stopping" and stabilizing the internal forms, of delimiting, distinguishing, and classifying units. In Bosch, the metamorphic process alters the internal divisions. It creates an undefined becoming (an outflowing temporalization) of the beings placed within a fixed framework. There things pass, flow by, change.

The space within which these transformations take place at first appears to be an abstract, regular field constructed by geometric distinctions within a square, which makes up the sides. Thus we have, in the central panel, an overall division into three areas, one on top of the other (I, II, III, counting from the top; see fig. 1); then a star-shaped subdivision of the lower area (III), further subdivided by three angles converging on a common central apex, each of which is bisected by a median (hence the segments 1 through 6, in III; see fig. 2); last, within each of these segments, an arrangement of figures that echoes that of the top area (I) (see fig. 3). The entire painting is a blueprint of places to build. It does not presuppose a ground of reference, like Brueghel's urban sites or fields of wheat. It is cartographic in nature— a matter of geometry in space. It is a taxonomic table allowing for homogeneous projection and the classification (by "locale" or by function) of encyclopedic information. This map is an "art of memory." Each section is a sort of compartment in which a geographical variant may be placed: woods (III, 1), swamp (III, 2), lawn (III, 3 and 4), and so on.

The whole constitutes an ensemble of places destined for pathways and crossings: for gathering and hunting (nomadic activities) but not for agriculture or planting (sedentary activities). This bias is connected with a *"nomadization" of space* (and not just of beings or of things), either by increasing the number of cartographic strata within the same space, or by the drifting of the borders defined by each of these maps.

There are, indeed, other constructions that may be added to the one I have isolated: for example, in the central panel, the triangle formed by the three owls (at either side of the middle zone and in the middle megalith); or the structure formed by the bearers of red fruitballs in the four corners (the two figures in the foreground and the two winged figures in the sky), whose diagonals meet in the middle of the central pool; or, in the bottom zone, the equilateral triangle formed by the three fruit-giving birds; and so on. These maps, the more of which we see the more we look, all occasion their own classification and treat-

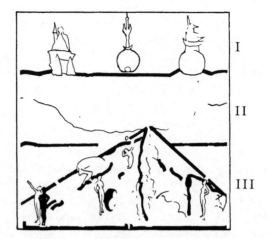

Figure 1.

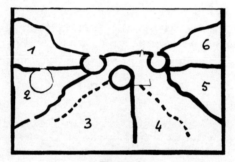

Figure 2.

Figure 3.

Figure 4. *A well-tempered geometry* (central panel, lower half)

ment (for example, the monuments and activities of the city, or the geography and symbols of paradise, etc.). They pile up, like different, stratified taxonomies. They also interact, as in the "model" of space that Freud constructed in imagining what Rome would be if each of its spatial configurations had remained intact and interpenetrated with all the others.[24] In Bosch, the space produced in the same framework is a proliferation of heterogeneous and coexisting geometries. It bursts apart *from excess*, but without each of the "orders" from which it is composed disappearing. It is a Babel in which the maps accumulate and mix without dissolving. A spatial polyglotism.

Moreover, the boundaries seem to be there only in order to be crossed, or, more precisely, crossing each other. Various techniques are used: imperceptible slippages (for example, from water to land, in III, 2 and III, 3); transverse crossings (for example, the lovers lying across the border between III, 4 and III, 5); arabesques that bind two figures above the line of demarcation between segments (for example, the tendrils crowning the boat-orange of zone III continuing into zone II with the nervous curves formed by the legs of the horses in the cavalcade); the points and stripes that advance from one place to another (for example, the spires of the megaliths, the man-birds and flying fish that soar from the horizon into the sky, etc.). The spatial setting keeps being disturbed by these border effects that posit in an *equally* artificial way both the boundary and its being crossed. It is well known that the bridge is a formal figure dear to Bosch, the iconic motif of "deviltry." It is generalized to become an organizing principle by which distinction itself becomes a means of deviancy.

### A Universal and Teratological Language

The above also holds true for beings, the parts of which only become the object of so precise an analysis and anatomy so that they may be combined with or substituted for other parts, in accordance with rules that defy the norms. The two dominant processes involved here consist either in "sticking" incoherent elements *next to one other* or in putting *one* (foreign element) *in place of the other* ("natural") *one*. An example of collage, the flying ensemble welds together, at the upper left, the green branch, the red starling(?), the pink horseman, the pale green griffin, and the blue-green bear: an aerial synthesis in which the colors contradict the forms, this carnivalesque configuration simultaneously posits and negates the distinction between orders. An example of substitution is the blue plum that the reclining lover has in place of a head—a fruit offered to his beloved, whom he kisses. By being repeated, these techniques of *coincidatio* and *substitutio* produce a proliferation of monsters, indicative of possible combinations and movements among species (an enormous fecundity), but dangerously transgressive in relation to the classification that postulates a stability of biological forms.[25] They quietly introduce a mixing of genres everywhere (animal, vegetable, human), an iconic analogy of a universal language made up of all languages.

In the end these "disorderly" combinations rely more on proportion (miniaturizing, hypertrophy) than hybridization (by substitution, inversion, and collage). It is true that a make-believe based on the human body organizes mixed beings (a bird replaces the head; a flower, the torso, etc.) and face-to-face encounters (man-bird, man-fruit, etc.) that disturb both the order of things and of proximities. But the most visible technique consists in modifying the scale of beings. It does not just set up, as in *Gargantua and Pantagruel* or *Gulliver's Travels*, an arbitrary but stable norm of relative sizes. It changes the norms constantly, enlarging the oyster, the pineapple, the strawberry, the duck, the tawny owl, alongside little human beings; miniaturizing the herons placed next to a monumental hawfinch or aglossa moth; reducing the freed bird next to the incandescent stalk of the pineapple, and so on. The differences themselves are unstable: "Bosch's *disparities*," as they were called as early as the sixteenth century.[26] That plasticity in proportional relationships jars through and through the spatial postulate of an order, that is, the permanence of a scalar relationship, *one sole* measure.

### NARRATIVE WANDERINGS

"In the work of art, pathways are laid out for that spectator's eye that is engaged in exploring, like an animal grazing in a field."[27] Bosch's garden offers ways to get lost. Landmarks point out possible ways to wander; detached, as in a dream, from any assured meanings, they come from afar. Their reappearances here and there in the painting suggest travels marked along the way by strawberries, cherries, eyes that are spheres or sexual organs, oral or anal obsessions. These pathways of nonmeaning, like a network of endless anamneses, constitute the Elsewhere of a paradise that is not that of an esoteric doctrine, a myth of the past, or a contemporary carnival

> *Mais le vert paradis des amours enfantines . . .*
> *Est-il déjà plus loin que l'Inde et que la Chine?*[28]

> But the green paradise of childhood loves . . .
> Is it already farther away than India or China?

Yes, because the Indian allusions of the landscape, its Chinese ornaments (such as its crystals), and its Turkish elements (for example, the treelike demon) are the metaphors of a different exoticism. To name these treasures of the Orient, as Baltrušaitis does admirably, is to deploy a vocabulary, not the sentence. A dictionary, not a poem.

Certainly it is true that the iconography of ancient Greece and Rome, and of medieval Asia, has furnished some elements of Bosch's garden, and that other sources also contributed, with the heritage of the *Hortus Deliciarum*[29] or the theological tradition of the *paradisus voluptatis*, that Eden which is *hortus voluptatis*.[30] The gems thus mounted and "cited" shine with a sudden sparkle before the erudite eye that recognizes them in passing. But their strange way of being set in the painting puts them beyond the range of academic explanation. It gives specific form to a certain delight. Remembrances, already the more or less hidden pleasures of scholarly research, here find a garden to wander in. Knowledge finds its places to play hooky. But this activity is no more or less "true" than the pleasures guided by the reapparitions of the purple strawberry, or stationed at the crossroads of the coral red tent, a flamboyant clearing, the most commanding center of this painting, an unexpected sun from which the entire panorama of the colors opens out.

One can "go strawberrying," pick blackberries, go after cherries, or "pluck the raspberry." This painting, the earliest known name for which was *La Pintura del Madroño* [The Painting of the Strawberry Tree], permits all the double entendres to emanate from the fruit with which it is studded. On that earth not violated by the plow (*immunis rastroque intacta*), the inhabitants pick, to the beat of the Ovidian dance, "the fruit of the arbutus tree and mountain strawberries"— *arbuteos fetus montanaque fraga legebant*[31]—the only "offspring" [*fetus*] in that Golden Age when adults are still so young. This fruit also calls to mind the mysterious child offering the then-adolescent Suso, on a day of "spiritual carnival," "a pretty little basket of red fruit resembling perfectly ripened red strawberries."[32] It is equally a "symbol of impurity," roundly asserts the historian,[33] the object of gluttonous greed, or blazon of that feminine body Clément Marot was to celebrate in poetry,

> . . . *Au milieu duquel est assise*
> *Une fraise ou une cerise*
> *Que nul ne voit, ne touche aussi* . . . [34]

> . . . ·In the middle of which sits
> A strawberry or cherry
> That no one sees, nor touches . . .

There are also journeys suggested by cherries, blackberries, or raspberries, points of glowing red or purple across the garden; the triangular path of the owls; the rising procession of the six fish, ecstatic idols held or carried by hands everywhere (from the sailor lying on the ground at the bottom to the aerolith that at last escapes gravity, alone, at the far right of the painting);[35] the comings and goings of the birds between the bird section, bristling with bills and beaks on the west side of the painting, and the stereotyped birds that, like so many signals of beakful feasts (sometimes recto, sometimes verso), are strewn over the east side, and so on. New ways that are but paths leading nowhere stretch out before us endlessly. Endless narratives, pleasurable discursivities.

## CALLIGRAPHIES OF BODIES

The "jubilant bustling"[36] of the bodies seems to be dictated by a strictly ordered mise-en-scène. Groups and dances form geometrical shapes upon the stage. Thus, in the lower zone (III), a large central triangle is formed at its base by a rhythm of human arches and columns, and on its two sides by the slope of bodies turned toward the apex. From that triangle, other spaces, also triangular, no longer made up of groups of human beings but of environments, can be discerned: the bird sector and swamp on the left, the clearing and lawn on the right. In that central portion, the bodies *are the architecture*, like the angels or the *putti* in a baroque church. The middle zone (II) is even more visibly constructed by the ellipse of the horsemen around the three groups of nude girls whose garland delineates the ellipse of the pool in which they are bathing. On the other hand, higher up (I), between the pink and blue masses of the megaliths forming a parallelogram underlined by the woods and still further emphasized by the water, the human beings get lost, tiny in that huge public square, gregarious and active players, often clownish or half-metamorphosed, and climbing, like insects, on the aerial branches of the monuments from which they fly off into the sky.

Caught up in this rising maelstrom, the bodies move with neither name (no attribute gives them personal individuality), nor age (there are no children or old people), nor occupation (the "savages" of the New World were to be thus described).[37] They have almost no shadow on the ground (but reflections in the water). Their volume is scarcely indicated. They are forms, beautiful or strange, similar to the anthropomorphic foliage of medieval architecture. An anonymity of elegantly turned curves.

These bodies do not in fact bend except at a small number of points (the neck, the buttocks, the knees, etc.). Thus they form only a very small number of angularities, although they are presented in various positions (see fig. 4): variations on a few geometric themes— a well-tempered geometry. Thus (for example, in the bottom zone of the picture), set off from the background by those nude bodies, the repetition of the curves (obtuse angles on the sides, acute angles in the center and at the edges) and straight lines (standing bodies stretched out by the parallel legs and elongated feet) are repeated in cadence, forming a frieze across the partitions of space. Like a treatise on postures or a film shown in slow motion, the painting shows the possible series of a few beautiful movements in their formality. It also intermingles them to produce abstract and complex figures. That is the case with the astonishing Shiva isolated in an area on the right, made up of two reversed bodies with a flower for a torso and a horned owl's head, a multiple jugglery (like the rapid movements in cartoons), an oriental divinity, an androgyny halfway burst open, an enigmatic acronym, a Chinese character. These bodies form flowery downstrokes and dropped initials, a chain of forms and strokes, in short, a *beautiful but illegible handwriting*. They write without "speaking." The opposite of the men-symbols of their immediate past, these are neither words nor meanings but silent graphemes, straight, slanted, reversible, and changeable, written without one knowing what one is writing. Lost to themselves, they describe instead a musicality of forms—glossography and calligraphy.

Hermetic hieroglyphics, interrelated by aesthetic rather than semantic relationships, they also lose their bodily unity. Parts come off, combine with others, or are substituted for them. A given part may disappear (head, feet, etc.), either due to a lapsus as in a dreamed body or because the biological body does not have a stable organicity (there is a collapse and loss of members or organs). Here, the feet are grouped in a marvelous marquetry of arabesques; elsewhere, they disappear, eliminated under various pretexts (the shape of the terrain, the levels of water, perspectival effects, etc.). All by themselves, they come out of an orange, a tower, or the water. Cut-off heads, looking like strange bunches of fruit or balls rolling themselves into a corner, produce a symmetry in relation to the interlaced feet, and a counterpoint to the bodies without heads, or with fruit or birds for heads. Sometimes the head substitution begins with the kiss, a near metamorphosis, between the strawberry or the tawny owl and the head of a man. Decapitated, dismembered, cut-up bodies that can be assembled or disassembled like Bellmer's dolls, bodies falling into pieces that the artist seizes upon to create his jewelry. Neither ephemeral nor perishable but already dead in their springtime beauty, the fragility of which a gaze, from a remote vantage point within the painting, assesses.

That defection of a bodily logic of symbols (or cohesion) spreads to each individual the nostalgia that only concerned the original androgyne in Plato's *Symposium*: "We were of one sole piece." And then it happened that "he cut men in two, like those who cut the fruit of the service tree to preserve them, or like those who cut eggs with a hair."[38] In Bosch, that half, already walking by hopping along, disintegrates in turn, once the logic of symbols that allowed medieval Christianity to hold its parts together and keep them stitched to one another has been broken up. That half reveals its internal contradictions, according to the model of the Shiva made up of two human beings back to back, with no other connection than a flower torso and a tawny owl's head. No doubt the dance of dismembering (orgiastic? eschatological?) has as its counterpart a parallel in the painting: the lovers in the bubble. But this iridescent dream is also cut off, being unapproachable behind its glass, the illusion of a ravishing aspiration. In any case, this oneiric union reiterates, by its perfect curves, the thing that "responds" to the reality as it is painted in the picture—a reality made up of peaks, beaks, arrows, and sharp points: an anal and oral poetics, a marvelous animality of asses and mouths, a greedy flowering of amorous play.

The musical gestures of this garden weave together the dispersed pleasures of bodies that are lips. A formal beauty articulates avid, at times agonizing, needs (there is an anxious immediacy) upon a decomposition of meaning. Thus, that beauty leads toward the "hell" that is no less our own—nor any less delicious perhaps, like Sade's nocturnal theaters. There, tortured bodies, written by a law, move about beneath *Melancholy*, whose look, underscored by the line that crosses the two panels, also dominates "Paradise" and creates their reversibility.

The *elsewhere* has a hundred other forms, from amorous threesomes or agonies of desire to avian or equestrian gracefulness in the carousel. At the end of my first travels, however, I am no better informed about this country into which I advance like a swimmer into the open sea. I "expected to see"; in reality, by the effect of a slow inversion, I am seen. "Paintings look at us."[39] A woodcut from 1546, either a reproduction or a plagiarism of a Hieronymous Bosch, has the innocence (which is hardly Boschlike) to instruct the viewer with an inscription: "The field has eyes, the forest, ears." *The Garden* looks. It is full of eyes that "observe us" (I counted at least eight or nine of them). Everywhere the look of the other looks down. The painting does not present us with an image in a mirror (mirrors are rare and diabolical in Bosch), but rather a disturbing deprivation of images, organized by the questioning element emanating from the painting. It is as if, entirely transformed into a close-mouthed sibyl, a sphinx, it were saying to the onlooker: "You there, what do you say about what you are, while you think you are saying what I am?" But it is already too much to ascribe it the status of an enigma, a statement that tells "the truth" to the extent, and only to the extent, that it means what we make it say. The aesthetics of *The Garden* does not consist in generating new lights for intelligibility but in extinguishing it.

✳  ·  II  ·  ✳

# A
# Topics

"At nova res novum vocabulum flagitat." In the middle of the fifteenth century, Lorenzo Valla, in opposition to Bartolomeo Fazio and others, claimed the right to use terms unknown to classical antiquity. He affirmed the right of words to be born: "A new reality requires a new word."[1] This thought itself was novel in that it connected languages with historicity more than with a structural order. In the sixteenth century, this notion spread and developed into a duty to increase the linguistic family ("the more words we have in our language, the more perfect it will be"), a claim to fame for the progenitor ("I made new words," said Ronsard), and a literary agenda, to which Joachim du Bellay devoted an entire chapter of his *Deffence et Illustration de la langue francoyse* (volume 2, chapter 6: "To Invent Words").[2] A Malthusian countercurrent very soon attempted to regulate, and would eventually limit, these verbal births. In 1640, however, Sandaeus said the same thing, using almost the same argumentation, as Valla. But it was no longer a personal statement of conviction; it was, rather, a view attributed to the mystics. "Where the thing [*res*] demands it, we must, *they say*, command words and not serve them."[3] He was already speaking of the past, summarizing a lexical creativity he catalogued in the *Lexicon*. It was a heritage, part of which

75

had become unintelligible, that he collected, explained, and defended in his *Pro Theologia mystica clavis*. In classifying it, he marks the conclusion of an immense production of a "mystic" language over three centuries. It would be another century before a comparable linguistic inventiveness would appear (though in different areas of human knowledge), stimulated by the sudden development of the science of economics, by giving attention to the special vocabulary of the trades, or by the "mystic neology" of the French Revolution.[4]

The term "mystic" is a particular case that specifically designates a lexical proliferation in a religious field. The word appears abundantly at the close of the Middle Ages. It designates an operation to be carried out upon the terms to which it is applied, for example, "rose," "garden," or "sense." It has both a pragmatic and a metalinguistic scope: it designates a way of using and a way of understanding the expressions it overdetermines. At first it is an adjective: it is added, as if to designate a specific usage, to noun units already constituted by language. It designates "ways of doing" or "ways of saying," ways of using the language. Little by little, these adjectival usages, becoming more complex and more explicit, were grouped within a domain of their own, their specific designation identified, toward the end of the sixteenth century, by the noun form: "la mystique".[5] The nominal form marked the will to unify all these operations, hitherto dispersed, that were to be coordinated, selected (what is truly "mystical"?), and regulated under the heading of a *modus loquendi* (a "manner of speaking"). Thus the word no longer modeled itself, as the adjective had done, on the noun units of one sole great ("biblical") Narration in order to connote the many spiritual appropriations or interiorizations of the biblical text.[6] It became a text itself. It circumscribed the elaboration of a particular "science" that produced its discursive forms, specified its procedures, articulated its own itineraries or "experiences," and attempted to isolate its object.

At the juncture of discursive practices and the naming of a new field [*lieu*], a new discipline was born. It took its place within a modified distribution of scientific fields (for example, "positive" [theology], "scholasticism," etc.) that would henceforth be distinguished by procedures more than by degrees of knowledge—by "methods" (that general device to mark distinctions during the period) rather than hierarchical levels of meaning or being.[7] This discipline was set within a configuration of knowledge that distributed the practices of knowledge in a different way, giving formality to new ones, reshaping or accommodating to old ones, in accordance with a general criterion of operability governed by rules of production. The rise of mystical science is, in fact, part of a larger movement. In retracing the steps by which this science became an autonomous entity, other transversal problematics come to light—patterns that also govern the reordering of neighboring fields. In its singularity, this mystical science was the symptom of multiple redistributions.[8]

This new science, unlike others born at the same time, was not destined to last. As an entity giving historical form and theoretical coherence to a set of practices, it dissolved at the end of the seventeenth century. Its ephemeral existence, bursting with the wealth of works it produced, has furnished the framework and object of this book. Why did it not last longer? How can that brevity be explained? Once it had become substantivized into a noun, *mystics* had to determine its procedures and define its object. Although, as we shall see, it succeeded in carrying out the first part of this program, the second part was to prove impossible. Is not its object infinite? It is never anything but the unstable metaphor for what is inaccessible. Every "object" of mystical discourse becomes inverted into the trace of an ever-passing Subject. Therefore, *mystics* only assembles and orders its practices in the name of something that it cannot make into an object (unless it be a mystical one), something that never ceases judging *mystics* at the same time that it eludes it. Mysticism vanished at its point of origin. Its birth pledges it to the impossible, as if, stricken by the absolute from the very beginning, it finally died of the question from which it was formed.

For a while, this science was sustained only by the poem (or by its equivalents: the dream, the rapture, etc.). The poem was the substitute for its scientific object. It was a paradoxical alliance. Mystical practices, to the extent that they become separate from the poem, the shadow of which delineated a space for them, drifted away to become autonomous sources of interminable discourse, destroying the very unity for which they had furnished the principle. These detached procedures would perform their tasks in other fields, especially literary ones. In the place once occupied by *mystics*, there remained only: stockpiles of psychic or somatic phenomena, soon to be subjugated by psychology or pathology; "exercises" of meaning, colonized by theology, which transformed them into practical "applications"; and radical questions, forgotten since then or taken up by philosophy.

Of that passing and contradictory science there has survived a ghost that continues to haunt Western epistemology. In pious memory or by habit, we still call what is left of that science in contemporary formations "mystical." This phantom of a passage, repressed during periods secure in their knowledge, reappears in the gaps within scientific certainty, as if ever returning to its birthplace. At such times it evokes something beyond verifiable or falsifiable systems, an "inner" strangeness that borrows its form from the faraway regions of the Orient, Islam, or the Middle Ages. In the remote corners and on the borders of our landscape, this fantastical passerby furnishes the radicalness necessary to those itinerants who flee or lose sight of the institutions that supply knowledge or meaning. Thus, in a thousand and one different ways, all of which recall the "mystical" turns of the ancient *modus loquendi*, the sayable continues to be wounded by the unsayable. A voice comes through the text, a loss transgresses the ascetic order of production, an intense joy or suffering cries out, the sign of a death is traced upon the display windows of our acquisitions. These noises, fragments of strangeness, may again be adjectives, scattered as memories always are, dislocated, but still relating to the substantive figure of the past that furnishes them with the reference point and name of what has disappeared.

*Chapter Three*

✠   ✠
✠

# The New Science

In summarizing this history, I have postponed the presentation of the analyses upon which it is based. Now I must go back to the faint trace that serves as a first guiding clue. On the soil of language, the evolution of the word "mystic" outlines a new form, just as, according to an old legend, an angel once drew in the snow the form of a basilica to be erected precisely there. But this word, traced by the angelic finger, will assemble practices within a common space. The combination of a noun (chapter 3) and practices (chapter 4) will allow us to locate precisely the place in which mystical science was formed.

## "CORPUS MYSTICUM," OR THE MISSING BODY

We take up the complex evolution of "mystic" toward the end of the Middle Ages, after the word has already traveled widely.[9] Of its medieval career it will suffice for us to recall just one stage, relating to the expression "corpus mysticum" (mystical body). It is but one "case" among others, but it has the advantage of having been the object of a detailed theological study to which my history might be the sequel.[10] Above all, this "mystical body," delineated by doctrine, immediately focuses our attention on the quest in relation to which it represents the goal: the quest for a body. The mystical body is the intended goal of a journey that moves, like all pilgrimages, toward the site of a disappearance. There is discourse (a logos, a theology, etc.), but it lacks a body—social and/or individual. Whether it be a question of reforming a church, founding a community, constituting a (spiritual) "life," or preparing (for oneself) a body to be "raised in glory," the production of a body plays an essential role in *mystics*. What is termed a rejection of "the body" or of "the world"—ascetic struggle, prophetic rupture—is but the necessary and preliminary elucidation of a historical state of affairs; it constitutes the point of departure for the task of offering a body to the spirit, of "incarnating" discourse, giving truth a space in which to make itself manifest. Contrary to appearances, the lack concerns not what breaks away (the text), but the area of what "makes itself flesh" (the body). *Hoc est corpus meum*, "this is my body": this central logos calls back one who has disappeared and calls for an effectuality. Those who take this discourse seriously are those who feel the pain of an absence of body. The "birth" they all await, in one way or another, must invent for the verb a body of love. Thus their quest for "annunciations," for words that take on body, for childbirth by the ear.

This quest concerns a question always in suspense, despite the misleading obviousness of our answers: What is the body? Mystic discourse is obsessed by this question. What it focuses on is precisely the question of the body. It haunts the suburbs of the body, and if it enters, it is in the manner of the Hebrews who once marched around Jericho with their trumpets until the city opened of its own accord. The body had not yet been colonized by medicine or mechanics. As a hypothetical model, that enigmatic focal point may be represented by a center, constructed from three points that shift according to variations in their interrelationships. These points represent: (1) an event pole (the surprise of pain, pleasure, or perceptions, which institutes a temporality); (2) a symbol pole (of discourse, stories, or signs, which organize meaning or truths); and (3) a social pole (a network of communications and contractual practices that institute a "being there" or an "inhabiting."

Thus the triad:

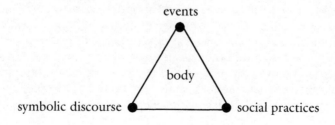

These three poles can be analyzed at different levels according to the type of experience represented, its content, the basic unit to which it refers, its function and the reference that it introduces:

|  | EVENTS | DISCOURSE | PRACTICE |
|---|---|---|---|
| CONTENT | pain/pleasure | meaning | communication |
| BASIC UNIT | surprise (happening) | signifier (naming) | relation (binding) |
| FUNCTION | historicity | symbolization | sociality |
| REFERENCE | time | truth | place |

The search for a body will bring these three elements into play according to variable modalities and emphases. Mystical literature composes scripts of the body. From this point of view, it is cinematographic.

But, in its Christian guise, a common preconception or postulate, which excludes a priori any hasty generalization into other religious traditions, affects it entirely. Christianity was founded upon *the loss of a body*—the loss of the body of Jesus Christ, compounded with the loss of the "body" of Israel, of a "nation" and its genealogy. A founding disappearance indeed: it defines the Christian experience in relation to the assurance that holds the Jewish people anchored in their biological and social reality—in relation to a body that is present, distinct, and localized, separated from the others by being chosen, wounded by history, and engraved upon by the Scriptures. The Christian word takes on "Catholic" (universal) and "Pentecostal" (spiritual) form only when it is separated from its ethnic origin and a certain heredity. In the Jewish tradition, the Text does not cease writing, correcting, and displacing a living body, which is its other, the body of the people or of its members. It will also make way for a medical tradition. In the Christian tradition, an initial privation of body goes on producing institutions and discourses that are the effects of and substitutes for that absence: multiple ecclesiastical bodies, doctrinal bodies, and so on. How can a body be made from the word? This question raises the other haunting question of an impossible mourning: "Where art thou?" These questions stir the mystics.

These same questions were already present at the evangelical beginnings. Before the empty tomb stood Mary Magdalene, that eponymous figure of the modern mystic: "I do not know where they have put him." She questioned a passerby: "If you are the one who carried him off, tell me where you have laid him."[11] That question, articulated by the entire primitive community, was not limited to one circumstance. It structured the apostolic discourse. In the Gospel of John, Jesus has no presence other than that which is divided between historical places in which he no longer is, and the unknowable place, says Jesus, "where I am."[12] His "being there" is the paradox of "having been" here previously, of remaining inaccessibly elsewhere and of "coming back" later. His body is structured by dissemination, like a text. Since that time, the believers have continued to wonder: "Where art thou?" And from century to century they ask history as it passes: "Where have you put him?" With events that are murmurings come from afar, with Christian discourses that codify the hermeneutics of new experiences, with community practices that render present a *caritas*, they "invent" a mystic body—missing and sought after—that would also be their own.

The medieval evolution of "corpus mysticum" marks a moment in this work. After the middle of the twelfth century, the expression no longer designated the Eucharist, as it had previously, but the Church. Conversely, "corpus verum" no longer designated the Church but the Eucharist. The adjectives "mysticus" (hidden) and "verus" (truthful, real and knowable as such) were reversed. At first, the change was in the form of a chiasmus between the signifier and the signified. The signified (Eucharist) became the signifier of the other term. In the new usage, "mysticum" is simply a contraction of *mystice significatum, mystice designatum*.[13] The Church, the social "body" of Christ, is henceforth the (hidden) signified of a sacramental "body" held to be a visible signifier, because it is the showing of a presence beneath the "species" (or appearances) of the consecrated bread and wine. This chiasmus is accompanied by a whole set of shifts, some of which need to be recalled at this point, since they set the scene in which mystical science [ *"la" mystique*] developed.

## FROM THE TERNARY TO THE BINARY

The theological change is the most manifest. Henri de Lubac devotes his study to it. In conclusion he writes: "Of the three terms . . . that had to be ordered in relation to one another . . . historical body, sacramental body, and Church body, the caesura was placed between the first and the second, whereas it later came to be placed between the second and the third. That is, briefly, the fact that dominates the entire evolution of Eucharistic theories."[14] What was at issue was the punctuation of dogma. Where should the separation that determines the meaning be placed? The caesura has the effect of distributing in *two* (moments) the *three* (bodies). It reduces the ternary to the binary, but the old formula and the new one do it in two distinct ways, which indicates a difference in the articulation of the ternary onto the binary. These formulae can be reinterpreted in the following manner.

Semiotically, the old formula joins ($\wedge$) the sacramental and the Church bodies, separating ($\vee$) the historical:

$$\text{Historical} \vee (\text{Sacramental} \wedge \text{Church})$$

Or, in abbreviated form, putting in italics the term qualified as "mystical":

$$H \vee (S \wedge C)$$

The sacrament ("sumere Christum") and the Church ("sumi a Christo")[15] were joined (the term "communio" was, moreover, common to both) as the contemporary performance of a distinct, unique "event," the *kairos*, designated by the "historical body" (Jesus). The caesura is therefore of the temporal sort, in conformity with Augustinian theology. It separates from the original event the manifestation of its effects in the mode of the Church-Eucharist pair, which is the "liturgical" combination of a visible community or people (*laos*) and a secret action (*ergon*) or "mystery." The fact is, the linear series extending from the apostolic origins (H) to the present Church (C) is sustained in its entirety by the sacrament (S), conceived as a unique and everywhere instituting operation (the "mystery"), linking the *kairos* to its progressive manifestation. Distinct times (H and C) are united by the same invisible "action."[16] This is the paradigm of "the tradition." It is repeated, moreover, in many religious orders that suppose the "spirit" of the founder, after his death (temporal break), continues to operate in the development of his work. The term "mystic" is therefore a mediating one. It insures the unity between two times. It overcomes (*aufheben*) the division and makes them into a history. *"Mystic" is the absent third term that joins two disconnected terms.* It is the third element postulated by the construction of a temporal series. Last, we have a relation of anteriority:

$$H \; ant \; C$$

and one of implication:

$$(H \wedge C) \supset S$$

From the thirteenth century on, a new formula prevails in which the positivity of an apostolic authority (the historical body) and that of a sacramental authority (the Eucharistic body) are linked to one another and split off from the Church, which is their hidden extension:

$$(H \wedge S) \vee \subseteq$$

This new scansion distinguishes the functions (H and S) in relation to a totalization of their effects (C). It no longer distinguishes the times (H and C) in relation to their dynamic postulate (S) as the first scansion did. In this passage from a temporal (or diachronic) distribution to a functionalist (or synchronic) one, there is objectification of the manifest terms (H and S). On one hand, the kairos, the historical "body" (H), becomes a "corpus" similar to a Code that is the law and serves as the basis for endless commentaries unfolding its hidden productivity. On the other hand, the "mystery," the sacramental body (S), is recast in the philosophical formality of the sign, that is, as one "thing," which is visible, designating another, which is invisible. The visibility of that object replaces the communal celebration, which is a community operation. It acts as the visible indicator of the proliferation of secret effects (of grace, of salvation) that make up the real life of the Church. There are, therefore, two positivities—one readable, the other visible—that refer the Church body to a carrying out and a totalization that are still "mystical." The mystical third is no more than the object of an intention. It is something that needs to be made manifest. Little by little, with the growing awareness of the need for Church reform (from the fourteenth through the sixteenth centuries), "mystic" came to mean the body to be constructed, on the basis of two clear, authoritative "documents": the scriptural corpus (H) and the Eucharistic ostension (S).

A different conception of time and presence was therefore entering upon the scene. Another indication of this was the new position given the term "mystic." In the three-body scheme of things, the mystical occupied the last position (and often had, moreover, an eschatological value). It stood in opposition to the positive terms, as an invisible to a visible, a goal to creative functions, or the whole to motor organs. It revealed a different time, a different space. It beckoned toward the purpose of a productivity, or the direction of a journey to be undertaken "beyond" all present points of reference. It would henceforth be with the help of the legible body of the origins, and/or the visible sign of the Eucharist, that a mystical Church body would have to be "invented," in the same sense in which there was to be an invention of the New World. That endeavor was the Reformation. It was gradually divided into two tendencies: one (Protestant) giving a privileged status to the scriptural corpus, the other (Catholic) to the sacrament. The binary (visible/invisible) won out over the ternary structure of bodies (historical, sacramental, Church). There was either

H versus C

or

S versus C

Until the middle of the seventeenth century, the "mystical body" occupied the strategic position of being the other in relation to visible realities. Sometimes there was an attempt to give a "mystical" space to the hierarchical or scriptural organization, at others to give a social or textual visibility to mystical experience. The work of various reforms was carried out along that boundary; in certain cases (with Ignatius of Loyola, Borromeo, and Bérulle) asserting a parallelism between an ecclesiastical hierarchy and a mystical order. But in any case, its goal was to produce a mystic body. This problematic gave rise, among the mystics, to the invention of a different body, born of and for the discourse intending to produce reform—an alien body against which the institution of medicine would eventually win out in imposing a scientific body.

## A STRATEGY OF THE VISIBLE

A historical and anthropological change paralleled this theological shift. These transformations, let it be said in passing, confirm the reordering of historical periods that tends to place the beginning of the Western Renaissance and modern period at the end of the thirteenth and the beginning of the fourteenth century rather than in the sixteenth century. New socioeconomic structures, along with the conceptual models that made them thinkable, appeared simultaneously. From our present perspective, the history of the thirteenth to the fifteenth centuries might have as its general identifying characteristic the specialization of the elite classes and the marginalization of a majority of the population with respect to the codes of a world that until then had functioned as a network of relations.[17] Hence society became opaque.

Within the Church, there were many signs of this. Learned clerics were being separated from the common folk, and administrative power was becoming more highly organized and centralized. As theology became more professionalized and international, its knowledge became more technical. The divisions between different ecclesiastical levels of authority were politicized, and secular law was becoming autonomous. Rural culture and rural "devotions" were increasingly isolated from the emerging urban bourgeoisie. Individual paths of life were derailed as frames of reference were reified or crumbled away. An increase, first in the number of "heretical" or "spiritual" movements, then in those of *mystics* or witchcraft, reflects both the tenacity and the instability of the traditional modes of integration that were being thrust aside by the new social order. There were obsessive fears of the "end"—ends of a world, epidemic deaths, exiles from meaning, and so on. Within the area of our present inquiry, a few elements of this complex call for further consideration.

The Third Lateran Council (1179) had organized a political restoration of the papacy and an administrative reform of the clergy. The Church body gathered strength, became clericalized, opaque. *"Mystical" was becoming that which no longer had the transparence of the (communal) sign.* This new consistency of the social apparatus soon made possible, with the Fourth Lateran Council (1215), a sacramental pastoral that attempted a *reconquista* of the believers. After the *in capite* (at the head) reform came the reform *in membris,* a therapeutics of the "members." Predication and sacramental practice were the instruments of a campaign to free Christians from the grip of the first large popular heresies, autonomous communal movements, and growing secular powers. The clerics, who were literati, began to use the vernacular language and produced a literature that tried to adapt itself to different social milieus (for example, with the *sermones ad status*). In order to be convincing, they mobilized the rhetorical devices of images and exempla, thereby using, already at this early date, the technique of "showing in order to inspire belief."[18] The evil they wanted to remedy was the gap between the Church apparatus and the proliferating forms of a lived Christianity being disseminated in all sorts of "Imitations" of Jesus. This proliferation of private experiences, which was tied to the individualization of practices (from the development of the auricular confession to personal devotions), appeared dangerous. *"Mystical" came to designate what had become separate from the institution.*

The inner crusade, then, was concerned with reestablishing the link between that "mystic" life and the ecclesiastical apparatus. The "sacramental body" had a strategic function in that attempt. It constituted a focal point at which mystical reality became identified with visible meaning (it posited the principle of their oneness). Moreover, it consolidated the clerical power upon which it was dependent (it posited a hierarchic principle). In this instance the sign *was* the presence it designated, by an operation that was the priest's privilege. This Eucharistic "body" was the "sacrament" of the institution, the visible instituting of what the institution was meant to become, its theoretical authorization and its pastoral tool. Far from being a mere theological thesis, the inversion taking place during this period that put one (sacramental) "body" in place of another (Church) "body" was a response to historical constraints and the policy regulating a social body. Furthermore, despite the ups and downs of the papal states, from the Lateran Council until the reformism following the Council of Trent (1545–63), that pastoral (centered on the only body that could symbolize and sustain the restoration/institution of a visible Church) would have great stability. It was even to have a secular echo, with the transformation of the central statement "this is my body" into the formulation, equally of the Eucharistic type, "L'Etat, c'est moi."[19]

The clergy campaigns of the late Middle Ages developed procedures that made "mystical" experiences "return" to the field of the visible institution. The instrument common to these methods, their technical model, seems to have been the confession, which appeared in two complementary forms. One drew the secrets of private life into the realm of the Church, (the "exorcism" type); the other showed the public the "truth" hidden within the institutions (the "miracle" type). One exploited the avowal, the other the act of showing. Both reinforced the Church representation, either by diminishing the invisible that lies beyond its reach or by organizing more frequent performances concerning meaning itself.

On one hand, because of its widespread circulation (first via the confraternities), the auricular, or private, confession introduced into clerical knowledge the hidden deviations of everyday life; all kinds of escapism, the secrets of which were pursued, were named and rounded up under the term "sins." The confession infiltrated the maze of individual lives; it interrogated them, made them speak, and thus exorcised them.[20] In treatises of the period, the confession becomes more complex with the new organization of the city and of work.[21] It distinguishes and "brings out" the details of this new organization. The mystical confession also functioned as the response to the insatiable demand of clerics. Determined on the theological plane by the passage from dogmatics to the analysis of practices (moral and linguistic), clerical knowledge increased its power by feeding on information that the auricular confession (the equivalent of our interviews) wrested from society's penumbra. In systematically stimulating the practice of that sacrament, the pastoral worked to produce a visibility of the religious society.

On the other hand, the internal "mystery" of the institution had to be manifested. This was accomplished in several ways: by "popularizing" clear, simple ways of preaching adapted to each social group; by displaying the sacramental body (from the thirteenth century on, the elevation of the host, the "exhibitions of the Saint Sacrament," the ostensions of the Corpus Christi, and so on, offered the sacramental body to view, and even to visual "chewing" or "devouring");[22] by reforming the priests (called upon to be the public epiphanies of meaning and the speakers of the institution); by the "lives of the saints" (stories of inner lives unveiled and private lives made into decipherable meaning); or by tales of miracles (that so often relate how a secret reality, Christ's blood for example, replaces the sign, the wine, that stands for it), etc. To the law requiring the faithful to "tell all" to the minister of the Church ("all" means only what is hidden from him) there corresponds the law requiring the priest to "show all" ("all" meaning what remains concealed by the institution). On both sides, the pastoral attempts to bring the mysteries of the institution and the secrets of secular life into a space of visibility, a recapitulative theater that would finally be, like a map, the visual and encyclopedic assembling of the Church. The utopian impetus already behind the drive toward transparency is the same that assumes, in the seventeenth century, the (epistemological) guise of "representation."

The proliferation of religious confraternities and congregations contributed to that crusade in which the hunt for secrets took on the appearance of a witch-hunt. The objective of these communities was indeed to create a body that would make visible a "spirit" (a communication) in accordance with the prestigious model of the original *vita apostolica*. Nothing was to be withheld, nothing hidden: "All the believers together put everything in common—*Omnes . . . habebant omnia communia.*"[23] Individual poverty was but the precondition of mutual exchange. It divested one of any asset or held-back secret. It was essentially epiphanic. The stories of "brothers" or "sisters" worked in the direction of composing a legible scene. The point was to create transparent bodies. It was a Franciscan dream: that a body might preach without speaking, and that in walking around it might make visible what lives within.[24] The "spiritual guidance" that developed around the convents (especially the Dominican ones) also filled the lacunae of institutional discourse with a dialogue of "confidences." A buzzing of voices along the fringes tirelessly carried the unsaid back to the authorities and quietly introduced Church legitimacy into the orderly or haphazard course of private experience. These verbal exchanges in the confessionals or parlors also furnished the religious "directors" with "material" from which to construct a literature of edifying "lives" or practical "exercises."[25] Far from subverting ecclesiastical authority, this massively distributed material permitted the authorities to reconquer and "inform" the Christian people. The "privatization" of discourse, analogous to the personalizing of products in our present-day economy, had a social function: it articulated privacy within Church language. Hence, from the thirteenth to the fifteenth centuries, the pastoral resorts to such privatization.

Though the confraternities and congregations were mini-churches, early *ecclesioles*, laboratories in which the reconciliation of the social body with the mystic life was beginning to be carried out, they were also (being of an intermediate nature between the ecclesiastic administration and secular collectivities) parallel and particular institutions that duplicated the Church form, rechanneling for their own benefit the "devotion" of the faithful and constituting a third domain, often "exempted," even autonomous. Their success threatened the papal or diocesan pastoral to which they nonetheless supplied models. These communities, such as the Dominican convents, were therefore successively privileged, watched over with suspicion, and even fought against by the pope and the bishops when they were not being torn apart, like the Franciscan congregations, between "ecclesiastic" tendencies and "illuminist" movements. There was an eddy effect. It was there that groups of devotees found a culture (in the biological sense) in which they were both protected and supervised, now drawing the convent toward aspirations it made possible, now being brought back to the orthopraxis the convent defended. There was an interplay of thresholds as in a set of canal locks. To a great extent, the geography of these congregations corresponded to the map of the mystical currents. This "third world" was a testing ground for apostolic tactics and strategies now rejected, now taken up by the bishopric that eventually, at the Council of Trent, incorporated some essential points from the practice of religious orders into its own program.

In this multifarious history of a "sacramental body" in search of its "Church body," or of a visible "head" in search of its "mystical" members, one trait is of special interest in the question of the apparition of mystical science: the progressive concentration of these debates around *seeing*. Without this new focus, it would be impossible to understand how much was being instituted during that period in the visual mode: the revolution in painting in the fifteenth century ("the discovery of pictorial composition, 1350–1450," as Michael Baxandall says) and the invention of perspective; the cartographic encyclopedism of knowledge; the role of optics in modern scientificity; the theories of language as "painting"; the dialectics of the look and of representation; and so on. It was a real modification of man's experience: vision slowly invaded the previous domain of touch or of hearing.[26] It transformed the very practice of knowledge and signs. Even the religious field was reorganized in function of the opposition between the visible and the invisible; the "hidden" experiences, soon grouped under the name of "mystical," acquired a relevance they had not had previously.

From this point of view, it is not surprising that from the thirteenth century (since the Latin translation of John Scotus Erigena in 852, Jean Sarasin around 1165, and Robert Grosseteste in 1240—43) up to the time of Bérulle, Dionysius the Areopagite was the dominant reference. He posited a structural homology between the mystical knowledge of the "visionary" [*oratikos*] and the "ecclesiastical hierarchy."[27] The authority of Dionysius served as an antidote against history that broke the link between the visible and the invisible, opposing to it a discourse (held to be original) that made it possible to conceive their distinction and to transcend it in a dynamic circularity. In the doctrinal domain, it eventually played a role analogous to that of the pastoral programs in the practical domain. Dionysius haunted five centuries of ecclesiastic reformism, to which he offered a speculative utopia, a myth comparable to what would later be the Hegelian discourse during a century and a half of sociopolitical conflicts. But history, specifically that of *mystics* itself, will show the failure of the reconciliation that the theory of Pseudo-Dionysius made conceivable.

## SYMBOLISM: RHETORIC AND THEOLOGY

The change also affects the conception of symbolism, a central problem in mystical language. The series of theological "formulae" analyzed above has already shown how a binary form (real or *verum* versus *mysticum*) gradually replaced the traditional ternary form while at the same time the content was redefined by the opposition between the visible and the invisible. That double modification implies a restructuring of the relations between fact and meaning. The more difficult it becomes to think that facts spell out meaning—a meaning assumed to be brought to legibility by the things themselves—the more it appears necessary first to generate a system of "reason" through the texts and then to generate facts (an "experience" and/or a body) to match that system of reason. (A symptom: the verb "produce" passes from the meaning "make manifest" to that of "create.") This task takes on, successively, a scriptorial, pictorial, political, and scientific aspect. The requirement is to construct a "ratio" (an order) by discourse and to reform the real on this model, in other words, to create a theoretic body and give it a historical body. These are the two operations rendered necessary by the impossibility of recognizing and applying an order inscribed in things. To simplify, the illegibility of Providence lends urgency and universality to the production of meaning's body, a program as essential to the enterprise of Machiavelli as to that of the mystics.

This evolution is related to the way in which traditional theology grasped the relation between a system of meaning and the historical or cosmological organization of the real, that is, it is related to a theory of symbolism that disintegrates precisely at the end of the Middle Ages. Let us consider but one axis of that theory. It presumes there must be a real analogy between the procedures (logical and rhetorical) that organize meaning and the succession or disposition of the facts (in a "salvation story" or in a cosmos of revelation). The link between the rhetorical and the "ontic" has a strategic function here.

Indeed, to treat the connection between the production of meaning and the (historical or cosmological) disposition of events or things, Christianity of the patristic period extended and applied the "figures" of classical rhetoric to the understanding of salvation. With the help of this shift, linguistic processes allow relations between facts or beings to be thought.[28] A precedent-setting example of this transfer of the rhetorical to the theological is furnished by the Pauline use of the allegory. Abraham's two wives, one a servant and the other free, are considered by Saint Paul as an "allegory" that no longer characterizes relations between words (*verba*) but between facts (*res* or *facta*). Hagar and Sarah "are" (in advance) "the two successive Alliances with God, the Old and New Testament."[29] This reuse takes for granted the legitimacy of the transfer that moves the trope from a linguistic usage (an operation on the meaning of words) to a theological one (an affirmation concerning an "operation" of history). In patristic and medieval Christianity, this transfer from one field to the other was generalized over the entire exegesis going under the name of "spiritual."

The case of "allegory," which antiquity and the Middle Ages assimilated to the category of "the symbol,"[30] will allow us to analyze the functioning of that translation and the problems it raised: the connection between the *allegoria in verbis* and the *allegoria in factis*. Since Saint Augustine, ancient tradition distinguished two classes of symbols.[31] Some were *signa propria*, that is, things we use to designate something else, things that are therefore "instituted" to signify. Thus, they were called *instituta* or "intentional," or *voluntaria* (Bonaventure). They worked on the model of words, which were indeed instituted to say "something other" than what they are. The other category consisted of things (*res*) that, in addition to their proper meanings, received from God the function of designating other things. These were realities of nature (things, persons, numbers, places, times, gestures, etc.), but transposed (*translata*) into signs by the divine will.

These *signa naturalia* escaped the human codifications of meaning. It was therefore necessary to learn how to "interpret" them on the basis of an intelligence that ascended to the divine will, then descended toward its inscriptions in the opacity of "natural" things. They were the province of a "spiritual" or divine hermeneutics.

The *allegoria in factis* belonged to the latter category. It contrasted with the *allegoria in verbis*, which was linguistic in nature and functioned like a metaphor, in accordance with its Stoic origins.[32] Thus, in the Pauline example, the "allegory" did not bind words together but rather the "historical events themselves";[33] not the signified [*signifiés*] but the referents. Hence theological thought distinguished between the *allegoria verbi* (or *allegoria rhetorica, allegoria grammaticalis*, etc.) and the *allegoria facti* (or *allegoria theologica, spiritualis*, etc.) in the same way Augustine had already distinguished between the *allegoria sermonis* and the *allegoria historiae*. The latter transposed a figure of language into the domain of the real; it assumed that there was a type of relation between events or facts analogous to the type rhetoric produced in the linguistic domain as allegory. That transposition was subject to several validating conditions; we shall use this trope's various names to classify them.

(A) *Allegoria theologica.* In order for one event or fact to signify another (which would become its "figure"), a will to signify is needed which is no longer that of man, but of God. David, in loving Bathsheba, had no intention of signifying the love of Christ for the Church. Only Providence ordering the course of events can found the *allegoria facti*. In a single gesture, Providence creates things and disposes them in sequences, like a writer arranging the relations between his or her words. The *allegoria facti* refers back to that unique "orator," God, and to his "art of speaking." It is God's rhetoric. According to this manner of thinking, it is the function and privilege of theology to recognize this rhetoric. But that is only possible for a mode of thought capable of seeing things from "the point of view" of God, who uses the world as his discourse.

(B) *Allegoria historiae.* The *in factis* symbolism is inscribed within a chronology. The difference between a "before" and an "after" is what conditions the instituting of one fact in "allegory" for another. The temporalization of the allegory is, moreover, the "true specificity of the Christian exegesis."[34] There is the presupposition of a history—a progressive history, since it is always a "before" that allegorically designates an "after" and not the reverse (which would be the Freudian procedure). There is no reversibility. Hermeneutics also has a historical form: we must await the second event for the first to become its prefiguration. The transformation of facts into signs is the effect of subsequent events and therefore bound up with the constitution of temporal sequences.[35] Finally, history must be closed; an "end" or "achievement" must be marked in it (the *kairos* of the Incarnation) in order for stable sequences (or "allegories") to be legible. This break functions like the closing of a text. It institutes a time out of time, a sort of remainder, a space for reading (or manifestation) once the text is completed. The *allegoria facti*, without the "end of time" it postulates, would degenerate into an endless proliferation of random allegories, corresponding to future events capable of changing past events into signs.

(C) *Allegoria in factis.* Real and stable "similarities" are necessary to validate a historical symbolism between facts or events. For example, between water and the Spirit, or between Sarah and the Church, there must be homologies inscribed *in re*, in the things themselves. As Hugh of Saint Victor said, only those "qualities" that are "necessary and essential" to the facts form the basis of comparisons between them.[36] This type of allegory, therefore, postulates a metaphysics of "qualities" attached to, although not identified with, the substances, and an epistemology capable of formulating criteria that specify such "qualities." If it should happen that such postulates are undermined by a philosophical critique (as did occur, with the advent of Ockhamism), the trope, cut off from its realist anchor, can only be overturned and broken into "dissimilarities." It will either be excluded from theology as lacking seriousness or be reduced by new theologies to its rhetorical function as being its only rigorous one, that is, to being an *allegoria verbi*. Such were to be the choices facing the humanists, the Protestants, and the mystics of the sixteenth century, before the "symbol" (toward the end of the seventeenth century) replaced the allegory as its opposing term.

These three conditions for the *allegoria facti* (which depended on the status of theology, a certain conception of time, and a specific metaphysics) became less and less conceivable in the fourteenth and fifteenth centuries. It appeared impossible to see "from the point of view" of the divine *Potentia absoluta*, for the simplicity of his will transcended his own creations and consequently eluded all intelligence that, of necessity, relied on them. For Ockham, theology ceased being able to be a true science.[37] Similarly, the stable sequences, contained within a completed time lapse, scattered and became random relations between past terms and future ones. This occurred because (the apostolic period no longer looking like a closure but rather like a lost origin) time was reversed into a waiting period oriented toward an imminent end, or a third reign, and allegory served to prophesy an uncertain future (or present). Finally, in identifying the real with the singular, the nominalist critique and, more broadly, the new practices of discourse of which nominalism represented but a philosophical "moment," restored to the domain of words the relations, resemblances, and so on formerly attributed to things.[38] The indiscrimination between logic or rhetoric and metaphysics was rejected, and tropes were confined to the field in which the play of language was sharpened, intensified, and purified.[39] "The great and unique *allegoria facti*," which was the very "Christian allegory" itself,[40] was thus gradually dissolved. Another use of rhetoric would treat the relationship between language and the body it lacked.

## "MYSTICAL" AS THE ADJECTIVE OF A SECRET

In the sixteenth and seventeenth centuries, the theological formula that appeared in the thirteenth century was maintained: "Jesus," writes Bérulle, "has a real body and a mystical body on earth. . . . We adhere to his real body by the communion at the Eucharist, and to his mystical body by the communion of the Church."[41] There are countless examples of this. But the split, already perceptible at the end of the Middle Ages, between the "political" and the "mystical" body of the Church, became stronger.[42] René d'Argenson distinguished from political institutions a "mystical State," a silent and living "inner" realm, the reality of which eluded intelligence as well as sight.[43] This dichotomy made itself felt even within the world of Catholicism, which one moment, prompted by anti-Protestant apologetics, emphasized the exterior and visible character of the Church and the next sought in "spiritualism" a counterweight to the politicization of the State or worldly society.[44] The development of the adjective "mystical" marks the dividing line of this opposition and its effects on the field it restructured. It marks the division that cuts across Christian discourse.

### AN ADJECTIVE TRIUMPHANT

Where we speak of "mystics," a sixteenth-century author instead said "contemplatives" or "spirituals." Thomas à Kempis asks: "Why are there so few contemplatives?"[45] It was the traditional term, often commented upon by Bernard of Clairvaux,[46] Bonaventure,[47] Thomas Aquinas,[48] and so many others. Henri de Herp (in *Eden contemplativorum*, or in the treatise translated by Pierre Blomevenna under the title *Directorium aureum contemplativorum* [1509]) scarcely uses the term "mystique,"[49] which is never found in the vocabulary of his master Ruysbroeck.[50] The latter was himself presented as a "divine contemplative" by Jean des Anges[51] and a "very excellent comtemplator" by Dom Beaucousin, his French translator.[52] Similarly, to designate what will later be called "the mystical union," the terms "unitas supereminens animae,"[53] "estado perfectísimo de contemplación,"[54] "contemplación quieta,"[55] and so on are used. So writes Teresa of Avila.[56] John of the Cross treats "contemplation," and only uses "mystical" theology to designate the "negative" aspect of infused contemplation in reference to the apophatic tradition of Dionysius the Areopagite.[57] He refers to "contemplatives" or "spirituals" when he quotes those whose doctrine he follows.[58] In the seventeenth century, the venerable word still holds its own in numerous titles: *Jardin des contemplatifs* (1605), *Philosophie des contemplatifs* (1618), *De contemplatione divina* (1620), *Vie della contemplazione* (1626), *Tratado da vida contemplativa* (1627), *Sospiri profondi dell'anima contemplativa* (1651), *Les Contemplations* (1654), *Tractatus brevis de vita contemplativa* (1663), and so on. The persistence of "spiritual," which goes back to Saint Paul, is even more noticeable.

The adjective "mystical," however, had been edging its way into usage for a long time, first in addition to, then as a substitute for, the synonyms formerly preferred. *Le Verger spirituel ou mystique* (1542): the new word is slipped in after the old one, which codetermines its meaning. "Unio moralis seu mystica": Vasquez adds the second term as a concession, as if to say "moral union," or, as they say these days, "mystical union."[59]

Of course, the word is also connected with its former usages, determined by allegorical exegesis and/or the theology of Pseudo-Dionysius. It is precisely on the basis of a specific relation to the Scriptures that Luther scoffs at the "twaddle" ("merissimae nugae") of a "mystical theology" that he judges "plus platonisans quam christianisans," "ludens allegoriis suis," and in which he brings together an entire tradition, from Origen and Pseudo-Dionysius to Gerson.[60] Luther discredits the word "mystical" to attack an "ecclesiastical" hermeneutics of the Bible, a theological stronghold. In the seventeenth century, "mystical" refers primarily to a kind of "exposition" of the Scriptures. This is indicated in all the dictionaries, from the *Vocabulario degli Academici della Crusca* (1623) to the last editions of the *Dictionnaire de Trévoux* (1771). "There are two perfect meanings," writes Pascal, "the literal and the mystical."[61] While Richard Simon criticized "these sorts of mystical and spiritual interpretations,"[62] Fénelon, on the contrary, grouping in one sentence the two uses of the word, the old (a reading of the sacred texts) and the new (a personal experience), defends "these mystical and allegorical meanings for which the scornful scholars of recent centuries have so great a distaste and such outspoken disdain when they find them in the writings of the mystics."[63]

The term "mystic," used in place of "spiritual" by the sixteenth century to qualify such nouns as "pomarium" (1535), "rosarium" (1531), the "pomme de grenade" (1582), and so on, continues to designate a way of reading and a transformation of things into the vocabulary of a doctrinal or moral teaching, as it had in Bonaventure's *Vitis mystica* [The Mystic Vine]. But although the word retains the traces of an anagogical and scriptural practice, the rules of that reading drift and fade away. The allegory of biblical facts (the *allegoria in factis*) is extended to all kinds of things, changing them into living images of the secrets of experience. It can no longer be theoretically shaped in proportion to the "mystery" of the divine will. It serves to make perceptible the ineffable movement of things or of the inner life. It refers not so much to a theological intelligence of the divine plan inscribed in events as to a didactic or poetic process, a "manner of speaking," a "style." It becomes (again) a metaphor. Hence we see a proliferation of "mystic" discourses, elucidations, institutions, questions, or treatises.

The phenomenon extends beyond doctrinal or pious literature. This eminently successful process is not essentially Christian, although it bears the traces of its exegetic or initiatory use. Its spread is due to the fact that biblical exegesis is only one particular sector in the wider field of *hermeneutica generalis*, whose procedures were ultimately derived from law or medicine.[64] But around this hermeneutics, guided by a reworking of Aristotle's *Organon*, the sciences of interpretation flourished on all sides, often inspired by the books of Hermes (which were assumed to be Christian) or by the corpus of the Areopagite. It was the ambition of these sciences to construct a coherent language to explain, on the basis of constant "laws," the relations between the data of an encyclopedic storehouse of knowledge and a few basic elements, regarded as the true "secrets" of knowledge.[65] Models of "scientific languages" are thus produced in which the lexicological concern (confirmed by the publication of so many dictionaries during this period)[66] and the elucidation of mental procedures and "methods"[67] are more important than the later problem of experimental verification. In that fervor of linguistic and logical activity, "mystical" marks the point of intersection between the endless description of the visible and the naming of a hidden essential, or between the list of the determined and the formulation of a determinant. Thus the word takes on the appearance of a universal key in the most diverse combinations, from the *De mystica numerorum significatione* of Josse Clichtove (1513) to the "mystical figures" of Heinrich Cornelius Agrippa (1533), or the *Mystica Aegyptorum philosophia* (1591) of Francesco Patrizi. Polemics, reflecting current tastes, also adopts this marker of the shifting frontier between the shown and the hidden, as in the *Lettre mystique touchant la conspiration dernière avec l'ouverture de la cabale mystérielle des Jésuites révélée par un songe* (1602). In this symptomatic title, "mystique" espouses "cabale" while "mystère" slips toward "mystériel." The hidden begins to take on the aspect of a plot.

## THE PROBLEMATICS OF SECRECY

At this point the term "mystical" becomes the proper one to qualify any object, real or ideal, the existence or signification of which eludes direct knowledge. "Mysticum illud dicitur quod vel in religione, vel in disciplina aliqua, sacratum magis ac secretum est, atque a vulgarium hominum sensu magis dissentire videtur."[68] Here Charles Hersent, a learned and versatile dabbler, has already grouped three characteristic elements that were in the air—the passage from "sacred" to "secret," the commonality of the term "mystical" to various "disciplines," and the separation the term introduces between scholars (or "gnostics") and the "vulgar." But there are degrees of knowledge. Thus Pascal was to write against the semilearned: "Equity is made up entirely of custom, for the sole reason that it has been handed down. That is the mystical foundation of its authority."[69]

Secrecy is not only the state of a thing that escapes from or reveals itself to knowledge. It designates a play between actors. It circumscribes the terrain of strategic relations between the one trying to discover the secret and the one keeping it, or between the one who is supposed to know it and the one who is assumed not to know it (the "vulgar"). In accordance with a tradition illustrated by *El Héroe* (1637) by Baltasar Gracián, the secret binds together, by illocutionary ties, those who hunt for it, keep it, or reveal it. It is the center of the spider web spun around it by lovers, traitors, jealous protagonists, pretenders, or exhibitionists. The hidden organizes a social network. "Subtleties, novelties and various philosophies are expressed in mystical and figurative words," note the Academicians de la Crusca in their *Vocabulario.*[70] They are suspicious of what comes forward masked ("larvatus prodeo"). In a meeker tone, speaking of the fall of Rome, Bossuet mentions "the mystical and veiled manner in which [the Church Fathers] speak of this sad subject."[71] Whether it be in the guise of something veiled, enveloped, withdrawn, or something that is on display, imposing itself with authority, the secret concerns the utterance.[72] It is an address: it repels, attracts, or binds the interlocutors; it is addressed to someone and acts upon him. Let us dwell upon only three of its aspects, in connection with this expansion of the adjective "mystical." A semantic passion is revealed here: the conjunction of a passion (which desires and suffers the other) with a meaning (which is offered or refused). The secret introduces an erotic element into the field of knowledge. It impassions the discourse of knowledge.

First, the secret localizes the confrontation between a *will to know* and a *will to conceal*. This elementary structure obviously has many variants: the will (pedagogical, apologetic) to foster belief in a desire to know ("surely you are anxious to know") or to hide ("I am not going to tell you"), to which we may oppose the real or simulated refusal to know ("I don't want to know"); the art of revealing while seeming to obfuscate, or of hiding while showing;[73] and so on. Around the secret is woven a web of tactics. But basically these "subtleties" may be traced back to two wills that seek and/or dodge one another in all the possible modalities of "telling" or "not telling."

Second, through their quests, struggles and subtle verbal intercourse similar to some lovers' dialogue after Marivaux, the actors also capitalize on the difference between *being* and *appearing*. In this latter guise, the secret is characterized as a something that *is* without *appearing*. But, by that very fact, it is dangerously close to the lie or fiction, that is, to what *appears* without *being*. That which purports to conceal could turn out to be no more than a simulacrum. Indeed, "mystical words," in having a secret referent, are not only engaged in the entire set of seductions or manipulations generated by the hidden; they are themselves caught up in the labyrinthian relations of the fictions they produce with the realities they conceal. They fall into the very trap they have constructed. Those to whom such words are addressed may always find those words to be no more than pretense. Nor does polemical discourse refrain from doing just that, being all the more effective because it often draws out the doubtful status of the secret upon which "mystical" discourse is based: Might it not be just an illusion? Thus the endless task of "discernment," the struggle against deception. True, the secret's attractiveness can work in its favor, yet it remains suspect. In the final analysis, reference to a secret moves the "appearances" (whose credibility is based on the secret) in the direction of illusion, so that it becomes necessary, in order to maintain the secret's reality, to resort constantly to a visible institution. The "mystic" word is always inclined to seek the protection of some "authorities" (ecclesiastical approval, biblical quotations, etc.) against the "examiners" who in turn defend their position by reducing the mystic utterance to pretense.

Third, the secret is the precondition for hermeneutics. There can be no interpretation without the supposition of something hidden to decipher in the sign. But it must also be supposed that an order exists between the unspoken and what masks it, for otherwise the very hypothesis of an interpretation collapses. Now it appears that—given the widespread experience of cosmic disorder and social corruption— the fabrication of linguistic secrets (purely discursive effects) permitted at least the maintenance, through refinements, of the logical or rhetorical order that regulates linguistic operations, and the creation of the preconditions for a hermeneutics that would function henceforth on the level of the interplay of meanings or words. The proliferation of the adjective "mystical" modifying nouns seems to have produced in and by language an artificial equivalent of the interpretative activity that until then had deciphered the divine will in the secrecy of things. The hermeneutic apparatus still worked, and even continued to develop, but in a verbal or "literary" field. This shift might be considered comparable to the one being made in our own time by the detective story, born at the end of the last century with Arthur Conan Doyle (Sherlock Holmes), at the same time that medical semiology and psychoanalytic symptomatology were emerging.[74] The detective story produces secrets artificially in order to create interpretation; it connects the one with the other by "clues"; it composes scenarios or "fictions" of hermeneutics. Anything termed "mystical" becomes a mini detective story, an enigma; it requires a search for something other than what is stated; it introduces endless details having the value of clues. There a virtuosity had found a field in which to perform. This linguistic isolation allowed for a flourishing of rhetoric and logic. It was also manifest in the form of a baroque or flamboyant hermeneutics that followed fifteenth-century rhetorical writers and that became a distinctive "way of speaking, a style."[75]

Indeed, it was to a way of speaking that the flowering of the adjective "mystical" corresponded most often during the first half of the seventeenth century. *Le Pressoir mystique* by Jean d'Intras (1605), *La Couronne mystique* by Jean Boucher (1624), *L'Abeille mystique* by Nicholas Parent (1639)—dozens of titles, hundreds of pages contained the word. Louis Richeome went on collecting "mystical figures" in the folios of his *Tableaux sacrés* (1601). Francis of Sales raised this genre to the level of a masterpiece in the *Introduction à la vie dévote* (1609) but adopted a less flowery tone in his *Traité de l'Amour de Dieu* (1616). "In nineteen years, one learns and unlearns many things," he said, "one speaks one way to young apprentices and another way to old companions."[76] His thought had matured. The times had changed, too. In the middle of the century, the adjective assumed a different tone; it became specialized. It became rare in scientific language[77] and, according to the French academicians (1694), pedantically behind the times, "it is only used in reference to things religious."[78] But in religion itself, it was no longer sustained by the lyricism that made the enigmas and blazons proliferate. The term denoted a particular state it served to classify, to catalogue. Already Innocent of Saint-André singles out from the other sorts of prayer the "supernatural and divine, or mystical one."[79] In using the word "mystical" as a supplementary synonym accompanying traditional terms, he reverts to its theological use but with a meaning that is overdetermined by the progressive isolation of a mystical "science." Similarly, Constantin de Barbanson, using a demonstrative adjective that designates a particular milieu and an object set apart by this milieu, distinguishes, within wisdom, "that mystical and celestial sapience" and, among the spiritual ways, "these ways, mystical."[80] In his *Anatomie de l'âme* (1635), he does not offer, as one did at the beginning of the century, an account made up of allegories and figures but covers "the entire mystical affair," a field in its own right that has the form of a "mystical voyage."[81] About a decade later, the experience examined by Louis Chardon was characterized by a subsistence that was "not human, but divine; not in the least natural, but mystical."[82] The "mystical" region became separated from the "ordinary" or "common" pathways and tended to become identified with the "extraordinary." That categorization increased mistrust. Muzio Vitelleschi, the general of the Jesuits, worried that Louis Lallemant might be "totus mysticus," is afraid of seeing his disciples swept away "ad devotionem extraordinariam."[83] Later, "spiritual" professors would once again work to hierarchize neatly all these heady experiences, as did the antiquietist Gottardo Bell'huomo in *Il pregio e l'ordine dell'orazioni ordinarie e mistiche* (1678). (But Gottardo accepted the established definition in which "mystical" was the opposite of the ordinary.) A certain theology is discernable here, the very theology whose theory of the supernatural regarded as pure "modality" went the furthest beyond the positions of Bellarmine, Suarez, or Grégoire de Valence. This theology—having gotten from "philosophy" a secularized concept of nature, and opposing the "internal persuasion" of the Protestants in order to encourage a return to the positive authorities of tradition—affirms that man is incapable of recognizing the "truth," which is nevertheless his proper goal; that consciousness is closed to an "undeserved and supplementary" ("indebitum et superadditum") supernatural; and that any "feeling" of God must be considered as "illusory" or "extraordinary."[84]

## THE SUBSTANTIVE OF A SCIENCE

The movement that specialized the usage of the word "mystical" brought about the birth of a science organized around these "extraordinary" facts, reserving a special space for them: mystical science, which soon was to become *mystics*. In the late Middle Ages, Gerson had contrasted "sapientia philosophorum" with the ancient "sapientia christianorum," which he later specified as the "vera sapientia christianorum":[85] this addition of "verus," an indication that there was vying between several uses of the expression "sapientia christianorum," began a semantic evolution that eventually narrowed down the expression's meaning. Within the framework of the same opposition, "sapientia sanctorum" replaced the "wisdom of the Christians" and in turn became the "science of the Saints."[86] The prodigious success of this expression and its many variants in the sixteenth, and especially in the seventeenth century, is well known: from the "sanctorum vita" or the "dicta sanctorum" to the "doctrine of the saints," the "practice of the saints," the "madness" or the "wisdom of the saints," the "maxims of the saints." Which saints? Here, too, there was evolution. The traditional heroes of hagiography were progressively being replaced by those whom we today would call mystics. The figures of male or female saints remained, but their content changed: always extraordinary, to be sure, but by their "states" more than by their virtues, by their knowledge more than by their performances, by their "unknown language" more than by their miracles. The "interior and spiritual things" qualify the "saints who experienced them and left them in writing," like Dionysius the Areopagite or Teresa of Avila.[87] "The language unknown in the science of the saints is familiar to Teresa," says Surin. "The school of mystical theology is in her."[88] Such were the "saints" whose "maxims" or "doctrine" Fénelon would defend.

### A SPECIFIC LANGUAGE

It is not particularly astonishing that this "wisdom" should have taken on the name "mystical" explicitly. It is called "mystical sapience" by Constantin de Barbanson and many others,[89] "mystical science" by Luís de la Puente, Jean de Saint-Samson, and Surin.[90] Nor is it surprising that the "contemplatives" were the doctors of that science "doctrina que escriben los santos."[91] The saint who became mystical received a scriptorial function. He established himself in the field of language. In 1588, after Bonaventure was declared to be among the doctors of the Church and recommended as the equal of Thomas Aquinas, Teresa was in turn canonized (1615) and recommended to everyone for her "books of mystical theology."[92] From then on, "many scholars of the time called her Mystic Doctor," and on all sides of the "Doctora mística" there proliferated "doctores y maestros de mística Teología."[93] Ruysbroeck was already called "doctor," and Johannes Tauler, "very illustrious theologian." This title, tied to a science and a linguistic competency, became generalized. From 1630 on, the publishers of John of the Cross began to attribute to him, too, the title "mystical doctor."[94] In 1640, when Maximilian Van der Sandt (Sandaeus) published his vast survey of mystical vocabulary, it was by the relation of these "saints" to language that he defined the "mystical doctors" or "mystical theologians" whose works he analyzed.[95]

The corpus of Dionysius the Areopagite contributed to the emancipation of that "science," which, in turn, interpreted that corpus more and more in the nocturnal light emanating from its *Mystic Theology*. This "treasure" came from the Orient, as if mystical language had always to come from those prestigious countries. Jean Goulu, at the beginning of his translation (1608), shows the relationship between "theory" and travel. "Louis le Débonnaire," he writes, "sent envoys to Michael, the Eastern Emperor, to get this book."[96] That was in the year 827. Beginning in the thirteenth century, a new wave brought the "high thoughts" of the oriental "contemplator" to the West. It produced such rapture that, by the end of the century, Jesus Christ himself, in the *Exercitia spiritualia* by Gertrude d'Helfta (d. 1301), sometimes began to speak as Dionysius did.[97] In the sixteenth and seventeenth centuries, its printed circulation enlarged the audience of the Dionysian corpus, which continued however, by its "secrets," to produce innovation. Thus the *Onomasticon Dionysianum* Balthasar Cordier included in his voluminous edition of the *Opera* (Antwerp, 1634) maps out a new world of the mind, the lexicon of a different language, a "novum quoddam et inusitatum dicendi genus" as Pierre Lanssel said in 1615.[98] In addition to the editions of the Greek corpus[99] and numerous partial publications,[100] an entire tradition of commentaries was accumulated, then renewed. The sixteenth century published the commentaries of Johann Eck (1519), Denys le Chartreux (1536, 1556), Marsilio Ficino (1538, 1561), Nicholas of Cusa (1565), Thomas Aquinas (1588), and others; the seventeenth century, those of Charles Hersent (1626), Martin Del Rio (1633), Balthasar Cordier (1634), Joseph du Saint-Esprit (1684), and others. Also numerous are the translations, of which the most famous in French is that of Goulu (1608, 1629); and we must not forget those done by the best spiritual theologians for their own use and inserted in their books, such as those of Leonhard Lessius (1620)[101] or Louis Chardon (1647).[102] The "Apologies," "Defenses," "Lives," or "Glories" of Pseudo-Dionysius are no less numerous, especially when critical erudition, after 1640, undermined the apostolic authority of this supposed disciple of Saint Paul.[103]

For the humanists, for Erasmus, the "divine Jerome" was the "princeps theologorum."[104] The "divine Dionysius" wrested that honor from him, and more specifically the "Dionysius who wrote *Mystic Theology.*" He was the "prince of Platonists," according to Ficino, and later, according to Giordano Bruno, that man "drunk with God."[105] Dionysius, the "prince of the theologians" as Nicholas of Cusa called him, began to reach a wider public, but at the same time the city of which he was prince was dwindling. When the *Commentarii conimbricenses* (1603) in turn declared him "Theologorum princeps," they were dealing with a science more spiritual and positive than Platonic and speculative.[106] The same is true of Lessius, when he wrote to Lanssel that "it does not appear that anyone since the apostles should be considered preferable or even equal to him."[107] Soon the eulogies became litanies: "theologus divinissimus," "princeps christianae theologiae," "apex theologorum," "profunditatem altissimae theologiae assecutus,"[108] "summus theologus,"[109] "most sublime and ancient theologian."[110] But these laudatory appellations were displayed in works of spirituality and in the recent editions of Louis de Blois or John of the Cross for which Dionysius served as a seal of quality. To be authorized, one had to resemble him.[111] Such was the procedure adopted by Diego de Jesús, Nicolas de Jesus-Maria, or Quiroga to defend John of the Cross (1618). The Areopagite was the eponymous hero of an entire literature, just as Jerome had been before him and as Augustine would be during the second half of the century. He was no longer the oracle of an elite. His ensigns waved at the head of a "turba magna" of spirituals and devout followers. At the end of the sixteenth century, the composition of a panegyric of him was a school assignment.[112]

In attempting to resemble him, other "mystical theologies" were born, with other "doctors and professors of mystical theology," "princes of the profound and secret theology of Christians."[113] His authority both circumscribed and permitted the formation of a discipline, furnishing a linguistic as well as a theoretical referent, which was, no doubt, the main thing. His artificial "language," by its lexical coherence and originality—an object debated, commented, and endlessly adapted—presented the model for a new science. It was at once its precondition and its utopia. This was a role it had won thanks to its transfer from the East to the West, thanks to its "exotic" status. In the East itself, in the complexity of byzantine traditions, it inspired nothing comparable; no other discourse, even one graced with a foreign origin, succeeded in organizing the internal flowering of oriental spiritualities into a "science."[114]

In the West, a diversity of problematics had been recognized for a long time within one sole theology. The question was thus: "quomodo differunt inter se theologia mystica et scolastica."[115] A hierarchy of types of knowledge distinguished but also united the differentiated levels, like anagogic steps, in an architecture of the cosmos and of man: a proper or "scholastic" theology organized the domain of intelligibility; a "mystical" theology first ascended "ad supermentales excessus," then ultimately to the "contemplation," which only the "sapiens et perfectus theologus" experienced.[116] In place of that ternary distribution, which comes from Bonaventure, Gerson substituted the binary structure that he founded upon the cleavage between the three cognitive faculties and the three affective ones, the former rising up to the *contemplatio* (by the *intelligentia*) and the latter called finally toward the *dilectio extatica* or *theologia mystica* (which involves *synderesis*).[117] In these examples, as in many others, the "pathways" or figures of knowledge present diverse modal forms according to an anthropological or cosmological distribution; they remain accidental and quasi-"adjectival" in relation to the One Principle that innerves them, correlates them, and manifests itself in them. Something altogether different occurs when knowledge itself, reflecting a societal rift, is transformed. As the split between *litterati* and *idiotae*, rich and poor, town and country leads to the existence of heterogeneous cultural fields and types of experience—that is, as a society reorganized into distinct "spaces" determined by power relationships (political, judicial, and rhetorical) emerges in place of the former hierarchies of status or "station"—knowledge, too, is altered, articulated in a twofold formality of spatialization and operativity. Knowledge will henceforth consist of regions whose differences are insurmountable and whose methods are specific to each region.

Separation of experiences and privileged ways of doing things go hand in hand. These two movements undermine the unitary architecture of theology. They bring about a spatialization of knowledge, relative to the visual perception of a geographic universe, and the concern to specify the "actions" that either characterize each of the isolated domains or cut across them. Two elements are relevant here: place, which ascribes a different value to statements apparently common or hierarchized ("truth on this side of the Pyrenees, error on the other"), and operations capable of transforming place and/or linking it to other places. Hence a unitary principle is no longer recognizable in the positivities of history; it becomes their darkness or vanishing point. Hence the mystical journey that set out in search of the One, a self-imposed exile from the solidity of things. But this journey is first determined by the movement that reorganizes knowledge. I will consider only two elements of that movement here, both equally important for its transformation into a science in its own right.

On one hand, marked by various signs (the pauper, the *idiotus*, the illiterate, the woman, or the *affectus*, etc.), there is the identification of spaces that resist the speculation of theologians and professionals. Thus, in the blows that the *Devotio moderna* directs against rational activity,[118] there is a traditional aspect (an opposition of wisdom to knowledge), but also the recognition of another social and religious "region," the new awareness of a different reality that many spiritual currents take note of, single out, and cultivate, from the *poverello* of Assisi to the "Brothers of the Free Spirit" of the North or the Spanish *alumbrados*. Beneath the multitude of doctrines or experiences, this collective swell of countless muffled voices lends its strength— sometimes seductive, sometimes frightening—to an otherness within the life of the spirit. It lends widespread assurance to the construction of a mystic language. It is the elusive referent of a "place."

On the other hand, the work of the humanists on classical, biblical, or patristic texts develops, alongside the binomial contrast between scholastic and mystical theology, a third locus: that of "positive" theology. The separation between scholastic (or "speculative") and positive theology, which goes back to the difference (traditional in fifteenth-century logic) between the "science of things" (connected with the *artes reales*) and the "science of words" (connected with the *artes sermocinales*), became impossible to suppress with the famous "liber prooemialis" in volume 2 of the *Augustinus* (1641), in which Cornelius Otto Jansen affirms the incompatibility of philosophy, founded on the *intellectus*, with theology, founded on *memoria*, that is, the authority of the Scriptures and the Fathers.[119] When positive theology wins its own status, at the beginning of the sixteenth century, it is first a return to the doctrine of the ancients (a *veterum theologia*) against the medieval *neoterici*, whom the humanists blame for being deviationist innovators (*novi doctores*), abstract dialecticians, and cloistered Schoolmen (monks and/or "théologastres").[120] In reality, the autonomy demanded by a new intellectual elite in matters of doctrine, method, or scholastic institutions was acted out through objective operations. Textual commentary (which was assiduously practiced in the School) was freed from the formal apparatus that dominated it. The medieval *lectio*, which applied a theoretical framework and/or a corpus of dogma to series of *loci*, was replaced with the discovery or *inventio* of an inspired author who had the active role in his work. Therefore, problems of language (a grammar) and of discourse (a rhetoric) were considered to be an essential element that alone could make possible the transition from an antiquity recognized as being different from the present to the idioms of contemporary debate. Finally, the main goal was to "understand" and to defend a teaching (*documentum*) sprung from the origins but corrupted, decomposed in its manuscript versions, and rendered equivocal by historical change or temporal distance. Interpretation concerned the experiencing of language itself (through philology, textual criticism, translation) and a form of dialogue (through attention to what an author was directing to a reader by his words, style, etc.). These two aspects assimilated interpretation to the practice of an art of saying, in accordance with a *modus rhetoricus* that goes back to the Church Fathers or to antiquity.[121]

The "letter" is a modality of speech. The science that analyzes it is indeed a "spiritual" or theological dialogue but one made up of linguistic and "literary" experiences, in every case relative to a present/absent interlocutor in its discourse. It has its "way of proceeding" (*modus procedendi*). Its proper name, "positive theology," designates specific operations. It is undoubtedly related to canon law (*jus positivum, doctrina positiva*) and to the procedures of juridical hermeneutics, which were of decisive importance for all of the historical or exegetical work that, at that time, was becoming distinct from theology. But although positive theology was differentiated by techniques that would be isolated and assume the guise of critical erudition in the seventeenth century, it was still attached, in the sixteenth century, to a "spiritual" (and monastic) tradition, particularly by the central role played in that science by the return to an experience, to a "literature," and to an *oratio*, three poles of the *lectio divina* in the Cistercian tradition. (Bernard of Clairvaux "renounced everything, except the art of writing," said Étienne Gilson.)[122] An epistemology of enunciation is what these two modern theologies had in common. They differed rather by a cleavage, internal to that common problematic, between two forms of the writing that speaks: the text became for positive theology what the body became for mystical science. Each would follow the logic of the locus—and the transformations of the locus—it had selected.

In the Renaissance there were, then, two coexisting binomials: scholastic theology versus mystic theology, and scholastic theology versus positive theology. Despite the exchanges between the terms of the first or the second disjunction, despite the passages of mystic theology to positive theology (or vice versa), these two binary oppositions would eventually combine to form a ternary series—scholastic, positive, and mystical—in which each discipline was specified by its own field, this field being articulated by a referential discourse (a scientific "language"): an Aristotelian and nominalist language for the first; a scriptural and patristic one for the second (stabilized into an explication of the Scriptures according to the Fathers);[123] a Pseudo-Dionysian one for the last. This ternary list has a reconciliatory function, being a map indicating the diverse regions of one sole theology. But, placed transitionally beneath this unitary sign, the list will progressively reveal the heterogeneity it masks, as the names designating its regions become more specialized and each of the three sciences, ceasing to have the status of a variant in relation to a common theological *habitus*,[124] acquires its autonomy in passing from an adjectival to a substantive position.

Mystical independence, already marked by a relation to the Dionysian corpus, or by the predicates of an "extraordinary," "experimental," "affective," "practical"[125] doctrine, in fact, soon did become legitimate. At the juncture of the sixteenth and seventeenth centuries, the "mystic theologian" became "a mystic"; then, in turn, "mystic theology" became "*mystics*,"[126] during the same era, incidentally, when the "philosopher chemist," disengaging himself from a cosmological philosophy, was transformed into "a chemist."[127] The disciplines were diversifying. The noun "mystic" seems to have made its appearance within and in reference to groups that were furthest removed from the theological institution; like many proper nouns, it first took the form of a nickname or accusatory term.[128] Thus, the *Censura* by Thomas de Jésus (1611) against the *Théologie germanique* (so lauded by Luther) included a second part entitled *De aliis erroribus Begardorum et aliorum Mysticorum quos libellus iste continet.*[129] Here we have one of this noun's very first occurrences. Thomas exorcises, by nominalization, a race he excludes from theology. That distance between "mystic" and "theology," the word of which it was originally predicated, was on the increase. Thus Pierre Charron says

(1635): "theology, even mystic [theology], teaches us."[130] This is the moment at which the adjective separated and was transformed into a substantive. Soon, Sandaeus (1640) was speaking of "mystica naturalis"; Chéron (1657), of "everything that is treated in *mystics*";[131] Léon de Saint-Jean says (1661): "Let us grant *mystics* its expressions"; finally, Surin (1661) treated *mystics* as a "science completely separate from the others," and in that year wrote a treatise (unpublished) *De la mystique*.[132] The day was not far off when Bossuet would combat the "new *mystics*"[133]—so new, from a semantic point of view, that the word was still absent from the *Dictionnaire de Trévoux* in the eighteenth century and would not appear in the title of a published work until the nineteenth century.

## THE WAR OF WORDS AND "MYSTIQUERY"

This late birth is precisely what *mystics* is reproached with: innovation and jargon. Both accusations—aimed at a birth and a way of speaking—go together, being inseparable, as in the word "infancy," which notes the child's inability to actually speak (*in-fans*). The established language seems to be an untouchable, the hypersensitive skin of a body that is sick, unsure of itself. Throughout the sixteenth century, ecclesiastical institutions increased the number of warnings, treatments, or brutal therapeutics to defend their way of speaking (to save their necks?). Witness, for example, the strict measures taken by the Jesuits, in the very springtime of their Order, against the "modos dicendi novos" and the "new and uncommon" expressions,[134] or the lawsuit brought in 1558–59 against Bartolomé Carranza, the archbishop of Toledo (a Spanish Fénelon under Charles V and Philip II), because of his "palabras peligrosas y non usadas sino rarisimamente."[135] These words were "dangerous," sometimes deadly. Why? What such words threatened, what *mystics* wounded and opened to question by its use of them, relates to a shifting of ground, a shift of the essential to the linguistic front and a hitherto unsuspected seriousness of the "literary" issues. A new epistemology was coming to the fore, a linguistic one. *Mystics* was a Hundred Years' War waged along a verbal frontier. It was still the object of the same accusations when the war was over at the end of the seventeenth century.

According to Bossuet, mystical usage continued to be characterized by an "abuse of language," by those "profane novelties of language that Saint Paul forbids" and that resemble "gibberish."[136] Mystics should be "put in their place, which will be quite low," because, as Johnny-come-latelies, they had neither tradition nor genealogy. "The new *mystics*," he calls them, "our present *mystics*."[137] The term "new" was pejorative at that time. Pascal armed himself with it against the Jesuits, "new casuists"; the Jesuits used it against the Jansenists, those "new theologians"; the Schoolmen against the Pyrrhonists, "new philosophers." Louis XIV wrote to Cardinal de Janson on the subject of Fénelon, who had been accused of treason: "I never want to enter into anything that could have an appearance of novelty unless it be in order to impeach its progress."[138] Since they are authors who only "date back three or four centuries," Bossuet had little desire to know them: "a certain Ekard," he writes, a distant "Rusbroche" full of "strange . . . absurdities."[139] He was not ashamed of not knowing them, nor Benoit de Canfield, Jean de Saint-Samson, nor even John of the Cross ("Mother," Teresa, sufficed), nor even Francis of Sales's *Treatise on the Love of God*, which he barely opened.[140] Above all, of those he had read, he remembered the "extraordinary style."[141] He underscored the "absurd expressions" of the *Institutions* attributed to Tauler, although it was "one of the most highly regarded" of mystic books.[142] He passed the same judgment on the Pseudo-Dionysian corpus: the critical works of Sirmond and Jean de Launoy authorized his referring to that corpus as "books attributed to Saint Dionysius the Aeropagite" and written in fact by a "clever unknown author."[143] "All the mystics [he] has read," have "never given a very clear notion" of the naked faith of which they speak. Those "great exaggerators," "not very precise in their expressions," form nothing but "peculiar thoughts"[144] and "abstractions."[145] They are "refiners"[146] who "abuse" the "doctrine of the Holy Fathers" and "that of the School."[147]

Bossuet was no exception and therefore does not deserve the belligerence directed against him by mysticologists since Henri Bremond. He voiced a commonly held view. The excess of blame that, in his case, followed an excess of honor may be attributed to the fact that he based his theatrical sermon on a well-known topos and delivered it on a renowned stage. But a hundred and one others repeated the stereotype. Writes Matthieu Marais: "The mystics are moderns; you didn't see any of them among the ancients."[148] Even Boileau, that mentor of Letters, took up the same position: "The mystics are moderns."[149] He knew his theology when he associated the word with the *alumbrados* who were condemned by the Edict of Seville (1623), with those tried in Picardy (1630–35), and the Quietist ("indolent") disciples of Molinos, all of whom were prosecuted as "fanatics":

> *C'est ainsi quelquefois qu'un indolent mystique*
> *Au milieu des péchés tranquille fanatique . . .* [150]

Rancé, the great reformer of Notre-Dame-de-la-Trappe, wrote something similar to Nicaise in 1688: "Nothing is more worthy of compassion than these poor fanatics who make up their own brand of piety and who, under the pretext of being spirituals through and through, find the secret of making abstractions and separations."[151] It is on these abstractions that the meaning of the neuter substantive "the mystical" ["*le' mystique*"] is based, just as one says today "the religious." "A penchant for the mystical" singled Dupin out as "a trifle ridiculous."[152] Madame de Sévigné scoffed at Corbinelli for being "steeped in the mystical" (1689).[153] Whence that amphigoric "mysticity" that d'Aguesseau deplored in Fénelon.[154] At last the word "*mystiquerie*" appeared. Bérulle's followers had already been charged with it;[155] Richard Simon associated it with the "intellectual amusements" and "ingenious ornaments" of allegory.[156] It was deemed worthy of a separate entry in the *Dictionnaire de Trévoux*: "It has been said of Desmarets that while still young he lost his soul writing novels, and in his old age he lost his wits writing mystiquery."[157]

Pierre Bayle compared this "extravagant" style of *mystics* to that of the "speculative Chinese," and according to Pierre Jurieu it was "so obscure and peculiar that it is extremely difficult to make mystic science speak the language of men."[158] It required justification by its own authors against so many "examiners" who "attack us on our terminology."[159] Their defense was also twofold: on one hand, the invention of an ancient mystic tradition; on the other, the affirmation that the new words said "the same thing" as Christian antiquity. In other words, mystic modernity had a genealogical history, and what it expressed was no different than what its antecedents had expressed. Demonstrating this was not so easy. Seventeenth-century erudition, sharpened by the theological quarrels between Catholics and Protestants (quarrels that had moved from the Scriptures to the patristic texts), knew and kept an eye on all the movements in the terrain. In an intermediary strategy, certain defenders of the mystics appealed to "secret traditions," going back to the Scriptures and sidestepping a positivistic examination of texts.[160] But this recourse was as disturbing as what it professed to authorize, for it, too, raised the issue of a separation between words and their meanings. There could be no "secret tradition" without the introduction of a double reading, hence ambiguity, into the orthodox language. This was intolerable to theologians who thought they could hold onto things of the spirit with words, thus guaranteeing an institutionalization of meaning. Therefore the apologetics for the spirituals had to return to the erudite demonstration of a continuity. This continuity established itself henceforth on the terrain imposed upon it by its adversaries—one the mystics had rejected: historical authority. Fénelon, in his *Maximes des saints*, is a case in point. He appealed to historical erudition to give his doctrine the foundation of a tradition: "The method of his mystic theology is that of positive theology."[161] To legitimize the "moderns," he answered: "The Church of the sixteenth and seventeenth centuries, which authorizes them, carries no less weight than the Church of the earliest times."[162] In the first stage of the argument, the present-day Church is posited as not inferior to the primitive Church, whence one can already infer it is not different. Fénelon nonetheless admitted covertly the novelty of the mystic phenomenon. He was so clearly conscious of it that, in his conflict with Bossuet, he preferred to speak of the "passive man," the "contemplative," "saints" or "spirituals," rather than use a word that smacked of heresy. If he does use it, it is to identify the mystic with Saint Paul's "spiritual man."[163] From this comes a second stage in the argument, to "show that the mystics did not exaggerate any more than did the Fathers."[164] There was neither deviation nor excess in the new mystics as compared to the old. The third stage is nothing but the converse: "The saints of antiquity . . . exaggerated as much as the modern mystics."[165] Consequently, the accusations leveled at the latter strike the former. Ergo (the conclusion is framed in reference to the case par excellence, in Clement of Alexandria, of the identification of a "perfect" with the object of his contemplation): "The gnostic of Saint Clement and the passive man of the mystics of these recent centuries are but two names for one and the same thing."[166] A tradition had been recovered at the price of the insignificance of the new words. The acquisition of a genealogy had to be paid for, at least in the discourse of controversy, by the loss of a language that carried within itself a century of mystic struggles. No, conceded those defenders of the mystics, nothing new was being said, almost nothing. That manner of speaking said nothing that was distinctively its own.

While the "secret tradition" insinuated difference into the same words, this exegesis restored the unity of "the same thing" beneath the difference of the words. The interpretation is typically theological. (It is also to be found, by the way, in a certain tradition of historical writing.) For there is theology wherever hermeneutics reduces the diverse figures of time to "the same." Any theology eliminates the irreducibility of differences by the production of a "tradition," that is, by defining an "essential" that clerical knowledge singles out, claims as its own, and regards as the common denominator of an oceanic plurality. Thanks to the work of theologians who, beginning in the seventeenth century, conquered the space created by spirituals, *mystics*, too, crafted its own tradition, weaving out of the texts of the past a homogeneous corpus with criteria taken from the new "science of the saints." Thus its present, held in words, fades away as its past is constituted.

This curious history gives its due to the irruption of new ways of speaking, divergences or discontinuities in a homogeneous tradition. Like slips of the tongue, words insinuate a repressed alterity into language. Otherness reappears with these details. It is therefore not a matter of indifference that *mystics* should first manifest itself in the apparition of incongruous and unheard of terms. Teresa of Avila, though very sensible as well as being rather wary of theologians, knew what was at stake in the use of those words through which could be discerned, in discourse, the sound and perhaps the gaze of the other. Consequently, like Descartes who was "deceived by the terms of ordinary language," she hoped for and allowed "nuevas palabras" to come forth.[167]

*Chapter Four*

✢  ✢
✢

# Manners of Speaking

The new science's most highly visible features are its linguistic ones. It is chiefly a way of using language. In the same *Censura* against the *Théologie germanique*, Thomas de Jesús refers to the "phrases" (*phrases*), the "words" (*verba*), the "ways of speaking" (*modus loquendi*) that characterize the mystics. In contradistinction to "theo-logy," discourse on God, which it parallels, *mystics* is a "manner of speaking." This issue becomes the obsessive focal point of the debates and legal proceedings surrounding the Beguines and Beghards of the North, or the *alumbrados* of Spain: "the way of communicating," "the way of speaking about spiritual things" [ *"la manera de communicarse," "el modo de hablar en las cosas espirituales"*].[1] The theme recurs everywhere, modalized in a variety of ways: the "way of speaking" [ *"dire"*] of "several mystics" [ *"plusieurs mystiques"*];[2] "it is what the mystics call" [ *"c'est ce que les mystiques appellent"*];[3] "written and spoken words of the mystics," "ways of speaking that are peculiar to the mystics" [ *"mysticorum scripta dictaque," "modi loquendi quos mystici ut proprios habent"*], or "formulations of speaking of the mystics" [ *"mysticorum loquendi formulae"*];[4] "according to what the mystics teach" [ *"selon ce qu'enseignent les mystiques"*];[5] "what the most excellent mystics write" [ *"les termes et les phrases dont usent les mystiques"*];[6] "what the most excellent mystics write" [ *"ce qu'écrivent les plus excellents mystiques"*];[7] "after the style of all the mystics" [ *"selon le style de tous les mystiques"*];[8]

113

and so on. Quasi-tautological expressions, since in saying "mystical" [*"mystique"*] it is to a language that one is referring. Generally speaking, the terms *spirituels, contemplatifs* or *illuminés* are used when it is their experience that is intended, and *mystiques* is used in connection with their form of discourse. In the former case, one speaks of *la contemplation* or of *la spiritualité* (which stops short of implying the expression of an experience); in the latter, of *la mystique*.[9] The adjective *mystique* itself qualifies a literary genre, a "style." Added to the words "death," "darkness," and so on, it delimits the intended meaning of these nouns in discourse. For example, "the state of trial and purification that the mystics call the state of death" means the term "death" as they understand it.[10] What is "mystical" is a *modus loquendi*, a "language."[11]

## PRESUPPOSITIONS:
## A LINGUISTIC PRAGMATICS

These "manners of speaking" relate the struggle of the mystics to language. More precisely, they are the traces left by that struggle, like the stones Jacob blessed and left near Yabboq after his night of wrestling with the angel. These turns of phrase, grouped into a science and, later, "museographied" in dictionaries, but also gathered and carried (like old battle scars?) within the tireless memory that is any language itself, are primarily the effects of *operations* that connect historical circumstances to linguistic practices. In making a few preliminary remarks on the circumstances that surrounded the verbal inventiveness of the mystics, I would like merely to introduce the analysis of a certain number of the practices that made up this new "art of speaking," and by which the late medieval tradition of the *parleüres* or "manners of speaking," and particularly the "arts of second rhetoric,"[12] redefined "contemplative" discourse. In this respect, *mystics* is the Trojan horse of rhetoric within the city of theological science.

### THE POSTULATE OF A REVELATION

By means of this postulate, Christian epistemology links mystic knowledge to language. God has spoken. "The Word is become flesh." This constitutes an initial historical split if compared with other religious configurations. Thus, a Greco-Roman tradition leads the mind toward silence (*sige, siōpe, hesyche,* etc.) and designates with the term "ineffable" not only a critique of language but its absence; it departs in the direction of an unknown god (*agnostos theos*) who silences all thought because he is beyond being.[13] In the Plotinian ontology of the One, language is excluded from mystic experience. The Greek silence still runs through the Logos of Christian antiquity. It fascinates patristic theology. A long passage of time and autonomy from the Church was required for the Christian paradox of a mystic language to take shape. "It is only with medieval Latin that a true technical language of *mystics* will be created. This language takes as its point of departure certain paleo-Christian terms, but nevertheless constitutes a new, typically medieval creation."[14]

In the sixteenth century, the mystic ways of speaking seem to manifest the instability of that medieval success. They reintroduce into that "technical language" something of the great Silence of the past that returns with the ancient classics, or through Dionysius the Areopagite, or in Jewish and Moslem traditions. They are combinations of the new evangelical spoken word with the ancient mutism, solemn as an origin, of the "nothing speaks." The postulate of a revelation is equally present, however, in the conviction that *there must be* a "speech of God." The *modus loquendi* is the outcome of the opposition between the waning of trust in discourse and the God-affirming assurance that the spoken word cannot be lacking. It oscillates between these two poles and finds, nonetheless, ways of speaking. Moreover, behind the illocutionary tactics that invent "words for that," there is, ultimately, the principle of a "concord" between the infinite and language. In the seventeenth century, philosophy and mathematics, still so closely allied, were to discover other applications of this principle.

### OPERATIONS ON THE FRAGMENTS OF THAT LOST UNITY

The end of the Middle Ages is marked by the passage from Latin to the vernacular languages and by exchanges between idioms separated by the divisions between professions, milieus, and, before long, between nations. Since the thirteenth century, Latin had become both a conservative language (its evolution being controlled by a professional elite) and a technical one (having the certainty and precision of an artificial language). It was the instrument of a scientificity. It would be more precise to say that the scientificity developed by exhuming the logical possibilities of this Latin, but while it became more refined, it also became narrower as its language became restricted to the schools. On the other hand, the languages termed "vulgar" were developing, first in the commercial cities of Southern Europe (Italy, Provence) and of the Netherlands. A different, lay elite upheld, accredited, and perfected a narrative or realist literature—courtly, full of love, current scandal, and critique. The mystic and marvelous stories that were written in the vernaculars were a part of these urban movements: the autobiography of Beatrice of Nazareth (d. 1268) in the Thiois dialect, the poems of Hadewijch of Anvers (mid-thirteenth century?) in Middle Dutch, or *Miroir des simples âmes* by Marguerite Porete (d. 1310) in French. These narratives were produced by such groups as the Flemish Beguine communities, strongly independent and well-endowed republics of women, or Italian preacher monasteries, often of bourgeois origin. Socioeconomic advance went hand in hand with these linguistic creations, fostered by lay and religious institutions still modeled on monasteries that attained a social, legal, and financial independence from university and Church authority.

Linguistically speaking, the essential point is not the uneasiness or resistance of the specialists toward the "dialects" that forged new organizations of knowledge.[15] From their point of view, the concern was justified. There was indeed opposition (Tauler alluded to it long before Rabelais did) between the "ecclesiastic bigwigs and masters of schools" [ *"die grossen Pfaffen und die Lesmeister"*] and the "masters of life" [ *"die Lebmeister"*].[16] The important point is the spread of bilingualism. It modified the very use of language. We have seen it in the case of the preachers or biographers who began to use the "vulgar" language also. Even though it may have been motivated by political or missionary considerations, this bilingualism nevertheless shattered an identity. Therefore it also has a metaphysical significance. Already in the thirteenth century, the German sermons of Meister Eckhart represent primarily the introduction of the language of the Beguines into the professorial domain, a language he learned from them in order to answer them while continuing to think in Latin in his treatises. These two languages constitute two different modes of discourse between which there opens up the Eckhartian "detachment," a silence that flows back over them, an absolute transcendence of being, a "dying of the spirit." The distancing that the master of Cologne transforms into "annihilation" of language appears everywhere, in more or less theoretical or radical ways. A manner of mutism rends the configurations of knowledge. An impossibility wounds the expectation that awaits being in logos.

The lost unity inspired the project of combining and bringing together these dialects, which were still perceived as fragments of a symbolic language. The coexistence, often within the same speaker, of professionalized Latin (or, before long, of a Latin restored to its ancient and classical difference, its status of dead language) and local dialects brings about constant adjustments and shifts, importing or exporting from one language to another words dispersed in regional expressions but all belonging to a single language, shattered by time. Naturally, the dissemination of the referential language intensifies the transference to an originary language, which in turn becomes the utopian or scientific model for common artificial languages. But what is even more striking than these myths or scenarios of "the" language is the activity of mixing together, reusing, and collating words selected from all languages according to their "power" of speaking, which they were thought to have retained from their origin. The editor of Garcilaso de la Vega's works was not alone in thinking that, since the "good" terms were scattered throughout all the tongues, one must "often borrow from a foreign language a word of *mayor significación.*"[17] This collecting enterprise, which ultimately corresponds to the same principle as the great polyglot editions of the Bible (the principle of recreating a body from its disjointed members), struggles against division by *practices of transfer*, of which the various modes of speaking are but variants.

### GEOGRAPHICAL AND LINGUISTIC TRANSLATION

A network of geographical transfers must be added to the linguistic ones. From the time of Charles V (1517), relations increased between the Flemish countries and Montserrat, Zaragoza, and especially Seville; or from the mid-fifteenth century on, between Cambridge, London, Venice, and Padua. The circulation was carried out via travelers,[18] manuscript copies, and particularly printing, "el maravilloso artificio de la impreta publicada," as Bernard Boyl said when he published his translation of the Syriac mystic Isaac of Nineveh in 1489.[19] These texts, coming from the East, the North, or the South, escaped the university institution and its professorial interpretation. Languages became passersby, processions of words lived in and practiced differently at each stage of the journey, but continuing to undergo, from region to region, the implanting of thoughts and foreign expressions used in new ways. Between the accumulation and mobility of vocabulary, novel combinations were formed, preserving, extending, or restoring the verbal heritage by means of the transfers themselves and the compromises they brought about. *Mystics* also springs from this melting pot of languages; it wanted to be the interlanguage of these languages.

Translations and their extraordinary travels typify this sort of transfer. Just one example: the *Miroir de perfection* [*Spieghel der Volcomenheit*] by Henri de Herp (or Harphius; d. 1477), who was himself a vulgarizer and "herald of Ruysbroeck." His first Latin translator, Pierre Blomevenna, in 1509 already thought he had to justify the "modus loquendi hyperbolicus" and the "termes ambigus" of the *Spieghel.*[20] This "mirror" is a coherent system of exotic words and a logbook of the "soul" traveling in other regions. It was published not only in Flemish (Mainz, 1475; Antwerp, 1501, 1502, 1512, etc.) and in Latin (Cologne, 1509, 1538, 1545, 1556, etc.; Venice, 1524), but also in Italian (Venice, 1522, 1523, 1539), Portuguese (Santa Cruz, 1533), Spanish (Alcalá, 1551), French (Paris, 1549, 1552, 1586, 1595, 1599; Arras, 1596), and German (Cologne, 1600), not to mention the anthologies, its diffusion via manuscript copies (such as by the Carthusian monastery Escala Dei near Tarragon), and the publicity made for it by the numerous Dutch members of the Italian convents or monasteries, which had become centers of Rhenish-Flemish *mystics* (Subiaco in Italy; Santa Cruz in Portugal, etc.).[21] It also took meandering routes: the French translation of the Italian adaptation of the Flemish in the *Compendio,* the conveyance of the German version into Poland, the Japanese transplantation of the Portuguese version, and so on. A hundred and one other strands go into the making of the European spider's web of a population of immigrant words, displaced and transformable. This linguistic melting pot was a sort of spiritual pidgin. Until near the end of the sixteenth century, and well after the stabilization of the national languages, it made up a fermenting mass in which terms forged for estranged systems stimulated, by their exoticism, the shifts of adaptation, and the conjunction of opposites became a resource of linguistic creativity. It is a workshop. One minute there was the play of verbal equivocation while the next the meanings of a term were revised to make them more precise.

A language of the "other" was generated by the vast labor of these alterations. Mystic speech was fundamentally "translational." It crossed the lines. It created a whole by unceasing operations upon foreign words. With this hodgepodge of material, it organized an orchestral suite of misalignments as well as cover-ups and lexical quotations. This writing style is a permanent exercise in transposition: it therefore gives precedence to word usage over received definitions. From this perspective, the supple perspicacity of a Luis de León or a John of the Cross in their translations of the Bible is but one variant of a more general art of transposition. The phenomenon is very widespread. But the obscure heroes of mystic language are those who, whether with brilliance (like Surius, Beaucousin, Cyprian of the Nativity, etc.) or without, pursued the sole task of understanding the different modes of speech and making them intelligible to others. These translators "lose their own language in foreign countries." They have none but that of the other. The distance between the Middle Ages and the Renaissance could even be gauged by what separates this modern translator from the medieval copyist.[22] By and large, they were all anonymous. But the copyist transformed his body into the spoken word of the other; he imitated and incarnated the text into a liturgy of reproduction. Simultaneously, he gave body to the verb ("verbum caro factum est") and made the verb into his own body ("hoc est corpus meum") in a process of assimilation that eliminated differences, to make way for the sacrament of the copy.[23] The translator, who sometimes also exercised the profession of printer or typesetter, was an operator of differentiation. Like the ethnologist, he presented a foreign region, even though he did so to give an adaptation of it by allowing it to disturb his own native language. He produced otherness, but within a field that didn't belong to him any more than that other language did, a field in which he had no right of authorship. He produced, but without any place of his own, in that no-man's-land, on that meeting of the waters where the waves of language roll back upon themselves. The transcriber and the translator had the same reckless devotion, but the former more contemplatively, in a rite of identification, and the latter more ethically, in the production of otherness. The history of *mystics* may well have converted the "copyist" into this translator, the ascetic caught up in the other's language and creating possibility, by means of it while at the same time losing himself in the crowd. In any case, mystics' manners of speaking are the product of that drifting operativity that has no domain proper.

THEORETIC REFERENCES FOR AN ART OF SPEAKING

These manners of speaking, whether they fit foreign terms into a canonic language or quietly introduce the terminology of a legitimate science into a new form of speech, are translative practices. They are metaphorical activities (the metaphor is a *translatio*). They effect displacements; they attract words and change them. The logical interplay that was carried out within one stable linguistic system is now replaced by "transformations" from one system to another and by innovative uses or reuses of words in every field. While there had been a relative homogeneity between the sites of production for university or scholastic discourse, the sites for spiritual production are heterogeneous. Thus, each type of discourse that circulates through or remains within them produces motion from one of these sites to another. They constitute a body marked by transplanted concepts and metaphorized words, tattooed with implicit or explicit quotations; a body that tells the operations of which it is the effect and instrument. It is based on a pragmatics of communication between disparate sites (or "experiences"). It also aspires to overcome that diversity, to bind its elements together by endless ruses, and to restore a dialogical unity. Therefore, it often takes the form of a dialogue or narrative that combines a number of acts and places into a unified textual sequence, that is, an order (chronological, cosmological, etc.) capable of interrelating and classifying these operations and their original sites.

Once a de facto privilege has been granted to the "ways of proceeding," for reasons that involve the very structure of the field in which these metaphorical practices are carried out, it becomes important to know where to find the principles that allow us to order this proliferation of operations into a "sequence" (or, as it was called, a *discursus*), that is, into the history of a kind of communication. Within what strategy of signifying are these tactics to be placed? According to what criteria can we introduce order into these apparently haphazard movements? As we shall see, there are several types of production that answer this question. There is the narrativization of one's own life (autobiography is, for Teresa of Avila and many others before Descartes, a way of "ordering one's soul" and one's "spirit"). There is the construction of fictional and/or normative itineraries, patterns of spiritual "ascensions" or biographical models of "progress" (scenarios intended to classify and hierarchize chronologically chance operations). There is also the drawing up of lists of "rules" for "discerning the spirits" (that is, for judging these movements or "motions" according to their connections and aptness to form series). And there are others. In these various guises, what Surin was to call "the experimental science" was being elaborated. But that elaboration itself presupposes general points of reference that furnish hypotheses and categories applicable to the analysis of the chronicle of events and actions. It must be able to resort to a few referential theories that, though outside the field of practices to be ordered, nevertheless play the role of coherent sets in which principles, methods, and a terminology can be found, even though they have to be adapted before being applied.

The theoretic "authorities" that are relevant to the construction of a discourse on ways of saying are not that numerous. Let us consider first only those that are concerned with the art of speaking—the problem that gives rise to the new mystic science—leaving aside the architectures of medieval anthropology and cosmology (which did, however, serve as frameworks for many authors, for example, John of the Cross, through the scholastic instruction he received at the University of Salamanca from 1564 to 1568). We may select, from among the recent authorities, the following types.

First, there was rhetoric, an outgrowth of the medieval *tres artes* and, in particular, of the *ars dictandi*, or art of composition, especially epistolary composition. Of Italian origin and tradition (Monte Cassino, Rome, and especially Bologna), much cultivated in the Loire region (Blois, Orléans), dominant in Castilian rhetoric,[24] that technique was basic to university teaching. It specified, according to the intended public, the circumstances and the subjects treated, the various manners (or *modi*) of "dictating" (*dictare* means to speak something that is to be written, primarily to compose a letter but also to write poetry, hence the German *dichten*).[25] Transferring oral to written expression, running through the gamut of styles (from the most formal to the most informal), codifying the passage from the vernacular to Latin, this rhetoric presents series of interlocutionary "forms" that are also models of literary contracts and social uses of language. The *ars dictandi* was a theory of *addressed, efficacious,* and circumstantial discourse, the works of which would have been the ideal corpus for J. L. Austin.[26] Epistolography (letter writing) alone, though but a part of the whole field, is the most highly developed branch of humanist literature, so much so that Paul O. Kristeller considers the humanists "the successors of the medieval *dictatores.*"[27] This legal, almost notarial structuring of language became the object of a "lay" science (though it did have close ties with the liturgical and sacramental treatment of discourse, a fact too frequently overlooked), but it also furnished a technical framework of "ways of speaking" to a literature that, beginning with fifteenth-century letters of "direction," "consolation," or "confession," "addressed itself" to God or to a spiritual clientele. Even the treatises of this literature, by Suso, Catherine of Siena, Francis of Sales, or Surin, were mainly composed on the basis of letters. There is no doubt that, except for the brilliant but elitist and ephemeral productions of a logic of dialogue (or *nova dialectica*) that was constructed in the vicinity of the *ars dictandi*, the art of speaking (*ars dicendi*) or its substitute, the art of speaking a written text (*ars dictandi*) was to be gradually reduced to grammar, replaced by an "art of writing," and, in the seventeenth century, subordinated to an "art of thinking," which was no longer organized according to a problematics of the dialogical speech act but rather by a logic of statements.[28] *Mystics* is tied to the fate of these arts.

Alongside these social liturgies of saying/writing, there were the doctrinal and descriptive complexes that great religious institutions had compounded around the *oratio*. With subtlety and rigor, they analyzed the spoken language: acts of the divine revelations, acts of spiritual dialogue (or prayer), acts of fraternal communication, and so on. Linked to the metaphysics of the School, or detached from it but still taking it for granted, these theories traced all interlocution back to the absolute beginning of a primal Speaker. Words and things, in this system of thought, spelled out a language organized by the adventitious occurrences of a Word to be heard among the noises of the world, that body of metaphors in which a hearing schooled in the subtleties of rhetoric could recognize the passages and ruses of a founding voice, the voice of the one, the only. Particularly notable among these theories were the tradition of the Cistercian monks, which, since Bernard of Clairvaux (d. 1153), introduced the erotic element of the *affectus* into the dialogical work of the chorale of the *opus Dei*, and the Rhenish-Flemish mystics who, since Eckhart (d. 1328) and Ruysbroeck (d. 1381), conceived of the "births" of the Being in the "intellect" on the model of speech events. Equipped with precise terminologies and grammars, these doctrines were constructed on the basis of a dual condition of possibility that defined their site of production: the foundation of a monastic "ratio" and the stability of a cosmic "ratio," each forming a discourse (an order that speaks), the former being social, the latter natural, and conforming to/confirming the other. Two centuries later, when this dual postulate was lacking, when the monastic network had fallen apart or fossilized and words ceased being docile to the order of things, these grand syntaxes of speech would no more "hold up" than would their site of utterance. They broke, along with the pedestal that sustained them. Migrating from place to place, they arrived fragmented in relics or anthologies, or transformed into utopias come from afar, like dreams, like the Dionysian corpus, exiled from its Orient. They were still, and more than ever, authorities, but in the form of quotations that generated texts but did not structure them. They no longer functioned as entities organizing theoretic fields.

The mystic movements would concern themselves precisely with the institution of new sites of utterance ("retreats," *ecclésioles*, holy towns, "orders," monasteries) in which to restore (re-form) the social space that is the necessary condition for saying to take place. But the mystic movements already had at their disposal another theoretic space, a *linguistic* one, the importance of which grew in the sixteenth century because it replaced a narrowing or disintegrating configuration with a *fundamental language*. This question essentially concerns the relation of science to the universal through a language, but it is also the main focus of the mystic project of unifying knowledge in a new language. The question is therefore common to science and *mystics*, even though its means and fields of action are different. It is related to the project of the unification of languages, which John

Webster still expects to realize with some "mystic" idiom, a hidden center about which proliferates an orchestral circumference of sounds.[29] Medieval Latin had created the site, without equivalent in Rome or Greece, of a language that was also an articulation of the real. That site, which was then left unoccupied, delineated the form that a linguistic science thereafter tried to fill with the erudite and/or mythical production of a referential language. These "post-Babelian" enterprises tried to identify a mother tongue, the *lingua sancta*, in which the "fiat" of the creation was pronounced, or to fabricate artificial languages (rational utopias, encyclopedic discourses, imaginary or burlesque languages, but also learned languages of astrology or the Kabbala, cryptologies, etc.), or finally to invent a universal language.[30] These attempts present some traits that directly concern *mystics*.

Although these pursuits still retained from their medieval model the ambition of grafting reality upon speech with the help of theories on the derivation of languages or their pictorial character, nevertheless the genealogical, etymological, or iconographic "realism" of linguistic "representation" postulated a divorce between words and things. The traces of Ockhamism are apparent. Also, whereas in medieval ontology all treatment of language was in itself an experiment or a manipulation of the real, language would henceforth stand face to face with what "manifested itself" in it: it was separate from that real that it intended, depicted, and was confronted with. The *experiment*, in the modern sense of the word, was born with the deontologizing of language, to which the birth of a linguistics also corresponds. In Bacon and many others, the experiment stood opposite language as that which guaranteed and verified the latter. This split between a deictic language (it shows and/or organizes) and a referential experimentation (it escapes and/or guarantees) structures modern science, including "mystical science."

Sixteenth-century linguistics, as has often been emphasized, often takes the direction of a "*mystics* of the beginning" and a "*mystics* of unity."[31] But it must be understood that the origin sought after is not a dead past. It had to be a "voice" that returned under new guises, still breathing its "force" into present-day words. To have recourse to etymology meant going to an abundant wellspring.[32] The linguistic methods and manipulations strove to uncap the wellspring and develop within the area of its "abundance." These methods, therefore, oscillated between the art of *hearing* the flow as it reached people then, the murmur of an effectual word, and the art of *producing* combinations and artifacts of all kinds. That was the very formula of *mystics*. It set up a fabrication of words, of "phrases" and expressions (a language, henceforth, was something that could be produced), but within a region in which a voice that never ceased beginning could be heard. Such was the paradox of the "ways of speaking": a production of language in the field of an attentiveness to something that was still speaking.

## A LINGUISTICS OF WORDS

The sixteenth-century effort to institute the unification of knowledge by a linguistic production would lead, in the seventeenth century, to envisaging a "total reinvention of language" (with Wilkins, Lodwyck, or Leibniz),[33] but its ambition remained restricted by the technical and conceptual apparatus at its disposal. It was a word-based linguistics, the Aristotelian heritage of a logic of terms. Language was cut up into semantic monads, words (or, in a kabbalistic and/or phonological tradition, letters—consonants, in fact), in function of a more essential dichotomy that separated an atomized verbal material from those operations capable of making words into discourse—operations capable of achieving precision thanks to rules. We have here a founding, undecidable, and determining option: it separated the mental act from the field in which it operated and which it itself organized. That fundamental option was reflected in the grammatical theories. Thus, for a long time, up until the fifteenth century, the analysis of the statement gave a dominant role to the verb, which had an "influence" on all the other nominal expressions (reverting to a tradition of the Greek grammarians) and it rendered that categorization more specific by granting a structuring function to the opposition between "agent" and "patient," that is, between the positions governed by the verb.[34] This reign of the verb—a "verbal government"[35]—in a system of thought that favored a logic of the agent, appears to have been the linguistic expression (and determination) of a philosophy that autonomized intellectual operations from a world of signs and conceived the series of these operations on the model of the genesis of a universe-language by the creator-speaker. In that perspective language itself, being conceived as a space or layer of combinable units, had structures only through the act that uttered it, and it was to an "art of thinking" that the task of taking over its organization into discourse would be allotted.

In order for us to assess what is peculiar to this paradigm (and also to grasp the framework it imposed on mystics' production of a new language), we need only compare its postulates to those implied, in the Western world itself, by the logic and linguistics of the Stoics. Obscured in the Middle Ages by the Aristotelian corpus, by its Arabic commentaries and the Jewish contribution,[36] Stoic science undoubtedly made a comeback in the sixteenth century, but in its ethical or cosmological form, and piecemeal, as can be seen from the marks it left on mystic literature. Broadly speaking, Stoic science remained caught up in the framework of a word-based linguistics that the nominalist critique had maintained. In itself, however, Stoic logic offered an inverse option: the priority of discourse. In any semantic or sensory unit, Stoic logic recognized the fragment of an inner discourse; it assimilated "representation," which was the mode of action common to all parts of the soul, to a discursive organization. More fundamentally, it attributed a discursive structure to the physical scene of corporeal events, so that a physical "discourse" always preceded and founded its anamorphosis into mental discourse. In other words, in the beginning there was discourse because the physical and corporeal world, which was itself discursive, was represented in statements as well as in images. This interplay of inner and outer discourse implied a "representability" of nature—a question left open—but, ultimately, it rested upon a general physics in which nature was discourse.[37] This view was foreign to the dichotomistic conception that made language a verbal space organized by acts of thought.

The shift that took place from the Middle Ages to the sixteenth century was obviously not a return of/to the discursive materialism of the Stoics. On the contrary, it was characterized by an exaggeration of linguistic atomism, because of the progressive weakening of Latin, which played the role of a semiartificial, stable language, and as a result of the nominalist critique, which dissociated from beings, all of which were singular, the universality that words receive from a mental activity.[38] The dethroning of the verb was a decisive symptom.[39] In its role of strategic copula in the active or passive modes of signifying (the *modi significandi*), the verb linked the act of thinking with the linguistic statement. The calling into question of its domination liberated the semantic units. Now words were being disseminated in numbers that were swelled by the vernaculars and thrown out of the referential Latin order, and it was not enough to register them in genealogies and to regroup them into families. Contractual rules of a "concord"[40] between them had to be found—or the elements of "discord" exposed—and, for each one, the possible ties between the singularity of things and the generalizing activity they attest to had to be brought out. It was imperative to have a policy of language that would institute alliances between terms and ground their capacity for showing. Two main problems spurred this work on: one, in keeping with nominalism, consisted in inquiring into the sorts of pacts words can make with one another; the other, to alleviate the Ockhamist deontologizing of words, consisted in asking whence they could derive their "force."

The former question was related to a rhetoric, the models for which were often judicial, or even monetary;[41] the latter was related to the philosophies that, through an analysis of origin, inspiration, and passion, and with presuppositions from Platonism and/or the Kabbala, identified the "movements" (*motus*) from which words received power.[42] Solutions varied. The mystics also constructed their language on the basis of these two questions, most of them making the hypothesis that the "force" of words grows with their "discord."

This investigation was empirical. It collated facts and "usages," as the Ockhamists had been doing for a long time.[43] The fact that usage was privileged is not surprising. The expansion and heterogeneity of vocabularies, their daring and unsettling independence from things, as well as the late development of vernacular grammars—all these factors increased "curiosity" about the thousands of ways of using words. This observation was necessary, since it made it possible to map the spread of usages and formulate methods of classifying their ways of working. For the rules sought were ultimately less those of the language itself than those of the operations that produced it.

## METHODS

The importance that the Renaissance places on methods is related to a contradiction,[44] internal to knowledge, between its technicalization during the three previous centuries and the destabilizing of its disciplines. To the extent that the order of the sciences and the "artes" becomes more disturbed, their techniques appear to free themselves from the field in which they had been elaborated. They take to the byways and, crisscrossing, encountering and combining with one another, they take on the appearance, now eclectic, now scientific, of general methodologies. These generalizations, often hasty or ideological, were criticized by scholars in the seventeenth century.[45] But they were the outcome of transitional situations. The methods formed pragmatic (and "interdisciplinary") passages from one configuration of knowledge to another. Thus, from the point of view of their practicality, they brought regulated productivity into action; in so doing, they introduced a new principle of scientificity. But they continued to draw their postulates from the very epistemology from which they were distancing themselves. For example, the seduction that the ambition of universal validity exerted upon them came from the past and was at odds with the limitations without which there is no rigor. Similarly, in knowledge gained by experience, which was claimed to be a new foundation,[46] the observation of the "facts" (a requirement of seventeenth-century men of learning) was not yet clearly distinct from the mental activities themselves. Also, by the way in which they symbolized (or put together) opposites, these methods had mythical as well as technical significance. They were the "symbolic" practices of a period. Hence the fascination of which they were the object.

The method, a discourse of practical rules, was a type of product that the Middle Ages, in introducing both the name and the thing itself, had already defined on the basis of Aristotle's *Topics* and the commentaries of Boethius. According to Albert the Great, while "science" institutes rigor (*rectificatio*) in speculation, and "art" institutes rigor in operation, "method" is for both *demonstratio viae*, the pointing out of the path.[47] Being common to both, method surmounted their difference in that its role was to specify the general intellectual procedures that, though necessary, were subordinate to various disciplines. These mental programs of procedure already occupied a third or transversal position. Method appeared above all as a temporal way of proceeding from one site to another: its order (its "ratio") consisted in a historicity (a chronological series of distinct exercises) inscribed on a map (a distribution of differentiated sites). It was a "discourse" (*discursus*), a reasoned series of figures of actions, that was constructed on the same formal plan as the novel (which appeared precisely during the same period). It was also, then, a scientific novel, a travel narrative, that put successive operations in series. At the end of the twelfth century, the first "methodical prayers" presented the same model,[48] which reappeared, but personalized, in the biographies and autobiographies, classic examples of the story genre that classed operations and sites along a pathway of "progress" or spiritual journeys.

Because of problems peculiar to the Renaissance, this instrument of thought continued to occupy an intermediary (third) position, but one that became dominant. For this reason it acquired new characteristics. First, in opposition to the scholastic or nominalist "verbosismo," (this trait was common to all the methods of the time and to rhetoric as well)[49] its role as technically *and* socially effective discourse became more accentuated. The goal was to obtain progress, knowledge, and profit at one and the same time, and to repeat this progress by a pedagogical formation. The process was supposed to produce knowledge and mold groups.[50] The difference it overcame was no longer the separation between speculation and practice but, within the field of operativity, the possible rift between a shift in the intellectual landscape and a transformation of the social space. In varying proportions, method combined actions on things and actions on interlocutors (disciples, correspondents, readers). It produced change within the social space as well as in the realm of knowledge.

In its internal structure and not only in its purpose, it assumed a more specific profile. Three of its essential characteristics: method constructed rules instead of revealing laws; it valorized time (speed) in a work economy; it selected, on the basis of usefulness, the situations that served as its material. On the one hand, even though there were some indications that it remained tied to the idea of laws (celestial or moral) for which it spoke, and therefore bore the marks of a metaphysics, in principle it constituted a scenario that sectioned off from the natural order a series of human operations and placed it within a problematic of decision-making of the type: *if* you want Z, *then* do A, then B, then C, and so forth. In this way, it freed itself from an ethics or an ontology and introduced a logic of the game. And to the extent that it was a question of rules and not of laws, the concept of error replaced that of fault or sin. It was a praxis in the process of autonomizing and rationalizing itself on the basis of decisional postulates (you want to or you don't want to) that it took for granted without having to ground them.

On the other hand, method could be defined as a condensation of time: "compendaria ars . . . quae brevissima est et cito nos ad rei cognitionem ducens," says Agostino Nifo (1555) along with a hundred others, commenting once again on Aristotle's *Topics*.[51] "Abridged," "condensed," "short," "brief": these characterized that "art" or its "means." Method harbored an impatience. Pertinence of speed, by a reduction of time and space not without analogy with the map.[52] Time became the essential element in that work economy, in view of a space to be covered or constructed "faster." It became the highest value. Productivity made rapidity its test, whereas duration had been the test of an order. Besides, in a century and a half, the mass of information had been considerably increased and interrelated, by printing in particular. In order to manage and manipulate it, a radical procedural transformation was necessary. One no longer had the leisure necessary to devote oneself to the few texts owned in a place of meditation and to give them time. Their own quantitative increase and accelerated circulation forced the user to take in hand the economizing of his time.

Finally, method is a science of the useful. As a result, it responded to situations; it gave a scientific seriousness to the circumstances and to the interlocutors with whom interests and goals entered into competition. The circumstantial furnished it with its vocabulary: it played on it. Only later were insular spaces to be constituted within which method would develop in a closed context. This was not the case in the sixteenth century. But method was already selecting from the environment the data that met the criterion of usefulness. Discernment implies detachment. It is a technique of rupture. This art of doing was also an art of forgetting, a more scientific and more difficult task than remaining faithful, captive to the past. From this perspective, the breaks required by the spirituals and mystics in view of practical new beginnings were variants of methodological detachment, perhaps pioneering variants. In any case, there is no method without a departure. A break must be made with ideological or historical ties. The idea of usefulness allowed for the construction of a future to replace respect for tradition; during the Renaissance, it was primarily a deterrent. Leave your country, that was the first rule. Descartes did not invent it. An entire century recited and practiced it before him.

The spiritual ways of speaking were a part of that new pragmatic. Mystic science favored an exceptional development of methods. There are doubtless many reasons for this. It had at its disposal, with the monastic tradition, a mental and pedagogical technology that was already ancient and very refined. To take just one example, but a spectacular one, the Brethren of the Common Life gave that technology an impetus that, with the *Devotio moderna* and the *modus parisiensis*, was decisive for the entire spiritual and didactic methodology of the sixteenth century.[53] Further, by the space of exemption and propaedeutics of rupture they constituted, mystic groups formed laboratories facilitating the elaboration and exercise of methods. In conclusion, by making explicit from the start the primacy of experience (a present practice that could not be replaced by any memory or institution) and the absolute of a goal to be sought after (a final salvation, an ultimate place), they clarified the two terms between which a method could trace a path. It is true that the coexistence of a methodological advance and a mental "passivity" constitutes the paradox of *mystics*, the dynamics and the instability of its situation. But this paradox was present from the beginning, with the manners of speaking that, in the mode of a linguistic treatment, gave it something like a formal model.

## "MYSTIC PHRASES": DIEGO DE JESÚS, INTRODUCER OF JOHN OF THE CROSS

There is a document that may serve to introduce the reader to these manners of speaking. It accompanied the first edition of the *Obras espirituales* of John of the Cross, which appeared in Alcalá de Henares in 1618, more than a quarter of a century after the author's death (1591). In addition to its delayed publication, the edition was incomplete. In particular, of the four large treatises by John of the Cross, the

*Cántico espiritual,* which caused the most hesitation because of its audacity, was eliminated. A version of the *Cántico* first appeared in translation by René Gaultier (*Cantique de l'amour divin,* Paris, 1622) before being published in Spanish in Brussels (1627), while another version came out in Rome (1627) in an Italian translation that was to serve as a reference for the first publication of the original text in Spain (Madrid, 1630). So the text had passed into several manuscript traditions via European networks and was read, retouched, and translated (for example, into French at Bordeaux as early as the first years of the seventeenth century) before being published in any of its forms.[54] The erudite and often heated debates on the "authentic" version or versions of the *Cántico espiritual*[55] do little more than begin the critical task to be undertaken on works that are seemingly more "certain," such as *La Montée du Carmel.*[56] This text is a passerby. Its circulation was hidden for a long time; its identity remains illusive. It is made up of intervening strata that began with the successive writings and rewritings of the author himself.[57] It therefore bears witness to a collective labor, the rules of which are indicated to us by its presenter. Conversely, while the adjoining document had its own goals (first, to protect the work from being assimilated to the doctrine of the *alumbrados*), it was not only a reading of, an apologia for, the texts, it was part of the operation that produced them.

That introducer was Diego de Jesús (1570–1621), a Discalced Carmelite (like John of the Cross) born in Grenada of the "illustrious" family of Salablanca y Balboa, a professor (renowned) or superior (moderate) his entire life. An austere, modest, learned man: "mi doctorcito y Senequita," as the Archbishop of Toledo, Gaspar de Quiroga, used to call him—my little doctor, my little Seneca. Besides courses in Thomistic philosophy (partially published, Madrid, 1608) and some very Gongorist poems (posthumously published, *Rimas en conceptos espirituales,* Madrid, 1668), he composed those *Apuntamientos y advertencias* [*Notes and Remarks*] that were to accompany the works of John of the Cross nearly everywhere for three centuries, the purpose of which was, as their title specified, to *facilitate the understanding of the mystic phrases and the doctrine of Saint John.*[58] Just as Luís de León, thirty years earlier, had provided the first edition of the *Libros de la madre Teresa de Jesús* (Salamanca, 1588) without having had the time, before his death, to publish the *Foundations,* and had added an *Apología* and a *Vida* (1589–91) to it, so Diego de Jesús was, in turn, with even more difficulty, the first editor and "apologist" for John of the Cross, who had already been silenced before his death by the very order he founded. Father Nicolas Doria, the provincial since 1585, an "iron hand," began by attacking the Teresian "freedoms" to the degree that they compromised the authority of the male Carmelites over the female convents; then he attempted to do away with the teachings of John of the Cross, which were never quoted, sealed in oblivion because they threatened the politically committed and counter-reformationist idea he had of the Carmelite way of life. Just as the author had formerly been imprisoned in a dungeon in the Toledo monastery until he escaped (1577–78), so now his work was condemned to silence. There was a rumor that even opposed Teresians and followers of John of the Cross. Not without some basis, for Teresa's style was one of apostolic passion and was, in that respect, more in accord with the missionary perspective favored by second generation Discalced Carmelites. The doctrine of John of the Cross, even though it was written only for the purpose of instruction, presents a captivating contemplation surrounded by a void. By its rarefying radicalness, it seems to demobilize or contradict the crusade of the Counter-Reformation. Also, not to mention particular cases of rivalry or personal incompatibility, his critics within the Order apprehended a "spirit," the exaggeration of which they deplored. They did not reproach him with accusations of errors but preferred that that defiance, inspired by some alien necessity, should remain hidden away, like a family secret, good to know oneself but dangerous to tell others. That was Doria's position, with his usual sternness: he refused the Teresians the institutional autonomy they had won with such difficulty, that had been bequeathed to them by their mother; and he refused the followers of John the doctrinal autonomy founded on the spirit of "retreat," the absolute quality of which their father never ceased preaching.[59]

But the faithful watched and waited: disciples (Juan de Jesús María Aravalles, Innocent of Saint-André, Juan de Jesús María Quiroga, et al.) and Carmelites (primarily Anne de Jésus, heiress of the Teresian passion and itinerant founder, for whom John of the Cross wrote his *Cántico espiritual*). 1601: A first edition was finally authorized and confided to two "definitors," one of whom was Thomas de Jésus. 1603: The entire responsibility of the enterprise fell to the latter, a companion of Doria's and yet a leader of the Teresians, learned, a scholastic, successively hermit and traveling representative of the Counter-Reformation, a spiritual with a captain's style.[60] A expeditious man, he "arranged" the text, corrected it, and, it seems, already excluded the *Cántico*. But he had more pressing business than exhuming relics. 1604: He gave up the project. 1607: Father Alonso de Jesús, hostile to the publication, became general of the Order. Even the biographical works written since 1597 on John of the Cross by Quiroga were interrupted. Then came six years of standstill, corresponding to the reign of this dour, punctilious father who would occupy the same post from 1619 to 1625. Between these two generalships, Diego de Jesús took up the task left by Thomas, whose favorite follower he had been in the past (but not an "epigone," as some have said). He worked through the abandoned documents again. He writes in his *Notes*:

> Some people to help themselves [by this doctrine] and accommodate it to the mind by humanizing it a bit, or by explaining it in their own way and according to what they could learn from it, made as it were extracts or abridgements, by removing or changing things, or explaining it without understanding the text, as happened to me with an important person, so that the copies were so different that there was no conformity between them, and very few that were close to the original. Various writings and papers of these works have been compared attentively, and the originals carefully tracked down in order to make the printed text that is coming out conform to them.[61]

Finally, in 1618, the *Obras* were published, but the *Cántico* was omitted. There were alterations (though made by a lighter hand than that of Thomas) and justifications: at the beginning, "the life and virtues" of the author (a *Relación* written, in fact, by Quiroga); at the end, a defense and illustration of mystic language (the *Apuntamientos* by Diego).

The two essential points treated by Diego—the production of "mystic phrases" and the use of the "vulgar" tongue—are taken up again later and developed, often with the same arguments and the same quotations, by Nicolas de Jésus-Maria (Centurioni), a Discalced Carmelite strongly influenced by Quiroga, in a book first published separately (Alcalá, 1631; Cologne, 1639), and then included, from 1639 on, in the editions of the *Obras*: the *Elucidatio phrasium mysticae theologiae*.[62] This *Elucidatio*, translated into French by Cyprian of the Nativity,[63] will again be exploited, like a mine of authoritativeness, by Madame Guyon, then by Bossuet, under the shortened and revealing title of treatise "*des phrases mystiques*."[64] It is worthy of note that around the controversial and strategic bastion John of the Cross, Diego and Nicolas set up a double line of defense on the issue of manners of speaking. "Phrase," says Richelet's *Dictionnaire*, "means way of speaking." Furetière's dictionary specifies: "Manner of expression, turn of phrase or construction of few words," with the example: "That is an Italian, a Spanish phrase, way of speaking." The debate on *mystics* is centered on turns of phrase or usages that reflect a different practice of language.

From the outset, Diego (and Nicolas will follow suit) affirms the right of every science to constitute for itself its own language. It is the title of his first "discourse": "Each faculty, art or science has its own particular names, terms and phrases." Yes, "the art, science or faculty declares, by its very name faculty, the power it has to impose names, to seek modalities and phrases with which to explain and make understood the truths it professes." Therefore, it is "sometimes appropriate to use impropriety and barbarisms, and a great wealth of rhetoric, especially when it is a question of very important matters"; one should not be "limited to literal propriety of terms or elegance."[65] "Barbarisms" serve as a blazon for that declaration of the right to produce a language. They symbolize the artifact that frees itself from the ordinary laws of natural language. Hence the pun on "proper" in Diego: the "improper" according to grammar is constitutive of a scientific proper. We must separate ourselves from the natural language in order for there to be a produced language. Valid for alchemy as well as for mathematics and any artificial language, this principle claims at one and the same time, for a scientific language, a different status (that of being made and not received) and a different way of functioning (that of corresponding to intellectual operations and not an order of things).

At this level, it was not yet important to know what type of scientificity would determine that fabrication, but rather to begin by recognizing that *mystics*, like any other science, had a certain right. This right of naming was already affirmed by Teresa: "There is another kind of ravishment, and I call it [*le llamo yo*] 'flight of the spirit'"; "I call [*llamo yo*] 'supernatural' that which . . . "; "I am in the habit of saying [*decir*] 'suspension' in order not to say 'ecstasy,' which . . . "; "I call [*llamo yo*] 'transport' a desire that . . . ," and so on, and she kept her distance with respect to the terminology of others [*dicen*].[66] John of the Cross did the same—"here we call the lack of desire 'night'"— with the same way of distancing himself from similar languages.[67] A separation circumscribed this discourse in the making, setting it apart from the already-spelled-out world. The act of naming invented a new land, as in the tale of a voyage, or better still, as Adam did for the first time: "He gave names (his names) to all things [*Appellavitque Adam nominibus suis cuncta*]."[68] At the beginning of mystic language, the author's words repeated the Adamic act.

Diego also specified the problematic underlying that linguistic fabrication. The discipline he treated was defined by a site, Mount Carmel, the name of which "means *science of circumcision.*" That mountain was the silent foundation of the languages that crowned its summit. Placed beneath the authority of this mount—which is a name, a semantic "faculty"—discourse composed formations of meanings and of voices (*voces*, words and sounds) in which the spirit of the place was manifested. They were its effect and, as it were, the excess in the "abundance [*el lleno*] of a spiritual doctrine." Discourse was therefore instituted by means of a place. That position marks the difference between the second generation of Discalced Carmelites, based on the establishment that authorized a production (as in all scientific institutions), and the first (that of Teresa or John of the Cross), for whom discourse, far from presupposing the foundation, had to make it possible and organize it. From one to the other, the perspectives were reversed: the foundation—or its substitute, the founding—was no longer for Diego a question to be taken up by discourse. The very status of language was thereby changed. But behind the historical foundation of Carmelite cloisters, there was a Palestinian and biblical institution; a place, Mount Carmel, a physical and mythical presence to which the entire Western and Eastern monastic tradition was related since its origin, a fortiori the Carmelites born on its slopes in the thirteenth century; and also a long line of Jewish contemplatives.[69] Earlier, in the ninth century *B.C.*, that mountain received Elijah into its silence, or protected him after he had cut the throats of the enemies of Yahweh with his sword, and then it drew him out of his cave by "the noise of a light breeze."[70] In the Vulgate, a "whistling" of the breeze [*"sibilus"*] is the song of the mountain by which the Voice speaks to the wild prophet. In the sixteenth century, the same sound again seized the host who had withdrawn into the (Teresian) "castle" (that mountain of crystal) a "whistling [*silbo*] so soft that one could scarcely hear it" and yet so "penetrating" that "the soul cannot not hear it."[71] It was the spirit of the place. John of the Cross also unfurled upon Mount Carmel the "ascent" of his discourse and he has drawn the map of this Dantean heaven in the form of a fantastic body, the lungs of which chant (like biblical verses) "neither this nor that" [*"ni eso, ni eso, ni esotro, ni esotro"*],[72] a body divided by the central ravine in which the "nada" ("nothing, nothing, nothing, nothing") is repeated, its base covered with a vegetation of writings that become more rarefied as they go up. The site becomes the mute hero of the story. The foundation of mystic science is indeed that mountain of silence.

The spirit residing there was "circumcision," a labor of cutting. It is manifest immediately in Diego's text by two indices that point out the structure of mystic phrases and the tool by which they are made: the structure is *dual*, the tool a *knife*. First, the historical establishment of the reformed Carmelite order goes back not to one but to two founders, the "saint mother" Teresa and the "blessed father" John, her "very faithful coadjutor," "two parents [*padres*] who can be called children [*hijos*] and parents [*padres*] of the Carmelites." In this family tree, the "parents" of the reformed discourse are also the "children" of the silence of the mountain, and the gender difference takes on from the outset a theoretical and practical relevance. It takes *two* (masculine and feminine) for the new language to be born. That language is not celibate (it is neither theological nor clerical), and its entire development will be dominated by the division that governed its foundation. That duality (Teresa and John) reverses the Adamic model (Adam and Eve), but it reproduces the Christic model of the relations of Mary and Joseph.[73] The "mother" is more important than the "father," not only for reasons of apologetics (the suspect doctrine of John must be made to pass beneath the mantle of the respected doctrine of Teresa) or of history (Teresa came first), but also in the name of a structure that appears repeatedly in this period in the commentaries on the Woman of the Revelation[74] or in the Christian kabbalistic tradition of the *Shekinah*, femininity of the divine presence and of her habitation in this world.[75] A maternal "indeterminate" seems in keeping with the silence from which discourse arises. An unnameable fecundity of the mother corresponds to that mountain which serves as a "source" for the "fullness" of spoken words. Just as Mount Carmel raises a primordial totality, which is the figuration of the Real—a "neutral" (neither one nor the other of the two terms), undifferentiated reference—the mother is she by whom the spoken word arrives and becomes body or discourse. From the celibate and/or patrilinear genealogy of theological language we must distinguish the origin of the mystic manners of speaking, characterized by the sexual difference and by a precedence of the mother. The two founders establish the privilege of the *dual relation* that will define the form of language and the content of experience. They illustrate that privilege in the story of the founding. That priority of the relation [*Beziehung*] to the other already indicates a "spiritual" [*geistlich*] perspective compared to a more metaphysical perspective favoring the adequation or assimilation to being. Moreover, it will be translated by an insistence on the ad-verb or the ad-jective and the verb, elements of correlation or division, and by an erosion of the substantive. It is part of a problematics of alliances and processes that will later be termed "nuptial." But in Diego, the woman, assigned a central role, appears ambivalent. She is a mediation (or a passage) between two perspectives. As mother, her function is to link discourse or experience with the real; as spouse, it is to announce an insurmountable difference. She seems to waver between an ontology that she still protects and an erotics she presages.

On the other hand, it is especially in connection with the father that Diego, with a strange, almost wild sort of lyricism, becomes the apostle of the circumcision and raises the knife that is its instrument. It is true that the works of Teresa are "esteemed by everyone" because they "circumcise the desires and the affections." But there is nothing there comparable to the "precision [Gaultier translates 'incision'] and anatomy of the mystics" practiced by John of the Cross. "The doctrine of our blessed father in matters of circumcising, cutting off, mortifying, disappropriating, undoing, annihilating a soul (all these names do not explain the thing sufficiently) is so special, so penetrating and (if one may say so) without pity in cutting and separating all that is not the purest of spirit, that it stupefies whomsoever reads it."[76] The sword of Elijah animates this luxuriance of trenchant terminology that ends, as the cadence of the sentence falls, on stupor [*espanto*]. It is a passion, linking the surgical and scientific violence of the Renaissance with the prophetic Carmel of the Old Testament. In this doctrine, Diego recognizes that of Saint Paul, for whom "the spoken word of God is a knife that cuts with both edges," or that of the Book of Wisdom, which sees in the Spirit "something sharp like the point of a sword." The discernment that is expressed there, "pointed and sharpened to cut and circumcise," attests to the eminence of John of the Cross in "that mystic and spiritual science of circumcision."

Circumcision has the long and double history of the divisions between Jews and Christians, and of contracts between the body and the absolute. The Hebrews had adopted that Egyptian custom and made it into the sign of their separation from the other nations and the covenant with Yahweh.[77] A biblical account gives a primitive version of it as the act of a mother and wife, at the moment when Yahweh "sought to kill" Moses. His wife, Zipporah, "took a flint, and cut off the foreskin of her son, and touched the genitals of Moses with it, and she said: 'Thou art for me a bridegroom of blood.'" The text explains that "she had said 'bridegroom of blood' because of the circumcision."[78] The covenant, like marriage, is signified by the act of removal and cutting. Practiced among the Jews, abandoned by the Christians and becoming the demarcation between them (baptism having been substituted for circumcision), forbidden to citizens of the Roman empire by the rescript of Antoninus, reinstituted by the Christian sect of the Passagiens (twelfth to fourteenth century), considered proof of guilt in the trials of the Jews (sixteenth century), that bloody signature of the body marks access to the name of the father (to virility) by a submission to paternal power.⁷⁹ Just as Abraham raised his knife over his son Isaac to sacrifice to Yahweh, that is, to produce meaning [*sacer facere*], so John of the Cross cuts into the quick of the flesh in order to describe the way of union. Cutting off is the procedure of the covenant when it is question of the absolute describing itself by what it takes away. A labor of sculpting, dear to John of the Cross. Negative theology: it *signifies* by what it *takes away*. The sign itself is henceforth the effect of a taking away or division. One aspect of this already appears in Diego's theory on mystic phrases. The "spoken word" is whatever cuts the body of the mother tongue. It is recognizable by the cleft "words" it produces, that is, by a trenchant linguistic practice.

Diego himself explains that analytic production, which consists in producing by cutting ("analysis" is a dividing), with several examples:

> The moral philosopher, hearing the word *excess*, will say that it goes to extremes that depart from the mean, which is required by virtue, and hence that it is depraved and reprehensible. Nevertheless, we can find at every turn in the sentences of the Scriptures the term excess attributed to perfect and divine things. In Saint Paul: "Because of the excessive love with which he loved us." In David: "Blessed is he who fears God, he will love his commandments excessively."
>
> I say the same thing about these words, "pride" and "fury," which sound like reprehensible excess and dissolute, and yet the Prophet says of God: "The Lord has sworn by Jacob's pride, that is, by himself, who is the good pride of Jacob." And Cajetan reads from the Hebrew: "The Lord reigned, and covered himself with pride." And David, in his Psalms, often applies the term furor to God. . . .
>
> Neither does scholastic theology accept the word "stain" except where there is blame, and in mystic theology we term "stain" the slightest trait or particular representation of a perceptible object, and anything that prevents the greater glorification of God; and one speaks of "purgation" of the inferior angels, when they are glorified and illuminated by the superior ones, of which we shall treat more amply later. Of "annihilation," the philosopher and the scholastic theologian will say that it means to be totally lacking in being, so that there remains of being neither existence, nor form, nor union, nor matter, which is the primary substance which lasts forever in the generations and corruptions, whereas the mystic will say that "annihilation" of the soul is a saintly neglect and abandonment of self, such that neither by memory, nor affection, nor thought does it worry about itself nor any creature, in order to be able to transform itself entirely into God.
>
> That license to use particular and uncommon terms is permitted especially in mystic theology, because it treats of very lofty, very sacred, and very secret things, which concern experience more than speculation, and because it consists more in taste and divine savor than in

knowledge, and this in a very elevated state of supernatural, loving union with God. That explains the scantiness of terms and phrases used in speculation, which in matters as nonmaterial as these is extraordinarily surpassed by experience.

Saint Bernard declares this admirably in sermon 85 on the Song of Songs, where, after having treated the particular degrees of perfection that conduct the soul to the union and bliss of God, which can be in this life, he says: "If someone asks me what it is to enjoy the Word? I tell him to address himself to someone who has experienced it rather than to me. And if I had experienced it, how could I explain what is ineffable? Let us listen to one who has had the experience: either we enter into excess of spirit near God or we are levelheaded with you. That is to say, things happen one way with God as only witness, another way with you. It has been given to me to experience such things, not to speak of them. Oh, you who are curious to know what it is like to enjoy the Word, do not lend it your ear but your spirit. It is grace that teaches it, not language. It is hidden from the wise and prudent, and revealed to the littlest ones. My brothers, what a high and sublime virtue humility is, that merits that which is not taught to it, that is worthy of obtaining what cannot be learned, worthy of conceiving by and from the word what it cannot explain in spoken words. Why? It is not because it merits it, but because it was pleasing to the father of the verb the bridegroom of the soul our Lord Jesus Christ."

Saint Bonaventure in *Itinerarium mentis in Deum*, in chapter 7, after having dilated at great length on the passage by Saint Dionysius that touches upon mystic theology, where he discourses on how one must leave the visible and the invisible, concludes: "For by yourself, and all things by an immense and absolute excess of pure spirit, you will rise to the superessential ray of divine shadows, leaving all things and being entirely exempt from them. If you ask how that is done, question grace, not doctrine; desire, not understanding; the sighs of prayer, not the study of reading; the bridegroom, not the master; God, not man; obscurity, not clarity; not light, but the fire that inflames all, and that transports one in God by excessive unctions and very ardent affections. Of which fire he alone is inflamed who says: my soul has chosen suspension and my bones death. He who loves that death can see God, because it is indubitably true that the man who sees me will not live. Let us die therefore and enter into the shadows, let us impose silence upon solicitudes, concupiscence and phantoms."

Therefore in matters so lofty and spiritual (as these saints say) in which experience triumphs over doctrine; in which he who knows cannot say; in which grace rather than language is mistress; in which humility reaches that which takes to the air and flies away, and learns what cannot be taught; in which the substantial spoken word of the father works such marvels as one could not express, as Saint Bernard has said, and in which, according to Saint Bonaventure, we should not be governed by understanding nor by the rules of masters; in which the moaning of prayer, the communication of God as bridegroom, heavenly experience, and suavity are the school and the instruction, in which clarity is harmful, in which obscurity sheds light, in which one need only look at what one sees, which is not at all acquired by discourse, but the opportune moment and point toward which the fire of love inclines; in which death and a saintly despair are a true disposition to that divine life; how will we put order, or limits, or text, or means in the terms by which we must explain so lofty a thing, wanting everything that is immense and unsayable to be subject to the ordinary rules, without exceeding the common phrases and guarded terms of the schools of disciples and masters, of arts and manners that can be taught and known?

The mystic has permission (provided that we know that in the substance of what he says he does not contradict the truth), in order to enliven and emphasize, to make its incomprehensibility and loftiness known with terms that are imperfect, perfect, hyperperfect, contrary or noncontrary, similar and dissimilar, as we have examples of all that in the mystic Fathers, especially in Saint Dionysius the Areopagite, who in chapter 2 of the *The Celestial Hierarchy* composes a mystic word that includes nearly all this, speaking of the excellence of the joy and quiet these intellectual substances[80] enjoy (what would he have done if he had treated the uncreated and divine substance?). Therefore, in order to declare it in inadequate terms, or purposely going beyond the common ones, after having imbued them with furor, irrationality, and insensibility, all of that being understood beyond the understanding, as he says, coming to treat of the quiet they enjoy, he says: "Immanem quietem." That they have a "cruel repose." The most dissimilar and contrary thing to quiet that can be. Yet he did it with a divine counsel, since, by what he said of "quiet," he removed the imperfection of "fury," and in saying "cruel and furious quiet," he declared the perfection and excellence of this repose. For whoever hears "quiet" unqualified seems to be contemplating something lazy, insipid and cold, lax, of low value and mediocre perfection. But whoever adds that it is "cruel and furious," already removing the imperfection of fury by "quiet," communicates the power, perfection, and intention, and, so to speak, the unbearable and incomprehensible excellence of that "quiet," and the excess that it has over the imperfect that occurs within ourselves.

That is why it seemed to Saint Dionysius, in this chapter, that the terms that were entirely dissimilar and contrary declared as much about these high and divine things as similar ones that bear some proportion. Here is what he says about it: "If the negations of divine things are true and the affirmations defective, the obscurity of their secrets is manifested better by dissimilar forms, and I don't think there is any wise man who would contradict the statement that dissimilar similitudes reduce our spirit more." Hence Hugh of Saint-Victor is quite right in saying:

"Not only are the dissimilar figures probable, because they show the heavenly excellences, but also because they withdraw our minds from the material and corporeal figures more than similar figures do, and do not permit us to rest in them". . . .

Terms that are imperfect and, if one must say it thus, vicious by excess, declare much better, like saying "furor" and "pride." For we see plainly that the pettiness, the evil they represent when applied to ourselves, is very far from God: And thus to take these terms that mean excess and disordered, unregulated and unreasonable things, is to admit that the good to which we apply them is a pure, very perfect good, such that it surpasses all order, all means and natural agreement, and everything reason can attain. . . . That variation that mystic theology employs also declares marvelously the divine perfection and its ineffability, speaking one moment regularly, that is, with the terms it finds ordered and perfect, the next moment, not content with those words, throwing itself into a holy excess, as if of madness and dissoluteness, and which is the excess of Saint Paul, or "insanivimus" as the Syriac writer says, using one moment very imperfect terms, such as pride, drunkenness, and furor, the next moment more than perfect terms, as did Saint Dionysius in his *Mystical Theology*, beginning by saying with the first words, "the supersubstantial, superdivine, and superlatively good Trinity," unable to say anything more, nor show any greater thankfulness, than to go beyond our terms.[81]

Diego's *Apuntamientos* specify the production of what Sandaeus was to call the mystic "dialect": "Amor suam habet dialectum."[82] The claim to a "manner" of its own echoes that made by jurists,[83] historians,[84] surgeons,[85] or theologians[86] of the same period, and belongs within the group of works that sixteenth-century grammarians and logicians devoted to "manners" (of writing, speaking, etc.), now that—given the inadequacy of the models formed by Latin, that stable, homogeneous, and limited language—they tried to base the rationality of the "vulgar" tongues on "usages."[87] More specific is the fact that, of all the existent usages, including the "theological phrases," the "mystic phrases" were distinguished less by their structure than by the procedure with which they were constructed. What was important was a *process of fabrication*. Diego insisted on the transformation carried out by the author of the text, to which the operation it brought about in the reader would correspond. On both parts, a movement was essential. It was characterized both by a *shift of the subject* within the meaning space circumscribed with words and by a *technical manipulation* of these words in order to mark the new way in which they were being used. In short, it was a practice of detachment. It denatured language: it distanced it from the function that strove after an imitation of things. It also undid the coherence of signification, insinuating into each semantic unit wily and "senseless" shifts of interplay in the relations of the subject with others and himself. It tormented words, to make them say what they did not say literally, in such a way that they became, in a sense, the sculpture of the tactics of which they were the instruments. There is a term, in itself ambiguous, that might serve to define these procedures that detach the language from its natural functioning, modeling it instead on the passions of speaking subjects: *address*. For on one hand the destination of discourse takes precedence over the validity of the statement (it is a question of "addressed" words, without one ultimately being able to tell by whom and to whom), and on the other hand a certain dexterity strives to awaken within words, by their correlations with other words, the possibilities locked in slumber by the domination of the thing signified (a certain emancipating technique liberates, in the words, the moves and relational movements that had been impeded by a docility to the things for which they stood).

This bringing into play of addressed and adroit language links Diego's conception to mannerism. During that second half of the sixteenth century, the *belles manieres* of treating the motifs and themes that had been established during the preceding period distanced themselves deliberately from the naturalism of the early Renaissance. Virtuosity in what was also called "practice" was beginning to replace the humanist theory of "imitation." The *Maniera*, an elaboration of language upon itself, the subtle and sumptuous effects of which illustrated indefinite capacities, was exalted. This expressionism was made up of artifacts that exorcised the referential and set in movement a space shattered into contrasting fragments. In the paintings, the passions depicted portray mainly a passion of forms and colors subjected to the delicious tortures of an art.[88] These theaters represent less heroes or feelings than the variety of treatments of which a traditional scene is capable. They are operas in which manners of painting and "touching" the canvas are danced out. Therefore we can place mystic phrases within the context of Spanish mannerist settings, from those which exhibit an irrealism of objects (with Pedro de Campana or Pedro Machuca) to those which create an irrealism of space itself, with El Greco, the Cretan "genius" from Toledo—"evil genius" and "spirit" of that place in which he stages an impossibility of place.

From this point of view also, as J. Baruzi wrote, "the mystic language emanates less from new vocabulary than from transmutations performed within the vocabulary borrowed from standard language."[89] Properly speaking, it is not a new or artificial language. It is the effect of an elaboration upon existent language, a labor applied primarily to the "vulgar" tongues (to which preference is given), but extending also to technical languages. The uses that define it reflect the operations carried out by speakers. Mystic science was not constituted by the creation of a coherent linguistic body (that is, a scientific system), but by defining legitimate operations (that is, by a formalizing of practices). A paradox: that science that emerged into historical visibility as language could only maintain itself by characterizing the stable practices of which words were the unstable and variable effects. It therefore was to break up when it could no longer integrate these operations with one another.

That vocabulary is the index of mystic procedures is shown by the texts. One example may suffice. When, at the threshold of *Moradas* [*The Interior Castle*], that fundamental topos that involves the soul as human residence and God as the only resident, Teresa of Avila writes, "You must understand that there is a great difference between *being* there [*estar*] and *being* there [*estar*],"[90] she is distinguishing between two uses of the same word by the operation that separates them. Thus a term becomes "mystic" by virtue of the itinerary ("enter into thyself") that founds its new usage. A journey on the part of the speaker produces a shift in meaning. This is the very dialectic Montaigne cultivated and Pascal questioned: "truth on this side of the Pyrenees, error beyond them." In order to explain the phrases of John of the Cross, Diego refers back to the procedures they reflect.

The procedure he singles out as exemplary is the oxymoron. "Cruel repose" ("immanem quietem," which Diego translated as "cruel y furiosa quietud") places two antonyms, such as "dark light," in a syntactic relation. It is a trope. Sandaeus says clearly that mystic expressions are formed "per tropos" and that they are "tropicae loquutiones" (he explains himself more fully on these manners of speaking in his *Grammaticus profanus*).[91] Tropes, then, which characterize the elementary units of mystic discourse, are, according to Du Marsais, "manners of speaking" or figures "by which one makes a word take on a meaning that is not precisely the proper meaning of this word." They are called "tropes," "from the Greek *tropos, conversio*, the root of which is *trepo, verto*, I turn," because "when one takes a word in the figurative sense, one turns it, so to speak, in order to make it mean what it doesn't mean at all in its proper meaning." A tour and detour, a turn of phrase, a conversion, the trope stands in opposition to the proper meaning. It is the "way a word deviates from its signification."[92] This process of *deviation* is no longer based, as was the traditional allegory, on an analogy and an order of things. It is exit, semantic exile, already ecstasy. As "creative daring" [*"fingendi audacia"*], it drifts toward dissimilarity. This deviation creates strangeness in the order (or the "proper") of language.

The oxymoron, a close relative of antiphrasis and the paradox, "violates the code" in a particular way, although the contradiction it raises is not "tragically proclaimed" as in antithesis but "paradisiacally assumed."[93] It has the value of fullness, whereas the antithetical contradiction is unsurmountable tension. But each of the opposites brought together in the oxymoron comes from a different scale or measure. As such, they are not true opposites, of which Aristotle rightly says that they are of the same kind (for example, *good* versus *bad*). The terms combined in the oxymoron belong to heterogeneous orders: "cruelty" is not comparable to "peace" any more than there is commensurability between the terms combined by John of the Cross in "sweet burning" [*"cauterio suave"*] or "silent music" [*"música callada"*].[94] The combination is askew, as if heterogeneous types of space had come to meet in the same setting, for example a ghost in a city apartment. In this respect, the oxymoron stands in sharp contrast to the universe of "similarity."[95] It is a lapsus in similarity. It mixes kinds and upsets orders. Moreover, the oxymoron belongs to the category of the *metasememe*, which, like the demonstrative, refers to something beyond language. It is a deictic: it shows what it does not say. The combination of the two terms is substituted for the existence of a third, which is posited as absent. It makes a hole in language. It roughs out a space for the unsayable. It is language directed toward non-language. In this sense also, it "disturbs the lexicon."[96] In a world taken to be entirely written and spoken, therefore "lexicalizable," it opens up an absence of correspondence between things and words.

The oxymoron process, then, engenders the turns of phrase that are mixtures of displaced words. These strange linguistic beings, whose two halves belong to different orders and whose head, invisible, inhabits another space, seem to obey the same rules of production as the bodies presented by Ambroise Paré, in his *Monstres et prodiges* (1573) or the "dissimilar" beings Jean de Léry analyzes in his *Histoire d'un voyage fait en la terre du Brésil* (1578). They combine parts taken from heterogeneous wholes (like the *tapiroussou*, which is "half cow, half ass," "participating in the one and the other"),[97] and they are situated at the juncture of two worlds. In all these cases, the "monster" is made up of elements known but disposed in a hitherto unknown manner that designates a different space. They might have been painted by Hieronymous Bosch.[98] On a more lyric level, Maurice Maeterlinck mentioned the Flemish words that Ruysbroeck "led elsewhere": "Invented for the ordinary uses of life," these words "are unhappy, worried and astonished, like vagabonds around a throne, when from time to time some royal soul leads them elsewhere."[99] But before discovering a poetics in this, we must recognize a procedure, the gesture of a thought. In this respect, the oxymoron is a micro-laboratory. This apparatus produces the elementary units of the ways of speaking. Mystic discourse will increase the number and complexity of its features, but a few principles of the initial operation described by Diego may already be abstracted.

### The Cleft Unit, or the Interdiction

The smallest semantic unit is split. There are two *in place of* one. In other words, one is two: this is the first principle. A dichotomy organizes the elemental, which takes on by this fact the status of an in-between: an in-between speech and an interdiction. That "unit" therefore offers us the quasi-abstract formula for "excess": it is not reducible to either of the two components, nor to a third thing, which is precisely what is missing. It exceeds language. It points toward an outside, like so many raised fingers in mannerist painting. An original split makes the "ontological" statement, which would be the "said" of the intended thing, impossible. The mystic phrase escapes that logic and replaces it with the necessity of producing nothing more in language than effects relative to what is not in language. What must be said cannot be said except by a shattering of the word. An internal split makes words admit or confess to the mourning that separates them from what they show. Such is the initial "circumcision." An initiatory scotomization (it is a question of initiation) institutes a wounded word as the standard unit of mystic speech. Such incision has meaning but does not confer it.

### The Opacified Sign

In the classical theory, the sign is double-faceted: it represents a thing (recognizable "through" it) and it has a reality of its own (which makes up its thickness). By the first aspect, it is transparent; by the second, opaque. Thus the letters representing a meaning can be considered in their materiality; in that case, they cause the meaning to be forgotten or to disappear. Paradoxical by nature, the sign uncovers and hides. In point of fact, a relation of inverse proportion governs these two poles: the appearance of the thing signified increases as that of the sign-as-thing diminishes. The more attention directed to the sign-as-thing, the less one recognizes the thing represented in it. Now, as W. V. Quine has noted, the opacification of the sign (and thereby the erasing of the system of reference) is the result of whatever draws the attention back to the reality (be it phonetic, graphic, linguistic, etc.) of the sign. Thus, quotation marks or statements of propositional attitudes (of the type: Diego thinks that John of the Cross is Dionysian), which are the equivalent of quotation marks (Diego thinks: "John of the Cross is Dionysian"), constitute what Quine calls "referentially opaque contexts." Put in quotation marks, the word becomes opaque; it is looked at as a thing and no longer as a sign.[100]

That is what occurs in the mystic phrases. The use of the adjective "mystic" already bears witness to this fact. As we have already seen, that adjective, applied to a noun ("garden," "death," etc.), signifies "as the mystics understand or use it."[101] It plays the role of quotation marks. It turns the attention away from the thing being represented and focuses it on the way the word is being used, that is, on the sign-as-thing. It therefore opacifies the sign. By its action alone, it tends to make the thing signified disappear in favor of the signifier. It is the producer of a secret. The "phrases" analyzed by Diego are to be considered a part of this metalinguistic action (metalinguistic in the sense that the adjective "mystic" is a term that speaks of language itself and not of things); they, too, direct the attention back to the words as being unable to signify. In the phrases analyzed by Diego, the attention is diverted from "repose" and "cruelty" themselves in order to underline the status each word has of not being able to state what it intends. The mystic phrases therefore remove from these words their designative value and, in so doing, also remove their signlike transparency. That is the first way in which they are mystic: they obscure the things designated, or make them disappear; they put them into secrecy, render them inaccessible, as if, between the shown referent and the signifier that points to it, the meaning that linked them had fallen away. That break is the downfall of the sign. Remaining are words turned in such a way as to show their own status: an impotence.

IMPROPRIETY

An apology for the "imperfect" surrounds the mystic phrases and places them within a rhetoric of excess. Diego defends the "license" of using "imperfect, improper and dissimilar terms," "vitiated by excess," and of "stooping to improper similes." He alleges their style to be "immodesty," "throwing itself into a holy excess, as if by madness and dissoluteness." That impropriety has a double aspect: lexical and stylistic. To a grammatical license it adds a literary effect.

Grammatically, impropriety takes the form of the solecism or barbarism. In point of fact, it is authorized by the ancient tradition of the *lingua barbara*. Gregory the Great had already claimed the right to "barbarize" the language and to defy Donatus's iron rule; he refused to "serve" the classical *ars loquendi* and to deny himself the *confusio* of barbarism.[102] Many mystics acted the same way, including Angelus Silesius, whose verses were sometimes constructed "with disdain for grammatical correctness."[103] Sandaeus articulated their practice: "They do not avoid barbarisms, they have no scruples in using semi-barbarous terms and even entirely barbarous ones."[104] This barbarism has its own function: it marks the superiority of the speaker to the system of the language. In other words, the impetuosity of a declaration (or an "inspiration") shatters the order of the statement. The speech act makes a breach in lexical or grammatical correctness. In this way, an oddness of the speaker is marked in the language he speaks. This phenomenon is characteristic of the current or "vulgar" language to which, precisely, mystic discourse reverts. In the manner of "I know what I mean," "you know what I'm talking about," and so on, performance frees itself from competence. In this case, however, there is opposition, not just combination of the two. The primacy of one is indicated by the wounding of the other. Of course, this opposition was condemned by many of the Spanish religious rhetoricians of the period, beginning with the greatest among them, Luis of Granada (rather classic, it is true), who considered it possible and necessary for there to be agreement between the "impetus divini spiritus" and the "artis observatio," between a "motion" of the divine author and the exactness of human technique.[105] But the opposition had on its side a genealogy that went back to the double lineage of the Pauline *insanitas* and the Platonic "madness" of the *Ion*; it made impropriety the hallmark of the inspired.

To that enunciative index is added the artifice of a style. It had as its horizon the conception that, from Erasmus to Rabelais for example, associated the "power" of the author with the "abundance of words" (the *copia verborum*).[106] In relation to that aesthetics of the "horn of plenty" (the *cornucopia*), barbarism was a type of extremism that claimed to guarantee inspiration by lexical excess. The greatest grammatical disorder would make the disturbing presence of the highest word credible. It created verisimilitude. It was constructed, moreover, on the model of the miracle: each grammatical error designated a miraculously healed spot on the body of language. It was a stigma. That theater did more showing than saying. It favored the demonstrative. But while barbarism staged an erotics *in* language (absences, contradictions, mimed pursuits in the relation of words to their meanings), it corresponded especially to an erotics *of* language, a playing with the mother tongue, one minute rejected, the next called back: *fort–da*, gone away–come back.[107] It was a moment in a difficult relationship with the maternal linguistic world; it was an act excerpted from that world. It made a scene with language in the sense in which one speaks of a couple "making a scene." These were paradoxical games, however, for, at those points where the mother tongue was lost (disappeared: "all gone"), it became upset and returned to itself. Barbarisms departed from the language (they mourned it) and reveled in it (through a lucky linguistic find, a pretty or witty word). They were a departure from and a return to language. They did not "express" an experience because they were themselves that experience. The fundamental experience that, in the Middle Ages, had concerned the things implied by the manipulation of words seems to have continued here, but with the words having been abandoned by the things. That experience continued to question the origin and the frame of reference, but rather than this questioning occurring in an ontological mode, on the relationship of being with beings (or with Being), it occurred in a linguistic mode, on the relation that the subject maintained with his institution through the mother tongue when, by barbarism, he wanted to cut the tie he could not undo.

This erotics was also connected, as we shall see later, with the art of equivocation among fifteenth-century rhetoricians.[108] Earlier still, as early as the mid-fourteenth century, in that *ars poetria* that is *Las Leys d'amors* [*The Laws of Love*] by Guilhelm Molinier and company, Rhetoric, "a lady of great nobility," reconciles the three queens Diction, Oratory, and Aphorism with their enemies, the kings Barbarism, Solecism, and Allebole, three vices, and from their alliances the figures of a beautiful language of love are born. The improprieties of interlocution begin to flower within language.[109]

### CORPOREAL AND BIBLICAL DISSIMILARITIES

Diego does not call on that rhetoric of love. He turns to Dionysius the Areopagite, the "father of mystic theology," to vindicate "unlike terms" ("desemejantes"), an expression that Gaultier translates as "dissimilitudes." A renowned passage from chapter 2 of the *Celestial Hierarchy* is pivotal to his argumentation. According to Dionysius, in speaking of God, the "obscure and deformed" "likenesses of dissimilarities" surpass "similar images" because, instead of detaining the mind with deceptive analogies, they neither permit it to come to rest upon what they say (they are manifestly too "crude") nor to name what they say (they are contradictory).[110] This language loses the capacity to unveil: it veils. Its worth lies not in what it makes clear but in the operation it makes possible. Moreover, in Dionysius, there is a "holy fiction made up of dissimilar images," a set of "simulacra," a "scene of names."[111] It is an artifact intended not to say anything but to lead toward the zero degree of the thinkable. By their combination, the words are cut loose from their meanings and transformed into *operators* of detachment. The "dissimilarities" are not signs but machines for setting adrift—machines for voyages and ecstasies outside of received meanings. They do not give the intellect a mental object; they *fool the mind* into moving forward while taking away its objects. They are like the springs of a mechanism. They no longer answer to the principle of the medieval symbol, which was epiphanic and ontological; they already function like the modern scientific "symbol." Produced within a space of "fiction" (an artificial "scene" of "names"), they are characterized by what they allow to be done.

Two elements, correlated by Dionysius, specify that production and play a determining role in the mystic manners of speaking. On one hand, the dissimilar comes from perceptible and "*corporeal* things"; on the other, it is founded on a *biblical* use of language. The first element is not just a figure of speech. It is taken literally. The corporeal supplies the dissimilar by virtue of its paradoxical relation with the mind. The body, in its difference, with headaches or stomachaches, movements of fervor or delicious swoonings, with extraordinary or troubling sensations, composes dissimilarities, the status of which remain the ones assigned to it by Dionysius. The dissimilar, a discrepancy in relation to the analogy conceived by the understanding, becomes a body, transformed and altered, the movements of which form the illegible vocabulary of an unnameable speaker.

The Bible furnishes the model for these dissimilarities and the area of their first development. By that path, the return of the humanistic sixteenth century to the Scriptures is a resumption of the theological exegesis of patristics. But, in this case, the biblical reference authorizes a style and not a content. It has closer ties with rhetoric than with hermeneutics. What is quoted here has less to do with what the Bible says than with its way of speaking. The use made of the Bible changes. Undoubtedly it is the nature of the question demanding recourse to the Book that calls for this type of "reading." Because the Scriptures are considered from the point of view of the relationship between language and the absolute, that is, from above and globally, like a bird's-eye view of a city, their contents are leveled to the status of secondary details on an immense surface, stirred up by movements that "manifest" the attractions of God by means of "dissimilar formations" ("per dissimiles formationes manifestatio").[112] A passing to the absolute level conjoins all of the signs into a sole demonstrative that is language itself, distraught by what eludes it and is lacking. The interpretable text, seen from this perspective, apprehended at the zero degree of meaning and as a (mis)treatment of language, is transformed into a distorted body. One more step in that evolution and the dissimilar word, showing what it cannot say, will be the body itself, a body painfully or delightfully tormented by what haunts it, a body speaking and mute, attesting to what it can neither say nor know—a physical and unspeakable experience of the spirit. At this point the alliance between the body and the Bible occasions an identification. It is the body that is biblical, speaking in the mode of the dissimilar, while the Scriptures become a text-object manipulated by the technicians of meaning.[113]

This development relies on the isolation of corporeal and biblical dissimilarity. On this point there is an essential difference between the Areopagite and Diego. For the former, there is "implication" between the "dissimilar" symbols, presented by biblical language, and "resemblant" symbols, which belong to the liturgical discourse. Biblical impropriety bears a necessary relation to "ecclesiastic" propriety. It introduces into the analogical positivity of discourse carried on by the institution of meaning the "negations" relative to the subjective deficit of language (an *agnōsia*) and to the objective eminence of the "absolutely Unknowable."[114] There is, therefore, a plurality of theologies, no one of which is the law of the other and the common center of which is the Silence of the ineffable One. The tension between the similar [*gelich*] and the dissimilar [*ungelich*] can be found as early as in the works of Tauler, for whom propriety, ultimately founded on the sacramental institution, remains one of the poles of a spiritual dialectic.[115]

As for Diego, he gives priority to the dissimilar. It is as if one were still hearing, in his text, something of the storm that, in Plato, threatens the "pilot" of the world with "sinking into the bottomless ocean of dissimilarity."[116] An "unlimited" [*apeiron*] returns, indissociable from a disorder and discord of things, but it is called Yahweh. A madness of God remains, as in Plato, a "negative principle" that disturbs a cosmos, the order of which is conditioned by a limitation. But the dehiscence that shatters or "ruins" the rationality of discourse is henceforth (presumed) the manner in which the divine speaker leaves his mark on it. The prophesy of the Old Testament inverts the Platonic structure. It is noteworthy that the ecclesiastical institution, a sacrament actualizing the covenant between God and man, therefore the basis for an analogy and a "regulation" of discourse, here seems not to have enough weight to counterbalance with "similitude" and "proportion" the wounds that God's silence makes in language. Even though Diego builds his mystic theology on the Christic principle of a given spoken Word, a Verb grafted upon this world, the literary form he promotes by autonomizing *mystics* and defending John of the Cross (but apologetics is also a logic and the confession of a way of thinking) carries his theology towards the conception of a spoken word that seems to be essentially a distress of language, an afflicted body.

## THE SUBSTITUTE ORIGIN

The apology for the "imperfect" and for dissimilarity changes language into a system wounded by its speaker, and makes the spoken word into a song of this defeated medium. In fact, it is as if the dissimilar were an operation that stirred up language by an agony of the ineffable, a sort of tattoo or signature for the unsayable origin. What can no longer be laid down in the language as its principle and ground is insinuated into the whole range of its practice in the successive acts of speaking it, like a movement that folds it back upon itself and punctuates it with dissimilarities. Diego is justified in referring to *metalepsis*, which in Quintilian is a figure of transfer and passage, an "intermediary stage," a "transitus."[117] The unnameable origin does in fact make its appearance as a perpetual slippage of words toward that which deprives them of a stable meaning and frame of reference. But it does not give rise to a true designation. The words never finish leaving. There slippage is held back only by a correlation of heterogeneous terms. That mobility slips in between them and shifts them by the very act of bringing them nearer to one another. It keeps on moving language by an effect of beginning, but a beginning that is never there, never present. That agitation is nothing but the interval between words. It stirs them up without their being able to say what it is. A *je ne sais quoi* of otherness works them and preoccupies them; it has no name but that very motion—practice, a "manner" of speaking. An operation is substituted for the Name. In that respect, the mystic phrase is an artifact of Silence. It produces silence in the murmur of words in the way a "record of silence" marks a hiatus in the noise of a café. It is a mystic turn.

✠ III ✠

# The Circumstances of the Mystic Utterance

The sociopolitical instability and deterioration of frames of reference constituted, during the sixteenth and first half of the seventeenth century, the background against which the national *political* units that replaced Christendom were to appear, as well as the *spiritual* groups or networks that miniaturized the ecclesiastical model of a social organization of worship. In Germany, France, and Italy, political foundations and spiritual movements presented parallel responses to the historical deterioration. The *Machiavellian moment* isolated by J. G. A. Pocock, and the *invasion* of the mystics followed by their *conquest* celebrated earlier in this century by Henri Bremond, occurred in the same places, with the same re-forming intentions.[1] The former was characterized by the opposition between a form of rational voluntarism and an economic conjuncture. Machiavelli gave it its form: to serve Florence, faced with decline and stricken by cir-

153

cumstances (bankruptcy of the Medici bank, recession in the clothing industry, the threat of invasion by Charles VIII or by Cesare Borgia, moral decadence, the fall of the Medici in 1494 and of the Republic in 1512), he assembled a panoply of learning based on a *virtu* as much moral as political. Strength of character and of thought had to fight against *Fortuna* and *corruzione* [corruption]. This science, coordinated with an ethics, would produce a *vivere civile* that would prevail over chance and the disorder of things, figures into which Providence had been changed to the point of becoming unrecognizable. But it was also, in Florence, the time of Savonarola (1452–98) and Bernardino, visionaries of their city, condemned to the stake; of the prophet Martino who gave himself the name "madman," *il pazzo*; or of the mystic *Nativity* in which Botticelli set the angels, heralds of a new world, into frenzied dance, beneath the words: "This picture was painted by me, Sandro, at the end of the year 1500, during the Italian disorder, in the half of time that is after time, according to chapter XI of Saint John, in the second Woe of the Revelation."[2] During the same period, a constellation of Italian female mystics was founding the spaces of another country: Camilla Battista da Varano, Osanna Andreasi, Catherine of Genoa, and others.[3] There is simultaneity and an interrelatedness of projects between these mystics and the politicians.

The "Machiavellian moment" was repeated in England, in the seventeenth century, in the form of a neo-Machiavellian political economy and, in the eighteenth century, in the United States. In Richelieu's France, that is, in another conjuncture of menacing and violent circumstances, the recourse to Machiavelli (and to Tacitus, that "breviary of State") also informed the harsh "logic of self-interest" that created state-controlled enterprise, bolstered up by the mercantile system, the revival of Roman law, and so on.[4] This is precisely the time of the "invasion" and "conquest" of the mystics. The task of producing a Republic or a State by a political "reason" that would take the place of a defunct, illegible, divine order, is in a way paralleled by the task of founding places in which to hear the spoken Word that had become inaudible within corrupt institutions.

Admittedly, these two types of founding, being just as much restorative as innovative, still relied on the inherited model of an ecclesiastical and cosmological tradition—a unifying totality—but they treated it on specialized registers, isolating in one case the field of a "reason of State" and in the other a "community of saints." Moreover, on all sides there was a springing up of endeavors stimulated by the ambition of creating centers in which all the dispersed pieces of the past and present could be put in order: erudite encyclopedism, philosophical

Neoplatonism, metaphysical poetry, utopian urbanism, and, an instrument of visual totalization, cartography—an optical strategy for accumulating and classifying knowledge. However, this ambition was only pursued within concurrent areas, each one delineated and specified by "manners of proceeding."

The act of setting oneself apart from the rest is not a goal. Rather, it is a necessity imposed by the disorder from which one must escape in order to circumscribe the space for a new beginning and to define methods of construction. Therefore, microcosms were formed, "reductions" of the dismembered macrocosm. They were haunted by two biblical images: a mythical image of the lost paradise and an eschatological or apocalyptic image, that of a Jerusalem to be founded.[5] In an often chaotic multiplicity, each unit was lived in the past or in the future, in a relation to the lost origin or the approaching end. Thus a historical consciousness developed, but it could not be a theory of history. Far from one truth being articulated through the successive or coexistent figures of time, truth escaped them, like the absent beginning or end. The truth remained alien to this world, which was the domain of the will, the ethics of a "will to do." There is only a theory of history where temporal heterogeneities are thinkable (and comparable) within the space of the same meaningfulness.

In that present exiled from its first and last principle, but looking forward to a "great instauration," the conquests of reason and spirit tried to overcome the contradictions between the technical *parceling* of specific areas (a splitting up of the world and knowledge) and the need for a *unitary* language. Symbolizing "institutions" served as frameworks for a variety of pioneering endeavors. That is the case, for example, of astrology, which grouped the dispersion of the visible into an organicity of the stars and the hazards of fate into a stability of the heavens; thus it already furnished a language that spoke of universal laws.[6] Similarly, the alchemic or hermetic art, "philosophy" of the "conversion of the elements," was already reconciling the innumerable procedures of production with the recognition of one sole Nature. There was also universal recourse to the *spiritus* that, being "neither matter nor soul," "pervades the universe and carries the power of superior beings to inferior ones." That general agent of transfer and movement, implied by the Cartesian *materia subtilis*, by the Platonists' *anima mundi*, or the "universal spirit" of the chemists, circulated through the "objects" distinguished by analysis.[7]

Another globalizing framework, though less explicit, is present in the perception of the cultural landscape. Experience transformed lived space into a cartography of a receding or recurring Golden Age, that is, into a network of degradations and returns (on one hand, "corruptions" and losses; on the other, the discovery of ancient works of art or primitive mores of savages) that together compose, as in painting, landscapes "with ruins," movable scenes in which "inventions"—the labors of erudition, disguises and pastiches—play upon the relics of an abandoned reference that is no longer the Origin and not yet a past.[8] But little by little it was the monarchy (that of the French jurists or of *Leviathan*) that became the institution par excellence. In France the king, symbolic body of the nation, was supposed to triumph over time by the genealogical transmission of a "fundamental" bond with the people, to organize society on the model of the stellar order, to insure the agreement of reason with force.[9]

The "mystics" also knew and used these communal institutions of meaning. They referred to them, but they tried, above all, to "reduce all to one."[10] And like the other sciences, even more than other sciences, the "science of the saints" had to reconcile contradictions: the local *particularity* that it circumscribed contradicted the *universality* to which it claimed to attest. There was also contradiction between the question of the individual *subject* and that of the divine *absolute*. A tension of this kind may serve to define the "experimental science" that plays upon the dialectics of the *nothing* and the *all*, and that, rejecting the particular knowledge of the "understanding," receives its authority from a "universal and confused" *notizia* (or "notion"). The mystics, participating in the great recapitulative project that would find its last "modern" figure in the *mathesis universalis* (philosophical ecumenism) of Leibniz (it was not to be revived until Hölderlin and Hegel), had to confront the insularity of their foundations with the in-finite of the One.

*Chapter Five*

✠   ✠
✠

# The "Conversar"

A specific problematic determines both the circumscribing of the mystic "retreats" and the style of the procedures that make possible a "work" of the universal within them. Their question is essentially concerned with the relation. It involves a theory and a pragmatics of *communication. Mystics* is the anti-Babel, the quest for a common speech after its breakdown, the invention of a language "of God" or "of the angels" that would compensate for the dispersal of human languages.[11] Relative to that quest, a topics sets the mystic scene, just as a topics of the relations of power to space set, in Florence, the "scene of the prince."[12] In giving its specifics, an initial topography can be established.

## THE "DIALOGUE"

Speaking and hearing: this binomial defines the space in which the procedures of the "saints" (which is what the mystics were called) were carried out. The questions they treat are symptomatic. They can be reduced to two essential issues: prayer (from meditation to contemplation) and the "spiritual" relation, be it with other individuals or (in the form of "spiritual guidance") with the representatives of the ecclesiastical institution. The human and/or divine "communication" designates an *act*. It focuses on narrative accounts, treatises, and poems. In Spanish mystic vocabulary, it is expressed in a single word: *conversar* (to speak "with God," *con Dios*, or "with the others," *con los otros*), the equivalent of the Latin *colloquium*, which in medieval spirituality designates both prayer and oral exchange. *Orare* is "to speak" as well as "to pray," as in [French] "oraison" and "orant," and so on. Hence, on the subject of the contemplation or language of the mystics, the existence of so many theoretical and practical discussions on the *manera de comunicarse*. Above all, the name itself that symbolizes the entire mystic literature refers to that *acte de parole* (J. R. Searle's *speech act*) and to the illocutionary function (J. L. Austin): the Spirit is "he who speaks"—*el que habla*, says John of the Cross;[13] it is the interlocutor, or "that which speaks."

Now, that communication was perceived as having been broken off. The credibility upon which it was founded was crumbling away. The breaks, equivocation, and lies of language brought an insurmountable duplicity into the relation, which added to the silence of institutions and of things. Texts were produced on the basis of this lack. It is true that devotion tried to foster the belief that beings and books were speaking of God, or that it was God speaking in them, but their gossip or murmur did not console the mystics of the seventeenth century, inattentive to these noises and thrown by their desire into the experience of a great silence. The "letter" was not the word they awaited, nor was the world. These messengers "cannot tell me what I want" [*no saben decirme lo que quiero*].[14] That absence of the Verb was counterbalanced by an assurance: it *must* speak. A faith was attached to what no longer appeared. Belief founded an expectation. It sought support in the promise of the Scriptures: "I shall pour out my spirit . . . ; and your sons and your daughters shall prophesy."[15] But the waiting came head on against a fact: what *should be* was missing. How then, and where, would that voice speak? In what manner could the emptiness in which it might resound be prepared? Or perhaps there were no longer ears for what still spoke? "They have ears, and hear not"[16] Or might it be the nature of that spoken word to "run dry"?

> It was so
> That a voice would ask to be believed, and always
> Would turn back against itself and always
> make of its drying up its greatness and its proof.[17]

But if the voice fell silent, should not hearing be called into question? Learning to listen: that was another theme of the mystics. *Audi, filia*, the title of the famous treatise by John of Avila (Madrid, 1588), sums up a tradition. "Listen, my daughter," was addressed to the "soul."

The injunction was aimed primarily at attention to the speaking Word. But for John of Avila, as for hundreds of others, it also meant all forms of the *colloquium* or the *conversar*: the relation of the preacher to his public, of the "spiritual master" to those under his direction, of everyone to others and to himself. How could man (who has nearly always the feminine figure of "the soul") recognize the language that stirred within others or that he spoke unbeknownst to himself? A deafness distorted the relation. Teresa of Avila attributed decisive importance to her experience with confessors who deceived themselves [*engañarse*], deceived her [*engañar*], or whom she deceived.[18] Those "masters" who "do not understand her" will be supplemented by spiritual works (which, like love stories, tell her desires) or "talks" [*tratos*] and "conversations" in a *buena compañía*, or her own "dreams" and "follies." John of the Cross, for his part, wrote *Subida del Monte Carmelo* for those men or women who in vain sought someone to listen to them. His book strove to fulfill that need: "It is a harsh and painful thing for a soul not to understand itself and to find no one to understand it."[19] Due to a reciprocity conceptually related to the confusion of tongues at Babel (*por no entender ellos la lengua . . .* ), we cannot understand ourselves unless we are understood. Later, Jean-Joseph Surin alludes to the "superiors," "spiritual directors or fathers" who "were almost all mistaken": "I would not cease seeking someone to whom I could reveal my heart." But he found nothing among those "wise and grave" interlocutors but "incredible oppression."[20] A general interrogation extends to both sides of the oratio: its internal and external processes are indissociable. Nothing "Other" may speak to the soul unless there is a third party to listen to it.

Whatever the issues raised by "mystic" communication, the two verbs *speak* and *hear* designate the uncertain and necessary center around which circles of language are produced. Two points of reference, separated by a century, might be proposed to indicate the growing hesitation with which the desire for the Speaking Word is accompanied. In 1543, prefacing the edition of the *Psalms*, Calvin assured his readers, with a sense of modesty that is a trait of his style, "God puts words in our mouth as if he himself were singing in us."[21] The "as if" strips the human voice of the divine song that has become scriptural. That is the gap the mystics tried to bridge. Around 1653, when Angelus Silesius was converted to Catholicism, he cast the Scriptures themselves over to the side of "nothingness", as being opaque positivity, in order to know the "essence" of the Speaking Word of *Thou* and *I*, but he got nothing from that "consolation" beyond the expectancy that exalted his poetry from one end to the other:

*Die Schrift ist Schrift, sonst nichts.*
*Mein Trost ist Wesenheit,*
*Und daß Gott in mir*
*spricht das Wort der Ewigkeit.*[22]

The Scripture is scripture, nothing more.
My consolation is essence,
And that God in me
Speaks the word of eternity.

Between the divine *oratio* (the spoken word) and the *oratio* of the believer, the separation maintained by Calvin's "as if" became less and less tolerable to impatient mystics, as it became increasingly insurmountable.

In various ways, the speech act that determined the "spiritual" elaborations started out with the postulate that the act of knowing was situated *in the field of prayer* (or, as Saint Anselm always said, in the field of the *invocatio*). Allocution was for knowledge its condition and beginning. It gave it the formality of a "speaking to" that was also a "believing in" [*credere in*]. Therefore, mystic science questioned at the same time the nature of the spoken word (issued from a voice), of belief (the attentiveness of an ear, *fides ex auditu*), and of knowledge. It stopped there, on the threshold at which the possibility of speaking was the measure of a possibility of knowing: How could allocution give birth to a knowledge of the other?

That the *invocatio* should be the postulate of an understanding was not new. The philosophy of Saint Anselm, in many respects close to the theory of the mystics, placed itself from the outset in the field and, so to speak, beneath the domination of allocution. *Proslogion, id est colloquium,* he wrote at the head of his treatise to explain its title.[23] But when his reflection advanced to the extreme iconoclastic and apophatic border of language, when it was no longer held together by anything but a name ("God")—that is, the index that pointed to the failure of all signs ("Thou art something greater than which nothing can be conceived")—and when on the basis of this one little word (the linguistic equivalent of the burning bush) it tried to guarantee to the "madman" (who says in his heart: there is no God) the existence implied by this word, it still took two things for granted: a stable agreement between speech and the being that was expressed by it (the word was an epiphany, a *locutio rerum*); and an act of speech occasioned by an approach, like a call, the shouting out of a first name, responding at a distance in the street to the passing silhouette of the beloved. Five centuries later, the *invocation* continued to dominate the field in which a rationality of faith might develop, and it remains true today for a theory of love. But it was no longer based on the double postulate, epiphanic and allocutionary, that authorized it in Anselm. The very condition of knowledge became the problem against which mystic thought stumbled and became polarized. Upon that beginning "all the rest" depended. How was it possible to speak, to hear? That beginning that constituted a threshold for knowledge of the Other must itself have its beginnings (how to begin to speak or listen?), its history, its tragedies.

## THE SPEECH ACT

Thus the *invocatio* and *auditio fidei* were cut off. The "essential" they constituted was no longer a step along a path leading from the conditions of possibility of knowledge, that is, the allocution of faith, *fidens quearens intellectum*, to consequent knowledge. It became a separate question alongside knowledge: the question of what knowledge itself presupposes. In other words, the speech act [*énonciation*] was distinguished from the objective ordering of what was stated in speech [*énoncé*]. The former gave *mystics* its formality. Hence the importance taken on by the instauration of a new locus, that of the *I*, and by the operations of (*spiritual*) exchanges that made communication hinge upon the question of the subject, and also by all the procedures, rhetorical or poetic, capable of organizing a field of allocution per se. What was called "experience" connoted this field, distinguishing it from already constituted fields of knowledge. At a time when a "utopian space, opening up in the margins of a no longer decipherable historical reality, supplied a non-place for a new kind of reason to use its capacity to produce a world as text and make texts themselves generate worlds[24]—a mystic space appeared alongside the various fields of knowledge. It, too, was a non-place, but one created by the stirrings the desire for the other awoke within language; that is, by the reversal that emptied statements of their content in order to lay bare the prior question of the *colloquium*.

Initially, that question did not add a new province to the organization of the disciplines. Only from the middle of the seventeenth century on, when the inquiry that had given rise to the mystic texts had been forgotten, would they be brought together to form a science apart, the "application" or the "practice" of theological "speculation." Such was, for example, the *Práctica de la teología mística* of M. Godinez in 1681.[25] That hierarchization, the work of theologians, aligned *mystics* with the "applied sciences," which were then considered distinct from and dependent upon "theoretical" discourse. But in point of fact, *mystics* dealt with a question that did not run parallel to but across all the established disciplines. It is true that *mystics* did involve a distinction between theory and practice, but in the sense that the *speech act*, distinct from the validity of statements, concerned the oral realization and not the logical truth of the proposition. *Mystics* consisted in asking oneself, for example: (a) if and how one could *practice* (speak effectively) the language that continued to be considered globally true; (b) whether it was possible to *address* God [*tratar con Dios*] with statements that presented knowledge *about* him; (c) how to converse [*conversar*] between *you* and *me*, in the exchange with the Other or with others; (d) how to *hear*, as a voice that concerns *me*, propositions objectively accepted as inspired (biblical, canonical, or traditional); and so on.

Thus the ancient cosmological account of tradition was taken up anew in a different formality and treated according to a new "way of proceeding" on the basis of several strategic points:

1. *A present act* of speech relativizes the relevance of the knowledge guaranteed by an acquisition (a past revelation) and founds a historicity of experience (a relation existential and necessary to the present moment): nothing said yesterday to others can take the place of what I can say or hear, here and now.

2. *The "illocutionary" relation*,[26] relative to the act of speaking and to the fact that it transforms the relationship between speakers, gives the leading roles to the *I* and the *you* that it implies: the "objective" content of discourse can be grasped anew in its entirety as the history of that relation.

3. Between the speaker (he who makes the statement) and the addressee (the one to whom he addresses himself)—or between the sender and the receiver—a network of *conventions* is established, made up of presuppositions and contracts that discourse strengthens, shifts, and manipulates: a series of reciprocal contractual *operations* takes the place of the hierarchic classification of statements according to their degree of validity.

4. The illocutionary activity is manifested in speech by the privileged place given to "indicial," that is, pragmatic or subjective, elements of language in such a way that the language of the statement becomes the account of the conditions and modalities of its own utterance—*a dramatics of allocution.*

All these points, and others that remain to be made, relate to the speech act.[27] The "experience" that specifies mystic writings, moreover, has as its principal characteristics on one hand the *ego*, which is precisely the "center of the speech act," and on the other hand the *present,* the "source of time," the "presence in the world that the act of utterance alone makes possible."[28]

It is not, as in theology, a matter of setting together a particular coherent complex of statements articulated according to the criteria of "truth" furnished by the triple authority of a Scripture, a magisterium, and a majority practice of believers. Nor is it a question, as was the case of the contemporary theosophy, of letting the world-organizing powers appear of their own accord in narratives in which the speaking subject's only role is to be a witness—the mouth through which those oceanic noises of the cosmos make themselves heard. It is, rather, a question of *treating the common language* (that of everybody and anybody, not that of specific disciplines) in function of the *possibility for it to be spoken.* How does this language get transformed into a network of allocutions and present alliances? An initial double division is thus introduced. On the one hand, a dichotomy separates the *said* (that which has been or is now being said) from the *saying* (the act itself of being said). The changing of the "said" into a "saying" presupposes their distinction and the passage from one status of language to another. Rabelais's fable of the "melted words" may serve to give an idea of that first division: Will words that time has frozen become voices again (addressed by whom to whom?)?[29] On the other hand, the universe, be it compact or infinite, be it regulated by order or chance, is posited in principle as the vocabulary of a *dialogical* discourse between a *you* and an *I* that seek one another through language. The same things are therefore two-faced signs that the partners address to one another equally, yet without encountering each other. These things are divided within by an opacity that is the secret of the interlocutors from one another:

> *Adónde te escondiste*
> *Amado, y me dejaste con gemido?*[30]

> Whither hast thou hidden thyself,
> And hast thou left me,
> O Beloved, to my sighing?

Certain mechanisms follow from this problematic. Like the linguistic signs of the speech act, they concern neither a signified object nor a referential entity (they do not have a denominative function), but the power of discourse itself. They do not refer directly to a "competence,"[31] although there are questions of that order: for example, what are the required conditions for uttering "mystical" statements? They aim at the *exercise* of language—a "performance"and therefore, according to Emile Benveniste, the "conversion of language into dis-course."[32] Among these illocutionary mechanisms, I shall restrict my-self initially to three that set the "scene" of a "mystic" text: (1) the *break* that precedes discourse and that sets up a contract with the receivers (the agreement on a *volo*—an initial "I will"); (2) the "empty" *place*,[33] "site without a site," that marks in the discourse the locus of its locutor (the "I"); (3) the *representation* of that place by the narrative figure that forms the setting of the account (the insularity of the "soul": a circle, a castle, an island, etc.). As we bring out these elements through a few examples taken from the mystic texts of the sixteenth and seventeenth centuries, a "way of proceeding" comes into view, suited to the question that prompts them from within: How is speaking or being spoken constitutive of existence?

## A PRELIMINARY: THE *VOLO* (FROM MEISTER ECKHART TO MADAME GUYON)

The first mechanism was intended to specify a preliminary that would make illocutionary contracts possible between speakers. In a language that had become opaque, fragmented, Babel-like, it was necessary to *produce* what hitherto had been taken for granted, namely, common presuppositions that permitted mutual understanding. Conventions were needed that would determine the places where communication could be restored. That no longer went without saying. There was no longer any common a priori—neither on a sole universal Speaker nor on the link between word and thing; nor, therefore, on the principle of universal rules governing the verification or invalidation of state-ments. Language was diversified by *usages*, or various "ways of speak-ing." Different *practices* (which were within the province of rhetoric, no longer that of logic) modified the value of words and discourse. What became decisive were the "ways" of using the same statements, true or false according to the way they were used. So it was by defining a common practice of language that a "convention" was established by the "spirituals." Mystic discourse itself had to produce the condi-tion of its functioning as language that could be spoken to others and to oneself.

Because it concerned a practice, that condition rendered particu-larly relevant the *circumstances* of the verbal exchange: its time and place, its "manner," the nature of the speakers, and so on. *How* things were said was more important than *what* was said. A preoccupation with the "circumstantial" was consistent with the analytic work of the jurists, who were busy drawing up the most complete list of the various circumstances and addressees that would determine whether or not a procedure was "felicitous."[34] The spirituals intended to set forth the conditions in which speech would "work," or "succeed" in making communication possible. By determining pragmatic presuppositions, they wanted to erect places in which relation could occur. By elaborating the preliminaries and rules of the operations corresponding to a particular dialogical or conversational use of language, by including in this language its bodily (gestural, sensuous) aspects, or its circumstantial ones (time, place, lighting, sound, position and situation of verbal exchange or prayer), and not just its verbal element, they engaged in a *politics of the speech act*. They intended to *reorganize places for people to communicate* in the aftermath of the breakdown of a system that until then had implemented relation through a hierarchized and cosmological network combining ontological states (lineage, truth values) with stable alliances (social clienteles, or contracts between words and things).

Within its own register, that politics was in line with the objectives the theorizers of rhetorics set for themselves. In Italy, since the fifteenth century, rhetoric, in keeping with the privilege of making and acting over knowing, expressed in the art of saying the desire to found *la civile conversazione*. By the use of "vulgar" languages, by the importance given to concrete realities, by the primacy of techniques of persuasion over the logic of truth, discourse was supposed to bind new social contracts. It corresponded to a "political moment." As long as the real was stabilized by a rigorous infrastructure, deductive reasoning sufficed within the confines of departmentalized disciplines and in function of an immutable truth. But when that order gave way, persuasive modes of discourse became necessary in order to create agreement between wills, to make new rules and so form social units. According to Francesco Patrizi and many others, the rhetorical *oratio* has the power to found republics.[35] The *conversar* of the spirituals was similar in this respect. That art of speaking, accompanied by countless "methods" that implemented the superiority of the act to knowledge or that of speech to reading, was to bring about the alliances in the present that were, in Teresa of Avila for example, either communal relations (the *compañía*), exchanges with the Christian tradition ("spiritual direction"), or conversation with God (prayer). Practices erected places for speaking.

To set up these dialogical spaces, there was one essential preliminary condition. It always took the form of an exclusive restriction, of an "only," a "nothing but," or a "no one except." The relation was *only* possible for persons who were entirely resolved, or who "wanted it." A "will" constituted the a priori knowledge could no longer supply. It had to be present (no past decision or knowledge could make up for it), practical (it was an act), concrete (here and now, it committed the "I"), and absolute (without restrictions). Without it, there was no spiritual communication. It belongs to the Heideggerian category of the "not without," *nicht ohne*. Everything, from the first, depends on each speaker's own *volo*. The *volo* provides the opening for every spoken word.

This presupposition defined the addressee required by the discourse ("I am speaking *only* to those who . . . "). From John of the Cross, who addressed "souls already engaged in the path of virtue,"[36] to Surin, that "convention" was in all cases required. It defined a category. It set apart a way of using language that consisted in casting all of one's desire into it. In this way, the "instructions for use" were spelled out, distinct from other usages, and a tacit understanding was established. Superficially, the postulate of this *modus loquendi* was different from the linguistic practice proper to apologetics or predication, which posited, from the outset, statements generally accepted by all parties and then proposed, on that basis, to obtain ultimate adherence (a "conversion," etc.), that is, a change of will on the part of the addressee. In the usage we are discussing, it was the *volo* that was the a priori, not the result of discourse. In 1670, Malaval made the postulate that created the circle of communication more rigorous. "I write only for persons capable of inner things, those who have been fully mortified with respect to the external senses and all passion, fully drawn to God by his pure love and fully detached from all that has been created."[37] He went rather far, but his rigidity, in a time of political secularization, was very much in keeping with a tradition in which an act founded discourse.

A performative verb designates an act, hence a present moment: *volo.* "Not: I would like to . . . , but: I will," as Meister Eckhart specified.[38] Three and a half centuries later, Surin required that his interlocutors had already taken what he called "the first step," "a determined will to refuse nothing to God," and that this be "all at once,"—now and completely.[39] And yet he maintained that in that *instant*, the "willingness to act" was not identical with the "possibility of acting." Eckhart had already stressed this point. It was not a matter of carrying out an action but of being resolved to bet one's entire being on God. This *volo* was "absolute," not bound by any precise determination. It was defined by the disappearance of its objects. It was both *nihil volo* ("I want *nothing*") and "I want only God" (I want

"God to want in place of my will wanting").[40] A speech act delimited, by that decision that has no object, the position of the subject fit to "hear" mystic discourse. Consequently, it also defined what allows the production of that discourse. It is what Surin called "to form desire." A desire "bound to nothing," he added.[41]

In the beginning, then, there is an act. It stands out with the uniqueness of an event, giving the experience a "form" that will be repeated throughout one's itinerary. It stands in contrast. It is a beginning. The cleanness of that break inaugurates both a different "region" and a style—a way of moving and speaking within it. "Either you want to or you do not"—there is no middle ground. The first movement also excludes the time-consuming and cumbersome preparation that goes with the actual carrying through. We are talking about an inner lift-off, a "detachment." Eckhart speaks of a "liberation." Whatever the length of its preparation or its effects, the "it's *already done*" of the "intention" is born "suddenly," crossing the threshold of reasons, opening up a new landscape of data and problems. It is "all decided." It is similar to the way one can have "already left" in a flash, long before having packed one's bags. "I say you must form the desire all at once, but the execution takes place little by little."[42] In that moment, which has the lightness of a departure, the two aspects of a decision, the ecstatic (to exit) and the ascetic (to lose), coincide.

In requiring this decision of its addressees, the discourse sets for them the condition of its own functioning. This is the first rule of its instructions for use: it only *works*, it is only effective when supported by the *volo* of its readers. Otherwise it is inert. This prerequisite does not involve a truth considered to have been established (for example, that God exists or that the Gospel is true) nor a definition touching the status of a text (for example, taking it as a fable, a true story, a philosophical work, or a corpus issuing from an authority). The prerequisite is an act, external to discourse. It will produce discourse—or make it function—as mystic discourse. It is outside of the text. It founds, on the basis of its instantaneity, the time (the developments) of discourse. Upon an unrepeatable present, it founds a textual space amenable to the returns, the repetition and reversibility of readings. Upon the melting away of knowledge into will, it founds the didactic exposition of an itinerary. There is therefore a contradiction between these forms of discourse and the prerequisite demanded of the reader. The *volo* is both their point of departure and their vanishing point. This paradox comes into play variously. For example, with the "I want (everything, nothing, God)," discourse postulates, to be read, a demand it cannot satisfy. It makes the reader's disappointment the modality in which the text must be approached. That tension already introduces a "mystic" style in the writing or reading of the text.

The *volo* presents a certain number of characteristics. In particular, it isolates a modal verb (to want), a relation to power, a position of the subject, and a speaking function. These four points may already serve to delineate the "country" in which the *volo* represents the threshold.

### To Want: A Modal Verb

It is a wanting that institutes a knowing. Knowledge is made possible only by an initial decision: *volo*. This is indeed a general structure of modern scientific disciplines. There is no field that is not based on a set of postulates and definitions that are decisional. But that inauguration of a body of knowledge by the will, in this instance, is detached from the contents normally affected by epistemological decisions. The will is isolated from any possible knowledge. A white border surrounding mystic language—that cliff, the sudden difference in level—marks off its outer limits. It may be envisioned as a first approximation, as discourse encircled by the modality of will.

Linguistically, modality is "a complementary assertion affecting the statement of a relation."[43] In the examples "I *must* leave" or "I *can* leave," something is added to the content (the *dictum*) and specifies the relation of the speaker to the *dictum* "I leave." This complement introduces a modification of the predicate by the subject: "must" or "can" indicates an intervention of the subject in his action (*to leave*) or his attribute (I am *leaving*). Modality maximizes the instance of the subject. Semiotically speaking, it marks the investment of the speaker in his or her statement. For example: I do not *think* he will come, I *want* him to come. Within the wide spectrum of modals (or operators of modality), we first notice their lexicalized form under the kinds of modal verbs such as *can* (I can go away), *must* (I must speak), *to know how to* (I don't know how to pray), and *want* (I want to leave). Positioned, like all modals, between speaker and statement, the *volo* represents that particular modality that circumscribes and specifies the mystic domain.

Raised to the level of a regulating principle for the other modals (can, know how to, must), that discursive helm stands in isolation. The predicates are obliterated or replaced by "nothing" or "everything": I want nothing, I want everything, I want only God. Given the disappearance of particular predicates, the clause is weighted toward emphasis on the relationship between the subject and verb, in the modality of wanting, which puts in question the strength of the speaker's commitment to his or her statement. This commitment is here only tolerated in the present: "I want." This reinforces the elimination of the predicates or complements of the verb, which refer to a past or a future, that is, to a time other than that of the object desired in relation to the act of wanting. In this "beginning" marked by the *volo*, the disappearance of the content (the thing wanted) and the exclusion of the past (I wanted) or future (I would want) work together to produce the same effect, which is to inflate the act of wanting itself. Originally, there is an absolute volitive, detached from anything known or possessed. It is all the more powerful for being less determined by an object. Thus the preliminary to mystic discourse plants an event of the will in the middle of a desert. It is, on a linguistic plane, the equivalent of what Jakob Böhme posits at the origin of all existence: the violence, the furor even, of a Will.[44]

That advent is, moreover, of a tautological nature. The question concerns the inception of mystic language. How can it have a beginning? Answer: In order for discourse to begin, there must be beginning somewhere. When the question is asked about a poem, it elicits an appeal to inspiration or the Muse. Here, it is resolved in terms of will. The *volo* is the affirmation that birth can take place at any moment. It is origin in the present, the principle of beginning.

Finally, this *volo*, because it has no particular object and "clings" to *nothing*, changes into its opposite—not to want anything—and thus takes up the entire range, both negative and positive, of wanting. The will is stabilized (in affirmation or negation) only if it is attached to a particular object ("I want" or "I do not want" *that*) and, consequently, if there is a distinction between a particular subject ("I") and a particular object ("that"). Once this link to a particular has been removed, the will turns back upon itself and identifies itself with its opposite. "To want all" and "to want nothing" coincide. The same is true of "to want nothing" and "not to want anything." Once it is no longer the wanting *of* something and no longer moves in the orbits formed by the constellations of distinct subjects and objects, the *volo* is also the act of "renunciation of one's will."[45] It is a *not wanting* as well, for example, in the "giving up" [*Gelâzenheit*] and "detachment" [*Abegescheidenheit*] of Meister Eckhart.[46] The suppression of the object (I want *nothing*) will, moreover, have repercussions on the subject. *Who*, after all, wants? What is the "I" that wants? There remains, dislocated, the act of wanting, a force that is born. The verb is "tied to nothing" and not to be appropriated by anyone. It passes through times and places. In the beginning is the verb to will. It posits from the very beginning what will be repeated in mystic discourse by many other verbs (to love, to wound, to seek, to pray, to die, etc.), itinerant acts among actors who may be positioned at one moment as subjects, at another as objects. Who loves whom? Who wounds whom? Who prays to whom? Sometimes God, sometimes the faithful. . . . The *volo*, then, as beginning and center, vanishing point and keystone of mystic communication, is the operative principle (and a verb) that will exercise all language.

## THE "INTENTION":
### FROM WANTING TO BEING ABLE

The preliminary to mystic discourse initially posits the first link in a derivation or series of modal verbs.[47] From wanting there emerges a being able: *to want (will)* → *to be able (can)*.

Already Meister Eckhart wrote: "With the will I can do everything." And again: "To want to do something as soon as I am able, and to have done it, these are the same before God." Or: "What I want to have, I have."[48] Four centuries later in his *Pro Theologia mystica clavis* (1640), Maximilian Van der Sandt repeated these expressions without even giving references (he normally documented his sources meticulously), as if to indicate that they were commonplaces within the mystic tradition. He adds: "Per voluntatem possum omnia," by the will I can do all.[49] In this progression from willing to being able (if you want to, you can), the efficacy of the *volo* is associated with the "inner" act, "intention" [*intentio*].

During this period, distinctions were made among acts of the will, between "intention" (which is focused on the goal), "election" (which highlights the means), and *usus* (which concerns the execution). Among these intentions themselves, there were various degrees (beginning with the first, the *prima intentio*, in relation to the "ultimate goal"), types (for example, six of them, from the "perverse" intention, to the fourth which is "right," to the fifth which is "simple," to the sixth which is "deiform" and properly mystical), and modalities (for example, the "actual" intention or *actu*, which is explicit, and the "virtual" intention, or *virtute*, which implicitly prolongs a previous choice). From Saint Augustine to Madame Guyon, a proliferation of terms, definitions, and combinations pertaining to intentions made up a complex map of an "inner country" to which the mystic journeys refer.[50] What kind of country was this?

These maps of intentions are not based on classifications that list predicates according to levels of a structure of human being (for example, vegetative life/sensitive life/intellectual life, or body/soul/spirit) with a view to organizing knowledge about man by "states" or "degrees" of being. Naturally, these anthropological tables exist, too, and they provide the mystics with reference points for an ascension.

But they have a hierarchical form, whereas the classifications of intentions are topographical. They develop a space organized by *operations*. On one hand, they differentiate the formalities of spiritual "actions" ("actions" in the military sense of the term) and, on the other, like strategy maps or the *Carte de Tendre*,[51] they plot a landscape modeled on these "actions," which show positional values—such as coming close to, moving away from, or avoiding the goal—and which vectorize, increase, or decrease the extent of the region in which they are performed.

Intentions are, in fact, first and foremost, translational movement. These operations consist, according to the spiritual tradition, in "passing" [*transire in Deum*] and "tending toward" [*tendere*]. These are "moves." By their shortcuts or meanderings, these "passages" create an in-between space. They are instantaneous and secret. Intentions are imperceptible gestures. It is an odd domain, this "inner" country, this invisible and silent space where revolutions take place before news of them gets out. Behind the manifest aspect of history, events determine this domain without a sound. Surin calls these events "formal." Like the heavens in which the actions of the ancient gods were carried out, the "inner region" is a place of movements (decisions, victories, defeats, etc.) not yet leaving their mark upon the conjunctures of social life. The same is true of intellectual life. A "thought" can be formed "suddenly," before any attempt is begun to formulate it in phonemes or trace a path for it in writing. That "inner event" is sometimes so intense as to make its verbal or written production trifling or impossible. Why say it? How could it be transformed into the historicity of a discourse? Intentions are also sensitive to the ecstatic seduction that keeps them within an inner world in which they pass in an instant. That world, which is not the one in which history actually takes place, is nevertheless a space in which decisive things are at stake.

This placeless theater of instantaneous operations called "intentions" ("here" and "this very minute," say the mystics) is determined by a criterion that is present everywhere in mystical literature and was already central to Plotinus's conception of the "inner" when he wrote about the will. "The inner" is what "depends on us." "Do at once all that depends on you," the mystics request, and Plotinus tried to define just that: "what depends on us"or on the wise man. The border marking out the limits of interiority runs parallel to what does not depend on us, namely circumstances (which depend on "fate"), and in this way it isolates the domain of the intention. "We are not the masters of success," for we are not masters of what "happens" or occurs. Therefore "what depends on us does not extend to execution [*to prattein*] nor to its externality, but to the inner act [*eis tēn entos energeian*]." In other words, interiority is the region in which the will is "master of itself." It is a region of the "pure" (*psilos*, naked, simple) will, without any admixture of circumstances not arising from it—like a laboratory in which a body is being isolated.[52]

We shall see that this isolation of the will in a pure state plays a decisive role in the theories of "pure love." These theories also attempt to circumscribe "what depends on us" in connection with damnation or blessedness, which then appears as an ultimate circumstance, the randomness of God's fancy. "Even if he were to damn me, I would love him." From Ruysbroeck to Madame Guyon, this "pure" will is affirmed. In order to "form," the intention must free itself from what escapes its purview. It is true that the postulate of this inner place was never unproblematic. Already Plotinus wondered frequently about the status and location within the soul of the region in which things depend on us. It was not based on desire, which depends on the other, and "draws us toward the outside and carries away a lack [*to endeēs*]."[53] The mystics do say that desire manifests itself at the threshold of discourse as the mainspring of its development; but with the volo, the operation and decision of the will "within," they isolate the hypothesis, both theoretical and necessary, of an *autonomy* that is dependent neither on its objects nor on circumstances. The inner space represents a *liberation of the ethical principle*.[54] That free zone indicates a difference of the will with respect to the law of things or writing. It is the divergence created by the act that posits that difference and that, anarchistic per se, is not bound or determined by anything. It transgresses the order of facts, to affirm a place/nonplace of beginning. We are still within the realm of the problem of the beginning (or beginnings), but insofar as it has an ethical form. Mystic discourse opens up the field of a different kind of knowledge, by the ethical postulate of a sort of freedom: "I/you can be (re)born."

Among all the intentions distinguished by the tradition, this preliminary retains only a *prima intentio*. Furthermore, the "ultimate" goal that determines it is not, as in Thomism, beatitude (which was also to disappear from the mystic *volo*) but "God," or "nothing," or "all." Indetermination of the goal, and nonpertinence of the future. All that remains, like an axiom upon which the system is erected, is the act that instantaneously links the unknown extreme, the origin (a *voluntas*) to the uncertain extreme of the goal ("all," "nothing," etc.). As the coinciding of these two extremes, as present without duration, that act accomplishes in one leap the entire itinerary whose steps will be distinguished and whose proceedings will be defined by discourse.

The act gives it its formal schema, providing its placeless model as well as its condition of possibility: an inner decision.

### THE "PERFORMANCE" OF THE SUBJECT

The *volo*, to the extent to which it is also a speech act, may be further specified through a comparison with the "performatives," defined, since J. L. Austin, as acts of language that "do what they say." The notion that "wanting" should already be a "being able to," or that, according to Eckhart, "wanting to do" and "having done" should be "the same thing" before God—this in fact does call to mind that category of linguistic acts called "performatives" that Austin distinguished from "constatives." The *volo* is not a constative. It affirms no truth and is not subject to error. It describes no referential. It performs what it says. It is itself the act of the speaker: "I will." That act does not postulate a reality or knowledge prior to its utterance. Also in that linguistic form, it is the accomplishment of a beginning. Among the performatives, it belongs more specifically to the order of the "commissives."[55] The examples given by Austin (promise, am determined to, pledge myself, am dedicated to, declare my intention, etc.) are the same words that, in the mystic texts, mark the social manifestations of the initial *volo*.

But, as in the case of the "yes" of the spouses before the mayor, the performative only "works" within the particular setting of proceedings, conventions, and persons—in short, in expected and verifiable circumstances. For example, the "yes" must be spoken before witnesses, between marriage partners, at the town hall, and so on—failing which, the "yes" (I do) doesn't marry. If one of these circumstantial elements turns out to be missing, there is "failure" (infelicity).[56] The good or poor functioning is judged, in performatives, according to the opposition "felicity" versus "infelicity," and, in constatives, on the basis of "truth" versus "error." The circumstantial, in the area of performatives, plays the same role as the referential for constatives. The performative places the social network above the thing intended or thought. It is conventional in nature. It is inscribed like a social ceremonial within a set of practices governed by law, custom, seemliness, and so on. It exists in relation to a social management of illocutionary acts and the conditions of their contractual operativity. There is nothing resembling this in the *volo*, which, on the contrary, in order to be "felicitous" (to function well), presupposes the elimination of circumstances. It is therefore a borderline case of the performative. It leaves the field in which efficacity is measured in terms of the transformation of linguistic acts into social contracts. It is operative in the sense that it transforms the speaker into the subject of volition. Its performativity consists in *instituting a place* (that of the subject) and the autonomy of an interior ("mystic" by definition, free from the labyrinth of social controls) rather than in setting up a convention for dialogue. In doing so, the *volo* also creates a *difference* in relation to those texts and codes, an alterity that is a priori impenetrable or (which amounts to the same thing) a solitude that is what it says, and leaves its mark on language without articulating itself in it. It is still a performative, but of an odd variety, one that eschews all contracts unless it be that immediate one of self with self, in terms of the indeterminate (lack of object), the "bottomless" [*Gruntlôs*] and "nameless" [*Namelôs*], that is, the unknown.

That position of the subject can also be designated, as Suso does, by the act of "forgetting oneself."[57] The loss of identity, by the forgetting of name, objects, and addressee, is, in this view, the a priori form of the "I." "Pure" volition, or intention, creates in the mind and language a void, without determined contents. Its form is traced out by a blank, the "I," an "empty" spot, according to Benveniste.[58] As will be seen, the "I" is the substitute of the *volo*, which constitutes it as "actant."[59] In this "I" we may already recognize the hole that volition makes in language as it passes through. It is a linguistic effect of this passage, just as much as it is the opening (entrance and exit) giving this passerby, the subject that wills, the form of his linguistic "appearance." From this point of view, the "I" is language's other. It is what language always "forgets" and what makes the speaker forget language. Saying *volo*, opening that place of the subject, means entering that forgetfulness. The subject *is forgetfulness* of what language articulates. From the start, the "I" has the formal structure of ecstasy.

In a more discrete but insistent tradition, the "performance" of the subject is also taken to be marked by the "yes"—a "yes" as absolute as the *volo*, without objects, without goals. Whereas knowledge delimits its content through a procedure that is essentially a "no," a labor of making distinctions ("this is not that"), the mystic postulate advances a limitless "yes." Naturally, this is a postulate of principle, as independent of circumstances as the intention aimed at "all," "nothing" or "God." Its model is in the surprising statement of Saint Paul about Christ: "In Him there has been only Yes [*nai*]."[60] This paradox of a "yes" without limit in the compass of a singular (Jesus) outlines a contradictory and placeless theory of the (Christic) Subject. An infinite "yes" pierces the field of separations and distinctions practiced by the entire Hebraic epistemology. This "yes" is repeated later. The same historical lapsus (the same forgetting) recurs. In the seventeenth century, Angelus Silesius went even further. He identified the written expression of the Separated (*Jah*, or *Jahvé*) with the limitlessness of the "yes" (*Ja*). In the very place of the sole proper Name (a Name that distances all beings), he installs disappropriation (by a consent to all). The same phoneme (*Ja*) brings together separation and openness, the *No-Name* of the Other and the *Yes* of Volition, absolute separation and infinite acceptance.

> *Gott spricht nur immer Ja*
>
> God always says only Yes [or: I am][61]

There is identity between Christ's "yes" and the "I am" (the Other) of the burning bush. The Separated is reversed, becoming the exclusion of exclusion. Such is the cipher of the mystic subject. The "yes," a figure of "abandonment" or "detachment," is, ultimately, "interiority." In that land, a whole population of intentions cries out on all sides "yes, yes," like Silesius's God. Is that space divine or Nietzschean? The speaking word [*Wort*], originator of this place [*Ort*], participates in the "essence," which, according to Evagrius, "has no opposite."[62]

### THE LIE, OR THE FUNCTION OF SAYING

The *volo*, intended to make possible mystic speech and hearing, is therefore already both, and also their identity in a "yes." From this point of view, there is in language the function of the angel as the late medieval theories presented it: a pure speech act.[63] Again like the angel, the *volo* struggles against the lies and duplicity of discourse. It combats the equivocation insinuated by the enemy who, being diabolical, destroys communication. By hollowing out an "interior," the *volo* restores the possibility of mutual understanding or of "sym-bolization" in the name of the spoken word coming from *there*. It gives a *place* to the *speaking subject*. It is not so much a question of "wanting to say something" as of a volition out of which speech is born, or may be born: a volition that already contains the essential elements of all speaking. This volition does not have speech for object (as would be the case with a desire or a decision *to* speak). It defines the act of speaking. It *is* what all saying says: to say is to want. It poses the ethical principle of speech (as indetermination of volition: to say without knowing *what*), the ascetic rule (a loss of objects and goals) and the linguistic sign (the modal verb *volo* and its equivalents, "yes," "I," etc.). A beginning or childhood of saying emerges at the point at which the enrootedness of speech in an in-finite volition (the "inner yes") and its singular inscription within language (one little word to the exclusion of the rest; a "no" to all things) coincide. At the threshold of mystic discourse, an elsewhere is engraved upon language, like the naked footprint of a stranger on the shore of Robinson Crusoe's island. As a matter of fact, that "angelic" intervention does not win out over lies. It does not succeed in forcing them to retreat. Paradoxically, the intervention generalizes lying, as if, from an accidental illness, the lie were to become a structure of language. The *volo* does not, like the Cartesian *cogito*, initiate a field for clear and distinct propositions to which a truth value might be assigned. Far from making up a field of its own, it brings about a general metaphorization of language in the name of something that does not arise from language and that leaves its mark there. Instead of supposing that *there are lies somewhere*, and that by tracking them down and dislodging them a truth (and an innocence?) of language can be restored, the mystic preliminary posits an act that leads to the use of *all language as fallacious*. Taking the *volo* as one's point of departure, all statements "lie" in relation to what is said in saying. If there is understanding between speakers, it is not, then, based on an accepted truth but on a way of acting or speaking that uses language as an endless betrayal of the intention.[64] It is "taken for granted" between us—mystic discourse says in effect to its readers—that we use language as the metaphor of speaking subjects.

Thus the nature of lying is transformed. For the speaker, it no longer consists in *affirming one proposition* in place of another (such a problematics would be situated on the level of the statement), but rather in *being* language's *other*, indefinitely, which problematics concerns the speech act. It is no longer defined by the relationship of propositions to one another ($p$ is false because $p'$ is true) or to a set of external referents, but by the relation of the speaking subject to what he or she says. In this way, the lie ceases being the enemy that must be combated in order to affirm the truth. It is the strategic place in which "saying" is linked to what is "said."[65] It is the element in which mystic discourse is elaborated. Mystic discourse is itself split by the opposition between "discourse" (made up of a deceitful language) and "mystic" (relative to the question of the subject), and organized like an "inner" task within language. To reiterate, the lie is no longer that which, were it to be eliminated, would allow for a system of truth or an order of thought. It is the field in which the effects of utterance will be produced. Mystic discourse does not expel the demons of deception. Just as, in the past, monks would depart for the Egyptian desert to be, through their bodies, the operators of the Spirit on earth and the very tongue of the Deceiver, so this discourse is a spiritual practice of "the diabolical."

## Chapter Six

✠  ✠
✠

# The Institution of Speech

By that foundational act, the spiritual subject springs forth from the retreat or time lapse of the objects of the world. He is born from out of an exile. He is formed by wanting *nothing* and being but the respondent of the pure signifier "God" or "Yahweh," whose acronym, since the burning bush, has been the act of burning all the signs: I have no other name than what makes you leave![1] The initial expression of the spiritual is nothing but the decision to leave. This gesture also functions as a linguistic convention, since it adheres to a religious language in its focal and vanishing point (the signifier "God"). The *volo* concludes a contract with the speaker, a contract that transcends the (uncertain) terms of particular statements and affirms in a general way: "I stake my all on my language," or, what amounts to the same thing, "All my words go toward what they do not say." The putting at a distance of all possible content founds the "interiority" that will fray a path through historical and linguistic positivity. It seems to respond to the spoken word [*logion*] preserved in the Gospel according to Thomas: "Jesus said: Be passerby."[2]

## WHENCE TO SPEAK?

This preliminary is found throughout mystic literature, from Meister Eckhart to Benoit de Canfield (*Reigle de perfection*, 1608), Isabella Bellinzaga (*Breve Compendio*, 1611), or Madame Guyon (*Moyen court*, 1685). It delimits the field in which events will take place. Within that field, it makes possible the apparition of places, which will vary with the era. On the threshold of the *volo*, the beginner does not behold the same landscapes down through the centuries. Thus it is with the sign that increasingly marks, in the text, its place of utterance: "I." To the establishment of a convention with the addressees of discourse, there must be added the necessity, on the part of the sender (or author), the need to *found the place from which he or she speaks*. That place is guaranteed neither by authorized statements (or "authorities") supporting discourse nor by the social status of the speaker within the hierarchy of a dogmatic institution. This discourse, as "spiritual," is not accredited by virtue of its being a commentary on propositions (biblical, canonized, etc.) held to be true nor as being spoken from a position of authority (the chair of a professor, preacher, or specialist). Even if it uses these authorizations by quoting them, it does not posit those authorities as legitimizing powers, as the theological or pastoral discourse of the theologian or pastor does. Its value is derived from the sole fact of its being produced in the very place in which the Speaker, the Spirit, *el que habla*, speaks. It is authorized solely by being the locus of that "inspired" speech act, also designated by the term "experience." It claims to produce a present act of saying. In the text, the "I" increasingly becomes the index, at the same time as the instrument, of the question—an initial question—that mystic discourse must take up: who speaks, and whence?

Related developments, since the thirteenth century, have refined the usage of this I-sign, as a literature broke off from the institutions that authorized it. These elaborations are particularly bound up with poetic discourse, to which mystic forms of discourse are connected by so many characteristics. A progressive autonomy of the "I" may be observed. Thus, in the tradition of courtly love (or of *la fine amour*), the poems delimit more and more clearly the "I" of the speaker (subject or complement of the verb: *I* love her, she rejects *me*), and the prose commentaries gradually change the textual elucidations into stories about the life of the author.[3] The speech act (or its subject) becomes the system of reference for what is said. The "I speak" is the place of production that the poem spells out in autobiographical episodes (I have lost the woman I love, which is why I lament), the place the commentaries attempt to approach by accumulating biographical details about the poet. The text is transformed into successive revelations of its hidden center. It is made up of events that serve as metaphors for the poetic act itself. Tirelessly it recounts its own birth out of that surprising place, the "I," which is genesis of the spoken word, *poiesis*.

In mystic discourse, too, there is a narrativizing of the speaker, an endless circulation around that productive agency, that infinite and uninsured locus, the "I." But before writing stirs itself up into a seething "erosive focal point,"[4] it must break away from silence. Whence will it speak? Since institutions no more settle this basic question than do propositions handed down through tradition, it is the "I" that produces the openness. In the preface or prologue of the sixteenth- or seventeenth-century texts, the "I" serves as an introit to the writing. It is stationed at the threshold as if it were what produced the writing, like a voice that "sets its pitch" to bring about a linguistic body, but in this case the voice fades away—becoming an empty place, a hollow voice—into the body of writing to which it gives birth.

THE "I" PREFACING
*THE EXPERIMENTAL SCIENCE* (JEAN-JOSEPH SURIN)

The position of the "I" will become clearer, with all its reflections and reverberations, in a specific text. This work is already nearing the coast along which the mystic configuration will run aground at the end of the seventeenth century: the preface (unpublished) to *La Science expérimentale* (1663) by Jean-Joseph Surin. As the "foundation" of the autobiographical treatise in which a new "science" is exposited by the narration of a madness, the "I" is posited there as if resulting from an already long spiritual tradition, which it reveals. As an unstable and residual referent (in the text, it keeps "taking the place" of the "he," "Father Surin"), and polyvalent as well (is Surin a sick man, a mystic, a spiritual director?), this mobile "I" allows for the continual passage of the voice, taken over by a possession, to the level of a written production; from the tormented body to the didactic text; from suffering to an inner knowledge. It ensures the link between "experience" and "science," that is, the very status of the entire discourse.

If I begin by quoting that short preface, a program of writing, in its entirety, it is not just in order to present a first "case" in which an illocutionary mechanism may be observed. It is also to introduce the gap of an opacity—the singularity of a text—within the generality of analysis, and to give this fragment the possibility of rending the fabric of my commentary.

THE EXPERIMENTAL SCIENCE OF THE
THINGS OF THE NEXT LIFE
*Preface*

One can know about the things of the [mystic][5] future life in two ways, namely by faith and by experience. Faith is the common way that God has established for that, because the things of God and the future life are only known to us by hearsay and the preaching of the apostles. Experience is for the few. The apostles of Jesus Christ were of their number. Which is why they said: *Quod vidimus, quod audivimus, quod manus nostrae contrectaverunt de verbo vitae annuntiamus vobis;* and elsewhere: *Quod scimus loquimur, quod vidimus testamur.*[6]

In every century God has provided people who have had that experience in some measure. This century is no exception. For since theology agrees that by the possession of devils, supernatural objects—or at least objects beyond the human sphere—are declared to us, God having granted a famous possession to take place during this century and before our own eyes, in the middle of France,[7] we may say that things of the other life, hidden from our ordinary, common lights, have reached our senses. We can also tender these words: That which we have seen and heard and felt[8] with our hands of the future century, we announce to those who would read this work. That is why we have taken pen in hand to explain the extraordinary things we have experienced.

Yet all of this is in order to serve faith. For like the apostle Saint Peter in his Letter, having testified to the Christians about what he had seen on Mount Tabor and what he had heard from the voice of the Father, and saying that that came *a magnifica gloria,* he nonetheless prefers faith, to which he commends them, *sed firmiorem habemus propheticum sermonem cui benefacitis attendentes;*[9] all that we say we have seen and heard is only said to establish you in the faith that you have in the spoken word of the prophets, to whom you do well to make yourselves attentive, as to a torch lighting our darkness.

It is in the same spirit and with the same intent that these things that we have known through an adventure we have had during our century, and in which God's providence engaged us, are used in this discourse to affirm the faith we are engaged to profess by the Catholic religion, and to make us better Christians. All those to whom we speak in this book have an interest in these things. For them I would like to perform a service for eternity.[10]

This preface is in the difficult position, shared by many mystic "prologues," of having to establish a discourse that is in principle sustained solely by the "experience" of its speaker (*I*). Here it is not the institution that accredits the text. Deprived of the legitimacy that would be given to it by a social status (hierarchical, professorial, etc.), the author presents himself in the name of what speaks within him: the Real (in mystic discourse) or the Speaking Word (in prophetic discourse). But he still has to show that he is indeed in the very place from which he is presumed to speak. He must, by his text itself, make what founds his text believable. The qualification that is pertinent from a mystic point of view is not one derived from an institutional position. It is true that the same may be said to hold for a poem, a traveler's log, or a novel. But mystic texts also have to satisfy an ambition that is peculiar to them. Although they put themselves in a *different* position from that of the Church instruction ex cathedra, they claim nonetheless to bear witness to the *same* God. They have to prove, at one and the same time, that they speak from a *different* place (as "mystics") and that they draw on the *same* inspiration (as "Christians"). Though not emanating from the authorities, they must manifest the same Spirit as the authorities do. The spring born by surprise in the basement must bear the same Name as the house beneath which it appeared.

Frequently mystic writers neglect or abandon one or the other of these tasks. Sometimes they underscore their difference, to the detriment of their conformity with a certain Church tradition. At other times they emphasize their faithfulness, minimizing their distance from the criteria and rules of the institution. Between these two poles, an entire rhetorics is developed, which aims at maintaining the possibility, which for *mystics* is essential, of expressing the One and Only. We shall see how the combination of the mystic poem with its prose commentary, the former exempted from all authorization and the latter subject to Church approval, is one of the mystic ways of keeping these two contradictory tasks together by assigning a different mode of discourse to each. But the preface must deal with the work as a totality and establish the *position* of the whole within a geography of literary genres and contracts with the readers. Therefore, it reveals the textual operations that establish a topics of mystic speech act.

Surin's preface, intended to indicate and lend credibility to the place *from which* the text claims to speak, and which we have chosen as an example because of the dry precision of its movement, ties together a certain number of procedures (which are found in a good many other prologues). I enumerate four of them—threads loosed from the fabric:

(1) A distribution of *personal pronouns* (by order of appearance: *we, they, you, I*) makes possible, through two successive and decentered configurations leading from the *one* (at the beginning) to the *I* (at the end), a pronominal architecture of combinations that sets up the network of the illocutionary function. Schematically, *one* introduces (between "two ways") the disjunction on the basis of which the distribution is carried out. First, there is a traditional opposition between *they* (the apostles) and *we* (the believers). But *we* shifts toward the author ("we have taken pen in hand," "our experience") and stands in oppo-

sition from then on to *you* (the addressees). *We* then becomes the mask (*persona*) behind which the *I* at last appears. Thus the schema:

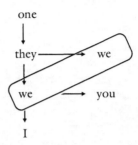

The slippage of the *we* allows for the passage from the *one* to the *I*, which will be the center of the text, sometimes as hero, sometimes author. It should also be noted that the pronominal positions of the first column (from *one* to *I*) *know* and say what is true, whereas the others *believe* it. The former mark the strata of "saying what is true": verisimilitude (*one*: the "of course," the "obvious," etc.), the apostles (*they*: a positive tradition), the author (*we*: "pen in hand"), and the *I* (the ultimately unsayable referent). There will be many tensions between these places of real utterances. Similarly, the ambivalence of the *we*, at once believing and mystical, already announces the author's strivings against lying: When is he in the place where the "word of life" [*verbum vitae*] is spoken?

(2) The use of *semantic oppositions* (faith versus experience, the past versus the present, much versus little, hearsay versus seeing, etc.) aims at containing these places, at framing them within a system of values by a sequence of alternatives (either this or that). Two types of distinction intersect here. One is *historical* or diachronic (the origin versus the present), with the mediation introduced by an intertime ("in every century"). That first distinction is reinforced by the two *linguistic* pairs opposing Latin quotations to their French paraphrases. The other distinction is *epistemological* and synchronic (experience versus faith) paralleled by a *numerical* distinction between "the few" (the apostles, "persons," "we") and many, and also by an *anthropological* distinction, which separates information gleaned through the hands, the eyes, the ears—through "our senses," in short—from information obtained through "hearsay."

It is a cleft structure organized by the principle of separation. This phenomenon is made all the more striking by the fact that in Surin it is the *writing* that both attests to and overcomes these divisions. The "book" produced by the "pen in hand" is a "work" of sewing between past and present, between experience and faith, the small number of witnesses and the crowd, the perceiving body and verbal knowledge. "I am here writing":[11] the act of writing symbolizes; a textualizing of the body (rather than the embodiment of meaning), ceaselessly it suffers and expresses what is divided. It is the present operation that re-ties. In this mystic text, as in many others, this "religion" (*re-ligio*, re-tying) concentrates within itself the belief, attention and interest normally attached to other institutions. It is the institution par excellence.

(3) The citation of a *historical body of evidence on the early days*, made up of founding "experiences" (Peter's vision on Mount Tabor, the ministry of the apostles, etc.) and canonical scripture (Saint John and Saint Paul), serves to establish a genealogy of the speech act—a genealogy concerning the act and place of speech, not the transmission or commentary on a specific content. The work of the text on this evidence advances in two phases, which are gone through twice, making four paragraphs. Two phases: first the reference to a historical time in the quotation, then its contemporary repetition by a new use or paraphrase of the quotation. The first time, that sequence posits the basis of the text, the experience, with the help of Saint John. The second time, the two phases indicate the intent of the text, which is faith, using Saint Peter. For here the discourse (like the traveler's account) derives its authority from an extraordinary "experience" (analogous to the *thōma* of Herodotus)[12] in order to produce a belief (an "ordinary") contrary to the other forms of discourse (by lawyers, politicians, preachers) that, on the basis of a belief, organize experience or practice. By the processing of a historical corpus, the primary opposition between experience and faith is transformed into the relation that the authorization (and content) of the text has to its purpose. Thus we have a four-part diagram:

| | CITATION<br>(past referred to) | REUSE<br>(present repetition) |
|---|---|---|
| I FOUNDATION:<br>*Experience*<br>(extraordinary) | 1. *St. John*:<br>the "living Word"<br>"quod manus nostrae<br>contrectaverunt" | 2. *The Possession*<br>*at Loudon*<br>"our hands have felt" |
| II FINALITY:<br>*Faith*<br>(ordinary) | 3. St. Peter:<br>From vision to faith<br>in the Spoken Word | 4. *The Book*<br>"to strengthen<br>faith" |

The transition from the original quote to its reuse does not obey the rules that define the relation between a textual authority and commentary on it. This hermeneutics is not that of the commentary, because it concerns the locus of utterance and knowledge, not the production or justification of meanings. Through the quoting of past experiences and writings associating Saint John with Saint Paul, a referential series is posited, of the type: see/touch → say/write → believe.

This sequence, being from the earlier times, serves as a theoretical model to the text that aims at ordering positions and functions. The reuse is intended to show that the sequence repeats itself in the present. The reiteration of the original experience in "this century" ("this one"), and the French paraphrase of the Latin scripture by the speaker ("we, too") serve to mediate between two historical figures of the same *formal series.*

It is because of the form, not the content, that there is continuity, even identity, between the past and the present. This has certain consequences. First, "apostolic times" are characterized by the combination between that form (which has archetypal value, even if it did occur historically) and contingent events (a content). They manifest for the first time a definitive structure of the Christian experience, but they are also connected with a past. To interpret those times is not to go back to a past moment and an authorized content in order to make them produce (dogmatic or historical) truths but to recognize the same form in the element of different events.

In this perspective, there is no longer any dependency linking the successive occupants of the same position in that series. The author of *La Science expérimentale* has the same authority as the first apostles. He can take their place. He is there "also." Similarly, his readers occupy the position of those who hear the apostles. Time, in this instance, does not hierarchize. It is not relevant from the point of view of the structure of the experience. Contrary to what occurs in theological or historical discourse, no essential value is placed on the past. Memory is above all the permanence of a form, to be recognized and manifested in every new present.

There is, however, a mark left by time upon content. The transition from the time of the apostles to the present era is marked by some modifications in the quotes from the early witnesses—differences that Surin does not feel the need to justify, since they are only signs of a different situation in which the same form recurs. They are the marks of facticity. They bring about a paraphrase of the original documents. There is no question of a "literal sense" (nor, therefore, of allegory either) here, where the point is to find the same "structure" through diverse "manifestations."[13] The author who is interested in the structural analysis of a formal sequence of experiences (or, as Ignatius of Loyola said, in a *discurso* of the Christian *conversar*)[14]—which is, properly speaking, the "spiritual sense" of the ancient texts—seems to have no hesitation in stating the historical differences. These variants concern two points, essentially: (a) in this century "a famous possession" replaces the speaking "Word of life"; (b) rather than to "announce," to write.

Time shifts the evangelical toward the diabolical and the spoken word toward the book. So we must wonder how God manifests Himself via the Liar and how the spoken word is produced in writing. These will be key issues in *La Science expérimentale*. The preface is content with noting that inversion as a fact and with situating the problem of spiritual/traditional revelation on the (more general?) plane of "things of the other life" or "supernatural objects." In any case, the original event was also ambiguous. The book's objective is to bring about the discernment of what "our senses" can perceive.

The preface, in setting up the formal path beginning with "what our hands have felt" and passing through "pen in hand," details the variants affecting the adventures of the hand. It makes that witnessing or producing hand a decisive actor with a history. It anticipates the story of the author. But the preface says nothing about the changes that would affect the third and final moment of the trajectory, faith. It seems, according to the text, that the same *act of believing* subtends the diversity of experience and modes of transmission. It is as if the "attention" and "interest" that characterized the faithful ear were to remain stable, as if it were a blank, an empty space to be filled. There is, between those diverse, mobile, active hands and that fixed ear, an odd remove. This suggests the division, dramatically lived through by Surin, between the outcast *I* of the witness and the unknown realm of the other. A madness haunts the scene in which the believing reader is a motionless phantom, necessary yet indeterminate.

(4) A progression of *modalities* (can, should, will) articulates the relationship to knowing/letting others know. It obeys a logical order (you can; furthermore, you should; so you are committed to, you will) in which the authorization to say and the intention of doing are privileged. It no longer reflects the form of experience but the movement of the preface itself. The first part is devoted to being able to say, the second to wanting to do, while "should" supplies the transition from one to the other: can → [should] → want to.

The succession of modals also has the function of progressively marking the difference between the text and its addressees by assigning different roles to each. The pronominal distribution is completed by a distribution of modalities. First comes *being able* (able to know, then say, and finally write), which, indefinite at first ("one can know"), is rapidly transferred to the benefit of the author ("we can know"). *Should* appears next, more discretely (in the guise of what "commits"), but in focusing on the readers ("you do well to"). The author is touched by duty ("should") only as a member of the Catholic Church, not as an author. On the other hand, his right to speak obliges his addressees to "be attentive." This maneuver has a double effect: the power ("can") of one brings about the duty ("should") of the others. Then the *will* ("want to") appears, reinforced by "intention," "is only said to," and so on. It is the author's prerogative. Further, the author, by the "service" he would like to perform for his readers, makes the latter into his debtors ("for eternity"?). Schematically, the modal checkerboard unfolds more or less as follows.

| | can (to be able) | | must (to have to) | to want to |
|---|---|---|---|---|
| author | to know ("one") | to say/write | | to perform a service |
| readers | | | to be attentive | |

On the author's part, there is a being able and wanting to do; on the part of the readers, there is a moral obligation. If the preface moves along a path that leads from the legitimacy of speaking to the intention of instructing, it ensures this transition by postulating an obligation on the readers' part (which also involves, secondarily, their interest). The readers' duty of expectancy, linking the two determining elements of the text, is what makes possible the author's will. On the latter's part, there is intent only in relation to a supposed expectation. That condition appears unquestionable: in fact, it is as fragile as it is fundamental. The readers' expectation is rather what the author *must* take for granted. But is he ever really sure, whatever the case may be with Surin himself, who has just emerged from twenty years of illness and isolation? The text of the preface, which has handled the affirmation with such aplomb up to this point, gives way at the last moment, when it finally introduces the *I* with the *volo*. The ultimate assertion is wounded by a hypothetical: "I would like to. . . ."

Doubtless the public, like the anonymous crowd in which the "mad-men for Christ" faded away, represents, for the mystic text, the real aspect of God sought after and presupposed by the solitary *oratio*; since, for the worshiper also, God *must* be there and "attentive" to the discourse addressed to him. Prayer counts on that expectation of the other.[15] But it is not sure of it. The worshiper may think he or she is not awaited and that God has turned away, as Surin was convinced for twenty years, believing himself to be damned. Similarly, the preface addressed to the readers seems like a prayer. While it makes a show of much certainty when speaking in the name of *we*, it becomes hesitant and troubled the moment it says *I*. At that point it no longer exorcises doubt. The *I* appears in its dependency on the other. *I* cannot express itself except in the desire emanating from elsewhere (rhetorically trans-formed into obligation on the readers' part). *I* speaks only if it is awaited (or loved), which is the riskiest thing in the world, even if, in principle, this very thing is guaranteed by the religious institution. Surin's madness was at first the violence of that improbable pass, the closing in of the *I* when it ceases believing itself to be awaited. The madness subsided (and he set himself to writing) when that isolation was transformed into the "extraordinary" surprise—inscribed on the body—of being called and heard somewhere. It is, he says, in that pos-sibility that one must believe, and he "takes pen in hand" to write it.

When the autonomy of the "inner," rendered explicit by the *volo*, is marked in language by a speaking *I*, it is an autonomy *bound* to what it is not. The *I* is not on its own. Its possibility of speaking depends, as with children, on a spoken word that precedes it and an expectation that it presupposes. The textual strategy that distributes and hier-archizes the illocutionary positions (the apostles, the author, the ad-dressees, etc.) finally arrives at this vanishing point, the *I*. With the *I*, speech only arises in the name of the other. The beginning of the mystic experience is thus to be found in the very operation (pedagog-ical and almost military) by which discourse takes up position. The entire complex of textual procedures seems to envelop—in order to protect its fragility or permit its (forbidden) avowal—the inner contra-diction of the speaker, or supposed "author." In the strong position of the text, the *I* is a sort of lapse. It is content with representing what speaks, or with taking the place of what prompts speech. It can only "take the place" constituted by others, the place founded by the past speech acts of the apostles and/or the place opened up by the "atten-tive" listening of believers. In these two forms (which themselves lead back to the divine Voice), the *I* speaks in the place of the other—in lieu of the other.

## THE FICTION OF THE SOUL,
## FOUNDATION OF *THE INTERIOR CASTLE*
## (TERESA OF AVILA)

To the extent that the world is no longer perceived as *spoken* by God, that it has become opacified, objectified, and detached from its supposed speaker, two orientations organize the ways of treating this new linguistic situation. One takes up the statements disorbed from the system that gave them the value of "spoken words" [ *"paroles"*], isolated from their Enunciator by history, to consider them as statements to be appraised and ordered according to internal truth criteria. The other focuses on the speech act itself, which made itself heard by faith: *I* speak, says God, and there is no one but me. The mystic is oriented according to this second perspective. Since the Speaking Word *must* exist even though it may become inaudible, he temporarily substitutes his speaking *I* for the inaccessible divine *I*. He makes this *I* into the representation of what is missing—a representation that marks the place of what it does not replace. Contradictory in nature, therefore, the speaking *I* (or writer) takes up the illocutionary function, but in the name of the Other. Like the position (also contradictory) of "author," the mystic sustains the question that cannot be forgotten but cannot be resolved either: that of the speaking subject. He "holds" this void in suspense.

This *I* who speaks in the place of (and instead of) the Other also requires a *space* of expression corresponding to what the world was in relation to the speech of God. A fiction of the world becomes the place in which a fiction of the speaking subject is produced—if by "fiction" we understand that which is substituted (provisionally) and represents (contradictorily) the cosmos that served as a language for the speaking creator. This figuration of space is also, then, located at the threshold of the mystic discourse. It opens, in an imaginary mode, a field for the development of this discourse. It makes a theater of operations possible. Thus it is the necessarily fictitious space of the discourse.

It also constitutes an internal theater. In an artificial field of representation, "objects" are articulable, the traces of a mute and ineffable interiority. In this displaced place, the metaphors of (secret) movements that do not take place (or space) are produced. What will manifest itself there, then, are the effects of a silence on a language that preceded the silence (language always precedes what is said in it). If one considers in the imaginary not primarily a lexicon (an iconic material, things seen or dreamt) but the *spatiality* that specifies all images, as well as the capacity that the imaginary has to produce a *scene* at a distance from the inner, immediate, undeveloped act; if one takes the imaginary to be space and, more than that, to be space-producing, then one can say that for the *volo* and the *I*, it is both their figuration (theater, metaphor, artifact) and their *illocutionary space* (the place of speaking for a speaking that has no place).

A speaking of what? Teresa of Avila specifies: of the *soul*. If the subject is an answer in search of what it is an answer to, this inner speaking is called "the soul." It is a speaking that does not know what it echoes. A "moaning," or a "murmur," whose space is lacking. In that respect, the soul is "the same thing" as "the spirit" ("el que habla"): "El alma y el espíritu son una misma cosa como lo es el sol y sus rayos," says Teresa.[16] This spirit is in search of a place, as vacant space, after the manner of the phantoms whose anxiety, while waiting to find a place of habitation, is told in the traditional legends or fantasy novels. The imaginary furnishes that spirit with a metaphorical locus, a "borrowed habitation."[17] It is a *fiction of the soul*, its production in a "mansion" not its own, the fictive place that makes possible the expression of a speaking that has no place of its own in which to make itself heard. This fiction might be defined as the image of an echo—the image, since it is spatial, like a page to be written upon, a circle to be played in, a garden to be walked in. But the soul, transported outside of itself in that borrowed space in which it can mark its movements, is itself but the inarticulable echo of an unknown Subject. In itself, the soul is silent, in that it is formed by being a response to that (God) which it does not know, in that it is the response to Unknownness: born of an Other and yet separated from that Other that would give it language, it is essentially believing and mute. Therefore, the image that offers the soul a space in which to speak can only be a fiction—an effect and an artifactor as Diego de Jesús said, a "turn" [*"tournure"*], a way of "turning" silence out from within, a "mystic sentence."

The fiction or configuration of the "dwelling" [*morada*] sets up a framework capable of representing at the same time the dialogical speech from which the believing subject (the *conversar*) springs forth, the inaudible speech that echoes this speech (the soul), and the language that brings to light these operations of the soul (the spiritual treatise). On these three accounts, it is, at the beginning of the *Moradas* [*The Interior Castle*], the sole "foundation" [*fundamento*] for a theory that simultaneously treats prayer, the soul, and mystic discourse. The fiction of the "inner castle," like the island of Thomas More's *Utopia*, does not concern the creation of an imaginary object but the opening of a space to saying, to the soul, and to a specific writing. It is a place for spoken words, a world of the soul and a framework of discourse. We will see that Teresa constantly passes from one theme to another, assimilating the soul to a "living book," or prayer to the movement of the soul, or else using the same spatial figure to order these three registers one after the other. In that respect, the "castle" does not merely make up a sole theater of representation for these three themes; it is a notational space that allows for the ordering of "modes" (or measures), parallelisms, and combinations from one to the other. It works like the projected geography of the lute in the tablatures of the period: positions on the six strings (or lines) made possible, by a system of letters, the production of songs for diverse "forms" of music and instruments. The castle with seven dwellings also organizes a formal space of transcription on which Teresa cartographs "melodies" played in turn, or simultaneously, on prayer, the soul, or the book. It conducts a concert.

Before quoting this beginning, which frames the spatial arrangement of the text, we must give an account of its position after another beginning: the opening of the *Moradas* (book I, chapter 1) is actually preceded by a "prologue" that specifies the place of the author and the circumstances of the production. This presentation also specifies what permits the book to be. But whereas in the first chapter the fiction of the castle is what makes the text possible, in the prologue what authorizes it is a received command. The opening move of the book: it will be a question of "things that obedience has commanded me to do"—*cosas que me ha mandado la obediencia.*[18] Is there competition between two authorities, one that "commands" (Doctor Velasquez, Teresa's confessor, and/or Father Jerónimo Gracián, her counselor) and the other that makes one write (the fiction, which "offers itself")? For Teresa, there is no contradiction. The "command" authorizes the author whereas the "fiction" allows discourse; the former comes from clerics while the latter is addressed to "sisters."

As in the preface to *La Science expérimentale,* the place from which to speak is here "framed." In her prologue, Teresa affirms, on one hand, her "will" [*voluntad*] to overcome the difficulty of the object to be treated (prayer) and the "weakness" of her body (headaches, infirmities, etc.) to comply with the demand made on her; on the other hand, in order to conform to "the Holy Roman Catholic Church" (about which she cannot judge on her own), she affirms her resolve to remain submissive [*sujeta*] to the opinion of "men of great learning" [*personas de grandes letras*]. There are, then, two elements: the strength of her will and the uncertainty of her knowledge. One is relative to the production of a work by the author; the other is relative to the judgment of her text by readers. Between these two poles the place of writing takes shape.

The first element concerns the work of writing. A "doing" [*hacer*] is the object that passes from the will of those who command to Teresa's will. "Do it," say the men of great learning: "write it." She answers: I want to do it, because the order comes from beyond them. Teresa does not hesitate: she must, she wants to, therefore she can. This "work" consists in losing something of one's own body in order for the text to be born, body-for-the-other. "Obedience," she says, "increases her headache," and so on. A pathos of the body inscribes its authenticating mark upon the will and pays for the scriptorial production. The "weakness" of this body [*flaqueza*] is aggravated by the suffering imposed upon it by the "strength" [*fuerza*] of her resolve. A pain certifies a childbirth in the bookish world in which the men of letters hope for a new writing. This feminine body, afflicted by its consent to the will which is communicated to it (like the angel's arrow in the statue by Bernini) by the message of the clerics, thus offers itself to its receiver like the first writing of Teresa: here is my body written/wounded by your desire.

The second element opposes her uncertainty of knowledge to the firmness of her will. For Teresa, it is no longer here a question of "doing" [*hacer*] the amorous work of writing but of "being" [*estar*] where she is awaited. How can I be sure it is really *there* that you want me to be or truly *that* that you want of me? It is a question of a meeting—the place and content of it. The will does not suffice; it must be enlightened. Henceforth what is "weak" is no longer the body but the text itself, the given response, the product of the labors. Teresa does not know. She is not sure of the place where she is, exposed to the perils as well as the intoxication of ecstasy. "Yo no sé lo que digo"[19]—I do not know *what* I am saying nor where I am. Whence has her "madness" transported her? She needs guardrails to tell whether she has inadvertently strayed out of, or whether she still remains within the region set out by the desires of "His Majesty." She has recourse to the *letrados*; she seeks out the purest ones, a permanent, almost obsessive concern; she counts on them to bring back her body wounded by love within the bounds of the field designated by the Scripture. Each time, their approbation is a "relief" [*alivio*] to her.[20] This tension between the speaking body and the scriptorial order was already characteristic of the *Libro de la vida*: an order of writing (the *libro*) does battle with the drifting and disorders of a passion (the *vida*). This autobiography is a theater made up of

Teresa's incessant "outbursts" ("dreams" and accesses of "madness"), followed each time by her "returns" to the place of meeting, decreed by an order ("let us return" . . . ). But bit by bit the order gives way, and in the last chapters, the amorous will goes off alone singing its "dreams" (Chapter 41). Similarly, at the threshold of the *Moradas*, we find a gallery of *letrados*, whose role it is to maintain the boundaries. As the writing, ecstatic, is about to escape, a recapture must be anticipated. The guardians of conformity to place can excise what strays too far. Teresa herself requests that her text be cut according to their judgment, just as her body is afflicted by their will.

She knows, however, that she has these *letrados* on a string (in spite of herself?). She becomes alarmed by her power and their pliability. She is therefore unsure of them as well. Their judgment is never any more than an opinion, what seems right to them [*parecer*]. So she always needs more "authorized" ones to certify to her that she has not unwittingly left the precincts. But their knowledge eludes the criteria of her experience. It is a knowledge both foreign and necessary to the "science" of which she speaks. It draws the boundary lines of the walls of the house, but in the form of a fluctuating border whose definition comes from the outside. Thus, once and for all, Teresa decided to submit to that necessary arbitrary, the law of writing, law of the other, law of the real.

The setting of the work is thus made up of (a) an order that derives the power to write from a price paid in physical suffering, and (b) a judgment that delimits what belongs within the Catholic space. It is a masculine setting. They are men, these same *letrados*, who both give the order and examine the product. But within this setting, a feminine discourse takes place: "mejor se entienden el lenguaje unas mujeres de otras"—"women understand better the language of other women." A plural. There is no longer an author but a language between women that love makes them understand: "El amor que me tienen les haría más al caso lo que yo les dijese"—the love they have for Teresa will inform them of what she is saying. A feminine circle, therefore—an inner one in this case—a circle in which the demand is collective and understanding shared. Between the command to *write* and the appreciation of the writing, both of which are masculine, the feminine act of *speaking* unfolds: "It is to these women that I shall speak [*hablar*] in what I am going to write [*escribir*]." The feminine spoken word insinuates itself within the masculine circumscription of writing. In the *compañía*, dear to Teresa, each sister understands that "when something comes to be said" [ *"cuando algo se atinare a decir"*] in this way, among women, it does not belong to an author—*no es mio*—but comes about through a speaking that escapes both individual appropriation and learned supervision. In this subtle combination, authority (of the Church) is masculine, as a social setting for the name of the father; the spoken word [*parole*] is feminine, as in the Jewish tradition of the *Shekinah*, a feminine figure of the Spirit that is speaking Word [*Parole*]. Teresa offers to that authority her body in travail and the text that it produces: it is *for them* [*pour eux*, masculine]. But the spoken word, a collective circulation, is *between them* [*entre elles*, feminine]: *between us*. The masculine authority dissects, circumscribes, orders, and judges *distinct* objects, but after all seems alien to the abundant and "indistinct"· speech that crosses over individual or scriptorial boundaries; it doubtless carries an implicit reference to the intensification of a feminine experience by that of the marranos. It is to this speech, to discourse itself, that a fiction will provide a "foundation."

Having made this clear, Teresa begins to speak in writing, to write in speaking. It is an oral text in fact, shot through with outbursts and breaks, interrupted by moments of impatience (that's not it, but, well, you know what I mean) and written in disconnected letters, with neither downstrokes nor upstrokes, hastily thrown on the paper like stones pulled loose, one after another, from the body of silence.[21] The moment in which the written body is produced. The moment in which it comes loose. All the witnesses say: Teresa did it *con gran velocidad*, "without stopping," the face "enflamed" (purple?), with blood rushing to the head.[22]

Moradas (Book I, Chapter 1)[23]
   While beseeching Our Lord today to speak for me, because I could find neither what to say nor how to begin to accomplish this obedience, there came to me that which I am going to say right away in order to begin with some foundation: to consider our soul [*alma*] as a castle made completely of diamond or very clear crystal, in which there are many dwellings,[24] just as in heaven there are many mansions.[25] Sisters, if we consider it well, the soul of the righteous man is nothing but a paradise in which, he says, He takes his delight.[26] Yes, how do you think the dwelling would be in which so powerful a King would take delight, so wise, such a pure one, so filled with all good things? As for myself, I cannot find anything to which to compare the great beauty of a soul and its great capacity. And truly our intellects, however acute they may be, can scarcely succeed in understanding the soul, just as they are unable to consider God, since He Himself says that He created us in his own image and likeness.[27] Well then, if it is thus, as in fact it is, there is no reason for us to tire ourselves out in trying to comprehend the beauty of this castle, because, given the fact that there is between the castle and God the same difference that there is between Creator and

creature, the castle is in fact a creature, it is sufficient that His Majesty say that it [the soul] is made in his image for us to be scarcely able to grasp [*entender*] the great dignity and beauty of the soul [*ánima*]. It is a great pity and confusion that by our own fault we should not understand [*entendamos*] ourselves nor know who we are. My daughters, would it not be great ignorance if someone were asked who he was and he didn't know, nor who his father or mother were, nor from what region [*tierra*] they came? Well, if that is great brutishness, ours is incomparably greater when we only try to know what [*que cosa*] we are in limiting ourselves to these bodies, while at the same time we know, in a general way, because we have heard it said and because our faith tells us so, that we have a soul. But what good qualities there may be in this soul, or who is within this soul, or its great value—this we rarely consider; nor do we give all our attention to trying to preserve its beauty. Everything engages us in the grossness of the mounting of the jewel or the outer wall of the castle, that is, in these bodies.

Well then, let us consider that this castle has, as I said, many dwellings, some above, some below, others on the sides. In the center, in the middle of all the others, is the most noble, the one in which things of great secrecy between God and the soul occur. It is necessary that you should be informed about this comparison. Perhaps, may God be served, I can, through it, give you to understand [*entender*] something of the favors that God, for his service, bestows upon souls and of the differences there are in them, as far as I have understood [*entendido*] that it is possible (no one can understand all of them, they are so numerous, and especially someone as wretched [*ruin*] as I am), because it will be a great consolation to you, when the Lord grants you such favors, to know that it is possible, and when He doesn't, to praise his great goodness. Just as it does not harm us to consider the things that are in heaven and that the blessed enjoy before we ourselves rejoice and try to attain what they enjoy, neither will it harm us to see that it is possible in this exile for so great a God to communicate with earthworms so full of foul odors, and that it is possible [for us] to love so good a goodness and such boundless mercy. . . .

Well then, to return to our beautiful and delightful castle, we need to see how we can enter it. It sounds as if I am saying something idiotic, because if this castle is the soul [*ánima*], it is obvious that there is no way to enter it because it is the same thing. Similarly, it would seem insane to tell someone to enter a room if he is [*estar*] already there. But you must understand [*entender*] that there are many ways of being there [*estar*]; and that many souls who are in the outer court of the castle, where those who guard it stay, have no desire to go into the interior, and they do not know what there is in such a precious place, nor who is inside, nor even what rooms there are. You have already heard, in some books on prayer, how the soul is advised to enter into itself; well, that is what it is.

A man of great learning [*letrado*] told me, a short while ago, that souls that do not pray are like a paralyzed or crippled body, which though it has feet and hands cannot control them. Those souls are exactly like that. There are souls that are so sick and inclined [*mostradas*] to dwell [*estarse*] among external things that there is no remedy, and they seem unable to enter into themselves. The soul, by becoming so accustomed to always being around the vermin and beasts that are in the precincts of the castle, has almost become like them; and though it is so rich by nature and can converse with none less than God, there is no remedy. And if these souls do not try to understand [*entender*] and cure their great misery, they remain transformed into pillars of salt for not having turned their heads toward themselves, as Lot's wife was for having turned hers.[28]

For, to the degree that I can understand [*entender*], the front door into this castle is prayer and consideration [*consideración*], I do not say any more mental than vocal: whatever prayer is, there must be consideration, because the sister who does not pay attention to whom she is speaking and what she is asking for, and who is asking, and from whom, I don't call that prayer, even if one moves the lips a lot.[29]

Rugged, rough-and-tumble sentences, torn by opposing impulses (I know, I don't know, etc.), punctuated with *pues* and *porque*, oral markers, sometimes of a hammering affirmation, sometimes of an appeal to the "sisters" who are right there, close by—thus begin the *Moradas*, which "are for *mystics* what Aristotle's *Logic* is for traditional philosophy."[30] This beginning, agitated by a plurality of modes of speaking, is not one of Teresa's "great literary texts," but it posits the foundation, relative to the initial question: "Who are you?" This treatise on the soul, prayer, and mystic discourse (or itinerary) is undoubtedly part of a long Socratic and spiritual tradition of the "know thyself,"[31] but it displaces that tradition from the outset in translating it into two other questions: "Who else lives inside of you?" and "To whom do you speak?" A problematic of being and consciousness is rerouted from the onset toward illocution, that is, toward a dialogal structure of alteration—"you are the other of yourself." The soul becomes the place in which that *separation of self from itself* prompts a *hospitality*, now "ascetic," now "mystic," that *makes room* for the other. And because that "other" is infinite, the soul is an infinite space in which to enter and receive visitors—"the Indies of God," said Francisco de Aldana:

> *¡Oh grandes! ¡Oh riquísimas conquistas*
> *de las Indias de Dios, de aquel mundo*
> *tan escondido a las humanas vistas!*

Whatever the sources were for the image of the castle in the *Moradas* (the third and fourth *Abecedario espiritual* by Francisco de Osuna, the *Subida del Monte Sion* by Bernardino de Laredo, etc.),[32] and the obvious references to the architectural symbolism of medieval thought[33] or to the imaginary spatial world of the novels of chivalry, which Teresa loved with a passion,[34] what is of consequence here is the use that the text makes of these things, which gives it the function of "beginning" and of "foundation" for the entire discourse. The image is transformed by the role Teresa assigns to it: it becomes the form of the theory by determining its space. In that respect, I will retain only three elements that have bearing on the mystic speech act: the crystal-castle is (a) a fiction that makes the reader believe in it; (b) the depiction of the soul as the place of the other; (c) the structure of a historicity (spiritual, discursive, etc.).

## A FICTION THAT MAKES THE READER BELIEVE IN IT

Whereas obedience does not suffice to make Teresa write (that "force" is, as it were, blind and encysted), a "comparison" gives her a "beginning." This shift opens a different field. It passes into a different genre. It is a metaphor. It occurs to her [*se ofreció*] and speaks "in place of" Teresa [*por mí*]—which is the very definition of the soul. Something from the other speaks in her and makes her speak. But that *other* is *nothing*, only an image, analogous to the "dreams" that people the *Libro de la vida*. True, since Diego de Yepes,[35] exegetes have attempted (without being convincing) to change that "comparison" into a "vision" and have tried to leaven that image with supernatural reality. The text itself says nothing of the sort. It has nothing to do with miracles. At the beginning, there is a fiction, analogous to a dream.[36] As on so many other occasions with Teresa, this "nothing," an idea, a symbol, permits her to write. *Fabrica spiritualis* or *spirituale aedificium*, fiction authorizes writing.

This space-creating authority fulfills the function of the quotation. It takes the place of the erstwhile "authorities" who did, in fact, make writing possible. But for Teresa, even if the castle is an image in which reminiscences (biblical, literary, etc.) are piled high, it "offers itself" as a space at once other and inner. It does not recall the (masculine?) gesture of "throwing" *outside* a *fragment* of oneself, an expelled, ejaculated object, which becomes the irreducible exteriority of being to itself.[37] With neither ejection nor fragmentation, it is a *totality* that is represented here, which is the infinite dimension of an inner foreignness. From this point of view the castle, an evocation of the internal Shadow, has an authorizing function. "Love can be made only among three," as Marguerite Duras said. The "comparison" is this third party —a symbolism (imaginary) that creates the place (without ob-jectivity) of communication. It is the scene, the third position, without which there is no *conversar* but only the silence of Teresa's finding "neither what to say nor how to begin."

Therefore, the writing born of this "dream" applies itself to emphasizing its beauty, *la hermosura de este castillo*. It is *todo de un diamante y muy claro cristal*. Nowhere is it a question of its truth. The "comparison" is doubtless to Teresa the equivalent of what the poem is to John of the Cross or Surin. Beautiful is what being does not authorize, what is valid without being accredited by the real. Thus "Beauty" in Mallarmé, identical to "Belief," is pure beginning. It is what no reality sustains: "She who ruins being, Beauty."[38] In this respect the aesthetic and the ethical gestures coincide: they reject the authority of the fact. They are not based on it. They transgress the social "convention" that wants "reality" to be the law. They oppose to this an atopical, revolutionary, "poietic" nothing, without which for Teresa there are nothing but bodies and a "brutishness." They consist in believing that there is some other, a "foundation" of faith.

### THE SELF, AS PLACE OF THE OTHER

It is, then, useless to "tire ourselves out in trying to comprehend the beauty" of this diamond that, like Marcel Duchamp's "Glass," is unbreakable and closed in upon itself like a precious stone, but transparent and open to light, as if offering it almost no resistance, and countable (seven), plural like a mathematical object. In this "enchanted castle,"[39] the forms of former dreams also proliferate. They sparkle in this translucent jewel like the fires of a thousand and one memories: models of the biblical Jerusalem (an apocalyptic image) or the Jewish one (messianic images of the return, so obsessive at that time among the marranos or the exiled); models of paradise (images of the origin), of the garden of pleasures (an erotics and an aesthetics), of the heavens (cosmological and astrological images); fictions of perfect architectures (mathematical and geometrical images),[40] military spaces (so frequent in Teresa), romanesque spaces (the chivalry of yore), and so on. With all these facets of the world, the soul shines, a new microcosm, an encyclopedia of histories.

This lovely object, one yet multiple, is nevertheless split into two opposing aspects: now crystal and diamond, now castle. The comparison oscillates between the untouched and the historical. That division quietly introduces into the mental icon the possibility of the text, which will play one against the other, developing the "surprises" of an itinerary through the castle and bringing these metaphors, or discursive transports, back to their mineral center. It is the work of division. The image, by its ambivalence, creates the movement; it incites to write, while at the same time positing the principle of the impossible identity. It is reducible *neither* to the castle *nor* to the diamond. It is itself already a play of in-between, a *Zwischenraum*. It is the same with the relationship that obtains, in so many mystic authors (John of the Cross is but the most famous example), between the poem and prose. There is unceasing return from one to the other. One must constantly go back through the story (the asceticism) analyzed by the (supposed) commentary in order to accede to the sonorous garden of the one and only. On the other side, the poem, corresponding to the primary function of the Teresian fiction, never ceases opening up new fields for history to walk through on its way to the prose of the world. This dichotomy is comparable to the mists that haunt certain rock crystals and trouble the immemorial by the shadow of time that it lacked. There is insinuation of the other as far as into the icon that represents the Other. An abyss of alteration: it goes on repeating itself from image to image, from mirror to mirror.

Another form of the alterity is marked by the "treats" [*regalos*] the castle-crystal offers. Here, too, the image, beautiful in itself (Teresa is overjoyed), an object of pleasure, is indicative of all the "delights" [*deleites*] that the King finds in his palace and that the soul finds in his company. Teresa's vocabulary spells out with precision, with a sort of gourmandise, the various kinds of sweet things to be found in this place: "tastes" [*gustos*], which relate to the mouth and are of the cognitive order; "delights" [*deleites*], sentient joys, of more tactile nature; "treats" [*regalos*], more delicate and more emotive; and so on. The body becomes the organ of all these spiritual "favors" and "graces"; it is played upon with these keys; it becomes their language. And this is for you, says Teresa to her sisters. "Despite the small enclosure in which you live," "you will revel," and "without permission of the superiors, you will be able to enter and go for a walk at whatever hour."[41] One can always enter the garden of love.[42]

To the question "Who am I?" enjoyment responds. Pleasure (as well as pain), a different space, introduced by fiction or a dream, is a mark of the other, the wound of his passage. It is an illegible writing, because it does not become separated from the one who feels it, but a writing that certifies by pleasure the alteration in which ex-istence consists. It is the voice, here, that is in a state of expectation; it calls, while waiting for the body to become the writing of the other—a body all the more blind, deprived of vision and knowledge, as the mad surprise of being "touched" is more profoundly engraved in it. Thus Teresa is like "someone who, candle in hand, is going to the death he desires, enjoying that agony with more delectation than can be said." She still dreams, romantic that she is, beneath the disguise of the masculine and, as it were, the theater of her last moments, the "agony" that she lives, "glorious unreason" [*glorioso desatino*], "celestial madness" [*celestial locura*].[43]

That mute ecstasy fills the void opened up by the "know thyself." It suppresses the discursivity of the *conversar*. It is no longer one nor the other but a third, the other of the other. It has a function parallel to that of the "comparison," having itself constituted the in-between of an essential, the soul. It also makes violence ("agony") and pleasure ("delectation") coincide, in the manner in which Louis Chardon was to describe the struggle of Jacob with the angel, a "war" that little by little turns into a nocturnal embrace: "They embrace, grapple with one another, and clasp one another," they become attached, they can no longer separate from one another, alienated and sustained one by the other.[44] *Where* are they?

## THE STRUCTURE OF DISCOURSE

But we must leave the non-place. Like the symbol of the castle, ecstasy itself is but a metaphor. There is "comparison," or ecstasy, only because one leaves it. As divergence and as divided in itself, the castle is a principle that makes possible the construction of a "story of the soul," that is, its discourse, if one does not lose sight of its being equally crystal and diamond. This opposition between the plural and the one, or between the detour of the metaphor and the return to the events, is but a reflection of the contradictions that make up this "marvelous" jewel, as was the philosopher's stone. One must enter it while already being there. Its center is equally its transcendental vanishing point, an exteriority. This sealed off area, sheltered from the "brutishness" of souls that have lowered themselves to corporeal life, is a place of enjoyment whose vocabulary is entirely corporeal. This is why the castle-crystal cannot be represented. Despite the attempts that have been made (and God knows how numerous they are), it cannot be drawn or projected onto a blueprint. It is not an image but a *discourse* (imaginary). In itself, it is a *coincidatio oppositorum*, the coincidence of opposites. It already has a narrative structure. Thus, the following analysis does no more than unfold the paradoxical place that it already constitutes.

But it is the same for the soul. Its contradictions entail a historical chain of events in which the succession of possible combinations between its elements will appear. It cannot be understood per se except by its *discurso* (a succession of events) and as discourse. And when Teresa produces this history, a progressive narration of these configurations of opposites, she finally reproduces the initial castle. Her text itself is the jewel that brings these opposites into play and "orders" them in function of what cannot be there [*estar*], unless it be in metaphors and passages. In this way, she can equally affirm that the castle is the book or the soul, that she is the author or that God is [*no es mio*], and that she is speaking of the writing, the soul, or prayer.

An analysis should be conducted of the differences between the Teresian castle and the innumerable "love palaces," "gardens," "retreats," "fortresses," "bubbles," and so on, all of which pertained, for Teresa's contemporaries, to the same question about the subject. Jean-Baptiste van Helmont wondered "quaenam in me esset Egoitas."[45] Far afield, the same appeal to the dream and the same imagery of the "inner castle" was in use. The "castle of health" that Robert Flud drew as a frontispiece to his *Integrum morborum mysterium*,[46] for example, is typical. But two essential differences become increasingly pronounced. One consists in making the image univocal (by making it into a map) and therefore isolating it from the operations that it represents or makes possible, whereas in Teresa the *comparación* is equivocal because it is an integral part of the contradictions and movements of which it is the working out. The other essential difference, one that will find expression in the myth of *Robinson Crusoe*, changes the process of alteration by pleasure (or pain) into one of appropriation by production (the writing of the island):[47] it is still about the subject, but the economic subject displaces the mystic one. The island factory replaces the garden of delights. The figure of the *I*, which always constructs a biographical novel, has become autonomized from what constituted it other than itself.

# · IV ·

# Figures
# of the
# Wildman

In the sixteenth century, the "castle" or "retreat" instituted a place of illocution; in the seventeenth, it underwent the transformations of establishment. The part that broke away in the form of isolated foundations of "new worlds" was either relocated in recognized abodes or relegated to the fringe of a new order. This separation reflected the inner division of the movement of the spirituals, the majority of whom became civilized while the others disappeared or were cast in the form of delinquency, soon destined to exoticism or exploitation. The initial great debates grew calm, retrenching on well-established positions that derived their legitimacy from the veterans and/or eliminated them. These second- (or third-)generation phenomena must also be analyzed, whatever the new formations that were proliferating during the same period may be. It is the problem Hannah Arendt raised, apropos of the second generation revolutionaries. What form did the mystic word take when religious orders and a science took it over? The following samplings have been taken from the period 1600–1660. They are relevant to the contradictory situation of a mystic "tradition," or, if you will, the repetition of the act of beginning within the place it constituted.

From a different angle, this section is about "wildmen." In the history leading from the mystic subject of the sixteenth century to the economic subject, the wildman represents an intermediary stage. As a cultural (or even epistemological) figure, he prepares for the latter by inverting the former and, at the end of the eighteenth century, he disappears, to be replaced by the primitive, the colonized, or the mentally deficient. In the seventeenth century, he is posited in opposition to the values of work, scriptorial economy, and territorial or social classification, which were being established by the exclusion of their opposites: he is without productivity, letters, or place and "condition." The mystics clothe themselves in this character as a clown puts on a costume, in order to find an outlet in the society that created him. He is an ambiguous actor, a transitional figure. He seduces (he turns from the path), but already with a touch of nostalgia. He traverses but no longer threatens the established order. He retains and even acquires symbolic value, as he ceases to command an organized force. He bears witness to another "world," but if he is arrested and tried, it is for transgression in this one. The great sociopolitical struggles (the *Frondes*, the *jacqueries*, etc.) no longer pass through his mediation. He plays a role exclusively in the institutions of meaning, in relation to a politics of the symbolic (in the churches and the orders), or in areas like the Cévennes, where the wars are still religious ones. In this respect, he really belongs to two worlds: he lives out a past reformism in a new sociopolitical order. He is in transit and bears witness to the passage from one world to another.

The forms of the wildman are multiple. He appears as the embodiment of "popular" wisdom in contrast with the networks of the "civility" and the professionalization of knowledge; as an "extraordinary" case in comparison with a normalizing of behavior and methods; as an aimless drifting within the space divided by the established Churches or the States that emerged from the old Christendom; and so on. The following examples represent no more than a few variants: the illiterate but enlightened man, later transformed into the legendary figure of the shepherd; the "little" heroes of the reform in an order, that of the Jesuits, which had won the reputation of being the official army of the post-Tridentine reformation; the wandering prophet of a message for which there is no longer a place. These are the modest histories of *mystics*, at a time in which it had gone underground and was wearing itself out in contest with institutions that have hidden its traces. During this period, mystic texts are no longer circulating freely everywhere;

rather, they have been turned into secret files. What happened to the son of a baker from Le Havre, some young religious zealots in Bordeaux, or Labadie traveling up through Europe from Guyenne to Denmark in search of a Church—this is not part of major literature; it belongs instead to a minor genre: detective stories of *mystics*.

Yet with these untamed spoken words, half lost along country roads and in back-room talk behind the scenes of history, something very old returns. The baker's son is the return of the "Friend of God," that poor layman whom Tauler presented as his master, or of the "Idiotus" celebrated by Nicholas of Cusa, or even of the nameless "idiot woman." The group of Bordeaux reformers repeats, in short, the adventure of the original founders of the Society of Jesus. They are their twins, but eventually they fail and are expelled from the heritage left by the founders. For all that, they are nonetheless members of a dynasty of spiritual pioneers. Labadie also belongs to the family of the prophets that counts Jan Hus and Luther among its members. He is a descendant of theirs, and also a mystic by the experience he relates, but he traces out both in his meandering travels and his innumerable texts the emblem of his unbearable disappointments. Is it the fault of the times? Is it their own? In any case, these different dynasties converge upon a central figure, the "wildman," that brilliant invention of the fourteenth and fifteenth centuries that preceded (and probably helped to shape) the Western discovery of the "savages" of the New World in the sixteenth century.[1] In this case, discourse once again preceded and prepared experience. Despite the variety of its representations, it presents the silhouette of untamed desire, now cruel, now seductive, issuing forth from the forests to haunt the marketplaces and homes, while a fledgling bourgeoisie learns the asceticism of a productive rationality. The wildman or wildwoman introduces on the level of symbolism what the city had exorcised, at a time when carnivals, excluded from town life as being too wasteful, reappeared in the form of sorcerers' and witches' nocturnal sabbaths. It is not surprising that a mystic discourse of irrational desires, repressed by the reason of State that served as a model to so many institutions, should also reappear in the figure of the wildman. In that form, he appears—he can only appear—as defeated. But this defeated figure speaks of that which cannot be forgotten.

*Chapter Seven*

✠　✠
✠

# The Enlightened Illiterate

The first dated letter of Jean-Joseph Surin (1630), which is also his first published text, marks the entrance of a bipartite personality. This account of a conversation with "the young man in the coach" presents two actors. It is hard to tell whether they are just one person, Surin and his shadow (his "angel," as he says), more real and more true than he is himself, or really two. Like the mystic phrase in Diego de Jesús, it is a cleft unity, apparently an "oxymoronic" apparition. It would appear that the mystic actor creates in narration the same structure that the mystic "word" creates in theory. In that form, which is more usual in the fantasy novel, Surin comes out of the "desert" in the "third year," that is, the third year of the novitiate, which, in the Society of Jesus, ended the process of a long formation that had begun with two initial years of retreat. He comes forth, "bearing a heart abstracted, solitary, estranged, incapable of getting along and adjusting to the ways of this land we consider to be an exile."[2]

It is only a letter, yet it sounds like a manifesto. His correspondents understood this: they showed it around, recopied it, distributed it. The "account of the young man in the coach" quickly made its way through France. It crossed the borders; soon it was published, and editions proliferated: four in Mons prior to 1649, four in Paris (1648, 1649, 1650, 1661), three in Lyon (1658, 1665, 1668), one in Malines (1648), one in Rouen (1649), one in Liège (1657), one in Brussels

(1661), one in Antwerp (before 1690), one in Cologne (1690), and doubtless many others (that we have not yet tracked down), prior to the editions (which in turn became classic and were often reedited) of the *Lettres spirituelles* in Nantes (1695) and Paris (1698). To try to follow the secret travels, reapparitions, and metamorphoses of a letter that, in the words of one of its first editors, "has passed through so many hands, and so many copies of which have been printed, that there is no longer any way of going back to the original"[3]—to trace, as well, the varied and successive milieus that carry out the diffusion of this text but betray themselves by correcting it, some amount of detail will be necessary. But the substrata of a critical apparatus constitutes a history of mentalities. It brings out, like a photograph, the stratification of superimposed readings, their combinations and interplay, which probably obey the same rules as complex combinations of historical and social strata within one sole period. It relates back, too, to the history and legend of the relations between the illiterate figure (who is sometimes one "not knowing," sometimes "of the people") and mystic "science."

Here, to begin with, is a version ("critical," of course) of the text that may be proposed:

My reverend fathers,

I wish I had enough strength to write out in full detail, and enough enlightenment to express well how felicitously our Lord received me as I left my region to encounter a thing of worth that it would be impossible for me to value too highly, that is, a soul of the rarest sort I have ever known, and from whom I have learned marvelous secrets. I found in the coach, placed very close to me, a young boy of eighteen or nineteen, simple and extremely crude of speech, totally unlettered, having spent his life serving a priest; but in all other respects filled with all manner of graces and such lofty inner gifts as I have never seen the like. He had never been instructed by anyone but God in the spiritual life, and yet he spoke to me about it with such sublimity and solidity that all I have read or heard is nothing compared to what he told me.

When I first discovered this treasure, I separated myself from the group to be with him as much as I could, taking all my meals and conducting all my conversation with him. Apart from our discussions, he was continually in prayer, in which he was so sublime that his beginnings were ecstasies that were, according to him, imperfections from which our Lord had freed him. The fundamental traits of his soul are a great simplicity, humility, and purity. And thanks to his simplicity, I learned many wonders, however many others his humility may have hidden from me.

I set him talking on all the points of the spiritual life I could think of for three days, as much in the area of practice as speculation, and I received answers that left me filled with astonishment. As soon as he became aware of what he was telling me, he wanted to throw himself down at my feet in humiliation, for we often alighted from the coach in order to be able to talk more comfortably and with less distraction. He thinks himself one of the world's worst sinners, and begged me to believe him.

He spoke to me almost the entire morning on the various states of the most perfect union with God, of the communications of the three divine Persons with the soul, of the incomprehensible familiarity of God with pure souls, of the secrets God had allowed him to know concerning his attributes, and particularly his justice upon the souls who do not advance to perfection though they desire to do so, and the various orders of angels and saints. He told me, among other things, that he would not give up a single communication that God makes to him about himself in the course of communion for what the angels in the state of glory and all men might give him combined. He told me that a soul disposed in purity was so possessed by God that it kept all of its movements within his power, even those of the body, with the exception of certain little deviations in which the soul sinned. These are his own words.

He told me that, to the extent that a soul was more in a hurry to attain perfection, it was necessary to do violence to oneself; that it was entirely the fault of the religious if they were not all perfect; people didn't persevere in conquering themselves; the greatest misfortune was that people did not bear up well under bodily suffering and infirmities, in which God had great designs, and he unites with the soul through pain much more perfectly than by great delight; too great care for health is a great obstacle; true prayer consists not in receiving from God but giving to him, and after having received, giving back to him by love; when tranquility of soul and flaming love attains rapture, faithfulness of soul at that moment consists in divesting herself of all, as God approaches to fill her.

I proposed all the difficulties of my inner self to him—by means of a third party, for otherwise I would have not been able to draw anything from him. In which he satisfied me in such a manner that I thought he was an angel, and that suspicion remained until he asked me, at Pontoise, for confession and communion: for the sacraments are not for angels.

He never agreed to promise to pray to God for me, but said he would do what he could; it didn't depend on him.

I asked if he was devoted to Saint Joseph. He said he had been his protector for six years, that God himself had given him to that saint, without his consulting anyone. He added that he had clearly recognized this holy patriarch to be the greatest of all the saints, after the Virgin; he had the fullness of the Holy Ghost far differently from the apostles; that he ruled souls whose virtue must be hidden in this world, as his had been; he was so little known; in compensation, God willed that only extremely pure souls be enlightened as to his greatness. He also said Saint Joseph had been a man of great silence; in the house of our Lord, he spoke little, but our Lady even less and our Lord still less than either of them; his eyes taught him enough things without the Lord's speaking. In short, he told me such a great number of good thoughts that I am not equal to writing them down. And I am sure that those three days have been worth many years of my life.

What I found particularly remarkable about this lad was an admirable wisdom and an extraordinary efficacity in his words. He told me the supernatural light that God pours into a soul lets it see all it should do more clearly than the sunlight shows sensible objects; and the multitude of things the soul discovers within is much greater than everything in corporeal nature; God in all his grandeur dwells and makes his presence felt in the heart that is pure, lowly, simple, and devoted.

When I pressed him to tell me whether someone had not taught him after all, he told me no, and said that there were some souls that could only be harmed by creatures. Even if the Gospel were to perish, God had taught him enough of it for his salvation. To these souls, God was ever present; in them dwelled nothing but him, and when they dealt charitably with their neighbor, they received very high workings; and even, during the night, when one must sleep, these souls lose but little time. And I asked him how it was that this took place; then he told me that I knew better than he did and that he was the most ignorant of all, and that our Lord had taught him particularly to excuse his neighbor and not be easily outraged.

He told me of wonders for the consolation and direction of a soul that, attracted to prayer and desirous of virtue, is held back by physical infirmities; God requires of it a most angelic patience—after which, if it remained devoted, it would atone for everything in one hour. One of the loftiest discourses was how God works within souls through the Word, and the relations they must have to God through the Word in all of their dispositions, even in their sufferings.

He told me the men of our profession who do not struggle against the pleasure of being praised by the world will never taste the joys of God; they are thieves; their darkness will ever increase; the slightest little trifle clouds the soul; what prevents the soul's freedom is a certain habitual dissimulation that holds it back. I use his own terms.

At last I took leave of him as he begged me a thousand pardons for having spoken with such pride, he who was so crude [and destined] to praise God and honor him, in the eyes of man, by humility only with simplicity, and not by spoken words; God obligates souls to secrecy and silence regarding the familiarities he grants them. I had to be very industrious, pretending to attribute no importance to him and persuading him that he was obligated by charity to converse with me by making some contribution on his part, since I couldn't talk all the time. And so he let himself go, and, being all ablaze with love, made no more objections but spoke on, following the impetuosity of his mind. As soon as I charged him to pray for me, he became less trusting and more on his guard. But being extremely simple and thinking himself the least of men, he revealed more of himself than he thought.

I am your etc.[4]

The manuscripts and old editions give either a short, primitive version, which I call "Northern"; a long, much later version; or an intermediary version, the latter two representing a "Southern" tradition. Here is a list of them, with capital letters referring to manuscripts and small letters designating the main editions.

### A. Attestations of the "Northern" tradition
MANUSCRIPTS

$R^1$: Chantilly, Archives. S.J., Collection Rybeyrete, no. 190, *Copie d'une lettre écrite par un père jésuite à ses confrères au collège de la Flesche.* [before 1640]

$P^1$: Paris, Bibliothèque Nationale, Fds fr. 19231, fols. 131r–132v, *Copie de la lettre du R. P. Seurin Jésuite à ses confrères du collège de la Flèche en forme de conférence.* [Seventeenth century. Reproduces a copy of 5 January 1631]

$B^1$: Brussels, Bibliothèque Royale, 2459, fols. 1–11, *Gheestelyck Discours van den Eerw. P. Surin van de Societeyt Iesu . . . met een ionghman oudt tusschen achtien ende negentien iaren.* [mid-seventeenth century]

S: Semoine, parish records, communal collection, cover of 1718 register, *Lettre du Père Burin.* (Guillaume was in charge of this parish near Arcis-sur-Aube from 1700 to 1730.)

PRINTED SOURCES

Le berger illuminé, ou colloque spirituel d'un dévot ecclésiastique et d'un berger. (Mons: de la Bruyère, 1648). See Bibl. cathol. Neerlandica, nos. 10260 and 10261. This is a fourth edition.

Gheestelijcke T'samen spreeckinghe tuss'chen eenen devoten persoon, ende eenen Scaephaerder . . . (Malines: Veuve Jaye, 1648). At Antwerp, Bibliotheek van het Ruusbroec-Genootschap.

Les secrets de la vie spirituelle Enseignez par Jésus-Christ à une Âme dévote, et par un berger à un bon religieux, en forme de conférence spirituelle. (Paris: S. Piquet, 1648), pp. 125–34. See Sommervogel, 3:581, no. 5.

Les secrets de la vie spirituelle . . . (Paris: S. Piquet, 1649). At Chantilly, SJ Library, W. 115.

Les secrets de la vie spirituelle . . . (Rouen: J. Besogne, *1644* [= 1649]). Private library of Louis Cognet.

Les secrets de la vie spirituelle . . . (Paris: S. Piquet, 1650). At Chantilly, SJ Library.

Colloque spirituel . . . (Liège: Tournay, 1657). See X. de Theux de Montjardin, Bibliographie liégeoise, and Bibl. cathol. Neerlandica, no. 11379.

Les secrets de la vie spirituelle . . . (Lyon: N. Vetet, 1658; according to the 1668 Lyon edition).

Les secrets de la vie spirituelle . . . (Paris, S. Huré, 1661). In Paris, Bibliothèque Nationale, D. 40063 and D. 51848; in Chantilly, SJ Library, E. 925.

Les secrets de la vie spirituelle . . . (Brussels: F. Foppens, 1661). In Chantilly, SJ Library, W. 115.

Les secrets de la vie spirituelle . . . (Lyon: P. Compagnon, 1665). In Lyon-Fourvière, SJ Library, 23678/6.

Les secrets de la vie spirituelle . . . (Lyon: Cl. Chancey, 1668). In Lyon, Municipal Library, 805615.

Le berger illuminé, Flemish edition (Antwerp, before 1690), according to Pierre Poiret.

Le berger illuminé, ou entretien spirituel d'un berger et d'un ecclésiastique, in [Poiret], La Théologie du coeur (Cologne: J. de la Pierre, 1690), 1:5–13.

## B. Attestations of the "Southern" tradition

MANUSCRIPTS

Ca: Carpentras, Municipal Library, MS 1816, fols 497–98, *1635. P. Surin, jésuite. Copie d'une lettre du Père Surin jésuite de la province de Paris.*
N: Paris, Bibliothèque Nationale, Fds fr. 24809, *Lettres pieuses du R. P. J.-J. Surin,* vol. 1, fols. 1–27, [end of seventeenth century]

PRINTED SOURCES:

c: Lettres spirituelles, by ***, vol. 1. (Nantes: J. Mareschal, 1695), pp. 1–16. In Paris, Bibl. S.J. des Études, J. 20.
$c^2$: Lettres spirituelles by ***, vol. 1 (Paris: E. Couterot, 1698). In Lyon, 334.265.

## TEXTUAL HISTORIES (1630–90)
### A "SOUTHERN" TRADITION

In the absence of the autograph, which would have provided a *terminus a quo* for this story, it is preferable to begin at the end: the letter "to Father Lallemant on the meeting of a young man marvelously enlightened in spiritual life," edited by Pierre Champion in Nantes in 1695.[5] His text is identical to that of a Paris manuscript from the end of the seventeenth century,[6] with the exception of a moment of distraction and especially an inversion,[7] probably caused by a misplaced sheet in the copy used by the transcriber (N). Since Champion did not reproduce that order, which in itself is as likely as his, we may conclude that he used a different copy of the same text. The Paris manuscript (N) comes from the Foreign Missions,[8] and since it resembles letters whose recipients often live in the region of Bordeaux, it is probably a collection assembled by Anne Buignon, a religious of Our Lady in Poitiers, closely allied with the Jesuits—the same collection she had sent to Paris in hopes of it being printed by the good offices of Messires Vincent de Meur and François Bézard, both directors of the Seminary of Foreign Missions, and by M. Philippe Aubery, who had "amassed in Bordeaux and elsewhere" writings by Surin.[9] The project failed, and the manuscript was later sent to Champion, after one copy was made, which would be the one kept in Paris. This text, then, leads us southward: to Poitiers and Bordeaux, around 1670, before the death of Vincent de Meur (1668), who often saw Madame la présidente de Pontac in Paris in 1665 and had met Anne Buignon in Poitiers in 1664.[10]

An older line enables us to trace this tradition up to 1661. At that date, Surin told Anne Buignon, who was already busy with a publication, that he himself had gathered some old letters with the intention of publishing them. "I had prepared some letters I considered very useful, which also failed, having been presented [to be revised by the Jesuit authorities]; they were written a long time ago and several of them have been printed. My thought was to make them into a volume, before getting to those that you had the idea of collecting, which I have written since our Lord has given me freedom to write [1657]."[11] Our text, which had already been printed several times, was to be a part of the "major" letters, about which Surin declared to the same correspondent, in April 1661: "I have given you the name of the person having most of the major ones." Who is this person? For other manuscripts, he mentions other holders: Monsieur de la Roche du Maine, general vicar of Pamiers; Madame la présidente de Pontac; the marquise d'Ars, and so on. In March 1661, having failed to receive from the authorities the "passport" for the publication of these letters, he added: "It was not my duty to appear. . . . I would just be sorry if something were to get lost."[12] The zeal of Anne Buignon, who "didn't dare touch" Surin's texts even when she noticed "a few crude terms," and who kept "the originals,"[13] is a sufficient guarantee that she neither lost nor adulterated the text: through her, the Champion edition takes us back to this period.

On 30 June 1659, Surin mentions, as we shall see, "the encounter I had with that saintly young man, on the road from Rouen to Paris," as a text he seems no longer to possess. But M. Pouget, a priest at Tulle, has a copy (apparently in manuscript form), a copy of which he must send to M. Poncet, "counselor at the Court of Aides, rue d'Anjou, in Paris"; at that time (1657–58) Pouget was sent Surin manuscripts either by Father Tillac, a Jesuit from Limoges, or by M. Friquet, a young member of the Aa[14] and attached to a Bordeaux family, friends of Surin's, the Du Saults.[15]

Similar to that version in all the stylistic detail and the thought that inspired it is the manuscript kept presently at the Library of Carpentras.[16] Although the variants in these texts are almost always identical, the latter text lacks a certain number of passages that, in the former, tend to justify and explicate the young man's spoken words,[17] or to complete them with comments on charity and the control of one's sensitivities[18]or even to correct them.[19] And we do not find in this latter text any indication of Father Louis Lallemant as addressee, nor the "my Reverend Father," which began and ended the letter in the Champion edition and the copy in Paris (N). The Carpentras manuscript is much older. It belonged to the famous astronomer and collector Nicolas-Claude Fabri de Peiresc, who died in 1637.[20] From 1623 until his death (hence prior to the writing of the letter in May 1630),[21] Peiresc remained in Provence, at Aix or at Belgentier, near Hyères. But in 1623, returning from Paris after a sojourn of six years, he went through Bordeaux to visit his abbey, Guîtres, and it was on this occasion that he and the "rector and syndic of the Jesuit novitiate" concluded a "concordat" on the subject of the tithes of Fronsac, a Jesuit property attached to the abbey.[22] This contract was renewed in 1628 and in 1629,[23] which is proof of the continued association between the scholar and the religious of Bordeaux. There is every indication that these ties explain the parallelism between the manuscripts of Paris and Carpentras, and that it was via Bordeaux that the letter got to Peiresc.

Another fact corroborates this hypothesis. On 1 July 1635, Father Mersenne wrote to Peiresc from Paris: "I do not know . . . whether you know that a Jesuit father, having gone to Loudun to perform an exorcism, was possessed or obsessed himself, as his own letters show." His friend answers, on the seventeenth: "If the possession or obsession of this good exorcising father goes on, it will be more noteworthy than all the other instances of this sort of thing, which normally befalls the spirits of weak little women."[24] Does Peiresc have some document about Surin? Apparently not from Mersenne. But on July 12 he received, from M. de Saint-Sauveur Du Puy, a close friend of Mme. de Pontac, née de Thou, a "little printing of Father Seurin," an edition of the letter in which Surin described his illness to d'Attichy (3 May

1635).[25] Peiresc answers Du Puy on the twenty-fourth: "This little printing of Father Severin [Surin] is most strange. Another written account was being circulated, that seems to be from him, and is not badly put together. I enclose it, though I suppose you already know about it; but just in case you may not have seen it, perhaps you wouldn't mind, because of the other one."[26] Might that manuscript "account" sent to Du Puy be the letter on the young man in the coach? In contrast with *La Relation véritable de ce qui s'est passé aux exorcismes des religieuses possédées de Loudun, en la présence de Monsieur* (which may be the text alluded to here),[27] the 1630 text had not yet been published, bore the author's name, and could have been known by a scholar in Paris, a city in which it was already circulating, though in a different form. Whatever its precise place may be in the southern filiation of Bordeaux, Poitiers, Tulle, Paris, Nantes, and so on, the Carpentras version did not contain, between 1630 and 1637, those paragraphs or clauses that, tightly interwoven within the Paris version, could not have been left out by accident; their content alone requires the hypothesis that they were added later. Although the question of an addressee remains open, and since the argument *a silentio* is insufficient, let us also note the absence, around 1635, of the homage rendered to "my Reverend Father."[28]

See the map of that southern circulation on the next page.

## A "NORTHERN" TRADITION

A northern circuit may be clearly distinguished from this southern one. At the periphery (both temporally and spatially) of its distribution, we find the opuscule (edited by Pierre Poiret in Cologne in 1690) entitled *Le berger illuminé ou entretien spirituel d'un berger et d'un ecclésiastique*.[29] In the preface, which presents the intent and content of the entire volume to the reader, Poiret says of the origin of the text:

> The Mons edition of the year 1648,[30] which was the fourth, and is the one we follow, bore the title: *Colloque spirituel d'un dévot ecclésiastique et d'un berger*. But we have elected to take the title from the Flemish translation that has just been published in Antwerp and is called: *Le Berger illuminé*. But we have kept to the French text of Mons, which is the original, except for a few words no longer current and a few obscure and cumbersome sentences that we have attempted to make clearer, leaving all the rest in its original simplicity.[31]

And he adds, to prove that the "adventure" was not made up "to give to the subject matter an attractive air of novelty":

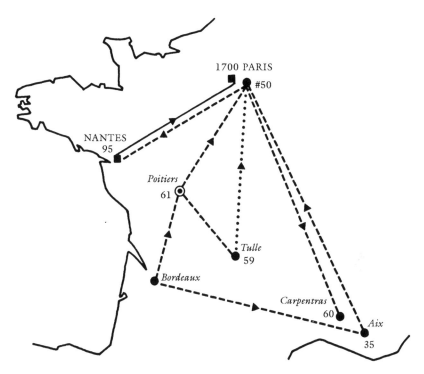

The numbers indicate dates (only the last two figures being given for seventeenth-century dates).

● Manuscript
■ Edition
⟶ Circulation of a printed text
- - - → Circulation of a manuscript
· · · · · → Assumed or deduced circulation

It is an entirely true meeting that really happened to the Reverend Father Buzin, a Jesuit of the Province of France, who, in a letter that he wrote on this subject to another religious named the Reverend Father François Poiré, tells him that it was he himself who met and spoke with that admirable shepherd, and he relates almost word for word a large part of those conversations. I found, among the papers of an ecclesiastic of great piety and who had many acquaintances everywhere, the beginning of a copy of that letter, which contains these particulars, and which I still possess.[32]

Poiret, a Cartesian converted to *mystics*,[33] the "spiritual son" of Antoinette Bourignon since 1676, was in Rijnsburg, near Leiden, where he had been living since 1688. Poiret had previously resided in Amsterdam for eight years, where, by a curious coincidence, he had been a close friend of the disciples of Jean de Labadie, to whom we shall return later.[34] Labadie was a frequent visitor to Surin in Bordeaux.[35] There is nothing surprising in Poiret's having known the Flemish edition and through it, no doubt, the Mons edition, which he reproduced.

The Mons edition was approved on 26 September 1646, in Tournai,[36] by Doctor Matthias de Nave, who was then censor of books and royal examiner. He had already enlisted his knowledge in the service of the new currents of piety—the devotion to Saint Joseph and the saints, the cult of the Holy Sacrament.[37] The Mons edition, already discovered by a fervent circle (the *Approbations*, as is well known, are often the indicators of alliances and groups during this period), born under the auspices of a theology concerned with "spirituality," presents a version that differs from those we have mentioned until now. It omits, compared to the Paris manuscript, the same passages as the Carpentras manuscript does; but it is written in a dry, sprightly style, sometimes awkward, often archaic, which attests by hundreds of variants to its authenticity, and which contrasts sharply with the more academic and more "pious" manner of the southern tradition. The comparison of the two texts shows a deeper difference: The "young man" of the Mons text is one of those "illuminated" simpletons who know more about God than the doctors. Having cropped up no one knows where,[38] faceless, unchronicled, an anonymous herald, he steps out of the crowd for the "Defense and Illustration" of the science of the saints. He is the "unknown soldier" in a spiritual battle. As for the "young man" of the Paris and Carpentras texts, he is a hagiographic figure. What he says matters less than what he is, his spoken words less than his virtues. Encountered on the road from Rouen, raised in our isolated rural areas, here, readers, is a saint in all his naïveté—a naïveté already clad in the prudent language that introduces him, duly valued, into the world of edification. Countless little strokes have retouched, transformed, the meaning of the story. We have here two different styles, two different pictures. One provokes, the other is intended to touch us; one presents the ignorant as witness to a science unknown to the learned, the other describes the virtuous innocence of a model presented for our admiration and imitation. It is the same story but its topic is different. Other indications temper the conclusions suggested by that divergence. In the northern edition, the young boy "is now a shepherd."[39] This literary identity, which is not present in the southern manuscripts, and which connects the story to the *Bergeries* of the times,[40] inspires other "conferences" that come later and that, equally attributed to "our shepherd,"[41] were certainly added to the text.

This text ends, moreover, on a remark (in italics, which is a sign of its spurious character), a seam between the two blocks and an artifice to link four new "interviews" [ *"entrevues"*] to the first: *"Everything above was the first conference."*[42] Thus, the first text is placed at the threshold of a larger body from which it remains distinct, however, by its style and doctrine, and which, as M. Viller has shown in detail, cannot be by Surin.[43] Clearly his letter served as a point of origin for later development. But the joint is visible. Poiret himself, who attributes the whole to the same author, points out the existence of separate pieces: the letter to Father François Poiré, an "almost word for word report of a large portion of these conversations"; or yet again "found among the papers of an ecclesiastic," "the beginning of a copy of this letter."[44] In all likelihood, this "almost word for word report" and this "beginning" both refer to the same text, that of the "first conference." Poiret presents them as additional texts, whereas they are in fact variants of the same. He knew the letter to "François Poiré" only through the copy made by that "ecclesiastic of great piety and who had many acquaintances everywhere." Working only on the Mons edition, he assumed the "copy" was only a "beginning," since it gave only the first encounter. He further assumed that that copy, being in letter form (which is not the case of the edited version that he copied), represented a *different* text, a hypothesis that was confirmed in his opinion by the "particularities" he found there, and which were absent from the *Colloque spirituel* published in Mons. These "particularities"—the epistolary form, the mention of an addressee (here Poiré; in N, Lallemant), the naming of the author (here Buzin; in N, Seurin)—all lead one to think that the "copy" belongs to the southern tradition, which had reached Cologne, but late and without having been published, since it had been short-circuited by the short version that had already appeared in Mons. According to Poiret, the "ecclesiastic" who attests to that northern branch of the long version seems to be dead by 1690; but he might have obtained this long text from the archdeacon Henri-Marie Boudon, who was intensely interested in Surin,[45] who had gone to Flanders and especially to Mons in 1687,[46] and who was himself "of great piety" with "many acquaintances everywhere."

Despite the advantage his "wilder" style gives him, must the text from Poiret and Mons be held unfaithful because of the supplement that condemns it, consisting of four spurious and pontificating "conferences," or because of the single occurrence of a term that imposes a pastoral disguise upon the mystic peasant? On the other hand, two older manuscripts confirm its authenticity. One, *Copie d'une lettre écrite par un père jésuite à ses confrères au collège de la Flesche*,[47] is part of a collection compiled by Father Rybeyrete (d. 1676) and contains very diverse pieces, nearly all addressed to Father René Ayrault, who died in La Flèche in 1644.[48] Contrary to what Father Michel thinks,[49] that copy is not from the hand of Father Ayrault.[50] It was enclosed in a letter "to the Reverend Father [Claude] Pasquier"[51] who, from 1628 to 1640, was the minister of the Collège de la Flèche.[52] While the author remains undetermined ("a Jesuit Father"), the same is not true of the addressees ("his colleagues at the College de la Flèche.") The ending and the details of the text (for example, the omission of "Rouen"),[53] as well as the general sense, are the same as in the Mons and Cologne editions. There is but one noteworthy variant: there is no mention of a "shepherd" in the Rybeyrete copy.

The other manuscript, *Copie de la lettre du R. P. Seurin Jésuite à ses confrères du collège de la Flèche*,[54] is identical to the preceding one except for a few insignificant details. But it ends with a note written by another hand: "All the above was the first conference." After this note there follows, on another folio, the "abridged points of the pious conferences of the angelic shepherd." Then, at the end, is a final note written in the same hand: "These conferences have since been printed in Paris by Sébastien Piquay de Gèvre à la Victoire in the year 1649, and the book is entitled *Secrets de la vie spirituelle enseignés par Jésus-Christ à une âme dévote et par un berger à un bon religieux en forme de conférence spirituelle*."[55]

That edition does in fact exist, in the form of a small volume in-16: *Les secrets de la vie spirituelle Enseignez par Jésus-Christ à une Âme dévote et par un berger à un bon religieux* (Paris: Sébastien Piquet, 1649). Signed "Paris, 20 December 1647," it bears the approval of Le Fevre and (who would have believed it?) Launoy—the famous Jean de Launoy (1603–78), one of the best theologians in Paris, the royal censor for theological works (1645–48).[56] One might well be astonished that the "*secrets* . . . taught by a shepherd to a good religious" (a suspect program, when put in parallel, in the title, with the "secrets . . . taught by Jesus Christ to a devout soul") and revealed in the course of an "extraordinary adventure" should be deemed "worthy of being given to the public" by that "iron-clad spirit," "bold critic," of whom it has too readily been said that "he removed one saint a year from paradise." But to be thus astonished would be to fail to recognize, I think, the problem hidden beneath the studies devoted by

Launoy, *veritatis assertor perpetuus*,[57] to the history of spirituality (Dionysius the Areopagite, *The Imitation of Jesus Christ*, Saint Bruno, Simon Stock, etc.). Of course, it would be wrong to place too much emphasis on the *doctrinal* aspect of an approval that was, after all, a matter of course ("I found nothing that is contrary to the Catholic, Roman, Apostolic Faith"). That approval is, nonetheless, a sign. At a time when the doctor was taking his position against the Jansenist thesis on satisfaction[58] and prepared to attack Aristotelian "science,"[59] thus rejecting both these theological allegiances, the old and the new, Launoy no longer had a scientific language for his (undeniable) religious convictions, and his *private* life, isolated from "positive" erudition, had no other means of self-expression but the path of devotion.[60] Wherever they appear, our "conferences," "excerpted," according to the subtitle,[61] "from a letter that this same religious wrote," seem to indicate, through the narrow canal of the text, a resurgence of the same waters: an "ignorant" spirituality, sometimes challenging, sometimes hidden. A movement of exodus is declared or unveiled.

According to Sommervogel, the book had an initial Paris edition in 1648.[62] We have never encountered it, although its date is compatible with that of the approval. In any case, there were other editions later, all identical, all accompanied by the same approval: Rouen, 1649, by Jacques Besongne;[63] Paris, 1650, by the same Sébastien Piquet;[64] and in 1661, by Sébastien Huré;[65] Brussels, 1661, by François Foppens;[66] Lyons, 1658–59, by Nicolas Vetet;[67] 1665, by Pierre Compagnon,[68] and 1668, by Claude Chancey.[69] The 1657 Liège edition belongs to this group.[70] The name Surin appears only in the Rouen edition (1649),[71] then much later, in 1661, in Paris (on page 133) and in Brussels,[72] and in 1668 in Lyons. But the addresses are identified in a preface that keeps reappearing with every edition.

> The account given by this religious known in France for his virtue and great capacities cannot permit any doubt that these conferences took place and that they occurred the way he himself set them down in writing in a letter that he addressed to those who were closest to him in a religious house that was very well regulated, very wisely led and very well considered for the holy exercises of piety and doctrine that are practiced there daily.[73]

All of these editions share two variants that distinguish them from both manuscripts: the condition of "shepherd" given to the young boy and the mention of "Rouen." Obviously they reproduce and are derived from one another.

To that northern circulation there must be added a branch in *Flem-*

*ish*, four geographical indices of which remain. The first is the Malines edition in 1648: *Gheestelijcke T'samen spreeckinghe tuss'chen eenen devoten persoon, ende eenen Scaepherder.*[74] This text, either already in published form or still in manuscript (which is more probable), seems to be the one Joanna Van Randenraedt read in Ruremonde before 1684 and entered in the list of her spiritual readings.[75] A third index is a Brussels manuscript that can be dated mid-seventeenth century. Its characteristics are that it names Surin as author and that it gives the title "conference" [*Discours*] to a text called "conversation" or "colloquium" [*T'samen spreeckinghe*] by the two preceding pieces.[76] Last there is the Antwerp edition, which appeared late in 1690, the existence of which is known to us only through Poiret.[77]

These four documents (or at least the two we can check) have their place in a different theological area. Instead of the approval of Launoy and Le Fevre, we have that of Matthias de Nave, the same approval that accompanies the French text of Mons and Cologne (but not that of Brussels) and to which was added, for the Flemish version, the authorization of Alexander van der Laen.[78] There was a transfer of authority as well as a change of territory. But the group placed beneath the aegis of Doctor de Nave was not homogeneous. It is true that, as a group, it is distinguishable from the circuit bearing the stamp Launoy-Le Fevre: absence of Rouen; replacement of "religious" by the more vague designation of "ecclesiastic" or "spiritual person."[79] On the other hand, the Flemish tradition represents, in relation to this group, a more "illuminist" avant-garde that drops the dogmatic allusions (to the Virgin, to the apostles)[80] and accentuates the opposition between the "illuminated shepherd" and the learned theologians. The title of the Malines edition, like that of the Ruremonde manuscript, speaks to us "of the great secrets and mysteries of the divine wisdom that God reveals unto pure and simple souls *for* the instruction of even the most learned."[81] These details reveal shifts in the meaning and function of the text. There are also traces of a Flemish subgroup (Malines, Ruremonde, and Antwerp) in the constellation formed by Mons, Malines, Antwerp, Cologne, and Brussels (ms),[82] which is itself connected to that other "northern" constellation already represented on the map: Paris, Rouen, Lyon, Brussels (edition) and, it seems, Liège. By a concluding note, the "Northern" manuscript of Paris (P') makes it possible to ascribe a common origin to both of these "constellations," and to clarify the relationship of the "Parisian" distribution with the printed text with which we began, that of Mons-Cologne (1646–90).

After having given the text, the copyist adds: "A copy of the same, dated 5 January 1631, was sent from La Flèche to Saint-Jean-d'Angély,[83] and from Saint-Jean-d'Angély to Reims by a religious of the Order of Saint Benedict."[84] This specification, let it be noted first, agrees with the date indicated by Champion, 1630, and there is no reason to doubt that, as he affirms with the manuscript N,[85] the letter was written on May 8 of that year.[86] What relationship brought about the sending of a copy to Saint-Jean-d'Angély? Perhaps in answering that question, we might succeed in identifying one of the persons to whom the letter was addressed. The information provided by manuscript P' already corroborates the identity and whereabouts of the addressees indicated by the editions of the short text: "to those closest to him, in a well-regulated religious house." P' specifies that the house is La Flèche. Among the Fathers present at La Flèche in 1629–30, several were among "those closest" to Surin: Jean Bagot and Achille Doni d'Attichy.[87] Further, we now know one of the paths by which the copies circulated. From Saint-Jean-d'Angély, whose old abbey, in 1623, had just been resettled by Maurists[88] (and their expertise really warranted the value of a manuscript!), the letter was sent to Reims. Whoever the Reims correspondent may have been,[89] the letter must have come into the hands of the Jesuits of the college where there was, at the time, a whole group of those "reformed mystics" who were dropped from history after having marked one of its spiritual crossroads.[90] From 1629 to 1632, René Ayrault was rector there; in 1631–32, François Poiré was spiritual father; Pierre Le Cazre, professor of theology; René de Trans, professor of rhetoric.[91] Once again, like Ariadne's thread, the circulation of the "relation" sketches out the map of spiritual centers and brings out the often invisible ties between them.

It was doubtless from Reims that the letter got either to Mons (perhaps via Pont-à-Mousson where d'Attichy lived, from late 1632 on),[92] almost unchanged,[93] or to Paris, where the presence of the Jesuits probably explains, first, the mention of place ("Rouen"), then, in 1661, the identification of the author ("Seurin").[94] But it is difficult to believe that the Paris printed text comes from Mons,[95] despite the similarity of the texts: they have neither the same characteristic variants nor the same mark of approval.[96] Though they both reproduce, as their first part, the translation (published in Douai in 1647 by Father Turrien Le Febvre) of a text by Father Gaspar de la Figuera, a Jesuit: *Dialogues entre Jésus-Christ et une âme religieuse, dans lesquels sont représentés et mis au jour comme en un tableau raccourci les secrets les plus cachés de la vie spirituelle* [Dialogues between Jesus Christ and a religious soul, in which the most hidden secrets of spiritual life are presented and brought to light in shortened form].[97] There is nothing there that could warrant our attributing the Mons edition to that same Turrien. It is more probable that the Paris and Mons editors each reproduced this text, adding to it as a second part the "conferences," which had reached them in manuscript form by different routes. Thus they offered the public, each with its own "approval" and "permission," parallel but independent volumes. The Paris copy (P') is not the origin of these works, since it mentions, as being contemporaneous with it, the Paris edition of 1649; but it attests to the tradition leading back to it and connected, by a carefully preserved filiation, to the 1630 text. As for the Rybeyrete manuscript, it must have been sent to Father Pasquier (hence to La Flèche) in order that the letter, already in circulation, could be checked at its point of origin. Father Ayrault had been sent there in 1635;[98] he remained there until his death in 1644.[99] So it is there, even if he had already seen the text in Reims, that he collected that copy, during or at the conclusion of Pasquier's stay, hence prior to 1640. After 1644, the document, along with others also gathered by Ayrault or addressed to him, passed into the possession of Father Rybeyrete. Given this set of circumstances, the manuscript possesses all the desirable guarantees.

See the map of the northern tradition on the following page.

### STRATA

Once this first state of the letter has been established, the dates, which also correspond to the locations of the text, can be determined, though the strata of the latest versions overlap. The establishment of that anatomy entails the resolution of two further points. First, in the southern tradition—the amplifications after 1635 and doubtless even later—the problem of the designation of Father Lallemant as addressee; second, the authenticity and nature of that "letter to Father François Poiré," as it is claimed to be by the Cologne editor in 1690.

In comparison with the northern version, the Carpentras text must be considered retouched. But though that revision, through numerous minor corrections, ends up changing the overall effect, no new elements are added. Inspired by piety and intended to edify, it nonetheless allows into the text many of those expressions that would later lead copyists to add explanations and justifications. Its intent is not to prove. It expands upon the traits of a lovely story. It reflects the way a pious reader read the text: it reflects the milieus in which the peasant militant was to appear in the posture attributed to saints. In that circulation, after the "mystic" period (represented by the northern tradition), it was the "devotional" period.

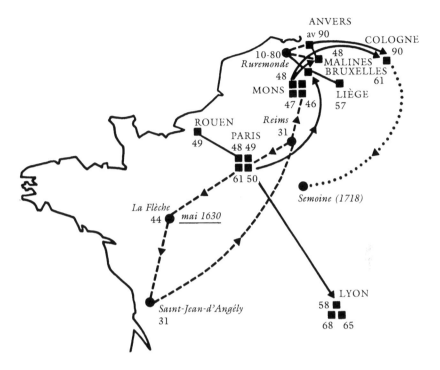

The numbers indicate dates (only the last two figures being given for seventeenth century dates.)

●      Manuscript
■      Edition
——→   Circulation of a printed text
- - -→   Circulation of a manuscript
· · · · ·→   Assumed or deduced circulation

Then there follows a new mutation, a third period, to which manuscript N attests. Encumbered with proofs, examples, rectifications, and moral considerations, the young man arms himself and goes on the defensive. He no longer throws caution to the winds. He counters. He strengthens his position. This transformation took place in the south between 1640 and 1660, at the time of the violent attacks on the spirituals,[100] while Surin was enveloped in madness, shut up in the "dungeon" of the Bordeaux infirmary, while his writings spread as if they were already posthumous.[101] Was he the one who, emerging from the shadows, armed and outfitted his hero? It is true that in June

1659, he sets Abbot Pouget on the trail of his account of the young man in the coach.[102] Later, in 1661, he contemplates the publication of his "major letters" (the "account" obviously being one of them) and appears to have prepared it.[103] During this period (1660–61), he corrected his manuscript and the *Guide spirituel* in order to clarify certain practical points and sharpen his critique of the antimystics.[104] He may have done the same with his account of the meeting with the young man. Certain traits of that version, such as the sudden appearance of "a horseman with scarlet coat," might be attributable to his style. But, all in all, the corrections are timid, solely defensive. That is not typical of Surin. When he amplifies, he goes further in the same vein, or else says the same thing in a different way. Would he have surrounded his young man with this "theological machinery" that he was to ridicule?[105] Would he have turned the illiterate mystic into a new doctor? That is hard to believe. Besides, he is known to have disclaimed the published versions and what they had *added* to his text.[106] But if he did not make the corrections, then who did? Perhaps one of his "friends" and users, better suited than himself to this work of textual revision. Whatever the case may be, during this period his letter assumed a new aspect, and at this stage in its history it is possible to discern, in its new ponderousness, the weight of a polemics.

The name Lallemant, universally respected, nearly the only one not borne off with *mystics'* receding tide, is a part of the same defensive campaign. He comes, with his unquestionable authority, to the defense of our controversial author. After his death (1635), he was "polished" by his editor, Pierre Champion, who revised him and freed him of any compromising association (with which his history is nonetheless replete). He became, at the end of the seventeenth century, the stamp of what seemed "acceptable" in the mystic strain of the beginning of the century.[107] His name appears (there being no earlier mention of him) as a new safeguard, a final precaution. But this mention of Lallemant does not square with the latter's relations with the young Surin, whom, in the third year of his novitiate, "he tested thoroughly."[108] Moreover, this name never occurs in Surin's works. Furthermore, as A. Hamon has noted,[109] it would be strange that a letter should be addressed to the instructor at Rouen when its author indirectly criticizes all theoretical instruction and affirms, speaking of his peasant: "All that I have read or heard [about spiritual life] is nothing in comparison to what he told me."[110] The corrector, preoccupied with his defense, overlooked the lack of verisimilitude of his tack. As for François Poiré, how could he have known and met with Surin? He had been in Dijon (1616–20), Pont-à-Mousson (1620–21), Nancy (1621–25), Lyon

(1625–28), and again to Pont-à-Mousson (1628–31), all years during which Surin, who was from Bordeaux, was completing his formation in Guyenne or in the Jesuit province of Paris. The reference Poiret gave is therefore surprising. But it can be explained if the copy of the letter came to him from Reims, as the similarity of the texts allows us to assume, and if Father François Poiré, a confirmed supporter of the "new spirituality,"[111] became the propagator of a text so much in keeping with his own convictions. Poiré might then have been taken for the recipient of the letter he was distributing. He was an active member in the more or less occult campaign carried on by the "spirituals"—a campaign in which, since 1631 and his first literary endeavors, Surin appeared to many as the standard-bearer.

## THE ANGEL IN THE WILDERNESS

Surin was thinking neither about polemics nor pastorals. For him, what Champion daringly called "the truth of history"[112] was located elsewhere. Prisoner of a different war, he gave little thought to shepherds' idyls. In his letter there is not a word, not a glance for the green countryside clamoring springtime beneath the soothing skies of Normandy. No one lives there. Nothing counts but this "young boy." The "company," a faceless decor, intervenes only once in this abstract setting, and merely as a fleeting shadow, quickly dropped.[113] All the other voices are absent. Just one solitary voice is heard in the wilderness: the words of an angel.

### THE "WILDERNESS"

At the completion of the third year of his novitiate, "on the road from Rouen to Paris," as he was to describe it,[114] Surin goes into "the wilderness."[115] "As I was leaving my country . . .": he is leaving behind the security of the recluse's life in God.[116] Judging from the date of his account (May 8), his time of departure was moved forward for reasons the letter will give. He is torn away from the mother house prematurely, by the decision of the "Father"—Lallemant. Sent back into the world he had fled to seek God, he is now excluded from the family by an order that nevertheless comes from God and that expels him, like Abraham, from his retreat. "Leave your country."[117] He obeys an incomprehensible order as he, in turn, "leaves his country."[118] His desolation is caused not only by these alien environs; it is more private, as is proved by the questions that this child, weaned too soon from his mother, puts to his confidant: "I proposed all the difficulties of my inner self to him." What are they? Two problems that are quite revealing come up several times. One involves the "physical infirmities" that most probably prompted Surin's departure. And the young man tells him of "wonders for the consolation and direction of a soul who, attracted to prayer and desirous of virtue, is held back[119] by physical infirmities." The "soul" who thus seeks "consolation" and "direction" is none other than Surin. He feels "held back" in his desire by the weakness that wounds him. He has within his own body an enemy that decreases the will within him to "do violence to himself." His defeat is already inscribed within himself by that alien who nonetheless is himself and who opposes his desire.

Even more insidious is the worry evidenced by the other problem. It is revealed through a response to which he attributes "particular" importance. "He spoke to me . . . of the secrets God had allowed him to know concerning his attributes, and particularly his justice upon the souls who do not advance to perfection though they desire to do so." The ending has an odd ring. It echoes those desires rendered ineffectual by infirmity, but it indicates something else. Surin comes back to it later, in noting a little "lecture" [*discours*] that can only be explained by the obsession, haunting this dialogue, with his alter ego: "He told me the men of our profession who do not struggle against the pleasure of being praised by the world will never taste the joys of God; they are thieves; their darkness will ever increase; the slightest little trifle clouds the soul; what prevents the soul's freedom is a certain habitual dissimulation that holds it back. I use his own terms." It is obvious that these remarks are an echo of the reformation trend; to an even greater degree, they take up the traditional teaching on the requirements of perfection. Lallemant had already said: "We spend entire years, and often our whole lives, haggling over whether we will give ourselves totally to God."[120] Surin, with many others, said it after him. But the vocation of religious is not presented here as the call to a more total giving; only the negative side appears. Just as a moment ago divine "justice" menaced those who do not progress, despite their desire to do so, now our attention is focused on a state of fact—the "darkness"and its logical development: "the darkness will ever increase." The situation is already determined and its future definite. The "thieves," having made off with God's glory, hear the Judgment. They are already discarded, destined for hell.

The cause of their condemnation is even more disturbing: "the slightest little trifle." Who would dare say he had avoided "the slightest little trifle?" How could one avoid these infinitesimal deviations that inevitably increase one's darkness? Are they even dependent on one's will? No, doubtless they are not, no more than is that vague "habitual dissimulation" that silently asphyxiates freedom without one's noticing it. If this is how things are, the fault lies in no particular act, and all action is caught up in a culpability that puts the person himself into question. Further, while there is no specific fault, one fact, precise and indisputable, looms large: darkness—spiritual uncertainty, discontent, dryness of soul. From that "darkness" the religious *must conclude* that there is within him, unbeknownst to him, sin. "It [is] entirely the fault[121] of the religious if they [are] not all perfect"; from their imperfection the fault can be deduced, a fault impossible to localize, destructive because identified with the self. For Surin, the problem is not fanciful. "Not all perfect": certain ones, then, have excluded themselves without realizing it. Surin knows full well of whom he is speaking, he who "propose[s] all the difficulties of [his] inner self . . . by means of a third party," and who, in this instance as in so many others, "draws," from a too "simple" interlocutor, truths that cut both ways, with which he nourishes his own sickness. Actually, these "men of our profession" are himself. They show the face of his anguish. For it is no longer a mere question of defeat, but of exclusion; and not only of an exile in the body but an exile far from God.

In order to understand his state, we must go back to his years of studying philosophy and theology. At that time, we are told, "being very bright, he succeeded perfectly in his studies and made an outstanding impression on all occasions."[122] He was, then, "praised by the world." He himself, in a letter written in 1634 to his friend d'Attichy, admitted the pleasure he formerly derived from these literary exercises. "I believe you are no longer in a mood to write nice, eloquent letters; as for me, I admit to you frankly that my tastes have changed radically for some time now."[123] Since nothing in his letters from 1630 to 1634 indicates such a "change," and since, writing to a fellow student, he refers to their common past[124] as students as being one of "niceness" and eloquence, the conversion must date from a crisis[125] prior to 1630 but after 1624. It was, in fact, during those years, 1626–30, that he describes his state to a female correspondent (unidentified):

> All consolations are taken from me, except the sole one of writing to you and hearing about you, which brings me some comfort. But it is only a little water on a great fire.

Or, written near Vitré:

> All this week I've had much business that has occupied me for a lot of the time, and my nature has had some release in this, and takes nourishment however it can from this fare, but being extremely gluttonous

and avid, it becomes excessively attached to these creatures, draws my reason and my entire sensibility in that direction. I do not see one moment that is not filled with unfaithfulness. I feel my outer self in dissipation and agitation; and when I think to look at it in that state, I fall into an acute anxiety, desiring on one hand to be faithful and detach myself from creatures, and, on the other hand, concerned about forgetting everything that has to do with me. Then, all of a sudden, I feel myself torn from myself and plunged into this dark void in which I am immediately lost and no longer see myself.

Or, written from Vitré itself:

Since my arrival in this city, I have gone through a severe physical and mental trial. Until now I have been taking remedies that have weakened me tremendously, having brought back my stomach upsets and vomiting which I had recovered from six weeks earlier, as I told you at Laval. Then, I was in the half-bath eight times. Rather than getting relief from it, I got only increase of pain, weakness and general languor, fever almost daily, continual indigestion, and an extremely poor appetite. And with that, an extreme distaste for my daily train of life.

Never had I felt so sick before. And as for the suffering and agony of my mind during all this, I cannot express it, so ardent is my suffering, for I had never experienced such abandonment and blindness, yielding to extraordinary impatience and hypersensitivity over the slightest pain, attachments and haste and worry over seeking relief in remedies, a taste for some particular food; making an effort to find some distraction and consolation among the creatures, in order to ease my pain a bit. And with all this, the Spirit of God does great violence, in all these outbursts, to my inclinations.[126]

Did the crisis, shifting to the third year of his novitiate, worsen? "It was in that holy solitude that he buried himself *all over again* in the tomb of Jesus Christ, in order to live only from death, saying an eternal *adieu* to all the creatures."[127] In his successes, did Surin recognize those "trifles," the least of which increases the soul's darkness? But where does the "trifling" begin? When does it become sinful? The evil is not attached to any particular act; it has no specific time or place. It is a bottomless well with no discernible sides. It becomes generalized, an evil for which death supplies the only remedy as well as the only meaning. To separate radically not only from the creatures but from oneself, to leave a life that is a "mixture"[128] or "habitual dissimulation"; to impose an absolute split between what is from nature and what is from grace; to break with existence itself and bury oneself in a tomb; to escape ambiguity by a definitive act and find "freedom" at last: this is the idea that haunts the prisoner of his own anguish. He is determined to "live from death."

In Rouen, he was not very encouraged by Lallemant. "He communicated his plans of such a great and long separation from created being to Father Louis Lallemant who was his director in that house of retreat. Being a man of grace, he tested him a great deal."[129] A biting phrase. Contrary to the peasant in the coach, the instructor refused to give his support to an act that, while putting an end to duplicity, opted for nothingness. Hence the departure, the "exit," to go to Paris or the provinces.[130] But anxiety is not to be reasoned with. This departure taught him nothing. The only result was the increased impression of having lost the chance for purity that death offered him, of being cast out into a darker night and sent back to this world in which his eyes could no longer see anything but a desolate wilderness.

### THE ANGEL

But then, behold, a "marvel": "our Lord" himself "receives" him! Behold, the exile meets a messenger of God, like Tobit, who, sent forth from his house, "found the angel Raphael standing before him, not suspecting he was an angel of God."[131] Filled with these ancient texts that he would often quote, he himself was raised up amidst these angels whose proximity and apparitions are so often mentioned in the most serious biographies of the time, just as they are in Carmelite chronicles: strange visibility of the Beyond, at the juncture of day and night, in the interstices of time and sight. Attracted to a presence by a desire that nostalgia for the Absent rendered more acute, Surin immediately suspects the true identity of the young man, who, like Raphael, "is familiar with all the roads,"[132] heals the blind man, and reveals the divine "secrets": "I thought he was an angel, and that suspicion remained until he asked me, at Pontoise, for confession and communion: for the sacraments are not for angels." It takes a theological argument to make him change his original idea. A mental rule is the only thing that can distinguish objects and decide, in the suspicion created by desire, ambiguous cases in which the eye cannot discern. But although there is a change in the nature of the object, it remains an apparition. Like the unforeseeable apparition of an angel, without any ties to the context, this "young man" rises up suddenly, "found" and "discovered" within the world's emptiness. Everything in him bears the mark of the "extraordinary": "extremely crude," "extremely simple," "sublime" in the prayers he says, he "says marvelous things." "I have never seen the like," declares the witness, and "all I have read or heard is nothing compared to what he told me." Foreign to ordinary laws and norms, incomparable in himself, the phenomenon transcends all that can be "expressed" or "written." It is outside of language and nature. It appears only to disappear again, like Klee's *Angelus Novus*, interpreted by Walter Benjamin as "the song of an instant before disappearing into nothingness." "He dwells in the things I no longer have. He makes them transparent, and behind each of them there appears to me the one for whom they were destined." He is the power of an absence, a place in which things disappear. "He moves away by fits and starts, receding inflexibly."[133] He creates a void in the objects in which he infiltrates what is behind them and behind him—an illocutionary act, an openness to otherness. One only "sees" it disappear until a man replaces what has disappeared.

As for Surin, he disengages himself from all those things that, compared to the gaze of the appearing-disappearing one, lose their thickness of reality or meaning. "I separated myself from the group to be with him as much as I could, taking all my meals and conducting all my conversations with him." His angel is a reconstruction of the "mother" retreat of which he had just been deprived.[134] "We often alighted from the coach in order to be able to talk more comfortably and with less distraction." He is at last "at ease," having taken refuge in loss. There is no longer any "trifle" in the extraordinary void opened up by this dual discourse. The opening of heaven creates a singular closure. The creatures fade away, like an insignificant decor, around this enclosure.

### THE PAUPER, THAT "TREASURE"

The "conversation" around which the story is organized evokes the combat described by Louis Chardon in 1647, when speaking of the struggle between Jacob and the angel. Seized by the victorious Enemy, Jacob first experienced in the dialogue "the terror of so sudden and unexpected an arrival of this Almighty who strikes before warning." But that war becomes an amorous struggle. "Instead of deriving despair from a combat that had begun with such heat between unequal parties," he "is moved to increasing confidence. The embraces of his antagonist reassure him. His grip swells his courage. His approach fortifies him. His rude attacks strengthen him increasingly. That war begins to please him, for the sole reason that the combatants' final goal is not separation, but union." The wound that weakens him binds him to the one who strikes him.[135]

This is the scene of a different struggle. Severing all ties with the others, Surin has no more relation to the young peasant than to them.

In his interlocutor he sees less a person than a miracle, an invaluable "good," "filled with all manner of graces and . . . inner gifts," from which he attempts to "draw" some "marvelous secrets." There is no conversation. Anyway, this is a priori impossible. One does not converse with the extraordinary. Surin is there, as if before his burning bush. He does not talk with anyone. He collects spoken words. He can do no more than lavish attention on the "treasure" he has "discovered"; listen avidly to whatever emanates from it; elicit revelations, of which he might be deprived by the least distraction, the slightest blunder. "With marvelous industry" he hides his fervor, "pretending to attribute no importance to" the inspired one, in order not to frighten him; and, at the same time, taking care not to forget any of the problems that might offer him the chance of a new oracle. "I set him talking on all the points of the spiritual life I could think of for three days, as much in the area of practice as speculation." He takes the precautions of a miser or a lover for the elusive object of his fascination. At last his "industry" pays off: the boy "revealed more of himself than he thought." This phrase, which ends the letter, proclaims the victory. Of what possession? In order to answer, we would have to know what it is. A love letter, in any case, made up of simulation, dodges, and seductions generated by a secret the spoken word opens and retracts at the same time. Furtive glimpses. In the story, the young man hides behind other "souls"; but through their invented graces, Surin recognizes those of his apparition, which themselves constitute the novel from which he is excluded. These "other" persons are to him the mirror of the one he meets, the latter being himself transformed into the mirror of the presence of which he is deprived. A gulf of disappearances—a network in which what disappears proliferates. Where is the body in which we may remain? An infinite play of relays narrates the absence of the Other. That unreal is the work of a passion, a passion knowing nothing save the strangeness impelling it.

But this boy eats. He certainly did exist—that much appears certain. There is evidence of it. First, there is the information given by the author of an early *Vie du Père Surin*:[136] "This young man," he writes, "was a poor boy, the son of a baker from Le Havre in Normandy, who, having served among the religious of Saint-Antoine in Rouen, went off to Paris to don the habit of a religious as lay brother."[137] He was, then, an employee in the hospital run by the Antonins in Rouen.[138] Yet another piece of evidence: Surin got a shock from that meeting that changed his understanding profoundly, making the hypothesis of a fictional narrative scarcely credible. If it was an illusion, we are forced to assume it remained intact thirty years later, for in 1659 he still spoke

of "the encounter I had with that saintly young man";[139] he was referring to an event, not a literary invention. One last indication seems just
as clear, though less obvious at first glance: the experience portrayed
by the words transcribed have their own coherence, and it is not
Surin's coherence. It is a coherence that has its place in a hierarchical
and mystic cosmos rather foreign to the Jesuit's thought. God the
Trinity stands at its origin; he moves by his Spirit the "various orders
of the angels and saints"; he "works within souls through the Word,"
pouring forth a life that brings light out of silence, and from that light,
action, until he appears at last in the charity, humility, and strength of
his creatures. By its various themes—God's attributes, the successive
"states" of spiritual life, the conception of contemplative prayer, the
critique of ecstasies—the teachings of this future lay brother remain
original. The young man has his own life, even in the mirror of this
account of it.

The issue here is not whether he existed, but what his existence
means to his interlocutor. Surin immediately discerns the value of his
discovery. He is not wrong about the quality of that gold. The spoken
words he transcribes let us perceive the resonance within him of his
interlocutor's experience: profound, cohesive, wild, unbending in its
affirmations, full of life in its uncompromising language. "Prayer consists not in receiving from God, but giving to him"—*non amari sed
amare*: the definition has its place in mystic truth, once the anxious
quest for divine favors has faded. The Jesuit is too deprived, too fam-
ished for those reassuring tokens for the Other, to be able to make so
pure a note heard within him. Such limpidity is not of his invention,
but he recognizes it. He listens to it as the voice for which he was
waiting. It also teaches him the secret of a silence that is not a void:
"He also said Saint Joseph had been a man of great silence; in the house
of our Lord he spoke little, but our Lady spoke even less and our Lord
still less than either of them; his eyes taught him enough things without the Lord's speaking." The alliance is so ancient. It precedes and
exceeds all communication. It no longer needs to draw attention to
itself by a special language; all things speak it. "Without the Lord's
speaking": How could Surin, haunted by a different silence and anxious to catch every word of the revelation,[140] have made up that expression of a presence that "engulfs" within itself any particular sign?
But he discerns the meaning of it, "filled with astonishment." It is the
event: in his universe, something supervenes. These are but words,
insignificant nothings that speak of nothing and talk "toward" this
treasure, poverty. And now, behold, like a poem they give voice to what
could not speak, "in-fans." They originate. They do not invent a body.

They do not even designate one. Even less do they express a reality; reality is uncertain, ambivalent, suspect. But they mark the place of reality, symbolize it or precede it, as the word "mystic" intends a body still absent.[141] They open a space not authorized by beings. They produce belief in what is not there. They create otherness. And, to use an image so often used by Surin, the drowning man, lost in the middle of his ocean, has just discovered, awestruck, a "new world."[142]

This land is that of the pauper. Neither positive knowledge nor good manners are to be found there. It has the external aspect of this "crude," "illiterate" boy. There is nothing of the polish that a subtle art introduced during this period, into even "the best conducted [religious] houses." Yet Surin, son of notables and members of the Parliament, is at home here. The confidence he has in a "simple person," who became his master in a few minutes, in the guise of a questioned child, contrasts with the difficulty he always had, by his own admission, in speaking freely with his peers or superiors. The poverty of the illuminated one is mysteriously in collusion with his own. Surin reveals himself, with a sort of haste reflected in the rapid, staccato movement of his letter. He is at ease; he can "breathe" in the space offered him by his interlocutor. He reveals himself on the other's stage. He speaks in that spoken word come from elsewhere, and the question of to which of the two it belongs is no longer an issue. The style of his letters and treatises will become a spoken word, a "song," born in and of the spoken word of his correspondents.[143] That word does not arise within oneself but within others and their hospitality: their poverty is what invents it. "You have hidden your secrets from the wise of this world and you have revealed them to the little ones, that is to say, the most humble souls": this is, as the Parisian editor of 1649 correctly perceived, the announced secret.[144] Surin was being summoned back to his country, which was none other than the one in which he lived, as the "child" and "beggar" he was.[145]

And that sufficed. There was no need of any other authority. Ultimately, that spoken word could do without the Scriptures. It was the structure of the Spirit, or of birth by grace. "When I pressed him to tell me whether someone had not taught him after all, he told me no, and said there were some souls that could only be harmed by creatures. Even if the Gospel were to perish, God had taught him enough of it for his salvation." Wisdom is no more bound to an oral or written tradition than the inspired one is bound or comparable to the realities of this earth. It is strange that the young illiterate boy should repeat to Surin the words that Ignatius of Loyola (that other self-taught mystic) said to himself while at Manresa (1522), and that he relates in his

*Pilgrim's Tale*: "Quite often he said to himself that if there had not been any Scriptures to teach us these truths of faith, he would be ready to die for them, solely because of what he had seen then."[146] The "father" seems to return in the person of this son of a Le Havre baker who restores the founding "authority." It is the roundabout return of the founder, in all his wild, pioneering youth. The shadow of the father appears like the spirit of the beginning, an angel in the wilderness.

## THE LEGEND OF THE PAUPER

In trying to go back from text to text to arrive at an original manuscript from which to extract the meaning, we are repeating what the successive versions made of the "relation": a legend, that is, a statement of *what must be read*. Each of the interpretations along the way of the story's circulation is a manner of understanding it as well as a revealing document about the group that "met" the young man or shepherd for a moment on its path. Our interpretation, today, is a part of that journey, marking but one more step in a story still moving, still placed beneath the sign of the coach. It is a textual journey, an immense unending voyage based on the fundamental formality of an interweaving between two people. There is no history but that which has been "revised and corrected." It mixes, as before, the reciprocal points of view of a "conversation" among several: it is at once our reading of Surin, his reading of the event, and our intelligence of the present through a "relation" with that past. The relation to the other plays simultaneously on those three registers. In the moment in which we are studying him, the "pauper" is equally Surin himself, his young man, and that part of ourselves to which an exchange gives a language. Each of the readings of the text is therefore both history and legend. True of our reading, it is also true of the version that parallels most closely the event of 1630.

### THE LAY DOCTOR

Surin's account is itself a reinterpretation of an older theme, and its success is doubtless due in large part to the resurfacing, in the form of a pamphlet and fervent recounting, of the myth that for three centuries had linked *mystics* with the ignorant one, the illiterate and illuminated *Idiotus*. It is in this sense that the event of the encounter, phantom object of and in our study, is itself the revival of a grand story, the historical return of a legend. It is the new "apparition" of a character whose trajectory draws, in its wake, the baseline of modern spirituality: the conversion of the theologian by the "Friend of God from the Oberland," an episode whose date, whether real or not, would be around 1345. By the time that the first edition of his sermons was published in 1498, Tauler was identified with the "Master of the Holy Writ," the hero of the "Marvelous Story" in which the layman, a Friend of God, declared to the man of learning, priest and Master: Christ "has taught me more in the space of one short hour than you would be able to teach me, you, Master, and all the doctors on this earth, from now till Judgment Day."[147]

The fact that the fable of the humble layman, spiritual director to a doctor, was quite probably the work of Rulman Merswin, a Strasbourg banker and friend of Tauler,[148] and that it probably also refers to a conversion of Tauler at about the age of forty,[149] has been studied elsewhere and is of less importance to us here than is another fact, which is patent in this text and explains its propagation: the *emergence of the laity* opposite the clerics; the taking up of questions common to all against the professionals who had appropriated meaning for themselves; the apparition of the nonpriest witness who reduced the master to a schoolboy and who, without having attended schools, without possessing the science of the Scriptures (the science of sciences), and by the sole fact of being illuminated, upsets the traditional hierarchical relations. Even if, as is probable, Merswin did not have polemic intentions and was not challenging the clergy directly,[150] even if he began by addressing his edifying novel to the community of Johannists gathered on Île Verte, even if he endowed his hero with the most reverent modesty toward the priest whose director he would become, his work is no less revelatory of a silent revolution, among the first witnesses of which were the Strasbourg "Friends of God." These laymen, yielding to the movement to "abandon themselves" to the Absolute [*sich ganz zu Grunde zu lassen*] to find their hidden abode [*in seiner verborgenen Heimlichkeit*], became "the foundation of the Holy Church."[151] It is an experience that was described. It did not yet need to defend itself, or did not, in its native fervor, think it was to occasion a polemics. But already, although in other terms, the "ignorant one" of yesteryear declares, like the young man in the coach, that, "even if the Gospel were to perish, God had taught him enough of it for his salvation." Already the theologian, his interlocutor, writes more or less like Surin: "He spoke to me [about the spiritual life] with such sublimity and solidity that all I have read or heard is nothing compared to what he told me."

The analysis of the manuscripts and printed editions of the Strasbourg "Meisterbuch"—if one follows its circulation and the corrections that changed it along the way—would show the responsive chords that lesson struck, as well as the subtle or violent "rehabilitations" that have tried to modify its meaning. One of the first and most visible of these shifts consisted in ascribing the story to Johannes Tauler, a priest and preacher. In the ensuing edifying *Lives*, the roles have been switched. It is the doctor, who, "converted in a strange manner," is the "Sublime and Illuminated Theologian," having achieved a "marvelous holiness of life."[152] Illumination, the sublime, and the marvelous have all changed sides. It remains only for the layman to become the wildman, by whom the cultivated man augments his value. But that is another story, which is not to be related now.

The fable of the Friend of God is nonetheless present in the works of an increasing number of theologians up until the seventeenth century, including all those who, like Bérulle (to name only the greatest among them), went looking in the suburbs or hovels and found beneath the cloak of the humblest trades the male or female Friend of God who would teach them the divine lesson. It is an ancient tradition that goes back to the "idiot woman" of Egypt,[153] a tension that already divided the primitive Church.[154] It marks out the fifteenth century with the legend-history of Schwester Katrei on the theme of "a simple woman" who "triumphs over a learned theologian."[155] It has its theoretical aspect in Nicholas of Cusa's *Idiota*[156] and also its popular one,[157] not to mention a literary tradition offering the age-old monument to the ironic wisdom of Sancho Panza.[158] Keeping to the religious sphere, one need but reread Bremond to find a hundred and one examples of the gesture that imitates the docility of the "Master of the Holy Writ." The "dearly beloved of God," an anonymous figure from the depths of Oberland, turns up everywhere, recognizable even though he receives new names or finally separates from Tauler after long association.

It is a theme dear to the spirituality of the era, placing the prophet beneath the sign of Amos, "taken from behind his cows." Thus it is (between 1610 and 1650) with those "wild" mystics who speak the "language of the mountains" and know nothing of books, but receive all from God, a God whom they "cannot get over."[159] Louis de la Rivière speaks of a peasant girl from Diois to whom "no one had ever given the least instruction," and whose "manner of speaking was in truth very crude and rustic, but seasoned with a marvelous wisdom."[160] Similarly, there was the "poor cowherd" of Ponçonas, in Dauphiné;[161] Anne Le Barbier, "keeping the sheep in the country," near Caen, and "having no other spiritual director but the Holy Ghost";[162] Barbe, the "poor maidservant" of Compiègne, "keeping the cows in the country," of whom Father de Condren used to say that he "had never seen anyone who had so much knowledge . . . of Jesus Christ crucified."[163] Countless other village women or poor "girls" burst in upon a learning that they tore to shreds in the name of an outlandish lore. And each time the learned man who "discovered" one of them declared, like Father Coton: "Her conversation did me more good than all the good books I ever read."[164]

Around 1650, the "true priest" M. Renar meets an illiterate carpenter who speaks admirably to him of Saint Joseph and of silence, and "had never used the reading of any book."[165] A few years later, the admirable "method of prayer" presented in the *Agneau occis dans nos coeurs* [Lamb slain in our hearts] was attributed to Jean Aumont, a wine-grower in Montmorency, a "poor villager without other science or study than that of Jesus Christ crucified."[166] But in this case, the doctor who is supposed to become the disciple of the illiterate is no longer a part of the text. His place is taken by the reader himself, to whom the "poor villager" gives this "notice" as the text begins: "This is no work of proper study, nor learned through reasoning, but by practice, grace, and divine infusion of divine Wisdom, uncreated, and by the ministry of his divine Spirit."[167] From that "terra incognita," the fields and mountains of the country, emerges a France of a different wisdom, a wild land that suddenly finds its way through the barriers of a society of "clerics" (in the later, profane sense of "clerks"). This was a moment of tension, before the illiterate took his place within the popular pastorals, "accompanied by his shepherd's staff . . . like a bishop or an abbot with his crosier,"[168] bearing the insignia of his erstwhile opposite for a masquerade. Soon the young barbarian would become the *Wise Three-Year-Old*, a famous "Christian instruction," a popular catechism "in which all the wisdom of the world is generously attributed to the innocent child."[169]

## THE "IDIOT" AND THE "PAUPER"

Leaving aside the manuscripts and printed books that A. Chiquot has painstakingly uncovered,[170] the theme becomes larger. The terms change. The Friend, for example, appears as a Solitary, a Hermit, a Pauper, a Beggar, and so on. The relationship, however, remains constant. It is structural. But it is affected by new problems that gradually shift the original meaning. Where there once was an opposition not only between the layman and the theologian-priest, but also between *mystic science* and *book learning*, the contrast now takes a social direction. Increasingly, poverty occupies the "place" of *mystics*. It takes on a revendicatory role in a society in which affluence and culture cease being Christian. The confrontation changes, no longer opposing two kinds of religious knowledge or two ecclesiastic categories but two social groups. The scholar becomes the rich man and "libertine" while the untutored man becomes the pauper and believer.

If we restrict our attention to the evolution of the theme from the end of the sixteenth century to the end of the seventeenth, there is first the opposition that sets one before the other: "[Myself], a layman and a poor idiot, and you, a great doctor of theology."[171] "Idiot" here is still, as in the original meaning of the term, the simple private individual, he who does not possess the official patent for theological knowledge and sacred functions. The adjective "poor" bears less the sense of modesty (which was the virtue of the Friend in the older version of the story) than of status. The criterion of work and of one's position within a hierarchy that was no longer religious but social was becoming decisive. Here, too, as in the case of *mystique, pauvre* ["poor"] becomes a noun rather than an adjective. It is a class, a condition, and also the myth of a different science. Let us quickly take stock of this complex evolution. In 1639, in the works of Nicolas Du Sault, a friend of Surin and a too frequently neglected spiritual writer,[172] Tauler's poor man has become a pustular beggar.[173] A few years later, in 1652, the same character is described as "a beggar, covered with poor rags, with bare and muddied feet, an object of pitiful appearance." The good Rojas overdoes it a bit, but his poor man is presented in French by Cyprian of the Nativity, the translator of John of the Cross.[174] Henri-Marie Boudon does not go that far, but he does establish an opposition between the "skillful" and the "poor ignorant one," that "wise idiot" who taught Tauler the "science of the saints" in making him pass through "a ridiculous life" in the eyes of the world.[175] Soon, at the threshold of the Enlightenment, a religious congregation would place itself beneath the insignia of "idiots." But Boudon himself, who returns several times to that "simple, poor man," quickly supplies contemporary examples. "I knew," he writes, "a poor married craftsman from whom the greatest prelates in the kingdom asked counsel and advice, even in matters of the greatest consequence."[176] What is significant in this text beyond the quality of doctor or priest, is the allusion to those "great prelates" and those "matters" of which a craftsman is the judge. A social relation takes the place of religious status or of a hierarchy of knowledge.

The shift accelerates. Myriad accounts or legends accompany that reinterpretation of a spirituality henceforth marginalized and invested in one of the terms of a sociocultural conflict: religion is now on the side of the poor. The narratives converge in a direction that is made clear by the case most interesting from a literary point of view, with its strange and elusive moment, the confrontation between Don Juan and the poor man, in Molière (*Don Juan*, III, 2). "The poor man," this "pauper," emerging from the forest, a nameless man coming out of no place, "withdrawn by himself into this wood for the last six years" like a hermit, is the sole interlocutor who forces the grand lord to yield; and he teaches him a lesson. He has no other power than that of responding to the bribes by saying, "No, Sir, I'd rather starve to death," which is perhaps the line for which that scene was written. Could it be that the invincible dignity to which a libertine does homage for "love of humanity" is the "science" that the poor man will henceforth teach the rich? And could it be on that basis that he is able to impose a different history (soon a revolutionary one) upon his master? That scene, an enigma at the heart of Molière's masterpiece, does not tell us. The other pauper, that of *mystics*, also survives. Madame Guyon's relation of her encounter with a dockworker is proof of it. It is the biographical twin of the letter about the young man in the coach, and it, too (as was already the case of the story of the idiot woman of the fourth century), falls into silence.

One day when I had decided to go to Notre-Dame on foot, I told the lackey who was following me to lead me there by the shortest way. Providence permitted that he get me lost. While I was on a bridge, a rather badly dressed man approached me. I thought he was a pauper. I made it my duty to give him alms. He thanked me, and told me he wasn't asking for them. And drawing near me, he began speaking of God's infinite greatness, of which he said admirable things. He then spoke to me of the Holy Trinity in so great and lofty a manner that all I had heard about it previously seemed as shadows by comparison. Going on, he spoke of the Holy Sacrifice of Mass, of its excellence, of the care one should have to hear it and take part respectfully. That man, who did not know me in the least, and who could not even see my face, which was covered, then said to me: "I know, Madam, that you love God, that you are very charitable, and give many alms" (and he said much more about the qualities God had given me). "And yet," he said, "you are far off the mark. God desires something quite different of you. You are fond of your beauty." Then, after he had depicted my faults naively but truly, my heart could not deny what he said. I listened silently and respectfully, while those who were following me said I was conversing with a madman. I felt distinctly that he was enlightened with true wisdom. He also told me God did not wish for me to be content with working like the others to secure my salvation by avoiding the pains of Hell alone; but he also wanted me to attain such perfection in this life as to avoid even the pains of purgatory. During that talk, the way, though long, seemed short. I didn't notice it until I got to Notre-

Dame, where my extreme exhaustion made me faint. What surprised me was that, having reached the Pont-au-Double and looking in all directions, I no longer saw the man, nor have I ever seen him since. I asked him, hearing him speak the way he did, who he was. He told me that he had once been a dockworker but was no longer. This meeting did not impress me as much at the time as it has since. At first I told it like a story, without saying what he told me at the end. But having realized what there was of the divine in it, I didn't speak of it anymore.[177]

*Chapter Eight*

# The "Little Saints" of Aquitaine

We encounter another kind of "Friends of God" around the same time, the 1630s, among the French Jesuits. It is no longer the case of a solitary in the "wilderness," but of a group living within a powerful, dynamic, well-organized institution not yet a century old: the Society of Jesus. The "wildmen" appear, in this case, within the most modern institution of meaning. Whereas that organization made reform its program, its crusade and "glory," these men demanded the Society's internal reform and a life more true to its origins. This handful of "young men," "little prophets and little saints," as one of their censors calls them[1]—in short, the brothers of the young man in the coach— start a movement similar to the one John of the Cross and his friends had begun in the old Carmelite Order by giving birth to the "re- formed" or "Discalced" Carmelites. They fought for a spiritual "pu- rity" within the very institution that asserted its value and gave it a social place. But history does not repeat itself. They failed where John of the Cross had succeeded. Were they perhaps too late?

Their situation is a paradoxical one. The founder, Ignatius of Loy- ola, had been dead for barely seventy years (1556) and had just been beatified (1609). He was "a man of this century," as Surin still said thirty years later. And already these "reformed mystics" arose like phantoms of a lost origin. Claiming to go back to the spirit of that origin and to Ignatius, they protested against the profane and worldly activities the Order emphasized in the distribution of its tasks and objectives. Oddly, their criticism and aspirations were similar to those expressed a short while earlier (1606) by the higher Jesuit authorities. But the moment these "reformed mystics" appeared, they were accused of introducing a doctrine that was "foreign" to the spirit of the Society of Jesus: a "dangerous," even "pernicious," teaching with respect to the rules that governed an apostolic mission, a trend characterized by two equally pejorative terms in the documents of the authorities—it was "new," and it was "mystical." There followed a series of marginalizing procedures that induced the "prophets" to toe the line, keep a low profile, or get out. Obey, keep quiet, or leave: three options for witnesses who made bold to bring the institution back to its "spirit." They were defeated, then, but without having opposed an Order to which they wished to belong.[2] They represented within it a mystic "resistance," the social expression of which could not be reduced to a denomination, nor even to a pressure group, and the failure of which would not prevent the development of a literary and spiritual posterity. Their lineage was born of their defeat. Within the Society, they had no more power than the "idiot woman" in her convent at Tismēnai. They were even determined to respect their "condition." They did not set another institution in opposition to the one that for them defined a "state." But they did introduce a *difference* into it. What difference, and in what way? This particular case should allow us to show how that "difference" manifests itself socially, and also how it sallies forth from its repression to go elsewhere—like those revolutionary chants that survive the failure of historical realizations and carry a spirit further.[3]

But first we must return to the institutional beginnings of this reformism, that is, to the form it took officially in the Society of Jesus, before the young mystic zealots made it their cause and paid the price.

## THE "DEFICIENCIES" OF THE SOCIETY (1606)

Reformism arrived in Rome well before the upset caused by its appearance among some young French members. In the space of one half century, the Jesuits had increased their membership tenfold (to over thirteen thousand by 1615), multiplied the number of their foundations, diversified their occupations, extended their influence, and increased their wealth. They were respected, feared, admired, and criticized. New problems arose, partly due to the qualitative changes entailed in quantitative growth beyond certain limits, partly to the mental transformation of Europe. Under the generalship of Claudio

Acquaviva (1581–1615),[4] two questions became increasingly acute: one involved the international character of the Order, which was developing at a time when the nationalities were affirming and separating themselves from one another; the other concerned the meaning and nature of its mission at a time when the practical ministries were becoming specialities increasingly independent from the spirit that induced Jesuits to exercise them. The necessary revision therefore involved the internal organization of the Society as well as its external activity. That revision had to make it possible to overcome the particular difficulties caused, within an institution that was still young, on one hand by the mutation of Christianity in Europe, and on the other by the secularization of philosophy, science, and human tasks then in process.

The first difficulty surfaced particularly in connection with the position occupied by the Spanish. Long predominant among the "professed"[5] and in the Roman hierarchy of the Order, they did not fail to react when that privilege, which seemed to have a basis in the origins of the Society, was challenged. Their side was supported by Pope Sixtus V (d. 1590), who needed the goodwill of King Felipe II. J. Acosta, the provincial in Peru, having returned to Rome with the help of the king of Spain, worked for their cause and won over Toledo (who was very influential in the curia and elevated to the rank of cardinal in September 1593). Whatever the role of pro- and anti-Spanish intervention may have been,[6] a fifth general congregation was decided upon by Clement VII (on 15 December 1592) and practically imposed on Acquaviva. The congregation met from 3 November 1593 until 18 January 1594 and addressed an already substantial docket of reformist projects. If the decisions of the delegates tended to impose more control over the power of the general by increasing the role of representatives in the Order,[7] or to safeguard the independence of the Roman government in the face of nationalisms,[8] it was because at the inception of the congregation, and central to the debates, was a tension between the new political patriotisms and religious unity. These deliberations and oppositions were accompanied by reports on the remedies called for by the "defects" [*"detrimenta"*] from which, from this point of view, the institutions of the Society suffered. The Portuguese Hernando de Mendoça would soon compose his *Advis de ce qu'il y a à réformer en la Compagnie des Jésuites* [Notice on what should be reformed in the Society of Jesus] for the sixth general congregation in 1608 (translated and published shortly afterward in French),[9] a text that was "presented to the Pope and general congregation." In this text, he calls into question the generalship for life;[10] he proposes that there be a general placed in charge specifically of Spanish affairs,[11] or at least the institution of alternation between a Spanish general and a "foreign one."[12] He asks for a reduced training time and adds "that an order should be given that not so many people should leave the Society, as happens every day, after twenty and even thirty years, so that there are more outside than in."[13] Other similar memoirs appeared, such as *Discours du père Iean Mariana, Iesuite Espagnol. Des grands défauts qui sont en la forme du gouvernement des Iesuites*, published in 1625, and perhaps in 1624 as well.[14]

To this type of reformism another must be added: spiritual reformism. Just as there was an opposition between the reality of national allegiances and the religious unity of the Order, a schism formed between the actual activities carried out and the spirit that had originally inspired them. In this respect as well, Jesuits examined themselves. The criticism engendered by their success was echoed from within their ranks. Still so close to their founder, were they not perhaps allowing themselves to be drawn by their works far from the "solid virtues" he had desired for his "little Company"? Were they not, as was charged in Rome and elsewhere, departing from the goals originally set for them? On 27 September 1585, Acquaviva asked Lorenzo Maggio to prepare a report on this issue. This memorandum, completed at the end of November 1585, and delivered to the general on 24 January 1586, is entitled *De naevis Societatis et remediis*. It analyses the shortcomings of the Society, their causes and possible remedies. It insists on the urgent need for a proper training for prayer.[15] In 1593–94, the question was taken up again and developed with the creation of a commission *Ad detrimenta cognoscenda*, which reinforced the fifth general congregation and was to continue its work. *Detrimenta*: the word itself recurs like a haunting leitmotif in the memoranda, reports, and controversies of the late sixteenth and early seventeenth centuries. It eventually became the theme of a sweeping inquiry—a procedure the general used on several occasions to bring about a raising of the collective level of awareness and the circulation of information.[16] In 1605, while preparations for the solemnities surrounding the canonization of Ignatius of Loyola and Francis Xavier (1612) were already underway, Acquaviva requested the examination *De detrimentis societatis* of all the Jesuit provinces. Every provincial congregation was to meet and send a report on the deficiencies they found, the remedies already applied and their results, and, finally, ways of ensuring greater faithfulness in the future. Every Jesuit also could send a memorandum on these same questions to

Rome. The entire file constitutes a generation's judgment of itself.[17] It is also a cross section of an entire social body.

For France, the responses are mainly focused on problems of spirituality. They are lucid and severe, and they come from remarkable individuals, among whom are the best spiritual writers of the day. The minutes of Lyon were signed by the provincial Louis Richeome; those of Paris, by Étienne Charlet, also a provincial, and his report is expanded by a personal memorandum from the hand of Pierre Coton, then the "royal preacher" at the court of Henry IV. The longest of these *Informationes de statu provinciae* comes from Aquitaine: twenty folios were sent to Rome on 4 February 1606. Judging from these French memoranda, the superiors took too little interest in the spiritual formation of their subjects and applied a purely external authoritarianism that was criticized insistently nearly everywhere. For example, at the professed house in Paris the superior "governs despotically" [*despotice*] "cares little for the people in the house and much for himself, behaves in too harsh and abrasive a way."[18] In particular, the Jesuits did not devote the time prescribed by the rules to prayer and spiritual reading, often considering these to be the occupation of novices. The Aquitaine report notes "an excessive propensity to omit, interrupt, or practice too negligently prayers, examinations of conscience, especially the particular examination of conscience, the reading of spiritual books," and "a difficulty in gathering one's thoughts, even during the spiritual exercises."[19] The religious appear too readily inclined to excel in science and to be more preoccupied with intellectual work than with the practice of the virtues.[20] There are several mentions of failure to keep the vow of poverty: for example, in Paris, the increasing use of the watch, which was, in principle, to be restricted to the provincial and to Pierre Coton[21] since the technological appropriation of time also went against the vow of poverty. But the most frequently noted of these *detrimenta* was a "great diffusion into the outer world" [*"magna effusio ad exteriora"*], toward "immoderate outside occupations that absorb the entire man."[22] This *effusio ad exteriora*, explainable by the urgency of tasks to be performed and the scarcity of workers, was, according to the collective reports, the "real root" of all the other failings. The law of work prevailed over that of contemplation.

Pierre Coton is the author of the most interesting personal memorandum,[23] a text that begins a long spiritual tradition (from Lallemant or Surin to Jean Pierre de Caussade and Jean Nicolas Grou) of internal criticisms targeting Jesuit activism. He limits himself, he says, to what he observed in the professed house of Paris, the only house in which he resided in this province. But there, he adds, "I believe I must say that the majority care very little about the inner man."[24] In the chapter "De cura spiritualium internaque cultura," he attempts to analyze the causes of the evil and its remedies. Among the causes, there is first and foremost a "bad training for the inner life" (with, as a corollary, an insufficient number of confessors and superiors who do know what the "inner cult" is); then there is the security found in "external" tasks; finally, a series of defects concerning superiors, who are managers more than spirituals, suspicious, scheming, untouchable, and sure of themselves.[25] In keeping with the request from Rome, this harsh judgment applied only to the responsibilities of the institution: education, the allotment of tasks, and the executives. But it also cast a negative hue on the solitary experience to which the Order was presumed to give a social form. To all indications, it was as if "spiritual" itineraries were "foreign" to the actual functioning of the Jesuit organization.

The remedies suggested by Coton were, in principle, measures the authorities could take to cure the ills and "save" the Order (as Maldonat, the great French Jesuit theologian had already written in 1579, "with just tears shed for the Society's undoing").[26] In point of fact, Coton presented a mixture of points concerning possible institutional intervention and general principles, of necessity left to the discretion of every individual. On the one hand, there was a need for superiors who were "good and spiritual," and for confessors "knowing how to teach and not satisfied with absolving," and so on. Also— and this is a noteworthy indication, coming nearly forty years before the campaign led by Antoine Arnauld in *De la fréquente communion*— one should "not indulge" in the Eucharist and the mass as one does when habit dulls its usefulness and thus one "disdains" the presence of Christ. On the other hand, the following are recommended: "the knowledge and disdain of self," "union with God and walking in His presence," faithfulness to the "motions of the heart" [*"motiones animi"*], conduct springing from the "inner affection of the spirit" [*"interior animi affectio"*] and not from sensitivity, custom, or ambition; a permanent self-examination of conscience and the assiduous, daily reading of spiritual books; and, finally, a life turned toward "God alone, the sole necessity."[27] The same insistence on the "motions of the heart" and purity of intention is present in the chapter "Ministeria zelusque animarum utrum langueant vel efflorescant," which upholds the primacy of the *affectus* over the *effectus*, that is, the priority of an obedience to the inner movements of the spirit over the objective interest presented by social activities. "Do not go from outer realities toward inner ones, but from the inner ones to the outer. . . . Heed not the call of the object [ *"non vocari ab objecto"*], but that of God."[28] It is the reversal of a strategy that would allocate tasks on the basis of their public interest. In relation to a dichotomy between the "inner" and the "outer," the movements of the "heart" should provide the criterion of what actions are to be undertaken.

The essential question is about the "subject" [ *subjectum*] and not about the "object" [ *objectum*]. All depends, ultimately, on the "disposition" of the former, not "on the quality or quantity" of the latter. "There are not fewer people who are avaricious for a small sum than for a large one." Similarly, one may be distracted by a trifle or by a great many matters.[29] The important point is not to transform tasks but hearts. Prayer [ *"oratio"*], is thus the resource of the reform: a return to the "inner," to the movement (at once *motus*, the motor principle, and *motio*, the inspiration of the moment) that comes from on high, to a "force" that, coming from within, gives meaning and direction [ *"intentio"*] to daily activity. It is the return to a medieval axiom, *actus sequitur esse* [action follows being], but the "being" set within a cosmic order is replaced by the promptings of the will of the absolute, and "action" manifesting that order is replaced by the operation that "produces" that internal prompting in the public arena. Thus, the reform consists in remodeling visible things on the basis of divine energies as those energies are felt by the heart (*voluntas* and *affectus*). This conception remains cosmic, but in the dynamic perspective of forces animating the human will, forces that must be assured passage out into the theatrical space of this world.

It is, then, in his chapter on prayer ("De studio orationis")[30] that Coton's views become explicit. They may be summarized as the opposition of two polarities, one designated by "spiritual luxury," the other by a few main formulations, such as "to want God in accordance with God" [ *Deum velle secundum Deum*], "to take delight in God" [ *Deo frui*] rather than to use him [ *Deo uti*]. The "mercenary" spirit, which profits from association with the divine for reasons of individual or collective promotion, and the spirit of "luxury," which turns love of God into self-love, represent typically "mystic" themes. They involve Coton in a development that (by prudence?) he eliminates from his final version: the luxury of the senses, blameworthy though it is, is less serious than the luxury of the spirit, which is all the more frequent among the religious, who have freed themselves to a greater extent from the pleasures of the "flesh." It is an "illuminist" leitmotif: true luxury, which makes the other into an object of profit, belongs to the heart, not the body. The latter is, after all, only the physical emblem of a more fundamental betrayal that perverts asceticism and puts the profitability of a position, relation, or authority in place of the hospitality of the heart.[31]

The positive direction is indicated by a series of maxims, spoken haltingly in fragments—like a path traced by little white pebbles:

> Keeping oneself untainted [*immaculatum*] by the world. . . . Wanting God according to God, that is, in the way he wishes. Finding joy only in what leads to him and suffering only in what distances one from him . . . Taking what we suffer for him who lived and died for us to be joy. Making a paradise for ourselves of what glorifies him. Annihilating oneself by oneself [*exinanire semetipsum*]. . . . Taking care to walk before the face of God, without ever (to the extent that this is possible) turning our eyes from him who looks upon us unceasingly with his fatherly eyes. . . . Speaking, discussing, studying, walking around, administering the sacraments not only according to God and in God's presence, but in God, as the birds move about in the air that surrounds them, or the fish in the sea, in such a manner that we may live in the experience of the God who is there and fills our actions. . . . The mercenaries prefer to use God rather than to rejoice in [*frui*] him; they only wish to serve him at his expense. . . . We must await God until, as long as, in the manner that, and for the purpose of whatever he wishes. Last, remaining available in whatever we are doing [*in negotio otiosum esse*], that is, with heart and mind almost never away from God, especially in external tasks that are easily compatible with that attention.

Such is the delineation of what is lacking. It uses some of the same propositions Lorenzo Maggio set down by 1585. It also echoes Italian spiritual groups with which Coton was connected, particularly the little network that formed in Milan around the figure of Achille Gagliardi, a Jesuit "spiritual director" who, in keeping with a frequent pattern, follows the experience of his "Philothea," Isabella Bellinzaga. This mystic traveler, like Dante's Beatrice, guides Gagliardi through the paradises, purgatories, and infernos of the soul. While Gagliardi becomes the interpreter and theoretician of his "directed one" in the *Breve compendio*, a book that is immediately very controversial,[32] Coton learns from her what "the purest" humility is.[33] He is more supple, more brilliant, and less vigorous than the Milanese Jesuit. But he, too, attests to "spiritualist" aspirations that murmur here and there in the visiting rooms of the Jesuit houses, and that seem, to the authorities, sometimes beneficial, sometimes troublesome or suspect, especially after the Spanish "affairs" of Antonio Cordeses and Balthasar Alvarez.[34]

By and large, the 1606 reports doubtless tend to paint the picture of the *detrimenta* in somber shades. It is a law of the genre. But they unanimously stress two decisive points in the contemporary scene and for the future: an antimony between a kind of apostolic work that had become excessive or captivating and the inner life, and the urgency of a (better) spiritual formation. This was a double surprise, a double break with respect to the tradition: works, due to their technicalization, can separate one from God; and "spirit," in a flourishing society, can be lacking. The enormous development of the undertakings (for the preceding twenty or thirty years, many religious were worried about their excessive or premature multiplication), the extension and mobilization of the Jesuits on all fronts of the post-Tridentine crusade, and the "secularization" of methods and practices destroyed the euphoric image of the original "little company" of "reformed priests." The *effusio ad exteriora*, before being the defect of the religious criticized in the 1606 French reports, was characteristic of the entire Order. In reaction to that effusion/diffusion, the hazard of growth, there was, at the beginning of the seventeenth century, a turning inward, an effort to defend an identity and establish a distinctive individuality.[35] Measures had to be taken to counterbalance the logic of the "external" occupations. Hence that reaction could not be bolstered by those occupations themselves, which, though still necessary, had become a danger. It was identified with a policy concerning spirituality. Its program intended *to construct an "interior."* Coton, the king's confessor, understood perfectly the institutional stakes involved in what the Society's secretary, Bernard de Angelis, called a "spiritual administration." This policy of *mystics* took shape in the vicinity of a borderline that required more rigorous demarcation, and that divided two areas whose names haunt the documents of the times: *nostrum* and *alienum* (or *peregrinum*)—what is "ours" and what is "foreign."

Central to this program was the necessity for the institution to take charge of the preservation of its "interiority," or of a "spirit." There was another frequent formulation of this strategic point: "the spirit of our Institute." Essentially, that did not mean that there *was* a "spirit" *in* the institution, but that the legal and intellectual organization of the Society (that is, its "institute") must form and guarantee a spirit that would be its own (the spirit of the house), even if it were in opposition to its own members, since the erosion, or as some said, the "downfall" of the Society was caused by the Jesuits themselves. It was no simple matter, that policy of the spirit. At any rate, if it fought against the shortcomings of the "inner life" of its workers, it was equally opposed to the manifestation of that spirituality outside the institutional norms. That policy took effect in three different ways.

First, a series of measures and laws were instituted that governed the novitiate (1580), the first years of study (1608), the "renewals" of religious promises (1608), the third year of the novitiate at the conclusion of studies (1593–94), daily prayer (1581), annual retreats lasting from eight to ten days (1608), the maintenance of spiritual life by the superiors (1598), the way of administering the *Spiritual Exercises* (1599), and so on. This administrative apparatus, by applying spiritual practices, tightened up an Order that was becoming "diffuse" due to its apostolic practices. That effort was seconded by a corresponding one in the academic area, with the *Ratio studiorum*, the first draft of which, in 1585, transposed methods taken from a spiritual discipline to the pedagogical domain. It was no doubt necessary for the Society to develop institutional rules regulating an interiority and its transmission, that is, a social economy of the spirit, in order to be able to produce a global, coherent pedagogical system.[36]

The production of a spiritual literature is another way of circumscribing a spiritual locus. It, too, was based on an institutional policy. It therefore was stimulated and controlled by Acquaviva. Until then, though there was a great abundance of "conferences" (or *"pláticas"*), "directories," and "letters," that production is devoted essentially to practical problems, "manners of procedure," and it especially develops, in the form of commentaries, the in-house tradition of Ignatius of Loyola's *Spiritual Exercises.* Beyond that, one might consult the great texts of the Rheno-Flemish, the Carmelite school, and the "lovers of Jesus Christ"—Gertrud of Helfta, Angela of Foligno, Catherine of Genoa, Madeleine de Pazzi, and others. The voices of these great contemplatives, coming from the "outside," contrast with the rather plodding texts of the "Directories," which are quite reserved about any mystical interpretation of the *Exercises.*[37] The former are intoxicating; they sweep you off your feet. Hence the drastic measures taken by Mercurian, in 1575, against a great number of these "readings" (Tauler, Ruysbroeck, Suso, Gertrude, Mechthild and many others were excluded).[38] Acquaviva encouraged a different style, already noticeable in the treaty, written at his suggestion, that Bernardino Rossignoli published in Ingolstadt in 1600: *Disciplina christianae perfectionis.* The texts became more technical, less affective. The references were no longer limited to an internal tradition but embraced all Christian literature. It was no longer just a question of techniques, but also of theoretical problems of Christian life and the great issues of the day. A doctrinal corpus was in the making. The following works appeared: *De vita spirituali* by Alvarez de Paz (1608), *Ejercicio de perfección* by Alfonso Rodriguez (1609), *De virtute et statu religionis* by Francisco de Suarez (1608–25), *Intérieure occupation* by Pierre Coton (1608), *Vida del V.P. Balthasar Alvarez* by Luis de Puente (1615), *De summo bono* by Leonhard Lessius (1615), and so on. These are major works, born of confrontation with the theological and mystic currents of the times; establishing, instancing, justifying what in Rome was called the *via regia* of spirituality, a "royal road," henceforth the standard for the entire seventeenth century. They inaugurated, under the influence of Acquaviva's directives, a language of the interior, a place of the spirit.

Last, an official image of the founder was put in place. It was the origin, revised and amended. The first generations of Jesuits had known the portrait, edifying to be sure, but informal, depicted by Pedro de Ribadeneyra in his *Vita Ignatii Loiolae* (1572). It had been a success: seven Latin editions, as many Spanish, three French, two Italian, one German, and one English. Acquaviva required Ribadeneyra, who showed little enthusiasm, to amend his book and give more attention to the institutions.[39] Another biography is requested from G. P. Maffei in 1573; in 1585 it was published simultaneously in Rome, Venice, Cologne, and Douai. It was the European launching of a different portrait: governmental, more "objective," a projection of the present work onto its genesis. The two texts were in competition: a double image of the father. But the second slowly gained ground; as in the iconography in which the knight, the pilgrim, the reformed priest wearing the Roman habit, and episodes similar to the *Flos sanctorum* were replaced by a founder in priestly robes, bearing like a monstrance, the texts of a law inspired by God. The institution had become the true founder. Whatever remained of the primitive "miracles" was there to prove that that institution was of "our" spirit.[40]

## THE PERSECUTION OF "EXTRAORDINARY DEVOTIONS" (1615–45)

On 15 November 1615, the seventy-four members of the Seventh General Congregation elected, on the fourth vote and not without debate, Muzio Vitelleschi to succeed Claudio Acquaviva. The following January 2, Jean-Pierre Camus, the friend and polygraphic admirer of Francis of Sales, introduced the new general to the rector of the college of Chambéry with the words:

> I join you in rejoicing over the very worthy general that your society has in the person of the Reverend Father Mutio Vitelleschi, a Roman

gentleman I have seen and heard with admiration in Rome. He is a person who in all things breathes nothing but holiness, and whose sufficiency is extreme, especially in the area of preaching. . . . I do not know whether Your Reverence ever saw him: he resembles Father Coton; I say this of his face, his words, and his conduct. May God bless this so canonical election with a success such as I wish for it, I, arch-Jesuit in soul and in all.[41]

This new Coton was a profoundly religious man (his prayers were accompanied by tears),[42] a rousing orator, erstwhile poet (in his "youth," which he evokes with tenderness in his old age),[43] and inclined to making compromises. He would repeat: "Beati non fortes, sed mites"—gentleness is better than strength.[44] His excessive prudence contrasted sharply with the daring authority of Acquaviva; it had caused some hesitation among his 1615 electors. He did, in fact, drop some of his predecessor's projects, such as the formation of a black clergy, the creation of centers specializing in scientific research, and so on. His conduct was the same in spiritual matters. Acquaviva, though he may have channeled the mystic currents, at least recognized them, often in contrast to certain of his assistants, such as Hoffaeus.[45] Vitelleschi saw them as a "danger": the terms *periculum, periculosum*, which come up repeatedly in his letters on the subject, reveals his underlying opinion.[46] But he himself traced this portrait with lucidity: "If I couldn't avoid opposite extremes and achieve the happy medium, my character would lead me to prefer excessive caution to reckless zeal, and I would rather be too timid than too daring or bold."[47]

His correspondence lets us witness the rise of a mystic peril in France. The disturbances [*turbationes*] took place around the years 1625–35. From Rome, Vitelleschi gives the impression of a person following, on the map of France, the progress of a contagious disease of which the locals are insufficiently aware. The first symptom appeared in 1626: a tendency toward "revelations" in the college of Poitiers—a "matter of great importance," wrote the general, who told the provincial of Aquitaine to be alert to avoid the worsening of the situation.[48] In June, then in December of the same year, there was further mention of this college, disturbed "under the pretext of devotion" by the spiritual "illusions" of certain Jesuits. That "novelty" was serious and risked spreading if order were not restored as soon as possible.[49]

What local measures were being taken? No one appeared particularly upset. In 1627, Vitelleschi comes back to that "extremely dangerous" affair, which he thought settled. "This new and foreign spirit of devotion," "that peculiar spirit," was totally "distant from the common conduct of the Society"; it had to be fought by those responsible locally before it crept in everywhere. This time, the general was writing to Bordeaux.[50] But in Limoges, too, three Jesuits, stricken by "extraordinary devotions," recommended an "inner spirit," declared that "the Society must be reformed," and wanted "to introduce I know not what improvement."[51] In Lyon, in Paris, the "fire" was spreading.[52] In Bordeaux, among certain young Jesuits (Pierre Cluniac, Jacques du Tertre, "still others"), these "extraordinary," "new," "peculiar," "dangerous" phenomena were observed. The "contagion" had to be stopped by punishing the ones involved, by isolating them, and, if possible, by dispersing them, before using more violent remedies if those proved insufficient.[53] For years, the number of injunctions grew, addressed again to Bordeaux,[54] to Paris,[55] Nancy,[56] Dijon,[57] and so on. They were very detailed. Within that vague, unfocused "novelty," they attempt to focus on key details. For example, in the houses of religious formation, they forbid the devotion of a "new and nontraditional" cult to Saint Joseph[58]—who, since Saint Teresa of Avila, had become the standard-bearer of *mystics*, and, according to Surin, "the patron of nearly all the great souls of this century."[59] Or else they request that any allusions, even in jest, to the "illumined" be dropped from conversation,[60] which might indicate that the announcement in France of the Seville decree (1623) against the Spanish *alumbrados* or the affair of the *illuminés* of Picardy (1630–35)[61] was on the minds of the young Jesuits.

Rome's uneasiness, sustained by numerous local informants, was motivated at once by a regional particularism that threatened the Order's unity, an illuminism that replaced apostolic activity with a contemplative "inaction," and a "spirit of novelty" that eluded the institution or "spiritual administration." The first point, always a sensitive one in the Ignatian organization of obedience, crucial between the years 1580 and 1610, lost some of its urgency after the centralization achieved by Acquaviva. The two other concerns filled a whole administrative and spiritual literature directed against the *neoterici*, who "exclude all human action" and define perfection as a pure "inaction" of God.[62] Certain general problems determined a setting, both imaginary and political, within which the countless details sent by informants were placed. The experience with Spain, haunted by the sixteenth-century *alumbrados*, and also the repeatedly turbulent Italian experience, gave a somber cast to the interpretation of reports from France. Roman officialdom, still predominantly Spanish, used the Castilian or Andalusian past as a frame of reference for construing current events from Lorraine or Aquitaine.

Seen from the French perspective, the facts were different, especially in the still dominant southern provinces. Those "young men" did not seem so "dangerous." After all, their ambitions were not so very different from those of certain "elders," such as Pierre Coton, back in 1606. Also, the religious wars had just subsided. The style of Louis XIII predominated. The suspect young men, feather in hat, practiced that "heroic virtue that uses excesses and the grandeur of the passions"[63] and that went with a "baroque" ostentation.[64] Their crusade was one of prayer. As schoolboys they had read the *Vie* of Teresa by Ribera, translated by Jean de Brétigny with a Franciscan freshness, full of "cheer" and miracles (1601, 1607, etc.). It was even proposed to pupils as a composition subject. In Paris, in 1614–15, Claude Bernier, one of those accused in 1627, was thirteen when he was enlightened by that book, which a classmate had given him.[65] In Bordeaux, in 1613, Jean-Joseph Surin (also considered "dangerous" by Vitelleschi) was the same age when he was gripped by the same book.[66] Many others had exactly the same experience. Ten years later in 1625, in Nancy, François Poiré (an elder) also said that "the example of Saint Teresa" (he was alluding to her *Vie*) had made him attentive to the "intimate movements" of the heart and led him to value above works "that silent Spirit that prompts him."[67] There was a French Teresian style. It was itself borne up by a deeper, older wave. In citing the ancient and mystical texts of Hermes Trismegistus ("most great Mercury") Guillaume du Vair characterizes that undercurrent with the phrase "that movement of the heart that most great Mercury calls the *inner spoken word.*"[68]

"Extraordinary devotions" are not limited to the Society of Jesus; they are found everywhere. It is a current that runs through institutions. Essentially it does not derive from them, though it is colored, precipitated, or channeled by the places through which it flows, as is water by the ground through which it runs. Therefore, before examining a case study, the Bordeaux group of suspect Jesuits, we must at least mention the existence of many other "little prophets" and "inspired women" whose passing is scarcely noted in the archives, and whom history, acquiescent to the logic of the documents produced by the past, knows only through the censures, trials, or banishment to which they have been subjected. These "middle-sized and small figures," far more numerous than one might think, and tending to form networks (as in Italy),[69] abound in Bordeaux.

Let us therefore open the windows of these religious houses onto the city of Bordeaux; a breath of fresh air, in passing. It was a city of intermingling nationalities. The Irish had their college there; the Flemish were very numerous at the Chartrons; the Spanish, the most influential group, played an important role in the instruction at the College of Guyenne (Juan Gelida, Francesco Suarez de Villegas, et al.)—they even had books in their language printed locally.[70] Merchants, jewelers, doctors, Portuguese Jews (approximately five hundred of them during the mid-seventeenth century) intensified the exchanges between European countries (family ties connected Bordeaux to Lisbon, Amsterdam, Genoa, and Naples), between religions (those "new Christians" lived on the borderline between institutions and returned in droves to Jewish practices at the end of the seventeenth century), and between languages (Spanish, Portuguese, but also Hebrew, the teaching of which, along with explanations of the Talmud, was publicly announced on written bills by Julius Otto in 1630).[71] No doubt a certain sort of Marranism is discernible, as is the case in Spanish mystic literature,[72] even among the religious writers who are sensitive to the passing of one selfsame "spirit" across institutional barriers—such as canon Jérôme Lopès, one of the best theologians of Bordeaux, who was of Portuguese Jewish origin and closely connected with the spirituals of the city.[73] In fact, Bordeaux was also a city of reformist and spiritual proliferation. In a little over twenty years (1602–26) foundations sprang up: the Capuchins (1602), the Daughters of Our Lady (1606), the Ursulines (1606), the Dominican Sisters (1608), the Minims (1608), the Carmelites (1610), the Sisters or Orphans of Saint Joseph (1616), the Mothers of the Assumption (1618), the Carmelites once more (second convent, 1618), the Nuns of Saint Joseph (1622), the Discalced Carmelites (1626), and so on. There was intense ferment, associated with the social rise of the lawyers, who supplied a great number of the novices or "donators" to these foundations before being threatened by the "ormist republic" of extremist merchants and bourgeois (1648–53). As they were forced to obey the royal power, their privileges were diminished or devalued.

Among the "extraordinary devotions" that accompanied, like music coming from a different country, the active and even hasty founding of reformed institutions, a sole example will suffice. It took place in May 1627. A "vicar" wrote to his archbishop, the cardinal of Sourdis, who was carrying out the reform *manu militari*. His name has been "eaten away by time" in the letter in which he refers to himself as the "valet" of the great lord his bishop, to whom the letter is addressed. He testifies to the "whiplash from on high" that has stricken him. For that "accident" that opened up the breach of a different dimension within the rites of the mass, he asks advice and castigation from the authority on liturgical rules.[74]

The congregation was held on the thirteenth of the present month, at Saint-Palais. Your valet was saying high mass, when an accident happened to him that was a whiplash from on high. While the ecclesiastics were singing the rest of Gloria in excelsis, your valet began to meditate when he thought he had an extraordinary devotion, but it was an indevotion instead, as I have been able to gather by what happened.

Which was that, the *Gloria in excelsis* being over, having said *Dominus vobiscum* and *Oremus*, I said: *Emitte Spiritum tuum et creabuntur.*[75] Having regained myself, I said the requisite prayer—although I had to consult the Holy Spirit to find out whether my consolation, accompanied by tears and sweetness, was from God and not instead some indevotion from the enemy of the salvation of souls, who is always at our heels and sometimes puts on the robe of light to make us fall down. Thus did I act.

And I also said that I would no longer be so pious, though I fear I have never been pious in the way one should, for which I beseech God's forgiveness and that of his Most Illustrious Lordship, subjecting myself to whatever punishment it may please Your Greatness to require of me.

I was supposed to be sitting. But because I found myself in a situation in which there was but one stool for the celebrant and not for the deacon nor the assistant deacon, it bothered me to be sitting while a priest, who is my equal, was standing.[76] For this reason, I occupied myself with meditation during the *Gloria in excelsis* and the Credo.

I beseech Your Greatness to write to me whether I should absolutely reject all extraordinary devotion.

Father Charles[77] advised me some time ago neither to reject it nor to seek it out. Obeying Your Greatness, in this and other things, I believe I am pleasing God, for the Apostle said: *Obedite praepositis vestris.*

This incident evinces no resistance to the Church authorities but the experience of something other. This anonymous and modest *illuminé* could be the representative of what was "happening" to many others, within the very institutions they respected. "Accidents" carried them off elsewhere. These were releases for aspirations that no longer had a language in those institutions. They were not indications of a rebellion but of escapism.

That the "spirit" might flee the Order, that the desire for the absolute might become alienated from the apostolic projects of the post-Tridentine Church—this was the "danger" the Jesuit Roman authorities clearly perceived. These "accidents" called into question the very link between the hierarchic organization of tasks and the divine "source" upon which the legitimacy of goals and the investiture of individuals was based. The very nature of the Society was at stake. In a larger sense, after the Council of Trent, Catholic theology and pastoral teaching tried precisely to reconcile the visible and the invisible, a vital link for which the endless debates on nature and grace sought the theory. Little by little, that combination, while it was affirmed in principle, was undone by history. Practices became independent of the spirit on which they were supposed to depend.[78] The "extraordinary devotions" were but the harbingers of what quietism made manifest by displaying the breach between the process of knowledge or action and a love that was "purified" of all knowledge and vested interest. It was the failure of the post-Tridentine Reform. But it was these "children" who first pointed to the break, whereas the institution claimed to guarantee reconciliation. They did not challenge the authorities. On the contrary, like the "foreign vicar," they often confessed to what, in their lives, did not correspond to the liturgical or apostolic norms, as if they were confessing to something that was their fault. They simply could not do otherwise. It would slip out. They confessed their inability to be simultaneously faithful to the inner inspiration and the objective works demanded of them. In the discourse of the Order, it was a lapse, the indecent return of a repressed division.

An expression dating back to the origin of the Society can be used to gauge the change that had taken place. This oft-repeated saying neatly dichotomizes a choice. The apostle, it was said, must "leave God for God," which Ribadeneyra clarified and nuanced in the following way: "Leave God [known] in himself [*Deum ipsum in se*] sometimes for God [sought] in one's neighbor."[79] In other words, leave the God you find in prayer (*relinquere Deum*) for the God you serve in action (*propter Deum*). This could also be translated: cease speaking *to* God to speak *of* him. Presupposing an exclusive disjunction (one or the other but not both), the expression is an invitation to pass from one to the other, leaving behind the inner scene of desire. It posits the principle of an equivalency or an exchange: one in place of the other. This goes back to an ancient tradition: "Leave your country, your kinsmen, and your father's house, and go to a country that I will show you."[80] The advice to "leave God" repeats (and transposes) a mythical and founding act. But at that moment in history it connected work, or the mission, with an exile far from the inner paradise: instead of God it was "the Glory of God." At the beginning of the activity, a loss defined what the activity was seeking on the outside, *ad exteriora*. A separation made it possible. The historical practices had their origin in the mourning of an intimacy. This also delineates, with respect to the relation to God, a problematic of "modernity": the task of production becoming the lot of those who have no longer any place in "the house of the Father." Further, in the Ignatian use of the expression, it was the religious institution that assumed the responsibility of replacing the "find within yourself" with a "seek outside." It assured the transition from one to the other. It transformed prayer into obedience. That exchange produced an apostolic history from the *mystics* of its subjects. The institution itself was the law of mourning. It seized the language of desire (prayer) to make it into social practices (an expansion of the Society). But also, more fundamentally, it put itself in the place of God, in whose name it organized and hierarchized research activities. It was itself the *propter Deum* that replaced *Deum in se*; it set itself up in the place of the Other. Therefore, it made its subjects "go out" of the interiority that symbolized their desire (the house of the Father) to send them off to do its own work. The "leave God for God" does not, therefore, just define the movement of the subjects but also the mechanism of the institution that leads them from their (undetermined) interiority to its (determined) tasks, and that produces its activity by having them "seek" what the institution is replacing. The institution must be constructed at the very place in which desire speaks in a prayer (without a special spiritual training there can be no religious Order), in order to be able to substitute its own social history for the Silence of God. The institution cannot allow either of the two elements to escape it, since its mainspring is the transformation of one into the other. In that way, it "accomplishes" (it objectifies and articulates), but it also destroys (it exploits and replaces) the ab-solute unnameable desire, which it transforms into its own service; it "finishes" it, in both senses of the word.

But the problem is precisely that that operation no longer works with the "spirituals" who cannot accept that exchange—or else it begins to work too well with the "good ones" who have forgotten at what price it works. For the former, the formula is no longer about the passage from prayer to action; it is an exile internal to prayer. It separates from the institutional question, as if the external activities ceased being relevant once one could no longer be distracted from what was happening inside. The desert was within. "Leave God" became the sign of a spiritual "dryness" and a "perfect disappropriation." One had to leave the "consolations" to seek God "purely," without profit, in the privation of the *regalos* ["sweet motions"] of which Teresa of Avila spoke. In 1587, Giuseppe Blondo, the Milan provincial and a friend of Gagliardi, took up the formula again, but in the form: "Deprive yourself of God through love of God."[81] Nothing must deter you from the feeling of being abandoned and "left" inside. Compared to this "emptiness," activities are no more than a distraction. Desire stops short in the place where it has been deprived of the sole object it cannot forget. The experience of that "deprivation" was to be intensified until it took the form of a possible damnation, a definitive exclusion from "the house of the Father." It was not the institution (nor the success it achieved) that could provide consolation for this mourning; the institution was precisely where it took place. Like the baroque high altars, the institution's "glory" was centered on a void. Those worshipers therefore stayed where they were, watchmen of a Silence.

For others, the traditional formula justified men of action for whom prayer had become difficult or impossible. Unable to "converse with God," they invested themselves more fully in the institutional tasks that were a substitute for it, and they supposed that, by their services, they were "leaving God for God"—an expression that from then on was scandalous in the eyes of the "spirituals," and the use of which Surin, for example, criticized sharply.[82] It remains to be seen whether the adversaries were not opposing one another on the basis of the same exile—one group trying to compensate for a loss by its work in the service of an Order that was standing in for an absence (those were probably the "moderns"), and the other group, like the Greek Antigone, reviving the mourning upon which an active Order was founded, and therefore necessarily marginalized in a society forbidden to hear them and unable to make use of them.

This expression, leaving for a moment the field of history, seems to begin speaking on its own. It contained from the start, but unveils little by little, the dangerous truth of a schism between the God of the heart and the God of a society at work—between the God who speaks, transformed into "extraordinary devotions" and "miracles," and the one who justifies, transformed into an ideology and a program for an institution. It becomes the incisive flint of a signifier. It may be the stumbling block of this Christianity: that the quest for God (*propter Deum*) begins with an irreparable loss, expressed sometimes as an inaugural fault (to have abandoned God), sometimes as a remoteness from God (he abandons us). Returning to the "little saints" of Aquitaine, one is struck by the fact that they share with most of their local superiors the consciousness of something essential having been lost. This reformism is no longer triumphant. It is burdened with an anonymous "sin" of the times, which refers back to a corrupted nature. It stands in the context of the weight of history. Thus, the "mystics" are less certain of their desires, and men of action less sure of the institution, within which, modestly (might this not already be more of an ethics than a faith?), they practice a dull gray discipline.

## "A KIND OF ILLUMINATI"

In 1655, a Jesuit from Aquitaine, Nicolas Du Sault, alludes, as one might to ghosts, to "a kind of illuminati," who had appeared "in various places" several years earlier, inspired by "three or four rather good-looking young men" who "did not lack good natural qualities." Fortunately, he said, "there is nothing or almost nothing left" of what he elsewhere terms "our reformed mystics," "our new reformers."[83] "Pure fantasy," thought Henri Bremond.[84] The fact is that, in addition to numerous unpublished letters between Rome and France that track these "new mystics" everywhere, their confessions and autobiographies still exist in the archives. They were intended for secret circulation, not public readership. They are internal explanations, confidential letters that exclude any nod toward an audience. I hesitate to bring them to light. Is it indiscreet? But these shades, who have become improbable even for a collector of "souls" like Bremond, tell a story that restores to *mystics* its status of being lost in the crowd, the anonymous extravagance of a desire disturbed by the visibility of its excesses.

These "rather good-looking young men" were more numerous than Du Sault says. By locating their texts, one can draw up a list of these hidden heroes, these Polyeuctes of a "new spirituality." They were (listing the Jesuit province to which they belonged): Jean d'Argombat (Toulouse), Achille d'Attichy (France), Jérôme Baiole (Aquitaine), Claude Bernier (France), Jean (?) Bonnet (Aquitaine), Pierre Cluniac (Aquitaine), André Dabillon (Aquitaine), Bernard Dangles (Champagne), Jean Jacquinot (Champagne), Jean de Labadie (Aquitaine), François Poiré (Champagne), Étienne Petiot (Aquitaine), Charles Séglière (France), Jean-Joseph Surin (Aquitaine), Jacques du Tertre (Aquitaine), René de Trans (Champagne), and others. Many were approximately the same age. Most were southerners: should importance be ascribed to the proximity of Spain and Italy, familiarity with the origins of the Society, regional traditions (since the Albigenses!), coexistence with the Calvinists of Languedoc and Saint-onge, influence of Bordeaux and Marseille? In any case, statistics are irrelevant: there are too many unknown or dubious "cases." Among them, there were some adventurers of genius, such as Surin and Labadie, whom we study elsewhere.[85] Among the others, choices are necessary, in order that we may hear at least a few of those accounts and autobiographical letters that were written between 1627 and 1632, contemporaneous with the confession of the "vicar" of Bordeaux.

The least known of these "little saints" is Pierre Cluniac. The "Relation by our Brother Pierre Cluniac of the Extraordinary Things that Happened to Him during Prayer or Otherwise, Written by His Hand, and Signed" is addressed to Vitelleschi.[86] The manuscript bears the Roman expression *per manus*, an indication that it had to be communicated to the general's assistants, who, in fact, each initialed it after reading. This was a state matter for the "spiritual administration."[87] The text was sent toward the end of 1627: on 25 February 1628, Vitelleschi let Bordeaux know that he had received Cluniac's and du Tertre's memoranda, which had been sent the preceding November.[88] Cluniac was twenty-one years old. Born in Périgueux in 1606, where he studied at the Jesuit college, he entered the novitiate in Bordeaux on 4 June 1622;[89] professor of grammar at Saint-Macaire in 1625, philosophy student at the college of Bordeaux from 1626, he began his studies in theology there (1628), then completed them in Pau with two other students (1629–30),[90] doubtless in compliance with the order given by the general, at the end of 1627, to isolate and scatter the suspects.

By 23 March 1627, Vitelleschi questioned the provincial and the rector of Bordeaux about the young philosopher who, like a "native of Poitou beguiled by the evil spirit," was reported to have predicted the hour of his death, and who would have to begin his novitiate over again if he disobeyed the rules.[91] Eight months later, the general thanked the rector for assuring him that Cluniac had less of that "alien spirit" than had been reported, but he added, other Fathers had given him reports quite to the contrary, and mentioned that the student had "disciples and imitators."[92] What was that "alien spirit" that seduced Cluniac in speaking to him of his imminent death? To explain himself, the young man sent his "Relation" to Rome. In it, he points out that as a child he had been terrified by an apparition of Satan as a "menacing beast," and that the "presence" of Jesus and his mother, driving out all fear, had shown him the path of salvation. That initial fright can be found everywhere at that time. It was even the background against which quietism appeared: "the anxiety to be overcome and the 'quietude' to be found."[93] As for devils and angels, they haunted the imagination of the day. One proof of this, among countless other examples, is "A Few Remarkable Points of the Life of the Reverend Father Coton" (who died that year, while serving as the Paris provincial), written in 1626 by the rector of the college of Tournon. Coton, that noteworthy Jesuit, confessor of the king, "would often see the angels, specifically his own and those of certain persons whom he directed, and learn from them the needs and doubts of those persons. . . . That good Father, entering the Church of the Acoles in Marseille, saw, beneath the square bonnet of the priest, instead of a man's head, a frightful head of a toad."[94] The universe of Hieronymous Bosch still filters through this edifying story. The perceived world, mutable and porous, remains a depiction of the passions, a scene in which good and bad angels circulate. Why should what was "remarkable" in Coton have become suspect in Cluniac? Cluniac goes on to describe that "extraordinary" prayer that had raised questions. After the novitiate, a time of dryness (because of the strictness of methods?), there came the "abundance of consolations." Here is his description of his current way of praying.

> As soon as I go into prayer, although I have already prepared the subject, it is as if God, rather, had himself prepared what he was to present to my soul [ *mens* ]: a truth occurs right away (such as: God must be loved, God loves us, God has become incarnate, it is glorious before God to suffer persecutions and afflictions for Christ, etc.), with such light and so filling my mind [ *intellectus* ] that it finds total repose, is captivated by that vision and, held in suspense by a truth whose light shines forth, is won over without any reasoning. At the same time, the will is suffused with a sweet adherence to God, not, it is true, with the continuous repose that the mind knows, but at times with a very simple complacency in an object, the love and attraction for which enrapture me with such gentleness and ease that the inclination seems innate and not having come from him.[95]

There are two questions concerning this prayer. It does not conform to the method that would require the meditation of daily circumstances as so many opportunities to practice some programmed virtues—a method whose victims Surin compared to "animals tethered to a stake, who can only go as far as their rope will stretch, and then do nothing but go around in a weary circle."[96] However, it was compatible with the practice of the virtues and stimulated by work, far from being contrary to them. For Vitelleschi, that was the main thing.

> In prayer itself, I can rarely apply myself to the virtues occasioned, in a more definite way, by daily life. However, when, outside prayer time, I examine my conscience on this subject, I find a very great desire to undertake the most difficult things, and experience itself has shown that prayer alone, more than any other thing, is a source of improvement in my ways of acting. Moreover, that blessing of prayer not only lasts during the entire time devoted to prayer, it extends to other moments

with greater or lesser intensity, so as to be nearly perpetual in me and the attention and love for God as present hardly stop. That inner occupation and attraction of the soul [*mens*] distract me so little from inner and outer tasks that both motions intensify rather in proportion to my application to study or other things.[97]

The analysis, made up of details, hinges on the border between what comes from the "inside" and what comes from the "outside." How can "inclination" be made to coincide with the rules of a religious institution? Poorly. Disaffection with the methods taught, the consciousness of being doomed to a "storm of afflictions," the assurance of dying at the age of twenty-one (before confronting theology):[98] these are meaningful admissions in a letter written to prove one's conformity with the Order. Cluniac also had "disciples" among his colleagues.

> Among them several came to me totally against my will, saying they had been specially prompted to do so by God, and others joined them, having been persuaded by the former ones, without my knowledge. At first I resisted. But being constrained both by their insistence and by an admonition, celestial as it seemed to me, telling me it would be beneficial to them, I yielded in the end and communicated with them, too enthusiastically no doubt, even outside the authorized times for conversation, and more frequently than was required by the charity we owe to all.

What was the content of those passionate discussions? They turned on the problem of knowing how "to try to express in one's life the perfection" required by the Order. But there was never any "criticism of the Society"—never, in spite of "whatever rumors tend in the opposite direction."[99] There was, then, an atmosphere of suspicion and denunciation. The documents give the impression of a great deal of informing between the individuals and Rome, in contrast with the relatively sparse free communication between them. The small group of fervent followers gathered around Cluniac to discuss the issue of perfection seemed jarring, subversive. What was to be done with their youthful hero? In 1633, he was named professor of philosophy at Bordeaux. In 1634, perhaps because he turned down this supposedly excellent but too intellectual position (just as André Baiole that same year refused a chair of theology because the work was not "spiritual" enough),[100] he was a preacher at Pau; in 1635, at Périgueux; in 1636–38, at Poitiers; in 1639–40, at Angoulême. There were incessant moves, as if, ever a stranger "where he is, he wandered in search of a spiritual place" in that society. Finally, in 1642, he left the Society of

Jesus.[101] Within two years, he had taken on the value of bad example. There, wrote Vitelleschi, is where the new spirituality ends up![102]

Another case. Jacques du Tertre, the subject of a Roman "examination" at the same time as Cluniac. Older, born in Saumur in 1591, du Tertre had studied philosophy and theology at the college of Bordeaux (1612–21)[103] and, ordained as a priest in 1621, returned there to teach. On 4 November 1627, he, too, sent his autobiography to Rome. It was written, he said, "by the order of the Father provincial."[104] Before becoming a professor of philosophy (1626–27), then of theology (1628), this man, "raised to mystical states,"[105] had been a missionary in Béarn, a region overwhelmed by witchcraft and burnings at the stake, in the same year (1622) in which Pierre de Lancre, royal councilor at the Parliament of Bordeaux, a "disciple and imitator of Montaigne,"[106] told how he had sentenced to the stake hundreds of these "magicians," among whom he included both the *alumbrados* and the Rosicrucians.[107] In the midst of these social and spiritual wars, there was the same worried vigilance on Vitelleschi's part. In 1624, he recommended the "solid virtues" to du Tertre and criticized his excessive tension of mind ("religiosae mentis contentio").[108] In 1626, he feared that du Tertre's continued presence at Bordeaux might sow "turbulence" in the college.[109] In 1627, du Tertre himself wrote to Rome that "various rumors are circulating in the house, according to which he is in illusion and follows a way of praying and acting that is contrary to the Order." To which he added that his superiors saw nothing to blame in his "ardor," and the provincial, Nicolas Villiers, even told him that he "counted on him to spread the divine fire throughout the province."[110] This provincial, who finally asked du Tertre to send his autobiography to Rome (by way of justification), was precisely the one that at the same date Vitelleschi repeatedly put on his guard against "the extraordinary and new devotions."[111] Where then was the true spirit? Between Rome and Bordeaux, there was a misunderstanding that du Tertre himself alluded to and feared.[112]

In his report, which was more mature than Cluniac's (du Tertre was thirty-six years old) and entirely devoted to the *ardor animi* (an expression that is the leitmotif of the text), he set forth, with a vocabulary inspired by Teresa of Avila and Catherine of Siena,[113] how the will to "be in closer conformity with the Order" arose in him out of a presence that inflamed and bared his heart, inundated it, enraptured it or settled it in profound peace.

> That ardor of mind holds me in several modes. Sometimes my soul strips itself of all it knows in order to clothe itself with God; sometimes

being submerged in God fulfills it; sometimes, forgetting all else, it remembers only God and feeds on him; sometimes it loses itself in praising God, putting all its strength in the service of his glory; more rarely, about once a week, it is suddenly enraptured in God, adores him profoundly, submits to him a thousand times and thus gradually finds a sovereign rest in God. Finally (I skip an infinite number of other modes that make me know and love in God a spouse, master, king, and father), the usual and permanent mode consists in a delectation that unites me with him, present and succouring in all places, and also in every undertaking.

From that *ardor animi*, du Tertre distinguishes an *ardor cordis*, more intense and violent, which, he says, is becoming increasingly rare. "Sometimes that ardor of the heart seems to project, make bubble up,[114] and liquefy and spread and nourish a fire for which the outlet is always too narrow." This volcanic landscape contrasts with Roman prudence. A kind of "furor" of mind lived within that man, a wildness that found rest in a silence no less foreign to the Order. It is striking that, for du Tertre (and the same is true of many others), the institutional norms provided a constraining framework that made possible the necessary practice of humility and the virtues of sociality, yet the source from which his mind lived was elsewhere: an unknown spring was welling up from cellar of the house.

A troubling strangeness: Vitelleschi was right about that. In his response, he acknowledged the sincerity of his correspondent, but requested that he not "regress by some new path" that would deviate from "the common norm of our Institute"; he reminded du Tertre that obedience was the only way to avoid "the total and lamentable shipwreck to which one's own sense and one's own will lead."[115] Du Tertre was to respect the law of his "condition," as just about everyone did in the seventeenth century. Sick (with what fever?) for the past few years,[116] he sought some remote place to live out his passion. When La Rochelle was taken by Richelieu's Catholic armies, the general asked the provincial to send a few zealous priests into that brokendown Protestant city.[117] It was a difficult mission. The "mystic" was appointed to go, but he died the following year, in Bordeaux, on 7 March 1630.[118]

At the time when Cluniac and du Tertre were writing their confessions, there were many others at Bordeaux who were suspect—"alios atque alios," Vitelleschi writes.[119] In October–November 1627, one of these, the young Surin, who was taking theology courses at the college, was hastily sent to Paris.[120] But there, at the college of Clermont (where Louis Lallemant was teaching scholastic theology), he found other witnesses of the same spirit, particularly Claude Bernier, another "case" about which Rome was disturbed.[121] He was twenty-six years old. He, too, had "disciples" and admirers among his fellows: François Chauveau, who became the distributor of his hero's papers; François Ragueneau, who asked, at one and the same time, the general's permission to go to Canada and to "be allowed to discuss his progress and the perfection of his soul with Father Claude Bernier";[122] and there were still more. Around him, admiration and entreaties increased. In 1618, Le Gaudier, an authority on spiritual matters, asked for a "catalogue of illuminations" in writing from his novice, and then is reported to have said "that he had never known a soul more predisposed to saintliness."[123] In 1623, the rector of the college of Nevers, where Bernier was a young twenty-two year-old professor, asked him to write and circulate his spiritual notes.[124] In 1625–26, Coton "orders him to write what happened to him during his life," a text Chauveau circulated widely.[125] Filleau, who succeeded Coton as provincial at Paris, took up Bernier's defense in Rome, where his faithfulness to the "royal way" [*via regia*] of the Jesuits was questioned.[126] What is more "extraordinary" than the devotions feared by Vitelleschi is the curiosity they raised, the craze for travel narratives to a world that was other, the eagerness with which the experiences of that "beyond" were collected and listed, written down, traced in the text of this earthly world, and transformed into relics. In Rome, witches were hunted down. In France, through innumerable networks, the avatars of a "spirit" that seemed lost were sought out. It was the fact of their having become rare, and not their delinquency, that made them "extraordinary." Hence the hagiographical overvaluation of these journeys, ultimately as solitary as that of the "idiot woman" of old; hence also their equivocal success among "disciples," young or old clerics, seeking a voice or a body touched by the *elsewhere*, seeking a "wild" element that their new and disappointing technicalization would enable them to articulate.[127]

Bernier was, in fact, a sort of peasant, lackluster and uncompromising, advancing with his measured tread toward the "purity" he craved, slow in his studies,[128] shrinking in the presence of his admirers,[129] modest, and on his own. Born in Orleans in 1601, he was ten or eleven years old when he used to "go off ruminating and imagining plans for a better life" as he said in his autobiography. At thirteen, Teresa of Avila's *Life* was a self-revelation: "I became extremely fond of prayer. . . . As God offered me within a way to follow him wholeheartedly, by means of a close union with him, I liked reading that *Life* so much that it seemed to me I had found all I was seeking, and I had it always in my thoughts, words and deeds."[130] It was his Bible, since, for him and his "spiritual" fellows, all that remained of the Old or New Testament were a few crucial sparks, fragments that still spoke within a corpus that had been transformed into an object of erudition.

Like Teresa and Catherine of Siena, authors to whom he refers,[131] he was taken with "clear-cutness." In him, something in the body was "touched," which founded the severity and restraint of words. While a novice, he said (he was speaking to God, not a superior), "it seemed to me that, by an inexplicable touch, I felt myself in you and you in me." It was the birth of a body that eluded discourse. It generated a stiffness in language, a literalness knowing no play, like the rigidified speech of someone in pain whose thoughts are elsewhere. "I similarly felt a great spirit of truth that dissuaded me from using, as one did rather frequently under pretext of eutrapelia [when joking], any jocular expression, even out of charity; and to flee all words that would have shown the least sign of special friendship with anybody. . . . That spirit inclined me to be serious with everyone and to say naïvely all I thought on any subject."[132] He recognized "that there were excesses," but didn't really change. "Puritas, puritas, puritas," such is the program he wrote as the heading of his diary. A purity to be attempted—risk and temptation—surrounded by universal compromise.

There was also independence in his conception of the Order. He mentions no received teaching, as he writes, in an address to God:

> I want to number among your countless mercies the tribulations I have had since entering the holy Society. . . . [During my novitiate], you know I was sorely grieved to see the ways of conduct of some of our number, ways that seemed to me so strange and afflicted me so that I had no rest. . . . But when it was pleasing, a few years later, to your goodness to have me know the spirit of the Society and of Saint Ignatius, not only were all these difficulties completely swept away, but also I saw how it had been incomparably other in every sense and more perfect than were the ideas of those persons who professed to be learned.[133]

The objective knowledge of the Society is that bitter knowledge of its "strange" defects (through "tribulations" and "sufferings"), which is displaced by the inner revelation of its "spirit." "I know, but still. . . . " For Bernier, the re-presentation of what is being lost replaces what he actually sees. It is as if, in order to stay *there*, Bernier was himself to produce the ideal object of love of which experience had deprived him. His "disciples" reinforced the process of that idealization necessary for their work in the service of the Jesuit Society. A case in point is François Chauveau, the silver-tongued spokesman of the group, when, on 16 August 1631, he wrote Étienne Charlet (the assistant for France in Rome) "at the end of the third year" from Rouen (where he was taught by Louis Lallemant). He begged him to ask Bernier to compose a *Life* of Ignatius of Loyola,

> in place of all those that have appeared thus far, for all four[134] are failures and far below the idea one should have both of that great saint and of our Society; it would contain all the good elements of each, and would give conceptions that are as equal as possible to the great deeds of that great saint, who remains unknown even to the majority of his sons.[135]

To redo the portrait of the Father and to construct a founding Image: this production of a mythology, in keeping with the needs of the era, was nothing more than a resumption of Acquaviva's spiritual policy, but in reverse. While Acquaviva wanted to place the administrative framework developed under his generalship within the authorized space of the Origin (or of the Jesuit "primitive Church"), the group of "spirituals" desired to put an "idea" totally opposed to the so-called "learned" in that space and to make Ignatius the mirror of their *mystics*. The "return to Ignatius," that is, to a figure of the Father who had clearly been "misunderstood" and remained "unknown" until then even to his own sons—this meant the invention of a third, or of an *n*th image: an effect of fragmentation marking the distance from the model.[136] The origin was, actually, the subject of a debate between two different "reforms," two "spirits." Chauveau, recalling the period during which Bernier "was greatly perplexed because of the faults of several who did not proceed in keeping with the spirit of the Society" (the "alien" spirit was, in this case, on the other side), adds:

> I don't know whether it was then or at another time that he wrote about the idea he has of the spirit of the Society. But I am quite certain that it is one of the most beautiful and most spiritual pieces I have yet read on such matters, and its inspiration is so lofty that I personally consider it to be, relative to spiritual matters, what the *In principio* of Saint John is in relation to the divine Scriptures.[137]

In spite (or because) of the exaggerations of Chauveau and other disciples, in spite (or because) of Bernier's silence (his notes are known not because he distributed them but through indiscretion on the part of others), this was tantamount to a new Gospel. Vitelleschi was not wrong on the fundamental issue: that alien "spirit" tended to replace that of the Institute. Whereas, in spiritual matters, Acquaviva commanded an administration, Vitelleschi waged a war. What worried him, and what strikes the historian as well, was the speed and ease with which that *mystics* permeated all of France. True, the general had countless informers on his side who sent him information (intelligence gathering was crucial in that secret war), but he soon discovered that the "danger" was not just a few young reformists and the small groups of enthusiasts surrounding them (which was enough to put the future in jeopardy). It was also the sympathy they met with among the authorities and notables of the Society. These alliances and affinities were indeed astonishing. Many cases have already been mentioned. Just one last example, but a major one, since he was the best-known Jesuit spiritual author of the seventeenth century: Louis Lallemant.

Chauveau, who had known Lallemant and Bernier at the college of Clermont in Paris (1627–28), becomes lyric in speaking of them: "I have never seen two saints symbolize[138] and fraternize as they do. Already during my theology studies, when I was pupil to one and fellow student to the other, they seemed to blend in with each other like two drops of water."[139] He relates how they used to have discussions "alone in the room" of Bernier on the nature of the angels, and the "wild" student would instruct the theology professor. The scene in the coach would merely reenact this conversation that took place in a cell, with Surin in Lallemant's role. A letter from Lallemant shows his relations with Bernier's family.[140] That "symbolization" was also true of others. In 1625, "while [Pierre Coton] was provincial and visited the Rouen college, he learned that Father Louis Lallemant . . . had much communication with a devout who was said to have had revelations. He forbade the Father to see that man until there was time to determine by what spirit that man was being led."[141] During those years, the extraordinary devotions of Lallemant (especially devotions to the mystic Saint Joseph, which Vitelleschi disallowed at that time to all Jesuit students) brought down on him "the disdain and at times the insults" of his fellows.[142] It was, then, not particularly astonishing that the general, in 1629, should in turn be "astonished" that his recently named third-year novitiate instructor, the guardian par excellence of the spirit of the Institute, was considered a total mystic [*totus mysticus*], who wanted "to lead everyone toward an extraordinary devotion."[143] A new "affair" resulted from this.

It was sixty years before Louis Lallemant's spiritual notes—*Doctrine Spirituelle* (1694)—were published by Surin's disciple, Pierre Champion. By then, as Nicolas Du Sault had said in 1655, "there is nothing or almost nothing left" of that "sort of *illuminés*." Labadie had left the

Jesuits in 1640, Cluniac and Dabillon in 1642; d'Argombat had become a Dominican; Surin was "insane," locked up in a "cell" of the Bordeaux infirmary; du Tertre died in 1630; d'Attichy in 1646; Bernier in that same year of 1655. They were dispersed. There was, around the years 1630–40, an overall adoption of a tough line within the Society, which was unable to endure the logical effects of that "effervescence" for a long time. This tough line was noticeable in theology as well as spirituality and was compensated for by an excessive amount of activity *outside* (a normal inversion of measures recommended in 1606) and by an asceticism of faithfulness *within*. But "there can be cases, after all, when the defeated were not wrong."[144] At the end of the century, in his "Far West," Pierre Champion collected the brightest bits and pieces of those forgotten mystics from the materials with which the previous generation had supplied him. He collated Lallemant's papers as he had first done for the texts of Surin, his hero, whom he called "the most enlightened man of this century."[145] There, after a span of time just slightly longer than it had taken to publish John of the Cross,[146] arose a marmorean monument, a serene masterpiece, freed from its past environment (suspect at the time, later forgotten), partially constructed on the model furnished by Surin (both closer to Champion and more intense), ennobled by a limpid, lapidary prose (that of Champion himself). It is first and foremost within that monument, the tomb of an entire generation and beginning of its anonymous story written postmortem, that the little *illuminés* of the past are to be sought. They are lost in that text, like the "madmen" of ancient times in the crowd.[147]

*Chapter Nine*

✠   ✠
✠

# Labadie the Nomad

*Wandersmann,* both wanderer and migrant: a "walker."[1] A man of the South by the models that inspired him, Labadie went north, ever further north, like Marguerite Duras' beggar, who keeps going south.[2] From Guyenne, where he was born and became a Jesuit, he went to Paris, Amiens, Montauban, Orange—his French oscillations—then he thought perhaps he would go to London, no, it was Geneva, then the Netherlands, Utrecht, Middelburg, Amsterdam, then farther, to Altona in Denmark, where he died surrounded by a little group he had formed ("the sequestered of Altona")[3] that continued its migration to North America without him. The "tireless wandering" of this baroque hero gives relevance to a spatial problematic.[4] The inner journey was transformed into a geographical one. Labadie's story is that of indefinite space created by the impossibility of a place. The stages of the journey are marked by the "religions" he passes through, one by one: Jesuit, Jansenist, Calvinist, Pietist, Chiliast or Millenarian, and finally "Labadist"—a mortal stage. He passes on. He cannot stop.

He brings to mind John the Baptist, the walker, sculpted by Donatello, in the instant at which movement is a loss of equilibrium. That falling becomes walking if *it happens to be the case* that a second place exists to follow the first, but the artist, by isolating the figure, makes that hypothesis uncertain. How can we be sure whether he is falling or walking? With Surin, to walk is to propel oneself outward, to jump out of the window. Labadie falls out of the places that cannot hold him, and that becomes a walking. It ends up being a story because each time, miraculously, other places "receive" him, or, more precisely, as he constantly repeats, they "preserve" his body from falling by "supporting" him. Each of these places provides, at the last moment, "another ground," he says, where normally he could have presumed there would be emptiness; and when, at the end of his life, after another departure he sees the lack of a new "support" (as if, by chance, he had arrived at the end of possible worlds), he replaces it with delirium. He is, then, forever expelled from the place where he is, and surprised by the place that comes next: the former intolerable, the latter providential; the former a sign of the corruption of societies, the latter proof of his election. He goes from disequilibrium to disequilibrium, from miracle to miracle. The only "natural," ever imminent thing, is the movement of falling. His life is the reverse of a pilgrimage. It is the "theory" (development in the mode of an itinerary) of a divorce between "grace" (miracle) and extension.

It is during the moment in which the fall begins (again) and the appearance of "another ground" remains improbable that Labadie's writing proliferates and rushes forward, as if to fill the gap between the two with discourse. The writing is also nomadic, endless, pamphletary, and prophetic, hastily executed, its rhythm determined by the interval between the place he condemns in leaving it behind and the (uncertain, necessary) one he announces as an imminent miracle. His texts do not make up a system. They are the effects—wordy, excessive—of a way of experiencing space: Labadie suffers from space as one does from a stomachache or headache. His writings form the strange, fantastic punctuation of a landscape progressively emptied of the real, which they reject as they discover it; they are filled with the extraordinary they project without ever finding it. Each time, they construct a land of fiction relative to a lacking institution. These processes of transfer, tied to the disappointments and expectations of successive stages, continue to adhere to what they release. They cannot be made into an autonomous whole. They are fragments of the framework of an autobiography that has no text proper. Each fragment appears only to say: the "I" is no longer here. This literature, an exorbitance and defection of discourse thrown in its entirety toward an exteriority (which is itself disseminated like space), produces an "a-topia" that cannot be (since all history constructs a legitimacy) the history of a "Labadian" institution, way of thinking, or figure. This account, proliferating on thresholds, relates events that, in various circumstances, are always falls avoided by miracle. But each text, fixed at the present moment, like an ec-stasy, forgetful of the preceding ones, unaware of those to come, taken up with an imminent fall and grace, is also a variant of "this cannot last." In this staccato form, all the texts taken together repeat an almost abstract form of the spatial experience: its uncertain and ultimately impossible character. The texts belong to no one; they are the texts of a "nowhere."

Thus it is not surprising that all Labadie said or did is covered with rumors. These rumors are the social, actualized form of that nowhere. No institution claims him as their own, which is, as is well known, a necessary "support" for the production of a historiography. He "betrayed" them all—in both senses of the word. He left them, going over to the enemy camp, but he also exposed an intolerable difference between their discourse about themselves and their actual functioning, between their "truth" and their reality. He wounded them at that articulation, which cannot be touched within the Church, the political "party" or the social organization, entities legitimated by a "truth" of militancy. He did not settle for the compromise that presumes, in order to "save" the institution and be morally justified in remaining within it, that its "truth" had retracted into the lower part of its body (that mystical "inside," whose equivalent in revolutionary history is "the people" or "the masses"); that it is only corrupt or contradicted by those in charge; and that it would therefore suffice, in order to restore the truth, to reform the higher part of this body. He judged the spirit on the basis of what he saw, a spatial perspective (once again) that does not posit, hidden behind actual behavior, an autonomous reign of symbols. His utopian reaction was the result of a "realist" analysis. Faced with that offensive perspicacity, the institutions responded with rumors that assailed the credibility of the speaker. A stock ploy. In Labadie's case, the frequency of his "apostasies" caused the proliferation of those legends that take hold of the body of the accused to drown out his discourse: his temperament, his social class, his illnesses, his acts of violence, his madness, his voyeurism, especially his sexual obsessions, were the terrain of choice for defensive maneuvers. Sex discredits the text. It would be pointless to rehash those bits of gossip, echoed by none other than the erudite, the critical Bayle himself, in a cleverly chosen entry of his *Dictionnaire*: the article "Mamillaires," a history of breasts. What is more striking is the sequence repeated by each institution in which an excess of honor is followed by an excess of indignity: honor, when upon his arrival Labadie affirms that it is superior to its rivals; indignity, when he pronounces in leaving that it is no better. All these "indignities" added up. They buried the traitor.

They still cover him, although, since a hagiographic article published in *La France protestante* in 1856,[5] a reappraisal is underway.[6]

Labadie, being hidden both by his own texts and the rumors of others, cannot really be presented. Nor can he be forgotten on the mystic stage, where he played nearly all the roles. Perhaps he should be cast as the hero of a novel, as he was by Van Berkum, with careful erudition, but in the style of his contemporary, Alexandre Dumas.[7] In a dramatic mode and in the domain of spirituality, this hero belongs to the tradition that reaches from the Don Juan of Tirso de Molina (*El Burlador de Sevilla*, 1630) to *Rameau's Nephew*: seductive "traitor," traveling "demon," spirit in search of an impossible body. There also remains the possibility that his fleeting silhouette may pass through the theater of the text. Numerous traces (published and, more frequently, manuscript) punctuating his journeys, sketch out the singularity of a passage (rather than the presumed psychology of an individual or the configuration of a doctrine). They also summon up that element of "spirituality" that was already declining and passing with him. In what follows, therefore, we have but a shaft of light flashing across *mystics'* (false) display case.

## A SPIRIT IN SEARCH OF A PLACE

At the moment of leaving his Catholic "friends," Labadie declares: "In changing communions, I have not changed vocations."[8] That is the theme, or rather the musical motif, of a *translatus*: a mystical and geographical "transport," which constitutes a transgression of the law specific to each place, and endless transplantation. Born 13 February 1610, in Bourg-en-Guyenne, where his father, Jean-Charles, was lieutenant of the citadel, Jean de Labadie felt from childhood that he was marked by God "as much by the inner grace of his Spirit as by that of his Scripture," two sources that for him always came down to the inner word. "As far back as I can remember," he added, "I recall having felt the impressions of his Spirit that my childhood did not permit me to discern when I received them, but I have known perfectly well and felt that I was not, nor had ever been, anything but his." That inspiration became distinct from himself only by a later effort of apprenticeship and language. But at first it was an instinct, an "innate inclination," as Cluniac said in 1628.[9] Something was born within him that was him. Also, "at that early age," he was "touched by that saying that it was good that a child should bear the yoke of God early."[10] That reference to a founding childhood separates from the outset the "savage" from enlightened education, according to which it is necessary to "rid ourselves of the prejudices of our childhood."[11]

Labadie entered the Jesuit novitiate of Bordeaux on 28 December 1625; he was fifteen years old.[12] Those first two years of training[13] were already taken up with the composing of "treatises" on *mystics.* After his philosophy studies at Bordeaux (1628–31) during the time there was discussion of the "extraordinary devotions" of Cluniac, du Tertre, and others,[14] he went to Périgueux for two years (1632–33), then to the college of Agen for one year (1634), before returning to Bordeaux to do his theology. In 1639, he was said to be a priest.[15] By 1637, Muzio Vitelleschi, the general of the Society of Jesus, was upset to hear that Father Jérôme Baiole was spreading the word that "a young theologian named Labadie . . . was living *per modum puri spiritus* [in the manner of a pure spirit], had reached the state of beatific vision, and other things totally alien to the spirit of the Society."[16] Despite the Roman admonitions, the talents and vigor of the young prophet were attracting an increasing number of admirers, such as André Dabillon, who entered the novitiate in 1622,[17] a professor of logic who left the Jesuits to follow Labadie in 1642,[18] because "he found only one good religious in his life"[19] the very same person to whom Jean du Ferrier attributed "such a beautiful beginning," like that of a "rising star."[20]

"His society," the erudite Nicéron said (not without exaggeration), "considered him a prodigy of spirit and piety." Why? "He preaches the old teachings of the Apostles before everyone."[21] Such was the prestige of the early Church, which was the locus of the Spirit. Differing on this point from the "little saints" who were his fellow students in Guyenne, Labadie went back to the origins of the Church, not just those of the Society. By this return to a beginning, he nonetheless belonged, as they did, to the category of those "reformed mystics" whom Vitelleschi feared like the plague. He intended to rally the "regenerate." But how was that founding Spirit known to him other than through the spirit of his own childhood, by an inspiration making him contemporary with that past, which by his time had become corrupted? "I saw . . . that to make a true copy or painting of the Christian Church, it had to be drawn from its live original; this live original was the first Christianity, as founded by Jesus Christ, promised by the apostles, called for by the Gospel and described by the Acts. . . . God, maintaining me in a great desire for this great work, showed me soon thereafter that . . . his plan was to have me work" for that reformist crusade.[22] The first operation therefore consisted in producing a representation: doing or "drawing" a portrait, as they said in the seventeenth century, meant constructing an image, as in the "admirable artifices" dear to catoptromancy, which was then developing among the Jesuits themselves.[23] Probably no era was more conversant with the ruses of the image. If "vision" makes what is *not here* spring up (a deceased person, a past, or the king), it exposes in so doing a doubling of the ego. What I see in the image of the other is me; I am not here where I am but elsewhere, in the mirror representing the absent other, and I didn't know it: this was the iconic theme of those years. The other who appears through vision is an unknown me. The "pure mirror" (*speculum sine macula*) is therefore the "enigma," the "obscure word" that bespeaks an absence from oneself. It is but a fiction or simulacrum of the soul. The clarity of the perceived object designates the darkness separating the spirit from itself. It is an "artifice," but an inner one. Labadie is part of this "baroque visionary *mystics*,"[24] but the "copy" or the "portrait" he draws of the origins is precisely the nowhere of his spirit, a "borrowed residence," a metaphor, a transport outside oneself. His vision itself informed him that he was not at home. He was deprived of himself by the place in which he was.

The act of leaving the Jesuits was nothing, fundamentally, but a logical result of that experience. He writes that into the plan to make the "copy" of the origin effective—the plan of at least *being* in the Image (that alien truth) or of making it coincide with a place where he was: God "inserted a clause that at first astonished me, but did not, for all that, throw me into true defiance; it was that I would not serve in that plan except outside of the place where I was and separated from the society to which I was joined." It is a striking characteristic that that "clause" is also made known to him by the word of another, a word that functions like the image of the other in telling him that he is not, there where he is, in his truth (God). "A person as luminous as pious" tells him: "Do what God wants and what he prompts and urges you to do, which is to go out from amidst the Jesuits."[25] He speaks in the word of the "luminous person" just as he inhabits the image of the ideal Church, but that word and that image are outside the place he occupies (his body, and that social body). They teach him his alienation. But it is (it will be) especially the image, that other space, that makes him *see* his exile. Vision itself is exilic. More broadly, it seems that the minds of the seventeenth century, in constructing an optic universe,[26] distanced themselves from realities that had shaped their identities. In any event, to return to a specific case, Teresa of Avila, who complained of having no imagination, experienced the indetermination of an unfathomable, divine interiority rather than a "nostalgia" for visible and therefore distinct objects, capable of spelling out her impossible truth outside herself.

Labadie "went out from amidst the Jesuits" in the spring of 1639. During the preceding year (1638–39), he resided with Jean-Joseph Surin at the college of Bordeaux. Fate had already brought them together several times. Surin, older by ten years, returned wounded from his battles as an exorcist at the site of the possession of Loudun. He was sick, mad, suspect.[27] Labadie continued to command general admiration, but his heart was already elsewhere. Their confrontation measures up to the level of their strange and different characters. In 1663, Surin referred back to the time when "by order of my provincial, I communicated with him." It was supposed that he could be helped, in his sad state, by the counseling of the young prophet. Surin's reflections:

> He had some very good things, and several similar to things I had received, and if God had not given me the desire not to rely on my opinion and never to waver from my first vocation, and especially from obedience, I have no doubt that, in that mixture of spirits, I would have foundered as well as he. . . . I spoke to him about his delusion. . . . He let himself be guided by the extraordinary spirit that, in my opinion, was good at the beginning and had been approved by several great servants of God, but, because of that great failure to be humble, for having preferred himself to the spirit of his vocation . . . and for having abandoned himself to his instincts, he ended up believing himself inspired by God, let himself be fooled by false apparitions and revelations. . . . Pride undid him to the point that he went astray, drifting through the bushes.

Labadie's response: "He told me he saw many things of the Spirit of God in me, and that I could do great service to God and advance much, but that obedience would always hold me down and tie my wings: for that reason I would never go far."[28] One word marks the divide: "vocation." Surin defines it as a social positivity that imposes upon a "universal" spirit the limitation of a body, a reality, and a death; Labadie defines it as an inner revelation for which the chosen one must invent a body. Two systems of symbols also stand in opposition to one another—each running as deep on either side. Surin's symbols are maritime (he himself being caught up in a hurricane): "his ship foundered," he says, "abandoned" to the winds by presumptuousness and swept ("drifting") toward the reefs. Labadie's symbolism is aerial: a spirit held "down" and whose "wings" are tied. One, a sailor of the open sea, condemns a reckless "guidance" that eschews bearings; the other, the prisoner of a place, looks with scorn upon a force that, by cowardice, refuses to spread its wings.

When Labadie asked to leave the Jesuits at the end of 1638, he surprised the authorities. The reasons he gave concerned health problems (particularly lack of sleep). After expressing his astonishment at never having heard any mention of this,[29] Vitelleschi drew a lesson from this departure that would be repeated again and again. "As for Father Jean Labadie, we have there the shattered dreams of those who had written whole pages on his merits and drummed them into our ears. May they now at least recognize the nature of their haste to praise him."[30] "At his request and by reason of his ill health," Labadie was therefore "released from all obligations to the Society" by a letter signed by the provincial on 17 April 1639.[31]

Labadie, trying to found a "secret school for the simple,"[32] was "received" in various places: Bordeaux, Paris (several sojourns), Amiens (1643–44), Abbeville, Toulouse (1645 and 1649), Bazas, La Graville. . . . Not that, being a secular priest, he wanted to become an itinerant. On every occasion, he answered an invitation that provided him with "another ground" the moment he fell from one place. They are statutary positions: he was the holder of a preaching chair in Guyenne, canon at the church Saint-Nicolas in Amiens, director and confessor of the Tiercerettes in Toulouse or the Ursulines in Bazas, and so on. Soon, very soon, his eloquence captivated some and repelled others. "May it be well taken that I say the truth as it should be said, that is, a bit strongly."[33] That was his oratorical maxim. The spoken word divides the place. The nowhere of his discourse slices into the opaque stratification that makes up the cohesiveness of each group, plunging into it the knife of a dichotomous fiction: "God calls . . . some, by justice, to eternal torture, and others, by mercy, to his glory."[34] A surgical, "anatomical" operation, as in Diego de Jesús,[35] which attempted to carve out of the real something that could offer a place to the Image.

It was the time of sympathies, then disaffection with Port-Royal.[36] There were doctrinal affinities. Subsequent ties, either personal or intellectual, have even been proposed between Labadie and Pascal.[37] Is the story as unbelievable as Sainte-Beuve (not wanting to mix the pure with the compromised) assumes? Like the Jesuits, the Jansenists have destroyed the evidence of the seducer after his treachery. But, as Freud said of this sort of repression, "the crime is never perfect." Clues remain, for example, a Jansenist collection of written or spoken exchanges by "authorities" or friends of Port-Royal. Labadie is there, in the good company of Le Camus (the future "reforming" bishop of

Grenoble), M. Lombert (translator of *The City of God*), N. Manessier (theologian soon to become the Jansenist deputy in Rome), all notables of the establishment.[38] But each new apostasy brought on bad stories about Labadie. In the name of Port-Royal he was presented by Godefroy Hermant as a "libertine" of shameful morals.[39] In Amiens he was accused of sexual relations with the Sisters, from which there came a trial that went up to the level of Chancellor Séguier.[40] The same charge was made in Abbeville. In Toulouse, it was rumored that he was spreading the ideas of the Adamites and the *alumbrados* among the Tiercerette Sisters, or that he danced before the altar—a very beautiful characterization, one that only enemies could devise.[41] At Bazas, it was said that he had spread the poison of "the doctrine of Jansen" among the Ursulines.[42]

He published *La Solitude chrestienne* (1645) during these transitions and stormy circumstances. The book, one of his best (a work of his early maturity: he was thirty-five), bases union with God on separation from the world, as if he were taking from Port-Royal precisely that for which he would later criticize them. In this work, he deals with election more fully than contemplation. "Consummation in God," which extends "to unity in him by his adhesion" (an expression of Bérulle's), is inseparable for the elected from their "solitude," for they "live in a different soil and breathe a different air."[43] But that "solitude," that "retreat," or that "refuge" is not, as in the religious ideology of the time, the name of an established and protected place.[44] The "other soil" designates a nowhere. Man, being everywhere "outside" and "being unable to do anything on his own but lose himself," there is no actual experience other than that of falling. The "solitary" is a "vagabond," forever deceived by the soil that he thought he recognized as his own. His nomadic life is the spatial manifestation of the permanent relation in which he stands to the law of his loss. For him, nothing holds. It does not appear that Labadie had the certainty (born of an "annihilation" of subjective anxiety by an inner assurance) capable of facing (like certain stoics), accepting (like certain quietists), or forgetting (like certain mystics) the idea of "natural" predestination to an eternal death. He experienced the law of that fall of minds, which is also the law of a separation, in somewhat the same way that Aristotle envisioned the fall of bodies. An "ancient" menace, which originally concerned the breakdown of the cosmos, reappeared in a "modern" religious uprooting. The sole salvation: the miracle of being held, received, elected. Labadie's affirmation (reinforced by his need) of the miracle on his behalf was intimated to him each time by a repeatedly surprising event: the "support," reception, and election of which he was the object in a new location. But that welcome was not enough for him. He knew the "deceptiveness" of it as well as Surin did. He needed a firmer confirmation from the outside. He expected it from the very publics who dashed his hopes of finding a place with them. Their refusal was a surer guarantee than their admiration. He therefore provoked it. In his violence, he "tried" those audiences in order to draw from them precisely what they denied him. Their hostility won him the exceptional place of a martyr whose privilege was the nowhere into which their rejection pushed him. Thus, they upheld his election: a proof by negation. They made him a true "solitary." Their opposition was, ultimately, a more "efficient" grace than their initial enthusiasm.

This was an ancient mystic tradition, but with displacement. John of the Cross already held that suffering alone was without deception. Not that it constituted the essential feature of experience, but in questions of knowledge, that writing that altered the body attested to a difference, just as, in science, failure introduces reality into the framework of theoretical expectations. With Labadie, the suffering did not exactly concern his body, but the "union" he thought he would find with a social body: it wounded the articulation with the body that he thought he was giving to his mind. From this experience, the mind comes out "solitary" anew, "living on a different soil." Suffering restores the Image in its purity. Far from losing himself in the crowd (which is the social metaphor of the Real), Labadie never stopped provoking it. In his own way, he defied it. He laughed at it. Impatiently, arrogantly, he waited for the crowd's deceit to come out, since his inner election was bolstered by this deceit. The denunciation of the real became a source of truth.

His texts display a curious rhetoric. His style combines the art of winning credence and the need to attack. He is seductive and abrasive. There is much edification in his speeches, often of the monotonous sort. But beneath this anonymous mantle there gleams the knife with which he stabs the audiences and dogmas that are comfortably installed in a consensus. He cuts. He confronts the positivity of a well-established text with an inspired interpretation. He deprives ritual practices of their biblical justification. He separates the spirit made "to breathe a different air" from the social reality that holds it captive. His is a baroque language, made up of contradictory gestures that are nonetheless all disjunctive. He never stops practicing the evangelical "crisis": "I have come to bring division."[45] But where, in the final analysis, is the author of the scenes he enacts on so many different stages? Who is he? A man on the verge of death, saved by the miracle of grace? A Don Juan? An actor? The audiences discuss with great fervor the characters they think they recognize in his repertory. As for himself, he designates rather accurately the relation his vocation bears to all these false semblances when he calls it a "dark night of faith."

In 1650 he went over to Calvinism and got a warm welcome. The aggressivity between the Churches made any emigrant from one a coveted object for the other. But there was another decisive element in the milieus he frequented: the social code forced everyone onto an identifying square of the checkerboard of religious "openings" and "states." If you were not here, you were therefore there; if you weren't a Jesuit, then you had to be a Jansenist; if not a Jansenist, then a Calvinist. Labadie's itinerant career obeyed the law of the terrain, amenably following, from square to square, a preestablished plan. That order has an objective "meaning," as a direction indicated by the slope of history. From square to square, from model to model, he lays out a diagram in which the "primitive" ideal becomes more intense as the bond between the social group and the "presence" of its origin becomes looser. He develops the successive variants by which the Origin is historicized (and also fragmented into "the origins"). The Beginning, which was once a present sacramental act, becomes a past textual representation. There is a pivotal point in that evolution, which Labadie shows very clearly in the case of the Eucharist:[46] the sacrament, which is the dialogual realization of the union between man and God, splits into an ethical act (the challenge of faith) and a scriptural positivity (the original scene). Between the two halves, *mystics* retains the inaccessible mark of their junction. Calvinism, a key stage in this development, offers Labadie the wherewithal to "announce" the exploded, paradoxical relationship that a challenge (absolute, unbound) maintains with an Image (distant), and the incomprehensible election that connects them. In principle, Calvinism only circumscribes a place, the content of which is an unattainable regeneration. It delimits the borders of that place all the more inflexibly, since the interior is beyond any appropriation by knowledge, the will, or the senses. But by this very fact, Calvinism soon made it impossible for Labadie to tolerate authorities who had become political (civic and moralistic) in the very name of a "spirit" that eluded them.

The early years were euphoric. The priest who converted in Montauban (1650) was soon fulfilling his pastoral duties (1652–57), after having sent "his friends of the Roman communion" his long *Declaration*, followed by a *Letter* about himself.[47] He put his Jansenist friends in a very awkward position by affirming that "the doctrine of predestination and presupposed grace, as Jansen explains it and shows it to be the only orthodox and true one, is the pure and whole doctrine of the Reformed Church."[48] That was precisely the Jesuits' accusation of the Jansenists. A Jesuit pamphlet immediately used Labadie's assertion against Port-Royal.[49] It carried this to an exaggerated degree in a second edition "enlarged with the praises the Jansenists gave the said Labadie": in point of fact, it could do no more than adduce one page of the *Second Apology for Jansen*, in which Labadie and Dabillon are called "ecclesiastics of exemplary virtue."[50] In his rather embarrassed response Arnauld reestablished the differences that Labadie continually blurred by causing places to "circulate," as the traitor[51] or the cuckolded husband does in traditional stories. The convert is not content with leaving places; like a "shifter" (in the sense Jakobson give this term), he sets them in movement and shuffles them like cards.

From 1657 to 1659 Labadie was in Orange. The vice-legate of Avignon, Gaspare Conti, regularly informed the Roman Secretariat of State of the schemes of the "apostate" he calls "l'Abadia." There was a web of secret letters.[52] The phantom[53] was back in the Roman offices—those of "your Eminence" (Cardinal Pamphili), no longer those of "your Fathership" (Vitelleschi)—but with the same motif as before: "The corruption of what is good is the worst thing there is."[54] He had turned bad. The question was rather in which direction he would turn next. He fled the "persecutions" of which he was the object in Montauban; they resumed in Orange. He was in communication with London; a long report from there spoke of his merits:

> Sr. de Labadie, a minister of an exemplary life and singular teachings . . . having formerly renounced the Papist Religion, had retired in Montauban where his preaching had been so successful that a great number of people had followed his example; which had moved the last Assembly held in Paris to obtain by entreaty of the King of France that he should leave the Realm, and thus avoid his ministry's further progress in Montauban and its environs by the conversion of those who went to hear him. This minister, having withdrawn, to avoid persecution, to the county of Orange outside the Realm, met with no less success, the inhabitants of Avignon and the vicinity crowding to hear him, so that if the Legate had not ordered the people of the county of Avignon not to continue going, it appeared there would be much conversion in that land.[55]

The Reformed French Church of Westminster in London offered him a position as preacher (1659). After having consulted the pastors of the Reformed Church of Paris (Drelincourt, Daillé, Gasche), he accepted, with the intent of going through Geneva and Germany. But his success in the city of Calvin kept him there for seven years (1659–66). The "Register of the Company of Pastors" gives a weekly account of his transition from seduction to exclusion. Friday, 10 June 1659: "Arrival of M. de Labadie in Geneva." He preached there on 12 June. Tuesday, 14 June, due to "the satisfaction our people received from his sermons," it seemed well to "retain him here as pastor."[56] It was love at first sight. Already on 18 June, he explained to the Company "that his vocation [was] divine";[57] he was to repeat it over and over, first in a long autobiographical speech, on 21 June.[58] He was received as pastor, but they "obtained a promise from him that he [would] not take, nor [desired] to take part in the new things."[59] Such is the way of all institutions. On 29 July, the first difficulty arose: the sermons assigned to him in the temple of Saint Peter were "in conflict" with those of M. Turrettin. The Company compromised. In November, people were already speaking "a bit impatiently" about him.[60] In December, he was the one who attacked—on a detail, but an important one. In a sermon, he asserted it to be "necessary to remove the pictures of the Apostles that [were] in the windows of said temple" (of Saint Peter). The Company answered with scriptural arguments, an order by the Counsel, and appeals to ancient custom, but to no avail. In his judgment, those stained-glass windows "[were] an object of idolatry."[61] There was but one Image, the "picture of the Christian Church" within him. It was the relic of its spiritual body, something analogous to "the penultimate image" at which, according to Freud, the fetishist stops wildly because he *knows* he has seen the absence that will follow. The image protects, fictively, from an already known lack, which is precisely what gives it its importance. It is at once a place of protection and the witness of a non-place, therefore untouchable. Labadie could not make any concession. The Company ordered him "not to preach any more against (those) pictures" and also "to shorten his sermons." He was always too long-winded; he could not "stop himself." The difficulties were compounded: over professors and students of theology, whom he accused by name (an affair that lasted over a year, 1662–63); over François Mauduit's pamphlets published against him in Lyon and Grenoble,[62] to which he was asked to write a response and show it;[63] and so on. There were endless debates.

Yet this was an intense period. In Geneva, he met Philipp Jakob Spener, a poet of the *Seelensprache* (the "language of the soul," which was a maternal language and a language of the people), the prophet of a spiritual "awakening" through "practical piety," who is said to have received from Labadie the pietistic inspiration for his *Pia desideria* (1675).[64] There Labadie made his most trustworthy disciples: Pierre

Yvon (1646–1707), who later on became his successor as head of the Labadists; pastor Pierre du Lignon, who came from the Academy of Saumur; and others. In that eminently theological city, he preached on fundamental questions: christology, ecclesiology, the Eucharist, exegesis, the pastoral ministry. From this material he drew his most important doctrinal works (but they are not his most original ones): *Le Hérault du grand roi Jésus* (Amsterdam, 1667), *Le Triomphe de l'Eucharistie* (Amsterdam: A. Wolfgang, 1667), *La Puissance ecclésiastique bornée à l'Ecriture et par elle* (Amsterdam: J. Van Elsen, n.d.), *La Réformation de l'Église par le pastorat* (Middelburg: H. Schmidt, 1667 68), and so on. These texts were delayed: they proliferated after his departure from Geneva. They were issued from a place he had already left. They "came out" from Geneva. There was, in the meddlesome surveillance that shadowed Labadie since 1662 (he complained about it to the Company of Pastors frequently),[65] not only the repetition of former imprisonments, but also a theoretical question touching, once again, the authority that power assumed to discipline the spirit: "I deny that pastors or bishops are ordained as legislators over the faithful, to set up, as they please, rules to be lived by, or force compliance with their decrees or statutes."[66] He did not criticize the power of the State and the magistrates. On the contrary, he made himself their apologist and condemned the "Roman clergy" for having wished to sidestep that power.[67] But he challenged the spiritual authority that "civil power" attributed to itself and, above all, the reciprocal idea that a community of "regenerates" could constitute a hierarchized society.

During his last years in Geneva, the Millenarian theme developed. Now, the Church was obviously not where it was, in the "bastions" of that "holy city." But if Geneva itself was not its site, where was the reign of the Spirit to be sought? One would have to await a new coming of the Messiah a thousand years hence. Since places were deceptive, one had to rely upon time; and the less places appeared capable of capitalizing time—of building up the reserves of a history, a tradition or a meaning, that is, of being perceived as authorities—the more time escaped those places, was freed from their codifications, and transformed into pure events or miracles. Millenarianism is a result of the unbinding of meaning in conjunction with a secularization of places, even ecclesiastical ones, in the experience of the believer. It expressed a hope whose only remaining possibility was to entrust the Spirit to time, to charge time with that responsibility. It spread among the reformed, with, for example, the commentary on Revelations written by Pierre de Launay in 1635, but published, interestingly, in Geneva in 1651. Amyrault, the great theologian of Saumur, did not consider it a futile task to refute that work in his *Du Règne de mille ans* (1654). Nathanael Homes took up the subject the same year, and in 1664 Samuel Des Marets (the same who a short time later wrote against Labadie) again attempted to strike a fatal blow to Millenarianism in *Chiliasmus enervatus.* There is no doubt that this literature developed in the wake of frightening rumors touched off by disruption in the celestial cosmos—the eclipse of 1654 or the execution of King Charles I (1649), the equivalent of the falling of a planet.[68] For Labadie, these falling stars were probably no more surprising than the fall of societies or Churches. More important is the movement that causes the Image that was past—already distant, yet seemingly promised to return to the Churches—to flee into the future, that is, into the direction of forward progress. Millenarianism marks the crossing of a new frontier: the passage of the Churches into sects.

Having been invited by the Walloon community of Middelburg, Labadie arrived in Utrecht in June 1666, with a group of "poor people from Lyon." There he rejoined the Van Schurmans—Johann Gottschalck (a medical doctor) and especially the sister, Anna Maria, whom he has been said (erroneously) to have married,[69] but whose autobiography gives the best information on the last period of the prophet.[70] Anna Maria, that erudite *apasionada* stayed with him to the end. In intensely radical formulations, she plots a course set upon the "hatred" [ *"odium"*] that prompts God to act, as if all things spoke to her in the language of solitary and inconsolable fury, to which the response was an unrequited love.[71] This God who "comes out," but for a struggle to the death with his disappointing creation, a god outside of himself, on the boundary where he is exiled both from himself and from the world, furious with a desire lacking an object— perhaps he resembles Labadie in his last days. But it matters little, after all. The appeal to psychology explains nothing, for this nomad is the locus rather than the author of the passion that arises at the point where an outer space is lacking as well as an inner one. Anna Maria Van Schurman recognized, in its theoretical form, an "absolute" structure of desire. She was able to hear (the ultimate way of "caring for") a war that no longer set gods at odds, but raged within the god, as Jakob Böhme had already seen, putting "hatred" at the very beginning of the Deity.[72] This was the period during which Labadie, settled in Middelburg,[73] connected with the "reform party," close to Voetius (with whom Anna Maria had put him in touch), emphasizes Millenarianism—for which the Companies of pastors and the synods reproached him more and more emphatically.

But the most violent polemics were about the interpretation of

Scripture, that is, the status of "the true copy or picture of the Christian Church," which is Labadie's last "place." The quarrel was touched off by *Philosophia S. Scripturae interpres* (1666), published anonymously by Louis Meyer, a medical doctor, poet, Cartesian philosopher, friend and first editor of Spinoza, who was then in the process of writing *Tractatus theologico-politicus*. Under the pretext of refuting Labadie's *Philosophia* in his *De Scripturarum Interprete* (Utrecht, 1668), Ludwig Wolzogen, who taught at Utrecht, adopts the biblical rationalism of Johannes Cocceius. He set up natural reason as the criterion for what was or was not acceptable in the Bible. The biblical texts were supposed to make up a metaphorical and charmed space in which verisimilitude (which is not yet truth) was to be selected according to the criteria of a certain erudition and philosophy. There ensued a raising of defenses on the part of the synods and the spirituals: ten, twenty pamphlets. With Yvon, and in the name of the Middelburg Consistory, Labadie denounced Wolzogen before the synod of Flessinge in a fifty-five page booklet. For once he was brief.[74] Supported by references to the tradition of Reformation theology, the theses developed were classic: "Wolzogen wants to elevate Reason above the Scriptures. . . . The interpretation of the Scriptures . . . belongs to the Holy Ghost. . . . For that purpose, it is in every particular Faithful."[75] Labadie goes on to develop this last point: inner illumination alone can procure an understanding of the Book. He isolates a "mystic" conviction, already central in Teresa of Avila: the true "book" is read within the soul. It is the soul itself, to the extent that the soul is a "fiction" and "painting" of the Spirit. In short, the autonomy of the Bible no longer existed for Labadie any more than it did for Wolzogen: the former reduces the Scriptures to what inner illumination finds in them; the latter, to what reason recognizes as its own. The text has no obscurity, nothing of its own.

By a spectacular reversal which was nonetheless completely logical, the synod of Naarden, after a series of postponements and discussions, ruled in September 1668 that Wolzogen's position was perfectly orthodox; Labadie's, on the other hand, was deemed incorrect and in need of a public retraction. Labadie was outraged and wrote a new piece against partiality and the rationalism of the members of the synod.[76] In fact, these gentlemen were right. For the past fifty years, the pastors had been worried that although they kept the text intact, they were no longer governing the *meaning* the faithful gave it. The "letter" remained in the Churches but the "spirit" was spreading elsewhere. There was, paralleling a similar reaction in the Catholic Church,[77] a return to the "clerics" and the privilege that an institution had to define a meaning. From this angle, the ecclesiastic institution and the "academic" one came to one another's assistance in opposing subjective "separatism," especially if it credited itself with an "illumination." In reality, in this debate, it was not a question of the text, but of two *practices* of the text: one institutional, conducted by the clerics, functionally "orthodox," and the other individualistic, by which the faithful could escape and follow their own paths. When the opposition between these two practices became alarming, as was the case in Walloon country, the quarrels between pastors and professors quieted down and they joined forces against a common threat. In 1668, Labadie refusing to bow to authority, a commission censured his Millenarianism. He was dismissed from his position, along with his adjuncts Yvon, du Lignon, and Menuret; the members of the Consistory of Middelburg were nearly all changed. The following year, a group of cosignatory theologians confirmed Wolzogen's "orthodoxy," The condemned Labadie persisted. He arranged conventicules in his home. There followed another exclusion, by the synod of Dordrecht (in the spring of 1669). Finally, at the request of the new Consistory of Middelburg, the Zealand States ordered him to leave the province. The pietists themselves also rejected the separatist.[78] Under interdiction of sojourn, he was doomed henceforth to be no more than a Labadist.

The "community of saints" that remained faithful to Labadie reached Amsterdam in 1669. There they organized. They, too, despite the difficulties of installation, became an institution. Oddly, information about them becomes abundant. There is an abundance of documentation and studies on Labadie's last five years (1669–74) and on the "sect."[79] As an institution, it had the right to a history. It also had its "renegade" writer, Jacob Dittelbach.[80] It drew together (shared goods), recruited (through propaganda seeking "regenerates"), became hierarchized (in a very authoritarian mode), asserted discipline (sternly), defined itself (with rites and doctrines), and expanded (to The Hague, Rotterdam, Utrecht, Dordrecht). When it began to cause too much of a stir, the tolerance of the burgomaster of Amsterdam, Konrad Van Beuningen, wore out. He sought to restrict Labadie to the internal service of his community. Labadie looked for a house outside the city. The contacts with Antoinette Bourignon, that other northern mystic, for the purpose of a common establishment on Noordstrand Island, foundered. "The Labadists," she said, "did everything in their power to have me become one of them, and to come with me to Noordstrand, presenting me with tons of gold by way of assistance if I needed them to get the said Island of Noordstrand in order to settle there, but . . . God made me see, from my earliest acquaintance with them, that it was all treachery and the seeking of convenient human compromises."[81] Moreover, Labadist predestination revolted her, quite as much as the "quarrels and contentions" of the group. Things turned sour: Yvon published two pamphlets against the "saint" [Antoinette] whom Pierre Poiret was quick to defend.[82] An invitation from Princess Elisabeth of the Palatinate, the abbess of Hervord, came just in time to allow a few dozen adherents to settle in her lands. They were given a very poor welcome by the inhabitants and clergy of the town. Hence they spent two years in virtual seque-stration—two liturgical, laborious years. The community had at its disposal a printing house, which published the *Solemnis fidei declaratio* of the founding trio, beneath the title/program *Veritas sui vindex*.[83] It was a fundamental problem, "Veritas se patefacit," wrote Spinoza at the same time. Under what conditions is "truth" its own proof? In fact, how could truth have any other proofs? In any case, the question was posed on both sides in a way that ruled out inspiration, and, for Labadie, on the basis of the shocking discovery that the truth no longer had the power to convince.

Despite Princess Elisabeth's intercession at the Court of Berlin to implore the King's protection, the Labadists had to yield to the Hervord authorities, who wanted them out of their territory. They went to Altona, in Denmark (1672). After a few months, they were again forced to change houses (May 1673), so that the "brothers" from Bremen could join the group. Labadie, having fallen ill, was in a delirium. After a time of improvement, he died on 6 February 1674 (they buried him in the garden), leaving a community that went on to settle in Frisia (in Wieuwerd, until 1688), then exiled itself to Mary-land, after the exploratory voyage of Jasper Danckaerts and Peter Sluy-ter to North America in 1679–80.[84] Was it during his last years that Labadie wrote the poems published in 1680, after his death?[85] Per-haps, but he had already written and published some poetry, in *Le Triomphe de l'Eucharistie*, in 1667: "You have ravished me, my God, you rend me from myself. . . . / At last I am myself no longer, I am You."[86] A rending whose only possible outcome would eventually be poetry.

## THE INVENTION OF EXTENSION

Historiography can, from this point on, take charge of the homeless wanderer and assign him a place—tomb and garden. "Labadie, R.I.P." might serve as title for the historical studies: such literature, that with one gesture both honors and buries, abounds.[87] If we prefer to remain at a distance from the polemic or edifying biographies that appeared soon after his death, we must pause for a moment at least to consider the appraisal, made twenty years later, by the least prejudiced mind of the times. Leibniz placed Labadie among the "condemnatives," who "have an aversion for those who are filled with good intent, but do not give themselves over fully to their own opinion," whose conduct does not conform "fully," exactly, and uncompromisingly to their intent. Too wise to approve, but too discriminating and universal not to understand these "extraordinary ways, that offend more than they clarify" (they wound), he found it "a pity that their zeal is not accompanied by more knowledge and perhaps also by more general charity."[88]

This remarkable lucidity distinguishes two kinds of mind and behavior in an expanding universe in which places, ceasing to be hierarchized (up to a supreme point that was their unity), were endlessly juxtaposed. Descartes had already said (and this is a good indication of the emergence of a new anthropology): "Extended matter, which makes up the universe, has no limits, because, wherever we might wish to pretend they are, we can still imagine beyond them indefinitely extended spaces that we cannot even imagine."[89] In that "indefinitely extended," there are minds fascinated by "the general," and if possible in the two modes, "science" and "charity." Such is the ambition of Leibniz: to reconcile, by calculus and relation, the "infinite" of particulars. There were also minds for whom the work of the infinite consisted in refusing one by one every specific place. They spent their time "untying" themselves from local identifications. That passion for untying (for the ab-solute) reiterated at every step the gesture that says "this isn't it," "this isn't it," endlessly, till the end of one's strength. That latter gesture is the mainspring of mystic life. A subtle word designates it, a "nothing" of the Other, an infinite term, common and repeated indefinitely: "God." But in a hierarchized world, as the one that John of the Cross lived in still was, every departure appeared to be either a descent or a "climb," and if it was performed with discernment, it was classified as an "ascension." It became the movement of going *higher* (an indefinite comparative). The world in which Jean de Labadie circulated no longer really respected that cosmic and spiritual hierarchy, which had not yet been replaced by the equally rigid and subtle system producing a socioeconomic hierarchy; hence, a step forward only meant going *further*, and discovering, from step to step, that an order of grace and creation was being replaced by a different space: "extension."

This was probably the "major" discovery to which Labadie bore witness in his travels. He was still living on the founding myth that there was somewhere a place of truth (maps of terrestrial paradise were still being printed in his time); he possessed, within himself, a "true copy" drawn from the evangelical "live original" and was looking for its actual site, but with the growing surprise (and irritation) of observing that it was "not here," nor "there," nor elsewhere. He does not give way on his "calling," which he identified, once and for all and very accurately, with the sacerdotal function. There was, he said, a "divine seal on me, not only of commitment, but of the priesthood." "My great intention was to take part in the true Ministry of the original Church, the idea of which was in my heart."[90] One of his earliest texts (unpublished) was entitled *Du Sacerdoce*:[91] it was the motivating force in his life. The priest is the functional designation of the "being-there" of a Spirit. By his status and his service, he guarantees to a society that it is the *place* of *meaning*. Therefore society judges it intolerable that he should betray a local legitimacy for which the inhabitants always pay dearly. (Nothing is as costly as the "authorization" of a place by a truth.) But Labadie was, like a militant bereft of a cause, a priest who no longer had a Church. He retained the "idea" of a place coinciding with that vocation, but, by experience after experience, was robbed of the space for it. He no longer progressed toward an end defined by the inaccessible point of a truth focalizing, organizing a space. He was going toward his own end, a personal fall in time, on the outskirts of an extended space that had no center. Perhaps he kept going north the way Descartes, as "a man who walks alone and in the shadows,"[92] decided always to go straight ahead, the only way to find one's way out of the woods. In reality, Labadie's wanderings had a direction, a regular orientation: they led him to places where the "sacramental" conception of space was disintegrating more and more, that is, toward a horizon in which grace was more and more foreign to each place and where, from the view point of the hope of at last localizing sense, extension was more and more "nonsensical."

His writing developed essentially as a way of walking. There is not, properly so called, a Labadie "doctrine." It is a *patchwork*, weaving together references and theoretical fragments from all sources. His books were formed from day to day, or rather from "religion" to "religion," out of elements he drew from the religion in which he was received against the one he was leaving, or vice versa. Traces of the soil through which he passed stuck to his shoes. He did not create a work constituting his own place. He composed a kind of *junk mystics*, just as there is today a kind of *junk music*. If (as is obviously the case) the ideas and quotations he retained from so much (and often rapid) reading reflected a personal selection, his criteria for choosing those materials did not derive from their pertinence within a system under construction, but from the movement that took up, then freed itself, from works, just as he dealt with places. Thus he did with the mystics he read most during his Catholic period: Richard of Saint-Victor, Bernard of Clairvaux, Tauler, Harpius, John of the Cross, and others—texts in which he could read stories of exile relative to evangelical "mirrors." But in contrast with those works, his own text was his walking. He wrote with his feet, that is, geographically, a story in which his publications, however numerous and voluminous, are only the punctuation, fragments or milestones. In Labadie's case, a change of method becomes necessary, such as would make it possible to conceptualize in a "geographical" way the theoretical significance of that sort of writing.

Labadie, advancing thanks to the symbolic material (that is, the field of activity) furnished to him by each Church—material that sketched out the utopian fiction of a place before becoming its lie—did not stop there. Nor did he use his travels to accumulate a capital of information. His impatience had a strange power to forget and to lose what came before. He did not belong to the race of travelers—visitors of lands or of books—who gradually replace the assurance of infinite truth with the indefinite accumulation of knowledge. His discourse did not become stable any more than his position did. All that remained, as he said countless times, was his "vocation." It was a work in those different languages, an identical operation on changing elements. In that respect, it still belongs to the mystic "way of speaking."[93] Hence his affinities, for a time, with the *praxis pietatis* of the pietists. But what was first, in mystic science, a practice of truths (or content of statements), intended to make them into a *conversar* (or a speech act), becomes with Labadie a practice of places (social, geographical) in order to make them into a way of walking. There is no longer really any dialogue. The *oratio* is reduced to an eloquence through which Labadie does violence to a place, in the name of the image it should be, until the public's attachment is transformed "naturally" into untying and rejection. All that remains of "prayer" or "communication" is its negativity, the pure movement of leaving a system of places for a *je ne sais quoi*, the solitary gesture of leaving.

Opposite the isolation of that operation (the "vocation") there stood the neutrality of places, the "neither one nor the other" of extension, indefinite space of an absence of meaning. Labadie, I repeat, was the spiritual discovery of that extension. As far as the "vocation" is concerned, he learned nothing. It had been obvious to him all his life, like a "childhood" that always guided him and that he maintained uncompromisingly. But it gave rise to a series of betrayals that were in fact indices of the progressive revelation of a space deconstructed because deprived of holy places to structure it—a space without limits because it had no center, and disseminated because it was lacking meaning. In reality, from Labadie's point of view, it was space that betrayed him. It was a wilderness to be gone through without it being possible to "believe" in anything. It is not surprising that the wanderer should have ended up thinking of that expanse as the theater of a "hatred," that of its creator. That hatred was the still-possible relationship between traditional faith in a creator God and the "modern" discovery of extension.

Labadie was obviously not the only wanderer of his day. They abounded during that period in which the Churches ceased organizing space and before a political order was in firm control. There are all sorts of wanderers, from the little passersby (like those Jesuits who become Protestants, or the other way around, and about which numerous documents lie dormant in the Roman archives) to the great itinerants (such as Quirinus Kuhlmann, who went from Silesia to Constantinople, from there to Switzerland, then to Moscow, where he was eventually burned alive in 1689),[94] not to mention the often even more radical, but more silent, "conversions" that took place in large numbers among the conquerors captivated by the New World, Africa, or Asia. Perhaps those migrations through the institutions of meaning had as their "exemplum" and laboratory the passages from Judaism to Christianity, or from Christianity to Judaism, frequent occurrences in fifteenth- and sixteenth-century Spain.[95] The cultural model of the *converso* spread as the fundamental sign of a break between place and meaning—a break difficult to tolerate, but without which it would be impossible to understand, in the seventeenth century, the aggressive restoration of local legitimacies in a political and national mode.

Labadie, though only one among all those passersby, gathers together in his singular journey some of the lines of force essential to the *mystics* that constituted itself as a "science" a century earlier, and he is a lucid, if "condemnative," witness of their dissolution. Three axes may define the changes produced by a movement that remained true to that of the earlier *mystics* but outside the field it presupposed: the sacramental idea, the surprise of the lack of place, and the practice of conversion. These are three poles, corresponding to the schema proposed at the beginning of this study.[96] The *sacramental idea* splits open, as if the symbolic discourse that founded the legitimacy of a

Church, after having been the paradoxical ("oxymoronic")[97] language of the coincidence of opposites, Spirit and place, left nothing but the original subjective certainty of a "vocation" (as a relic of a millennial history). The *event* emerges as the reiterated surprise of the absence of place: this suffering has the value of a confirmation for the spirit, but traces within it a privation of body identical to the privation of place. Finally, *conversion*, which presupposes the Western paradigm of one sole truth, and which changes place (or allegiance) as a way of being more completely in "the" (or "one's") truth, ceases being a putting into social circulation of places of meaning in order to become the ethical gesture of defiance, crossing a desert of meaning.

> You are alone now in spite of these stars,
> The center is near you and far from you,
> You have walked, you can walk, nothing changes anymore,
> Always the same night that never ends.
> And behold, you are already separated from yourself,
> Even that same cry, but you do not hear it;
> Are you he who is dying, you who have no more anguish,
> Are you even lost, you who do not seek?[98]

The poem, as always, precedes our progress. But perhaps our progress made the poem possible, by one of those roundabout ways spawned by the wiles of history. In any case, we have indeed arrived at that expanse that no longer speaks to us, lies mute, and where the wanderer, if always possessed of the same cry, no longer has anything to "say" but the "lie" of an image. He no longer seeks a place in which to become lost, for he is lost everywhere. The task of isolating, from a particular life, the form of that experience that remains mystic, leads us to renew our inquiry on the status of the body, which is lacking here. We must, then, move through *mystics* once more, no longer exploring the language it invents but the "body" that speaks therein: the social (or political) body, the lived (erotic and/or pathological) body, the scriptural body (like a biblical tattoo), the narrative body (a tale of passion), the poetic body (the "glorious body"). Inventions of bodies for the Other.[99] Labadie has led us to the edge of a shore where there is nothing, formally, but the relation between defiance and loss. That "excess" marks a boundary. We must return to the "finite" place, the body, which *mystics* or the mystic "infinitizes,"[100] and let Labadie pass by—a man whose wanderings continue to elude the learned, who only see him cross the narrow field of their competency, and who, like Empedocles, leaves us nothing but his sandals.

# Overture to a Poetics
# of the Body

Most high love, if I should die
Without having learned whence I possessed you,
In what sun was your abode
Or in what past your time, at what hour
  I loved you,

Most high love that passes memory,
Fire no hearth holds that was all my day,
In what destiny you traced my story,
In what slumber your glory was beheld,
  Oh my abode . . .

When I am lost to myself,
Divided into the chasm of infinity,
Infinitely when I am broken,
When the present presently enrobing me
  Has betrayed,

Through the universe in a thousand bodies shattered,
Of a thousand not yet gathered instants,
Of winnowed ashes windblown to the heavens' void,
You will remake for a strange year
  One sole treasure

You will remake my name and image
Of a thousand bodies borne by days away,
Live unity with neither name nor face,
Spirit's heart, oh center of mirage
    Most high love.

~     ~     ~

*Très haut amour, s'il se peut que je meure*
*Sans avoir su d'où je vous possédais,*
*En quel soleil était votre demeure*
*En quel passé votre temps, en quelle heure*
    *Je vous aimais,*

*Très haut amour qui passez la mémoire,*
*Feu sans foyer dont j'ai fait tout mon jour,*
*En quel destin vous traciez mon histoire,*
*En quel sommeil se voyait votre gloire,*
    *O mon séjour . . .*

*Quand je serai pour moi-même perdue*
*Et divisée à l'abîme infini,*
*Infiniment, quand je serai rompue,*
*Quand le présent dont je suis revêtue*
    *Aura trahi,*

*Par l'univers en mille corps brisée,*
*De mille instants non rassemblés encor,*
*De cendre aux cieux jusqu'au néant vannée,*
*Vous referez pour moi une étrange année*
    *Un seul trésor*

*Vous referez mon nom et mon image*
*De mille corps emportés par le jour,*
*Vive unité sans nom et sans visage,*
*Coeur de l'esprit, ô centre du mirage*
    *Très haut amour.*[1]

This poem by Catherine Pozzi, first published in 1929, moves rhyth-
mically on to its conclusion, which is a return to the beginning: *Très
haut amour.* Its music bears simple words, rolling them onward as in
a sea, bewitching them. The meaning is under the music's spell. Musical waters inundate the house of language, transforming it and

sweeping it along. At the beginning, as in the ancient shaman or Hindu forms of *mystics*, there is a rhythm. Where does it come from? No one knows. It has taken over the words, sweeps them away. Its movement is repetition: it recasts phrases in the form of incantations (*je meure/de-meure/quelle heure*). It whispers the same syllables to the ear (*mille corps/encor/trésor/mille corps*) and the same phonetic insistances (the chant is a variation in *m: mou/meu/mais/mé/moi/mon/meil/moi-même/ment*, etc.). The sounds, resembling fragments of refrains, form an uncanny memory, prior to meaning. One would be hard put to say what it is the memory of: it recalls something that is not a past; it awakens what the body does not know about itself.

Thus do the Indian shamans enter the forest of innumerable sounds, in search of a certain music—song of bird or wind—that will give birth in them to they know not yet what. A "spirit" is said to be calling them. Once back in the village, they will spend their lives answering that strangely familiar "vocation." And thus the poem "came" to Catherine Pozzi, at night, almost in its finished form. The music hoped for and heard, echoes in the body like an inner voice that one cannot specify by name but that transforms one's use of words. Whoever is "seized" or "possessed" by it begins to speak in a haunted tongue. The music, come from an unknown quarter, inaugurates a new rhythm of existence—some would say a new "breath," a new way of walking, a different "style" of life. It simultaneously captivates an attentiveness from within, disturbs the orderly flow of thought, and opens up or frees new spaces. There is no *mystics* without it. The mystic experience therefore often has the guise of a poem that we "hear" the way we drift into dance. The body is "informed" (gets form) from what befalls it in this way, well before the intellect becomes aware.

The poem's canorous gait, then, traces out a novel path of meaning. It regulates the progress of a train of thought. It places all existence beneath the sign and quasi-jurisdiction of a "love song." The song orders thoughts as shepherds' flutes once gathered scattered flocks. In Catherine Pozzi, the rhythm gives experience its wayfaring form. It begins with the difference in time ("your time" is different, "past") and place ("I die" is set in opposition to "your abode") that separates "I" and "you." But the initial division, which makes the other unknowable ("without having learned whence I possessed you"), leads, in the middle stanzas, toward the disintegration of the present "I" ("lost," "divided," "broken," "shattered," "winnowed," etc.) and finally reaches, in stanzas 4 and 5, the expectation, unjustifiable and self-assured, of a reconstitution by the unknown, loved inter-locutor:

> You will remake . . .
> You will remake my name and image

The breakdown of the body and disintegration of time into instants will inexplicably give way to the "live unity with neither name nor face." From stanza to stanza, an itinerary takes shape that is the mean-ing of experience. It links, with certainty but neither cause nor reason, the broken "I" to its recreation by the "most high love." The truth undone by song (as passion undoes ordered tresses) is replaced by that form that orients the love story toward the sun in which it culminates and vanishes: "You."

In that dance of the "I" and "you," one of the partners dissolves and is reborn in the other. Passion of love: mystic passion. But the poem is not content with giving a structure to experience. It allows for countless variations. More intimate or accidental finds, amorous en-twinings, lie hidden in the poem's musicality—that is, in what is audi-ble, not legible. Thus the *mémoire/histoire* parallel allows us to hear the *moi/toi* duo, which the reader does not see. To the ear it intimates a closeness underlying the visible (legible) opposition separating the time of the Other (history) from internal duration (memory). That is but one example among scores of others.

By its musicality, the poem is a labyrinth that branches out the more we circulate within it and the more we hear its voices. It is a body of journeys. To one who repeats it to himself, it contains and reveals myriad secret analogies, unsuspected languages, similarities and con-trasts, surprises and unfoldings. In this way it becomes a house haunted by the experience whose essential note it gave at the start, simple as those of a melody. It is as plural as the voice whose inflections and accents say, to an amorous attention, more than fully formed senten-ces. In that multiple space, the journey and events that all relate to the movement hastening "I" toward "you" are no less inforseeable. Like the experience whose fable it narrates, the song itself is the relation between "a thousand bodies borne by days away" and the "live unity with neither name nor face": a game of surprises, driftings, fugues in all directions, but also the meeting place where "I" returns to lose itself in that crowd that is, with neither name nor face, the presence of "you."

Echoes of Catherine Pozzi's poems can be heard in the most varied historical settings. A thousand-year-old tradition, that mystic poetics passes from place to place and age to age. Everywhere there reappears the experience that in the thirteenth century Hadewijch of Anvers said is caught up in "an eternity without shores" and expanded "by the unity that absorbs it"—"intelligence of calm desires, consecrated to total loss in the totality of the immense." Mystic and poet, Hadewijch described those wanderers who move through history in search of what has befallen them:

> They hasten, those who have glimpsed that truth, on the dark path, Untraced, unmarked, all inner.[2]

They are, she said, "drunk with what they have not drunk": inebriation without drinking, inspiration from one knows not where, illumination without knowledge. They are drunk with what they do not possess. Drunk with desire. Therefore, they may all bear the name given to the work of Angelus Silesius: *Wandersmann*, the "wanderer."

He or she is mystic who cannot stop walking and, with the certainty of what is lacking, knows of every place and object that it is *not that*; one cannot stay *there* nor be content with *that*. Desire creates an excess. Places are exceeded, passed, lost behind it. It makes one go further, elsewhere. It lives nowhere. It is inhabited, Hadewijch also said, by

> a noble *je ne sais quoi*, neither this nor that, that leads us, introduces us to and absorbs us in our Origin.[3]

Of that self-surpassing spirit, seduced by an impregnable origin or end called God, it seems that what for the most part still remains, in contemporary culture, is the movement of perpetual departure; as if, unable to ground itself in a belief in God any longer, the experience only kept the form and not the content of traditional *mystics*. It is, as Nelly Sachs says in a poem, *fortgehen ohne Rückschau*, "leaving without looking back." And René Char: "In poetry, one only lives in the place left behind, one only creates the work one detaches oneself from, one only gets duration by destroying time." Unmoored from the "origin" of which Hadewijch spoke, the traveler no longer has foundation nor goal. Given over to a nameless desire, he is the drunken boat.[4] Henceforth this desire can no longer speak to someone. It seems to have become *infans*, voiceless, more solitary and lost than before, or less protected and more radical, ever seeking a body or poetic locus. It goes on walking, then, tracing itself out in silence, in writing.

# Abbreviations

| | |
|---|---|
| AHG | Archives historiques du département de la Gironde (Bordeaux, later Paris) |
| AHSJ | Archivum historicum societatis Iesu (Rome) |
| ARSJ | Archivio romano societatis Jesu (Rome) |
| BN | Bibliothèque Nationale (Paris) |
| *BSBU* | *Bulletin de la société des bibliophiles de Guyenne* (Bordeaux) |
| Budé | Parios, Belles Lettres, coll. des universités de France, published under the auspices of the Guillaume Budé Association |
| DDB | Desclée De Brouwer |
| *DHGE* | *Dictionnaire d'histoire et de géographie ecclésiastique,* ed. A. Baudrillart et al. (Paris, 1912ff) |
| *DS* | *Dictionnaire de spiritualité,* ed. M. Viller et al. (Paris, 1937ff) |
| *DTC* | *Dictionnaire de théologie catholique,* ed. A. Vacant, E. Mangenot, and E. Amann, 15 vols. (Paris, 1903–50) |
| *EC* | *Ephemerides carmeliticae* |
| *EE* | *Estudios eclesiásticos* (Madrid) |
| *GW* | Freud, *Gesammelte Werke,* 18 vols. (London: Imago, 1940–52) |
| *MGH* | *Monumenta Germaniae historica* (Berlin) |

| | |
|---|---|
| *OCP* | *Orientalia christiana periodica* (Rome) |
| *OGE* | *Ons Geestelijk Erf* |
| *PG* | *Patrologia Graeca*, ed. J. P. Migne, 162 vols. Paris, 1857–66) |
| *PL* | *Patrologia Latina*, ed. J. P. Migne, 221 vols. (Paris, 1844–64) |
| PUF | Presses Universitaires de France |
| Pléiade | Paris, Gallimard, coll. Bibliothèque de la Pléiade et Encyclopédie de la Pléiade |
| *RAM* | *Revue d'ascétique et de mystique* (Toulouse) |
| *REG* | *Revue des études grecques* (Paris) |
| *RHB* | *Revue historique de Bordeaux* (Bordeaux) |
| *RHE* | *Revue d'histoire ecclésiastique* (Louvain) |
| *RHEF* | *Revue d'histoire de l'Eglise de France* (Paris) |
| *RHLF* | *Revue d'histoire littéraire de la France* (Paris) |
| *RHR* | *Revue de l'histoire des religions* (Paris) |
| *RCL* | *Revue de littérature comparée* |
| *RSR* | *Recherches de science religieuse* (Paris) |
| Sommervogel | Sommervogel, *Bibliothèque de la Compagnie de Jésus*, 12 vols. (Paris and Brussels, 1890–30) |
| Vulg. | Vulgate, traditional Latin version of the Bible |
| *ZAM* | *Zeitschrift für Askese und Mystik* |

# Notes

## Introduction

1. This Heideggerian category seemed to me to permit my reinterpretation of Christianity. See my "Rupture instauratrice," *Esprit*, June 1971, 1177–1214. [Reprinted in *La Faiblesse de croire*, ed. Luce Giard (Paris: Editions du Seuil, 1987), 183–226. –Trans.]

2. Franz Kafka, "Before the Law," *Franz Kafka: The Complete Stories*, trans. Willa and Edwin Muir, ed. N. N. Glatzer (New York: Schocken, 1972), 3–4.

3. On the present-day importance of this theological motif, see Geneviève Javary, *Recherches sur l'utilisation du thème de la Sekina dans l'apologétique chrétienne du XVe au XVIIIe siècle* (Lille: University of Lille III and H. Champion, 1978). The *Shekinah* implied a spiritual indwelling, a presence, a glory, and, later, a femininity of God—themes that also played an important role in the Christian *mystics* of that era.

4. Kafka, "Before the Law," 4.

5. Juan de la Cruz, *Cántico espiritual*, strophe 6 (*The Complete Works of Saint John of the Cross, Doctor of the Church*, trans. E. Allison Peers, 3 vols. [London: Burns, Oates & Washbourne, 1934–35], 2:51).

6. See part 3, "The Circumstances of the Mystic Utterance."

7. The curve of that evolution may be compared to the sociological model presented by Jean-Pierre Deconchy in *Orthodoxie religieuse et sciences humaines* (Paris and The Hague: Mouton, 1980). The "mysticization" of belief takes up where orthodox forms of regulation (doctrinal authority or theology), demystified by scientific knowledge, leave off. It upholds a sense

of belonging by fleeing critical questioning. Therefore, this process obviously remains *internal* to the religious domain. Viewed in relation to a general consciousness of institutional "corruption" (not just to the triumphant advance of knowledge), "mysticization" certainly does act, in the sixteenth and seventeenth centuries, as a defense. But, as its history demonstrates, that "strategy" also has its own dynamics: whatever withdraws its objects from exposure to external critique also attenuates their vigor from within.

8. See my editions of Pierre Favre, *Mémorial* (Paris: DDB, 1960); Jean-Joseph Surin, *Guide spirituel* (Paris: DDB, 1963); and Surin, *Correspondance* (Paris: DDB, 1966).

9. This work obviously owes much to the great historical studies on the subject, from Henri Bremond's *Literary History of Religious Thought in France* (New York: Macmillan, 1926–36) [see my "Bremond, historien d'une absence," *L'Absent de l'histoire* [n.p.: Mame, 1973]), to Leszek Kolakowski's *Chrétiens sans Eglise: La conscience religieuse et le lien confessionnel au XVIIe siècle,* trans. Anna Posner (Paris: Gallimard, 1969) (see my "Mort de l'histoire globale, L. Kolakowski," *L'Absent de l'histoire*), and to works of modern history of religious mentalities, among which are the indispensable studies of Michel Vovelle (see my "Christianisme et modernité dans l'historiographie contemporaine," *Recherches de science religieuse* 63 [1975]: 243–68), or the thought of Michel Foucault (see my "Noir soleil du langage, M. Foucault," *L'Absent de l'histoire* [This essay on Foucault is available in English in *Heterologies: Discourse on the Other,* trans. Brian Massumi (Minneapolis: University of Minnesota Press, 1986), 171–84. –Trans.]) I am even more indebted to my former teacher, Jean Orcibal, whose subtle, nice modesty combines massive erudition with a "positive metaphysics" passed down to him by Jean Baruzi. See Orcibal, *La Rencontre du carmel thérésian avec les mystiques du Nord* (Paris: PUF, 1959); Orcibal, *Saint Jean de la Croix et les mystiques rhéno-flamands* (Paris: DDB, 1966); and my "De Saint-Cyran au Jansénisme," *Christus* 10 (1963): 399–417. Among recent works whose methodological contribution opens new vistas in the modern history of Christian spirituality, see especially Bernard Gorceix, *Flambée et agonie: Mystiques du XVIIe siècle allemand* (Sisteron: Présence, 1977); Walter Sparn, *Wiederkehr der Metaphysik* (Stuttgart: Calwer, 1976), esp. 61–92, "Die Begründung einer Logik mystischer Prädikationen"; Daniel Vidal, *L'Ablatif absolu, théorie du prophétisme: le discours camisard en Europe (1706–1713)* (Paris: Anthropos, 1977); and Charles Webster, *The Great Instauration: Science, Medicine, and Reform, 1626–1660* (London: Duckworth, 1975).

10. See "Histoire et mystique," chap. 7 of my *L'Absent de l'histoire,* 153–67.

11. Many studies have shown this, from the chapter Emmanuel Le Roy Ladurie devoted to "pathways to writing" in his *Paysans de Languedoc* (Paris: SEVPEN, 1966) to Elizabeth L. Eisenstein's decisive and polemic thesis on the sociocultural revolution brought about by printing in vol. 2 of her *Printing Press as an Agent of Change: Communications and Cultural Transformations in Early Modern Europe,* 2 vols. (New York: Cambridge University Press, 1979).

12. It was to the history of that triumphant writing that I devoted *L'Écriture de l'histoire*, 2d ed. (Paris: Gallimard, 1978); available in English as *The Writing of History*, trans. Tom Conley (New York: Columbia University Press, 1988). See also Michel de Certeau, Dominique Julia, and Jacques Revel, *Une politique de la langue: La Révolution française et les patois: l'enquête de Grégoire* (Paris: Gallimard, 1975). In this respect, *The Mystic Fable* could be considered the counterpart to that phenomenon, the history of a "leftover."

13. The lovers' bubble, a detail from Bosch's *Garden of Delights*, represents that "retreat" of the word in a space of "fiction," analogous to the psychoanalytic space: a monastery or "balloon" of speaking subjects. See cover.

14. See Marguerite Duras, *India Song*, trans. Barbara Bray (New York: Grove Press, 1976), 21, and *The Vice-Consul*, trans. E. Ellenbogen (New York: Pantheon, 1968), 1, on a beggarwoman who finally goes to the Ganges, "where she found the way to get lost" (*The Vice-Consul*, 145).

15. *Wandersmann* is the title given to Angelus Silesius's *Aphorismes spirituels et sentences rimées* (1675). Silesius was at once a "pilgrim" (in E. Susini's translation, *pèlerin*) and a "wanderer" (in R. Munier's translation, *errant*), and above all a walker.

16. A. Furetière, *Dictionnaire universel* (1690). In Pascal we find the same focus on "the way of writing" and, in the field of logic, on "the ways of turning things" or "propositions."

17. See Ludwig Wittgenstein, *Tractatus Logico-Philosophicus*, 6.44: "Nicht *wie* die Welt ist, ist das Mystische, sondern *dass* sie ist." ["It is not *how* the world is that is mystical, but the *fact* that it is." –Trans.]

18. See Wittgenstein, *Notebooks 1914–16* (New York: Harper Torchbooks, 1969), 51 (25 May, 1915): "The urge [*Trieb*] towards the mystical comes of the non-satisfaction [*Unbefriedigtheit*] of our wishes by science. We *feel* that if all *possible* scientific questions are answered *our problem is still not touched at all.*"

19. Virgil *Aeneid* 1.405: "Vera incessu patuit dea." It was the moment of her departure; the goddess can be recognized when she is leaving.

20. The isolation of this truth already appears in a linguistic mode, with the change of the word "mystic" from an adjective to a noun. See below, chapter 3, "The New Science," and the notes of Gotthold Müller, "Ueber den Begriff der Mystik," *Neue Zeitschrift f. System. Theologie* 13 (1971): 88–98. It must be pointed out that, in the vocabulary of the time, "mystic" referred essentially to a use of *language* while "spirituality" referred to the *experience*. See the two great interpreters, M. Sandaeus, dedication to *Pro Theologia mystica clavis* (Cologne, 1640), and Honoré de Sainte-Marie, *Tradition des Pères et des Auteurs ecclésiastiques sur la contemplation* (Paris, 1708), 2:601ff.

21. See Dom Porion's summary of the dating of the poems in Hadewijch d'Anvers, *Écrits mystiques* (Paris: Seuil, 1954), 26–29.

22. Since the publication of the study edited by Jacques Le Goff, *Hérésies et sociétés dans l'Europe préindustrielle, XIe–XVIIIe siècle* (Paris and The Hague: Mouton, 1968). See also S. Shavar et al., "Hérésie et champ religieux," *Annales E. S. C.* 29 (1974): 1185–1305.

23. See Jean Séguy's synthesis, "Les Non-conformismes religieux d'Occident," in *Histoire des religions,* ed. Henri-Charles Puech, 3 vols. (Paris: Pléiade, 1970–76), 2:1268–93, on the modern period.

24. Jean-Claude Schmitt shows how the social and linguistic functioning of the accusation of heresy changes in the course of two centuries in his *Mort d'une hérésie. L'Église et les clercs face aux béguines et aux béghards du Rhin supérieur du XIVe au XVe siècle* (Paris and The Hague: Mouton, 1978). These findings should be compared with the Quietism crisis within the "political" space of the end of the seventeenth century. See Jacques Le Brun, *La Spiritualité de Bossuet* (Paris: Klincksieck, 1972), 439–668.

25. From *Histoire de la folie à l'âge classique* (Paris: Plon, 1963) to *Surveiller et punir* (Paris: Gallimard, 1975), Foucault has equipped historiography with the appropriate conceptual tools to analyse the intellectual and social processes of exclusion. [Available in English as *Madness and Civilization,* trans. Richard Howard (New York: Vintage, 1963) and *Discipline and Punish: The Birth of the Prison,* trans. Alan Sheridan (New York: Pantheon, 1977). –Trans.]

26. Among the many studies that have been done, those especially deserving of mention are Séguy, "Possibilitat e Problèmas d'una istoria religiosa occitania," *Annales de l'IEO* 4, no. 1 (Fall 1965): 5–26; Robert Lafont, *Renaissance du Sud. Essai sur la littérature occitane au temps de Henri IV* (Paris: Gallimard, 1970), and *Le Sud et le Nord* (Toulouse: Privat, 1971); and, for their methodological quality (although religious issues are treated only indirectly), vol. 2 of the compendium published by Daniel Fabre and Jacques Lacroix, *Communautés du Sud. Contribution à l'anthropologie des collectivités rurales occitanes* (Paris: Union Générale d'Éditions, 1975), Collection 10/18.

27. See the work already done by Georges Duby on heresy, that "hydra," and the "radical transformation" from the Middle Ages to the modern era, in *Hérésies et sociétés,* 397–98.

28. Alphonse Dupront, "Vie et création religieuses dans la France moderne (XIVe–XVIIIe siècle)," in *La France et les Français,* ed. M. François (Paris: Pléiade, 1972), 538, 557–59.

29. *Histoire de France* (1713 ed.), preface to vol. 1, quoted by Michel Tyvaert, "L'Image du Roi: légimité et moralité royales dans les Histoires de France au XVIIe siècle," *Revue d'histoire moderne et contemporaine* 21 (1974): 521.

30. Blaise Pascal, *Oeuvres complètes,* ed. Léon Brunschvieg and Pierre Boutroux (Paris: Hachette, 1908–), 9:369.

31. See Dupront, "Vie et création religieuses dans la France moderne": on the one hand, there is "religious solidity" (492), "religious stability" (493), see 496, 507; on the other, there is "a bursting apart" (538), "secularization," "polarization . . . between religion and State" (545).

32. The "schism" has as its corollaries, in the time of Richelieu, an autonomizing (or "secularization") of political thought with theories on "reasons of State." See Étienne Thuau, *Raison d'État et pensée politique à l'époque de Richelieu* (Paris: A. Colin, 1966), and Friedrich Meinecke, *L'Idée de Raison*

*d'État dans l'histoire des Temps modernes,* trans. M. Chevallier (Geneva: Dròz, 1973).

33. Maurice Agulhon, in *Pénitants et francs-maçons de l'ancienne Provence* (Paris: Fayard, 1968), has shown the stability of a provençale form of sociability maintaining itself through a series of these ideological contents: Christian (brotherhoods of penitents) in the sixteenth century, Freemason in the eighteenth century, political under the Revolutionary government (the populist societies of 1792) or in the twentieth century.

34. This evolution is comparable to the one Pierre Francastel analyzes in *La Figure et le lieu* (Paris: Gallimard, 1967). In Quattrocento art, a different distribution of the figurative elements handed down by religious tradition introduced a new way of functioning of the painting or of the "place" [*lieu*] well before Botticelli and Magenta gave that aesthetic revolution its own specific "figures."

35. See the anticipated thesis of M. Beugnot (University of Montreal) on the "refuge" or "retreat" in the seventeenth centurya movement common to all the religious congregations, including the Jesuits. (After an initial expansionist period, the Jesuits established the "residence," enclosure, and the "internal" practices of the Order as the condition permitting external action; see below, 249–51.

36. Heribert Bastel, in *Der Kardinal Pierre de Bérulle als Spiritual des Französischen Karmels* (Vienna: Wiener Dom Verlag, 1974), discussing Bérulle's role with the Carmelites, shows how the cardinal adjusted "mystic theology" to fit in with the "ecclesiastical hierarchy" and inner grace to fit in with a social and sacramental order. Kolakowski errs in classifying Bérulle among the "Chrétiens sans Église" ["Christians without a Church"] in his book of that title, 349–435.

37. See my "Écrire, une pratique mythique moderne," *L'Invention du quotidien* (Paris: Union Générale d'Éditions, Collection 10/18, 1980), 1:234–42. [In English, *The Practice of Everyday Life,* trans. Steven Rendall (Berkeley and Los Angeles: University of California Press, 1984), 133–39. –Trans.]

38. On the Jesuit "reductions" of Paraguay, which projected the utopian model of a Christian "city" on foreign soil, see Luiz Felipe Baêta Neves Flores, *O Combate dos Soldados de Cristo na Terra dos Papagaios,* stenciled thesis, Museu Nacional, Rio, 1974. The author aptly calls it an "institutional pedagogy" (90), but it is a pedagogy that rests upon the condition of an inaugural cutting off, the demarcation of a "scholarly" place that encompasses the entire existence of the "learners." The same protective/educative project for the Indians is already described in Bartolomé de Las Casas (1474–1566). See Marcel Bataillon and André Saint-Lu, *Las Casas et la défense des Indiens* (Paris: Julliard, 1971); Las Casas, *Très brève relation sur la destruction des Indes,* trans. J. Garavito (Paris and The Hague: Mouton, 1974); and Philippe Ignace André-Vincent, *Las Casas, apôtre des Indiens. Foi et libération.* (Paris: Éditions de la Nouvelle Aurore, 1975).

39. Discourse takes its form from that practice of the caesura. On the "discourse of prophecy," see Vidal, *L'Ablatif absolu.*

40. Gershom Scholem criticized precisely this "ahistorical" tendency in *On the Kabbalah and Its Symbolism,* trans. Ralph Manheim (New York: Schocken, 1965), 5. See also his "Mysticisme et société," *Diogène* 58 (1967): 3–28. Kolakowski even claimed to "treat" mystic ideas and movements "as manifestations of social conflicts" (*Chrétiens sans Église,* 44–45) but did not keep his promise. On the relationship between *mystics* and society, the basic texts are Ernst Troeltsch, *The Social Teaching of the Christian Churches,* trans. Olive Wyon, 2 vols. (New York: Macmillan, 1956), esp. 2:729–806, "Mysticism and Spiritual Idealism"; and Ivo Höllhuber, *Sprache Gesellschaft Mystik* (Munich-Basel: Reinhardt, 1963), esp. 332–33 for his three theses on "the connection between language, society, and *mystics.*"

41. Lucien Goldmann, *The Hidden God,* trans. Philip Thody (London: Routledge & Kegan Paul, 1964), esp. 103ff.

42. Dupront, "Vie et création religieuses dans la France moderne," 535. The relationships retraced by Orcibal in vol. 1 of Fénelon, *Correspondance de Fénelon,* 13 vols. (Paris: Klincksieck, 1972–), are ample demonstration.

43. Jean Sainsaulieu, *Les Érmites français* (Paris: Cerf, 1974), 47–93. Among the seventeenth-century anchorites, there were more members of the older *noblesse d'épée* than there were *noblesse de robe*; there were also many Leaguers among them.

44. See vol. 2 of the present work, forthcoming.

45. See below, part 4, "Figures of the Savage," and Le Brun, "Politique et spiritualité: la dévotion au Sacré-Coeur," *Concilium* 69 (1971): 25–36.

46. See Marie du Saint-Sacrement, *Les Parents de Sainte Thérèse* (Paris, 1914).

47. Marcel Bataillon, *Erasmo y España* (Mexico City, 1966), chap. 4, and particularly Antonio Dominguez Ortiz, *Los Judeoconversos en España y América* (Madrid: ISTMO, 1971), 149–66. See also, by the same author, "Las ordenes femeninas," *Las Clases privilegiadas en la España del Antiguo Régimen* (Madrid: ISTMO, 1973), 321–36; the work of Francisco Cantera Burgos, *Alvar Garcia de Santa Maria* (Madrid, 1952) and his articles on the *conversos* in *Sefarad* 4 (1944): 295–348, *Sefarad* 27 (1967): 71–111, and *Sefarad* 28 (1968): 3–39; Albert A. Sicroff, *Les Controverses des statuts de pureté de sang en Espagne du XVe au XVIIe siècle* (Paris, 1960); and the curious case analyzed by Francisca Vendrell de Millas, "Retrato irónico de un funcionario converso," *Sefarad* 28 (1968): 40–44. On the innovative and fundamental works of Américo Castro, see *Américo Castro and the Meaning of Spanish Civilization,* ed. José Rubia Barcia (Berkeley and Los Angeles: University of California Press, 1976), esp. J. H. Silverman, "The Spanish Jews," 137–65. Important from the point of view of the role played by "madness" in a "mystic" freedom is the paper read by M. F. Marquez Villanueva ("Jewish Fools in Fifteenth-Century Spain," Toronto Colloquium on Marranism, 1 May 1979) on the "court jesters" who came from among the *conversos*—ironic fabulists of a freedom within the very precincts of power. On the *alumbrados,*

see Alvaro Huerga, *Historia de los Alumbrados (1570–1630)*, 2 vols. (Madrid: Fundación Universitaria Española, 1978), and Antonio Márquez, *Los Alumbrados. Orígenes y filosofía (1525–1559)* (Madrid: Taurus, 1980).

48. See Efrén de la Madre de Dios, "Tiempo y vida de Santa Teresa," in Sta Teresa de Jesus, *Obras completas* (Madrid: Biblioteca de Autores Cristianos, 1951), 1:162–71; Narciso Alonso Cortes, *Boletín de la Real Academia de España* (1947); and Gerald Brenan, *St. John of the Cross: His Life and His Poetry* (Cambridge: Cambridge University Press, 1973), 91–95.

49. See Friedrich Lütge, *Deutsche Sozial- und Wirtschaftsgeschichte*, 3d ed. (Berlin: Springer, 1966); J. B. Neveux, *Vie spirituelle et vie sociale entre Rhin et Baltique au XVIIe siècle* (Paris: Klincksieck, 1967), 330–59, 503–23, passim; and Gorceix, *Flambée et Agonie*, 33–36, passim.

50. England differs in this respect from the Continent.

51. Quoted in René Pillorget, *La Tige et le rameau. Familles anglaises et françaises, XVe-XVIIIe siècle* (Paris: Calmann-Lévy, 1979), 108.

52. Steven E. Ozment, in *Mysticism and Dissent: Religious Ideology and Social Protest in the Sixteenth Century* (New Haven, Conn.: Yale University Press, 1973), analyzes "mystical writings in protest against established Christendom" by authors whom Williams classifies as "revolutionary spiritualists."

53. The motif of the present being "wedded" to death is found in both sixteenth- and seventeenth-century iconography and literature. See especially Alberto Tenenti, *La Vie et la mort à travers l'art du XVe siècle* (Paris: A. Colin, 1952); Michel Vovelle, *Mourir autrefois* (Paris: Gallimard-Julliard, 1974); and Philippe Ariès, *Western Attitudes toward Death: From the Middle Ages to the Present*, trans. Patricia Ranum (Baltimore: Johns Hopkins University Press, 1974).

54. Simone Weil, *Écrits de Londres et dernières lettres* (Paris: Gallimard, 1957), 31.

55. Louis Massignon develops the notion of that "solidarity" between societal destitution and a "mending, saving grace" into the central hypothesis in his study on Hallâj, *La Passion de Husayn Ibn Mansûr Hallâj: Martyr mystique de l'Islam, exécuté à Bagdad le 26 Mars 922: étude d'histoire religieuse*, 4 vols. (Paris: Gallimard, 1975), 1:25–28.

56. "Christ's promise can be salvaged by the baptism of the little ones" (Ockham, *Dialogus*, in M. Goldast, *Monarchia Sancti Romani Imperii* [Frankfurt, 1614] 2:506). On Ockham's position, see Francis Rapp, *L'Église et la vie religieuse en Occident à la fin du Moyen Âge* (Paris: PUF, 1971), 359, and Y. Congar, *Dogmengeschichte* (n.p.: Herder, 1971), 191.

## Chapter 1: The Monastery and the Public Square

1. Marguerite Duras, *The Vice-Counsel*, trans. E. Ellenbogen (New York: Pantheon, 1968), 118 (see also 1, 81, 145), and *India Song*, trans. Barbara Bray (New York: Grove Press, 1976), 21.

2. See esp. José Grosdidier de Matons, "Les Thèmes d'édification dans la vie d'André Salos," *Travaux et Mémoires* [Centre de recherche d'histoire et de civilisation byzantines] 4 (1970): 277–328. See also, among works con-

sulted, E. Benz, "Heilige Narrheit," *Kyrios* 3 (1938): 1–55; G. Fedotov, *The Russian Religious Mind,* 2 vols. (1960; Cambridge, Mass.: Harvard University Press, 1966); I. Kologrilof, *Essai sur la sainteté en Russie* (Bruges: Beyaert, 1953) 261–73; and Thomas Spidlik, "Fous pour le Christ," *DS,* vol. 5, cols. 752–61; etc.

3. My thanks to Michèle Montrelay, Evelyne Patlagean, and Joseph Paramelle, who enlightened me in my reseach in various ways.

4. My translation of the text edited by C. Butler, *Texts and Studies,* VI (Cambridge: Cambridge University Press, 1904) 2:98–100 (with scholarly notes) and republished (without scholarly notes) in Palladios, *Histoire lausiaque,* trans. and ed. A. Lucot (Paris: A. Picard, 1912), 228–33. A longer, later version, which gives the name "Isidora" to the "idiot woman," is found in *PG,* vol. 34, cols. 1106–7.

5. See Georges Dumézil, *Idées romaines* (Paris: Gallimard, 1969), 61–78.

6. See Pierre Canivet, "Erreurs de spiritualité et troubles psychiques," *Recherches de science religieuse* 50 (1962): 161–205.

7. 1 Cor. 3:18.

8. Jacques Lacan, *Les Quatre Concepts fondamentaux de la psychanalyse* (Paris: Seuil, 1973), 241.

9. The term *Amma,* "Mother," or more precisely, as the text points out, "spiritual mother," is not present in all the manuscripts.

10. On the basis of the *Lausiac History* itself, it is difficult to come to a definite conclusion. Two young spouses address one another as *Kurie* [Sir], *Kuria* [Lady], *Kuria mou* [my Lady] (Butler, *Texts and Studies,* 27); Evagrius, a lay deacon, is addressed as *Kuri diacone* [Sir Deacon] (ibid., 118). What can we deduce from this other than a *possible* meaning? Titles of respect are sometimes used here derisively. For example, the title "Great" (*o megas,* the great) applied to Anthony with an attenuated, if not ironic meaning (ibid., 65) or to a crippled person lacking both arms and legs, with nothing left intact but his tongue ("Do you want me, my great one, *o megas,* to take you to my home?" [ibid., 64]). Whatever the case may be, the subtle interplay of titles and their instability is of central importance.

11. See François Perrier, *Psychanalyse* 2 (1956): 187, who quotes Luke 1:38.

12. Duras, *The Ravishing of Lol Stein,* trans. Richard Seaver (New York: Pantheon, 1966), 72. See Michèle Montrelay, *L'Ombre et le nom* (Paris: Minuit, 1977), 9–23.

13. See Claude Reichler, *La Diabolie. La séduction, la renardie, l'écriture* (Paris: Minuit, 1979), 41–46.

14. Roland Barthes, *Roland Barthes* (Paris: Seuil, 1975), 149.

15. See Reichler, *La Diabolie,* 11 n. 5.

16. See *Vie (et récits) de l'abbé Daniel le Scétiote,* ed. Léon Clugnet (Paris: n.p., 1901), 22–25, and Grosdidier de Matons, "Les thèmes d'édification," 287–88.

17. Grosdidier de Matons, "Les thèmes d'édification," 284–85.

18. Ibid., 306.

19. Ibid., 302–28.
20. A term taken from the manuscript, to be retained, despite L.Clugnet who corrects it to *exechoumenos.*
21. Greek text in "Vie et récits de l'abbé Daniel de Scété," ed. Clugnet, *Revue de l'Orient chrétien* 5 (1900):60–62; my translation. On this story, see Grosdidier de Matons, "Les thèmes d'édification," 288–90.
22. That is, the Patriarch of Alexandria.
23. "Vie et récits de l'abbé Daniel de Scété." Verisimilitude would seem to incline toward correcting the text, and toward supposing that the idiot attacks the old man, or at the very least that he calls out to the onlookers, shouting "Help." But there is nothing in the variants that would justify that modification.
24. On that "idiot" [*salos*] who laughs, in an Egyptian community (fourth century), see Grosdidier de Matons, "Les thèmes d'édification," 285–87.
25. Jean-Joseph Surin, Cantique 4 ("I want to go and run among the world"), *Cantiques spirituels* (Bordeaux, 1662).
26. See Evelyne Patlagean, "L'Histoire de la femme déguisée en moine et l'évolution de la sainteté féminine à Byzance," *Studi Medievali,* ser. 3, XVII, II (1976): 597–623.
27. *L'Evangile de Thomas,* trans. and ed. A. Guillaumont et al. (Paris: n.p., 1959), 57 [logion 114], quoted in Patlagean, "L'Histoire de la femme déguisée," 607. [In English, see *The Gospel according to Thomas,* trans. and ed. Guillaumont et al. (New York: Harper & Row, 1959), 57 [logion 114]. My translation is a close rendering of de Certeau's text; the English version of Guillaumont's translation reads: "Jesus said: See, I shall lead her, so that I will make her male, that she too may become a living spirit, resembling you males. For every woman who makes herself male will enter the Kingdom of Heaven." The divergence may be due to Patlagean. –Trans.]
28. Evagrius, *Histoire ecclésiastique* 1.21, quoted in Patlagean, "L'Histoire de la femme déguisée," 614 n. 56.
29. In these texts, sex is a "garment" one can remove. See Patlagean, "L'Histoire de la femme déguisée," 608.
30. Montrelay, *L'Ombre et le nom,* 147.
31. All of these stories define the site of madness by the proximity to waste, dross. The Tabennesiot nun is in the kitchen; the drunkard woman, near the toilets; Mark, at the baths; Simeon, in the women's bathhouses; Andrew, in the garbage or gutter; and so on.
32. Plotinus *Enneads* 2.4.6–13. Bréhier translates: "Of matter one says merely that it is other, or perhaps *others,* in order not to determine it overmuch by the singular, and to indicate with the plural its indetermination" (Budé, 68). Literally, it would be: "not determine it too much by the [term] *other* and indicate its indetermination by the [term] *others.*"
33. Simone Weil, *Ecrits de Londres et dernières lettres* (Paris: Gallimard, 1957), 31ff; see also 167, 180, passim.
34. Plato *Phaedrus* 242e, trans. Mario Meunier (Paris: Albin Michel, 1960), 63.

Chapter 2: *The Garden: Delirium and Delights of Hieronymous Bosch*

1. R. H. Marijnissen and M. Seidel, *Jheronimus Bosch* (Brussels: Arcade, 1975) list and provide the contents of these papers, 17–21.

2. Wilhelm Fraenger, *Le Royaume millénaire de Jérôme Bosch,* trans. Roger Lewinter (Paris: Denoël, coll. 1966), 17.

3. On the criticism leveled at Fraenger's resounding thesis (according to which *The Garden of Delights* illustrates the Adamite theology of the Brothers of the Free Spirit), see Marijnissen and Seidel, *Jheronimus Bosch,* 50, 99.

4. In *Ontcijfering van Jeroen Bosch* (The Hague, 1949) and *Beschrijving en poging tot verklaring van het Tuin der Onkuisheiddrieluik van Jeroen Bosch* (Amsterdam, 1958), Dirk Bax has painstakingly compared Bosch's scenes and figures with the proverbs, puns, or jokes of the old Dutch language. That ethnological and linguistic exegesis is without a doubt the most serious of the erudite approaches.

5. There is, in *The Garden,* neither square nor rectangle, except the format of the painting itself, which is almost square.

6. Paul Klee, *Théorie de l'art moderne* (Paris, 1964), 39. [Translated from "Schöpferische Konfession," *Tribüne der Kunst und Zeit* (Berlin, 1920), no. 13, 28–40. –Trans.]

7. A. Chastel, "La Tentation de Saint Antoine ou le songe du mélancholique," *Gazette des beaux-arts* 15 (1936): 218–19.

8. Novalis frag. 488, quoted by Fraenger, *Le Royaume millénaire,* 182.

9. See Paul Zumthor, *Langue, texte, énigme* (Paris: Seuil, 1975), 23–88, and *Le Masque et la lumière. La poétique des grands rhétoriqueurs* (Paris: Seuil, 1978), 125–75, 267–77.

10. See Raymond Klibansky, Erwin Panofsky, and Fritz Saxl, *Saturn and Melancholy* (Cambridge: Nelson, 1964), 241–74.

11. This point of construction and inversion, at once the *limit* of an indefinite series and the *principle* of their unitary reorganization, might well be compared with the *punctus convexitatis* of Nicholas of Cusa. See M. de Gandillac, *La Philosophie de Nicolas de Cues* (Paris: Aubier, 1941), 155–59, 223–27, passim.

12. A variant of the signature (see Chastel, "Signature et signe," *Revue de l'Art,* no. 26, esp. "L'art de la signature," 8–14), the emblem, to use the distinctions established by C. S. Peirce, replaces the "symbol" with the "icon" (see J.-C. Lebensztejn, "Esquisse d'une typologie," ibid., 48–56). It replaces the concept with the image (see also Zumthor, *Le Masque et la lumière,* 213–17). But rather than being an emblematization of the name, the little scenes in the three corners should be considered an emblematization of the picture, in a humorous style rather frequent in riddles of this kind.

13. Grylles, many-headed or headless beings, double-faced, heads with legs protruding, heteroclite hybrids, gradually begin peopling the iconography, which, during the fourteenth and fifteenth centuries, inventories the possible. They abound in the paintings of Bosch, which Don Felipe de Guevara, around 1560 (*Comentarios de la pintura*), even defines as "this sort

of painting" called *grillo*. See Jurgis Baltrušaitis, *Le Moyen Age fantastique. Antiquités et exotismes dans l'art gothique* (Paris: A. Colin, 1955), 11–53.

14. See Peter Glum, "Divine Judgment in Bosch's *Garden of Earthly Delights*," *Art Bulletin* 58, no. 1 (1976): 47.

15. See Guy Lecerf, *Les Fêtes et leurs représentations dans l'oeuvre de Jérôme Bosch*, unpub. thesis, Paris, 1975, 87–90, and P. Lehmann, *Die Parodie im Mittelalter*, 2d ed. (Stuttgart, 1963), 95ff.

16. See J. Van Lennep, *Art et Alchimie* (Brussels: Meddens, 1971), 213–22.

17. See Stanislas Klossowski de Rola, *Alchimie* (Paris: Seuil, n.d.), 7–8.

18. Astrology must also be taken into account, given the presence of the signs of the zodiac, the circular calendar (the merry-go-round), essential figures (the moon, the Bear, etc.). See Keith Thomas, *Religion and the Decline of Magic*, 2d ed. (London: Penguin, 1973), 335–458.

19. See Roman Jakobson, *Essais de linguistique générale*, trans. Nicolas Ruwet (Paris: Minuit, 1963), 214–21.

20. See Tzvetan Todorov, *Introduction à la littérature fantastique* (Paris: Seuil, 1970), 174–77.

21. Marcel Brion, in *Bosch, Goya et le fantastique*, ed. Gilberte Martin-Méry (Bordeaux, 1957), xxv.

22. A 1590 Antwerp inventory uses this term to refer to Bosch's paintings. See Leo Van Puyvelde, *La Peinture flamande au siècle de Bosch et Breughel* (Brussels: Meddens, 1964), 52.

23. Marijnissen and Seidel, *Jheronimus Bosch*, 16.

24. Sigmund Freud, chap. 1 of *Civilization and Its Discontents*, *GW*, 14:427–28.

25. See Georges Canguilhem, "La monstruosité et le monstrueux," *La Connaissance de la vie*, 2d ed. (Paris: Vrin, 1965), 171–84.

26. Fray de Siguença cites that common opinion and deems the term pejorative ("foolish things") and unworthy of Bosch (*Tercera Parte de la Historia de la Orden de San Gerónimo* [Madrid, 1605], 837, 841).

27. Klee, *Théorie de l'art moderne*, 38.

28. Baudelaire, "Moesta et Errabunda," *Les Fleurs du mal*.

29. See A. Straub and G. Keller, *Hortus Deliciarum* (Strasbourg, 1901), on this text written at the end of the twelfth century by Herrade de Landsberg.

30. "Paradise of enjoyment," says Denys le Chartreux in his commentary on the Pentateuch, no. 3 (Cologne, 1534). "Garden of Pleasure": Saint Bonaventure, *Tractatus de plantatione Paradisi*, in *Opera Omnia* (Quaracchi, 1891), 5:574. See Dagmar Thoss, *Studien zum locus amoenus im Mittelalter* (Vienna-Stuttgart: W. Braumüller, 1972), and Klaus Garber, *Der locus amoenus und der locus terribilis* (Vienna: Böhlau, 1974). Bosch perverts the *locus amoenus* by identifying it with a *locus terribilis:* the ambiguity of the place creates the fantastic.

31. Ovid *Metamorphoses* 1.101–4, ed. G. Lafaye (Budé, 1928), 10–11.

32. "Vie de Suso," *L'Oeuvre mystique de Henri Suso*, trans. B. Lavaud (Paris: Egloff, 1946), 1:126–27.

Notes to Pages 68–77 / 314

33. E. Delaruelle, "La Vie religieuse populaire en Occident dans les années 1500," in *Colloque d'histoire religieuse* (Grenoble, 1963), 30.

34. Clément Marot, *Poètes du XVIe siècle,* ed. A. M. Schmidt (Paris: Pléiade, 1953), 332. On strawberries, s.v. "Erdbeere," *Lexicon der christlichen Ikonographie,* I:656–57, 1. "Weltlust," 2. "nourriture des élus," 3. "plante du paradis," etc.

35. Two per zone, not counting the seventh, which has been changed into a bird and is being ridden by a *zeeridder* in the sky on the left.

36. Christiane Rabant-Lacôte, "L'Enfer des musiciens," *Musique en jeu* 9 (1972): 23, quoting the expression Lacan used to describe the child playing in front of a mirror, to characterize "fiction."

37. Michel de Certeau, *L'Écriture de l'histoire,* 2d ed. (Paris: Gallimard, 1978), 215–48. [*The Writing of History,* trans. Tom Conley (New York: Columbia University Press, 1988), 209–43. –Trans.]

38. Plato *Symposium* 189–93, [Aristophanes' speech] in *Oeuvres complètes,* trans. L. Robin (Paris: Pléiade, 1950), 715–22.

39. Klee, *Théorie de l'art moderne,* 26. [Translation of *Über die moderne Kunst* (Berne-Bümplitz: Benteli, 1945), a lecture given at Jena in 1924.]

## Chapter 3: The New Science

1. Lorenzo Valla, *Opera* (Basel: Henricus Petrus, 1543), 504. See W. Keith Percival, "The Grammatical Tradition and the Rise of the Vernaculars," in *Historiography of Linguistics,* ed. Thomas Sebeok (The Hague: Mouton, 1975), 255.

2. See Ferdinand Brunot, *Histoire de la langue française,* 3d ed. (Paris: Armand Colin, 1967), 2:161–73, 188–97, passim.

3. "Debemus, inquiunt, ubi res postulat verbis inperare, non servire" (M. Sandaeus, *Pro Theologica mystica clavis* [Cologne, 1640], 6); my emphasis.

4. See J. R. Armogathe, "Néologie et idéologie dans la langue française au XVIIIe siècle," *Dix-huitième siècle* (1973): 17–28.

5. [The term "la mystique" has no precise equivalent in English, which uses "mysticism" for both "la mystique" and "le mysticisme." In the present work, de Certeau never uses the broad, generic "le mysticisme," but always the historically specific "la mystique," which I translate as *mystics.* See "Translator's note."–Trans.]

6. Henri de Lubac, *Exégèse médiévale. Les Quatre sens de l'Écriture,* 4 vols. (Paris: Aubier, 1959–64). See Michel de Certeau, "Exégèse, théologie et spiritualité," *RAM* 36 (1960): 357–71.

7. See below, 126–29.

8. From this perspective, the new seventeenth-century discipline could be compared to the "ethnology" that Ampère "isolated," named, and classified in his general overview of the sciences. See G. de Rohan-Csermak, "La première apparition du terme 'ethnologie,'" *Ethnologia Europa* 1, no. 14 (1967): 170–84. Between these two "heterologies" (*mystics* and ethnology) there are, moreover, quite a number of analogies.

9. See the notes by Sophrone, "Le mot '*mystique*,'" *Revue pratique d'apologétique* 28 (1919): 547–56, and Louis Bouyer, "*Mystique*. Essai sur l'histoire d'un mot," in *Supplément de la Vie spirituelle*, no. 9, 15 May 1949, 3–23. The former already points out the semantic difference between the adjective and the noun (554). See also A. Fonck, s.v. "mystique," *DTC*, vol. 10, no. 2 cols. 2599–2674, and, more detailed but in a narrower perspective, Lucy Tinsley, *The French Expression for Spirituality and Devotion* (Washington, D.C.: Catholic University of America Press, 1953).

10. Lubac, *Corpus mysticum*, 2d ed. (Paris: Aubier, 1949).

11. John 20:13, 15. The rest of the text ("Mary," Jesus says to her, and she answers "Rabboni,") already falls within the province of mystical life.

12. See John, 7:34, 36; 12:26; 14:3; 17:24; passim.

13. Lubac, *Corpus mysticum*, 281.

14. Ibid., 288.

15. These Augustinian expressions characterize two "communions" with the Body: the act of "consuming, eating, receiving" Christ (that is, the Eucharist) and the act of "being consumed, received, assimilated" by Christ (that is, the Church).

16. This perspective insists on the *mysterium* (a problematics of the "operation") more than on the *sacramentum* (a problematics of the "sign" and, before long, of representation). Lubac reminds us pertinently that "a mystery, in the old sense of the word, is more of an action than a thing"; it is a "mutual relation" (Simonin), the operation of an exchange or of a communication between the terms distinguished (*Corpus mysticum*, 47–66).

17. See, among many others, Francis Rapp's synthesis, *L'Église et la vie religieuse en Occident á la fin du Moyen Âge* (Paris: PUF, 1971).

18. See *Faire croire. Modalités de la diffusion de la réception des messages religieux du XIIe au XVe siècle, Tableronde, Rome, 22–23 Juin 1979* (Rome: École française de Rome, 1981). See also Maria Corti, "Ideologie semiotiche nei 'Sermones ad status' del secolo XIII," *Il viaggio testuale* (Turin: Einaudi, 1978), 221–42; Corti, "La cooperazione di tre strutture semiotiche: 'allegoria in factis,' 'speculum' e modello sociale triadico," *In ricordo di C. Angelini* (Milan: n.p., 1979), 1–8; and the historiographic panorama of Carlo Delcorno, "Rassegna di studi sulla predicazione medievale a umanistica (1970–1980)," *Lettere italiane* 23 (1981):235–76.

19. See Louis Marin, *Le Portrait du Roi* (Paris: Minuit, 1981), 145–68.

20. See Thomas N. Tentler, *Sin and Confession on the Eve of the Reformation* (Princeton, N.J.: Princeton University Press, 1975). The canon *Omnis utriusque sexus* (Lateran IV), requiring confession at least once a year for all the faithful having reached the age of discernment, marks the beginning of this development.

21. This comprises a vast literature. See P. Michaud-Quantin, *Sommes de casuistique et manuels de confession au Moyen Age (XIIe–XVIe siècle)* (Louvain-Lille: n.p., 1962). There are countless treatises and handbooks (such as the successful *Confessionale* by Antonin de Florence, or the *Miroirs de la confession*).

22. See Édouard Dumoutet, *Le Désir de voir l'hostie et les origines de la dévotion au Saint Sacrament* (Paris: Beauchesne, 1926).

23. *Actus Apostolorum* 2.44 (Vulg.).

24. Francis, walking in the fields, "preaches" without needing words, those opaque mediators between man and nature. See Edward A. Armstrong, *Saint Francis: Nature Mystic; The Derivation and Significance of the Nature Stories in the Franciscan Legend* (Berkeley and Los Angeles: University of California Press, 1973), 5–41.

25. In the sense in which Freud spoke of the *Material* offered him by his patients and by historical and anthropological documents.

26. Lucien Febvre had already taken note of these sensorial polarizations in *Le Problème de l'incroyance au XVe siècle. La réligion de Rabelais* (Paris: Albin Michel, 1942), 393–403. [Available in English as *The Problem of Unbelief in the Sixteenth Century, The Religion of Rabelais,* trans. Beatrice Gottlieb (Cambridge, Mass.: Harvard University Press, 1982), 436–42. –Trans.] In opposition to his thesis ("the underdevelopment of sight" in the sixteenth century, a thesis taken up later by R. Mandrou) stands that of Johan Huizinga (*The Waning of the Middle Ages: A Study of the Forms of Life, Thought and Art in France and the Middle Ages in the Fourteenth and Fifteenth Centuries,* trans. F. Hopman [London: Edward Arnold, 1924], 261ff) on the predominance of the sense of sight during the same period. See also Robert Klein, "La Pensée figurée de la Renaissance," *Diogène* 32 (1960): 123–38. In any event, the question is of primary importance and is treated as such on both sides. Perhaps the theoretical hypertrophy of the visual was not yet paralleled by a modification in the common perception of things, and the privilege of sight was at first a speculative, revolutionary, "visionary" phenomenon.

27. In Dionysius the Areopagite, "hierarchical discipline, far from opposing mystical experience, protects and prepares the conditions of its fulfillment," so that one might "place the treatise *Mystic Theology* not apart from, but at the very heart of, *Ecclesiastical Hierarchy*" (René Roques, "Denys l'Aréopagite," *DS,* vol. 3, cols. 283–84).

28. Oddly, there is a similar transference in Freud, when, for example, in chapter 6 of *The Interpretation of Dreams,* "figures of speech" or their equivalents (displacement, condensation, etc.) characterize the specific operations of "dream-work," thus defining the formalities of historical procedures. [Certeau uses the term "formalité" to designate the situational significance of practices within a specific historical context and contrasts it with their "content." See his *Writing of History,* trans. Tom Conley (New York: Columbia University Press, 1988), 147–48, 156–58. –Trans.]

29. Gal. 4:21. See also 1 Cor. 10:11 ("All these things that happened to them were symbolic [*tupikōs*]"), or 2 Cor. 3:6 ("the letter killeth, but the spirit giveth life," which is another form of *gramma-pneuma* opposition).

30. In antiquity and during the Middle Ages, allegory "is" a rhetorical figure that consists in "saying something else" than what one wishes to signify. See Augustine: "Quid ergo est allegoria, nisi tropus ubi ex alio aliud intelligitur?" (*De Trinitate,* XV, 9, 15; PL, 42, 1068). Isidore of Seville calls it

alieniloquium: "Aliud enim sonat, et aliud intelligitur" (*Etymologiarum sive originum libri XX*, 1:xxxvii, xxii). See Jean Pépin, "La Notion d'allégorie," *Dante et la tradition de l'allégorie* (Paris: Vrin, 1970), 11–51.

31. On medieval allegory, in addition to Pépin's *Dante*, see Lubac, *Exégèse médiévale*, 4:125–262; Dunbar H. Flanders, *Symbolism in Medieval Thought and Its Consummation in the Divine Comedy* (New Haven, Conn.: Yale University Press, 1969); Johan Chydenius, "La Théorie du symbolisme médiéval" (1960), trans. in *Poétique* 23 (1975): 322–41; and Armand Strubel, "Allegoria in factis et Allegoria in verbis," *Poétique* 23 (1975): 342–57.

32. See Raoul Mortley, *Connaissance religieuse et herméneutique chez Clément d'Alexandrie* (Leiden: Brill, 1973), 39–58, on Stoic allegory as "allusive meaning," or *hyponoia*. In the medieval tradition (for example, in John Scotus Erigena) the term "symbolum" is often restricted to *allegoria dicti*. See Pépin, *Dante*, 19.

33. Augustine *De trinitate* 15.9.15.

34. Pépin, *Mythe et allégorie. Les origines grecques et les contestations judéo-chrétiennes* (Paris: Aubier, 1958), 478.

35. In *Interpretation Theory and Practice*, ed. Charles Singleton (Baltimore: Johns Hopkins University Press, 1969), 190–91, Paul de Man makes a distinction between the "symbol," a "simultaneity" of image and substance, and the allegory, in which time is the constitutive category. In point of fact, this problematics of noncoincidence, providing the basis for a "rhetoric of temporality" that situates the trope within the "void of temporal difference," goes back to the Christian use of allegory.

36. See Strubel, "Allegoria in factis," 350–51.

37. See Paul Vignaux, s.v. "nominalisme" and "Occam," *DTC*, vol. 11, no. 1, cols. 733–84, 876–89.

38. See Ernest A. Moody's analysis in *Truth and Consequence in Medieval Logic* (Westport, Conn.: Greenwood Press, 1953), 5–6: "The primary significance of what is called the 'nominalism' of Ockham is its rejection of the confusion of Logic with metaphysics, and its vigorous defense of the older conception of Logic as *scientia sermocinalis* whose function is to analyze the formal structure of language rather than to hypostatize this structure into a science of Reality or of Mind."

39. See, for example, Terence Cave, *The Cornucopian Text: Problems of Writing in the French Renaissance* (Oxford: Clarendon Press, 1979), 78–124, on interpretation.

40. Lubac, *Exégèse médiévale*, 4:140, 149.

41. Pierre de Bérulle, "Dédicace au Roi," *Grandeurs*, in *Oeuvres* (1644), 133. Following Bérulle, see Saint-Cyran, quoted in Jean Orcibal, *La Spiritualité de Saint-Cyran avec ses écrits de piété inédits* (Paris: Vrin, 1962), 21 n. 54. Bérulle translates "verum" as "réel" in accordance with tradition. See also Orcibal, *Le Cardinal de Bérulle* (Paris: Cerf, 1965), 124.

42. Lubac, *Corpus mysticum*, 131–32.

43. René d'Argenson, *Traité de la sagesse chrétienne* (1651), 111, 186.

44. See Orcibal, "L'Idée d'Église chez les catholiques du XVIIe siècle,"

*Relazioni* [Tenth International Congress of Historical Sciences] 4 (1955): 111–35.

45. Thomas à Kempis, *Imitatio Christi* 3.31. It is a characteristic fact that in the *Imitation* the word "mysticus" never appears; "mystice" appears once, and that is only in book 4, the only book that speaks of the sacrament (4.10); but "contemplatio" occurs eight times, "contemplativus" twice, "contemplor" four times, "spiritualis" thirty-seven times, and "spiritus" sixty-nine times (not counting "Spiritus Sanctus," which appears eight times).

46. Bernard of Clairvaux, *In Cant. Cant.,* sermo 52, 5 (PL 183, 1031) distinguished between *contemplatio* and the *consideratio* that preceded it. See Etienne Gilson, *La Théologie mystique de Saint Bernard* (Paris: Vrin, 1934), 164–77, and Christine Mohrmann, *Études sur le latin des chrétiens* (Rome: Storia e Letteratura, 1961), 2:347–67.

47. Bonaventure, *Il Sent.,* d. 9, praenotata (*Opera Omnia,* 2:240), who connects "contemplatio" with "conversio." See *Lexique Saint Bonaventure,* ed. Jacques-Guy Bougerol (n.p.: Éditions Franciscaines, 1969), 40–41.

48. See Tinsley, *The French Expression,* 78: "speculatio" is opposed to "contemplatio," which is "simplex intuitus veritatis."

49. It is in reference to Dionysius the Areopagite that the *Directorium* uses the adjective *mysticus* (2.22.30 and 32; ed. Verschueren, 134, 174, 184).

50. See Giovanna della Croce, in *Jahrbuch für mystische Theologie* 6 (1960): 75. More than two centuries later, the same is true in Alvarez de Paz: with the exception of the expression "theologia mystica," in reference to Dionysius the Areopagite (see *Opera,* 1623, 3:1230, etc.), he speaks "de gradibus contemplationis," the seventh and highest of which is the "spiritualis somnus" (*De inquisitione* 5.3), or describes the fifteen degrees of spiritual life leading up to the state in which the soul is "unus spiritus cum Deo facta" (*De vita spirituali* 2.1.9–11), without using the term "mystical."

51. Jean des Anges, *Diálogos,* I, ed. Gonzalez, 61.

52. *L'Ornement des Noces spirituelles,* composed by the divine doctor and most excellent contemplator Jean Rusbroche, Toulouse, 1606.

53. Henri de Herp, quoted in P. Groult, *Les Mystiques des Pays-Bas* (1927) 54; or "contemplatio perfecta," quoted ibid., 100.

54. Luis de Granada, *Libro de la oración y meditación* (1554), ed. Cuervo, 2:429.

55. Bernardin de Laredo, *Subida del Monte Sion por la via contemplativa* . . . up to "la contemplación quieta" (1535).

56. See Teresa de Jesús, *Camino de Perfección,* 4, 3, on the sufferings of "los contemplativos." On "contemplación perfecta," see ibid., 25, 1–2; and *Moradas,* 6.7.7 in *Obras* (Madrid: BAC, 1954), 2:148, 192, 450.

57. See H. Bouillard, "La 'Sagesse mystique' selon saint Jean de la Croix," *RSR* 50 (1962): 508–16. The identity between "contemplation" and "théologie mystique," affirmed several times by John of the Cross, is based in most cases on the "negative" aspect of infused contemplation (see the texts quoted by Eulogio de la Vierge, in *DS,* vol. 3; cols. 401–2): "contemplation" corresponds to the whole of what we call mystic life; "théologie mystique"

refers to *one* apophatic tradition, which ended up reading the entire works of the Areopagite in the perspective of "shadows." While it is true that the Dionysian influence is enormous during this period, conversely, the nature of that influence dictated a particular reading of Dionysius the Areopagite. Already at the beginning of the century, Luther does not use the word "mystic," nor does he quote Dionysius, except in connection with the theology "quae docet Deum quaerere negative" (Martin Luther, *Werke, Tishreden,* ed. Weimar, vol. 1, n. 75; vol. 2, n. 2031).

58. See Juan de la Cruz, *Noche,* 2.5.1; *Cántico,* 39.12 and 27.5. He also relies on "libros espirituales" (*Subida,* 2.17) that we would call "mystic."

59. *In D. Thom.,* III, 79, a.2, disp. 204, cap. 2, on the "consummatio charitatis quae fit inter nos et Christum in Eucharistia."

60. Luther, *Werke,* ed. Weimar, 6:561–62; *Tischreden,* ed. Weimar, 1:n. 644.

61. Blaise Pascal, *Oeuvres,* ed. Léon Brunschvicg and Pierre Boutroux (Paris: Hachette, 1908–), 6:89.

62. Richard Simon, *Histoire critique . . .* (1693), 6–7, quoted in Lubac, *Histoire et Esprit* (Paris: Aubier, 1950), 425.

63. Fénelon, *Le Gnostique de Saint Clement d'Alexandrie,* ed. Paul Dudon, 226–27. When his associate Bossuet speaks of the "mystic eagle of Moses" (*Oeuvres oratoires,* ed. C. Urbain and E. Levesque, 7 vols. [Paris: DDB, 1914–26], 5:114), of the "mystic wood" of the cross (5:608), it is also in order to designate the spiritual meaning of the facts related in the Scriptures in a "mystic language" (5:340). In the eighteenth century, M. A. Léonard, in his *Traité du sens littéral et du sens mystique* (1727), will tend to discount "mystic meanings," considering them to be the ancients' way of "compensating for their ignorance of the literal meaning" (preface, vi), but his use of the word is still traditional.

64. For hermeneutics proper, see Conrad Lycosthenes, *Apophtegmatum ex optimis utriusque linguae scriptoribus,* (Lyons, 1556); Lawrence Humphrey, *Interpretatio linguarum* (Basel, 1559); Michael Piccartus, *De ratione interpretandi* (Altdorf, 1601); Giacomo Zabarella; etc. To which must be added the works on law: Jean de Drosay, *Methodus juris universi justinianea* (Paris, 1545); Julius Pacius, *Oratio de juris civilis difficultate ac docendi methodo* (Heidelberg, 1587); etc. Similarly, for the field of medicine: Petrus Jacobus Toletus, *De methodo opus* (Naples, 1558); Celsus Martinengus, *De methodis commentarius* (Venice, 1594); Christoph Guarinonius, *De methodo doctrinarum . . . ,* (Frankfurt, 1601); etc.

65. See Frances A. Yates, *Giordano Bruno and the Hermetic Tradition* (London: Routledge, 1971), 1–156; Keith Thomas, *Religion and the Decline of Magic* (Harmondsworth: Penguin, 1973), 209–458; and Wayne Shumaker, *The Occult Sciences in the Renaissance: A Study in Intellectual Patterns* (Berkeley and Los Angeles: University of California Press, 1973), 1–59, 160–251, etc.

66. Such as Martinus Rulandus, Lexicon alchimiae sive dictionarium alchemisticum (Frankfurt, 1612). See A. E. Whaite's *Lexicon of Alchemy,* 1964.

67. See Allen G. Debus, *The Chemical Philosophy: Paracelsian Science and*

*Medicine in the Sixteenth and Seventeenth Centuries,* 2 vols. (New York: Science History Publications, 1977).

68. Charles Hersent, *In D. Dionysii de mystica theologia librum* (1626), 7.

69. Pascal, *Pensées,* ed. Lafuma, frag. 60 (Br. 294).

70. *Vocabulario . . . ,* 1623, 522.

71. Jacques-Bénigne Bossuet, *Explication de l'Apocalypse,* preface, 22; Bossuet, *Oeuvres complètes,* ed. F. Lachat, 31 vols. (Paris, 1862–66), 2:329.

72. An ancient tradition. See Henri-Irénée Marrou: "The obscurity of the expression, the mystery surrounding the idea thus hidden, is the most beautiful ornament of that idea, a powerful cause of attraction . . . Vela faciunt honorem secreti" (*Saint Augustin et la fin de la culture antique* [Paris: de Boccard, 1983], 488 ff). Or A. J. Festugière: "That notion of mystery, of obscurity, complements that of authority. The more hidden, secret a truth is, the more power it has" (*REG* 52 [1939]:236).

73. Hence the technique, the theory of which was formulated by Pico della Mirandola (*De hominis dignitate,* ed. Garin, 130), of "speaking in enigmas," of using an elliptic style and "sub aenigmate in publicum proferre," in such a way as to render the words "published and not published" [*editos esse et non editos*], (156). Celio Calcagnini, in his *Descriptio silentii* (in *Opera aliquot* [1544], 491–94), shows how "verbal ciphers," "hieroglyphics," and "enigmas" make it possible to both *say* and *not say* at the same time, or to combine speech and silence. See Edgar Wind, "The Language of Mysteries," *Pagan Mysteries in the Renaissance* (London: Faber & Faber, 1958), 13–23.

74. See Carlo Ginzburg, "Signes, traces, pistes: racines d'un paradigme de l'indice," *Le Débat* 6 (Nov. 1980): 3–44.

75. See Paul Zumthor, *Le Masque et la lumière. La poétique des grands rhétoriqueurs* (Paris: Seuil, 1978).

76. See Francis of Sales, "Préface," *Traité de l'Amour de Dieu,* in *Oeuvres* (Paris: Pléiade, 1969), 347, in reference to the *Défense de la Croix* (written in 1598) and to the *Introduction à la vie dévote.*

77. The term does not, however, disappear from scientific usage. Leibniz, if not Pascal himself, was to give the name "mystic hexagram" to Pascal's famous theorem on the properties of conic sections.

78. S.v. "mystique," *Dictionnaire de l'Académie française* (1694).

79. Innocent of Saint-André, "Prólogo," *Teología mística* (1615).

80. Constantin de Barbanson, *Les Secrets Sentiers . . .* (1623), ed. 1932, prologue, 27, 25.

81. Barbanson, *Anatomie de l'âme* (1635), 1:95; 2:178.

82. Louis Chardon, *La Croix de Jésus* (1647), ed. 1937, 22.

83. To Jean Filleau, provincial of Paris, 5 April 1629, ARSJ, *Franc.* 5, fol. 291r.

84. See Lubac, *Augustinisme et théologie moderne* (Paris: Aubier, 1965), 183–223, and Richard H. Popkin, *The History of Scepticism from Erasmus to Spinoza* (Berkeley and Los Angeles: University of California Press, 1979), 1–128. Fénelon, on the contrary, thinks the idea of "pure nature" is "foreign" to him (*3e lettre en réponse à celle de Mgr l'évêque de Meaux, Oeuvres,* 2:654,

664; see also Lubac, *Augustinisme*, 305–7, and Henri Gouhier, *Fénelon philosophe* [Paris: Vrin, 1977], 83–124).

85. Gerson, *Super Magnificat*, tract. 8, ca 3 in *Opera Omnia*, 5 vols. (1706), 4:374. On the opposition to *sapientia philosophorum*, see *Expositiones in Theologiam mysticam* (PL 122, col. 269). His constant refusal of negative theology (mystic theology is *ars amoris vel amandi scientia*) would later, in the *Elucidatio scolastica theologiae mysticae*, lead to his break with the philosophers. See André Combes, *La Théologie mystique de Gerson* (Paris: DDB, 1963), 1:86–90; 2:424–27.

86. See for example, Nicolas de Lyre, *In Joannem*, prologus, and Jean Dagens, *Bérulle* (1952), 250–52. Bérulle writes on the "science of the saints": it is "livelier and more perfect than the science common to the good and the bad, pagans and Christians" (*Correspondance*, ed. Dagens, 3 vols. [Paris: DDB, 1937–39], 2:187). Bourgoing presents his work as a "sapience" not based "on human science": "it is the true science of the saints, the science of salvation and an emanation of sapience and divine science" (Bérulle, *Oeuvres*, [1644], vii–viii). Saint-Cyran, too, ranks the "science of the saints" and the "inner library" above all of scholasticism (quoted in Orcibal, *La Spiritualité de Saint-Cyran*, 112). In 1609, François Solier translated Ricci's *Instruzione*, as *Science des saints*, a work often republished. In 1638, François Poiré published his *Sciences des saints*, and, in 1651, Antoine Civoré followed suit with his *Secrets de la science des saints*. See again Francis of Sales, *Traité de l'Amour de Dieu*, "Préface" (Annecy ed., 4:4); Pierre Camus, *La Carité* (1640), 604; Louis Lallemant, *Doctrine spirituelle* (1694), 1959 ed., 392; Bourguignon, *La Vie du P. Romillon* (1649), 38; *La Gloire de sainte Ursule* (1656), 353; or Pierre Boudon, according to whom Jean Bagot was "even more enlightened in the science of the saints than in that of the Schools" (BN, French coll., 25174, fol. 59).

87. Luis de la Puente, *Vie du P. Balthasar Alvarez*, trans., (1628), 167, 161, 163.

88. Jean-Joseph Surin, *Correspondance*, ed. de Certeau (Paris: DDB, 1966), 1250. Innocent of Saint-André says that he wrote his *Teología mística* (1615) according to the "doctrine of the saints."

89. Barbanson, *Les Secrets Sentiers*, 27.

90. God revealed to Balthasar Alvarez "the secrets of divinity and profound wisdom, through the means taught by the doctors of mystic science" (Luis de la Puente, *Vie du P. Balthasar Alvarez*, 160). See also Jean de Saint-Samson, *Oeuvres spirituelles* (1658), 135, and Surin, *Guide spirituel*, 4.3, ed. de Certeau (Paris: DDB, 1963), 182, on the interchangeable expressions "mystic science" and "science of the saints"; or *La Science expérimentale*, 4.5 (BN, French coll., 14596, fol. 49).

91. Luis de Léon, "Dedicatoria," *De los nombres de Christo*, ed. Federico de Onís, (1956), 1:9.

92. Decree by Pope Gregory XV (1615), quoted by Nicolas de Jésus-Maria, "Eclaircissement des phrases de la théologie mystique," in John of the Cross, *Oeuvres spirituelles*, trans. Cyprien de la Nativité (1642), 2:11.

93. Miguel de la Fuente, *Libro de las tres vidas del hombre* (1623) IV, cap. 14 and Thomas de Jésus, *Tratado de la oración mental . . .* (1610), 177.

94. It is exclusively in Spanish editions of the four treatises of John of the Cross (Madrid, 1630) that the title "mystical doctor" appears; it appears neither in the incomplete edition of Alcalá (1618), nor in the Brussels edition of *Declaración de las canciones* (1627), nor in the first Italian translation (Rome, 1627). From then on, John of the Cross will be known as "místico Doctor"— "our mystic doctor," as the Carmelite Nicolas de Jésus-Maria says ("Eclaircissement des phrases," 2:12; see also 2:7, 15, 18, etc.). It is also at this time that the *Obras* (1618, 1630) become, in André de Jésus's Latin translation, the *Opera mystica B. Joannis . . .* (Cologne, 1639).

95. M. Sandaeus, *Pro Theologia mystica clavis* (Cologne, 1640), 4.

96. Jean Goulu, *Les Oeuvres du divin Saint Denys Aréopagite* (1608), dédicace. More precisely, it was Michel le Bègue, in Byzantium, who sent this manuscript via legates to King Louis I.

97. See M. A. Fracheboud, in *DS*, vol. 3, col. 357.

98. "De S. Dionysio deque dius scriptis disputatio apologetica," on the title page of vol. 1 of his edition of *Sti Dionysii Areop. Opera omnia* (Paris, 1615).

99. In 1516, Florence; 1539, Basel; 1561–62, Paris; 1634, Antwerp; 1644, Paris.

100. "From 1580 to 1630," writes Paul Cochois, perhaps with some exaggeration, "there is a new edition of the Dionysian Corpus nearly every year" ("Bérulle et le pseudo-Denys," *RHR* 159 [1961]: 176 n. 3). R. Aubert mentions "sixteen complete or partial editions of the works of Pseudo-Dionysius during the first half of the seventeenth century" (s.v. "Denys," *DHGE*, vol. 14, col. 303). Also s.v. "Denys" *DS*, vol. 3, cols. 318–429, on Pseudo-Dionysius in the West.

101. See Albert Ampe, "Marginalia lessiana," *OGE* 28 (1954): 360–67. Léonard Lessius translates lengthy passages of *Théologie mystique* in his *De perfectionibus divinis* (1620).

102. Chapter 22, Third Conversation in *La Croix de Jésus* (1647) (1937 ed., 496–503) is a translation of *Théologie mystique*.

103. See Goulu, *Apologie pour les oeuvres de saint Denys . . .* (1608); E. Binet, *La Vie apostolique de saint Denys Aréopagite . . .* (1624); Milet, *Gloria Ecclesiae Gallicanae vindicata de suo Dionysio Areopagita* (1638); Gerson, *Copie de la lettre . . . en laquelle est montré que saint Denys Aréopagite . . .* (1641), and, by the same author, *Sainte apologie pour saint Denys Aréopagite . . .* (1642), Léon de Saint-Jean, in *La France convertie, octave en l'honneur du B. S. Denys l'Aréopagite* (1661), preached in that "high place" of Dionysius, the abbey of Montmartre, etc. Among the "critics" of Dionysius, let us mention J. Sirmond, *Dissertatio in qua Dionysii Parisiensis et Dionysii Areopagitae discrimen ostenditur* (1641); the various works of Jean de Launoy on the same subject, three in 1641, one in 1642, and a last one in 1677; and the critique by Dallié (1666).

104. Erasmus, letter to Pope Leo X, 21 May 1515, ed. Allen, 2:86.

105. See Yates, *Giordano Bruno*, 117–29, 284–86.
106. *Comentarii . . . Conimbricensis . . . in Physic.*, I, 8, cap. 6, qu. 1, a. 2, 2:514.
107. In *Sti Dionysii Areop. Opera omnia*, "Disputatio apologetica" (n.p.).
108. Binet, *La Vie apostolique* (1624), 449–54.
109. Louis de Blois, *Opera* (1632), 289 (*Instit. spirit.*, Epist. ad Florentium, 1).
110. Tamajo de Vargas, in *Oeuvres* of Jean de la Croix, 1641, approbations, 47.
111. A "mystic author" is, a priori, a disciple of the Areopagite. Saint Bernard himself is but "a second Dionysius from our France" (Léon de Saint-Jean, *La France convertie*, 215)—which is more than debatable (see Fracheboud, in *DS*, vol. 3, cols. 329–35).
112. See F. de Dainville, *XVIIe siècle*, nos. 80–81 (1968): 23.
113. Quoted in Orcibal, *La Rencontre du Carmel thérésien avec les mystiques du Nord* (Paris: PUF, 1959), 237, and Laurent de Paris, *Palais d'amour divin* (1614), 138.
114. On the problem of the mystic "Nights," see the hypothesis advanced by I. Hausherr, *OCP* 12(1946): 43–45.
115. Quoted in J. de Ghellinck, *RAM* 25 (1949): 290. See also Gerson, *Theologia mystica* (1420), I, pars 6a: "De acquisitione mysticae theologiae et de ejus decem differentiis ad theologiam speculativam."
116. See Bonaventure, *In Hexameron*, coll. 20, 21, Quaracchi, ed., 5, 424; Gerson, *Considerationes de mystica theologia*, VI, 28 (*Opera*, 3, 383–84). Jérôme Accetti still refers to that traditional distinction in his *Tractatus de theologia symbolica, scholastica et mystica* (1582), as Saint-Cyran does much later, (quoted in Orcibal, *La Spiritualité de Saint-Cyran*, 9), whereas Bourgoing, in presenting Bérulle's works, adopts the modern classification: "three theologies: the positive . . . , the scholastic . . . and the mystic" (Bérulle, *Oeuvres* [1644], vii).
117. Gerson, *De Theologia mystica*, consid. 9–19, Glorieux, ed., 3:256–65. See Combes, *La Théologie mystique de Gerson*, 1:86–109.
118. In the opinion of Gérard Grote (d. 1384), only "simplices idiotae" can be reared to mystic theology (quoted in Pollet, *Revue des sciences religieuses* 26 [1952]: 392–95). Later, the Carthusian Vincent d'Aggsbach, a fervent follower of Nicholas of Cusa and prophet of "Docte ignorance," went so far as to refuse to include contemplation in mystic theology, because it still implied a degree of knowledge (quoted in E. Vansteenberghe, *Autour de la "Docte ignorance"* . . . [1915], 208).
119. Jansen, *Augustinus* (1641), 2:1–29.
120. The name itself seemed to be used for the first time in a 1509 publication by Jean Mair in Paris (see R. Garcia Villoslada, "Un teólogo olvidado: Juan Mayr," *EE* 15 [1936]: 96–109). But Lope de Salazar y Salinas had already drawn up a catalogue of positive theology in 1457 (see Meliquiades Andrés, *La Teología española en el siglo XVI* [Madrid: Editorial Católica, 1976], 1:223, 250, passim). At the beginning of the sixteenth century, that

theology was concerned with the Bible and the Founding Fathers (who were themselves called "positive theologians"). By 1550, a distinction is made between "lo positivo" and "lo escolástico" (see ibid., 1:181–87, 303–7). To the former, what is essential is a breaking away, or a "liberation" from language ("el verbosismo") and from the institutions of the School. See Du Cange once again: "Theologia positiva dicitur quae scilicet ambagibus scholae libera est" (*Glossarium* [Basel, 1742], 3:pars 1, 380).

121. On the debates concerning positive theology, see R. Guelluy, "L'Évolution des méthodes théologiques à Louvain d'Erasme à Jansénius," *RHE* 37 (1941): 31–144.

122. Etienne Gilson, *Théologie mystique de saint Bernard* (1934), 81–82. [Available in English as *The Mystical Theology of Saint Bernard*, trans. A. H. C. Downe (London, 1940).–Trans.] See J. Leclercq, *L'Amour des lettres et le désir de Dieu*, (1957), 23ff, 189, passim. On the connection between the mystic tradition and humanism, see J. P. Massaut, in *The Late Middle Ages and the Dawn of Humanism outside Italy*, ed. G. Verbeke and J. Ijsewijn (Leuven: Leuven University Press, 1972), 112–30 (Erasmus and Rhenish *mystics*); or, on certain "mystic" texts of Erasmus, see Massaut, 69, *RHE* 69 (1974): 453–69.

123. So in Grégoire de Valence (d. 1603), Lessius (d. 1623), or Sylvius (d. 1649). See R. Guelluy, "L'Évolution des méthodes théologiques," 134–38.

124. See Grégoire de Valence, *Commentarium theologicorum tomi quatuor* (Venice, 1608), 1.1.6–7.

125. "Practice-practica," writes Sandaeus in *Pro Theologia mystica clavis*, 4. This point is emphasized. In his *Opera utilissima* (1531), Battista da Crema is presented as "maestro di scientia spirituale pratica" (quoted in O. Premoli, *Fra'Battista Da Crema* [1910], 101).

126. ["La mystique" (*mystics*) was originally an elliptic form of "la théologie mystique" (mystic theology).–Trans.]

127. See D. de Planis Campy, *Oeuvres* (1646), 447, on the "chemist philosophers," and N. Lemery, *Cours de chimie* (1675), préface, on the "chemists." See Debus, *The Chemical Philosophy*; the unification of the "chemical" approaches to nature is reflected in the formation of a separate science and by the emergence of the noun form of the word.

128. See F. Zonabend and M. Segalen, *L'Homme* 20, no. 4 (1980): ("formes de nomination en Europe"), 7–24, 63–76.

129. Quoted in Orcibal, *La Rencontre du Carmel thérésien*, 195.

130. Charron, *Sagesse* (1635), 2:21.

131. Sandaeus, *Pro Theologica mystica clavis*, 11, and Chéron, *Examen de la théologie mystique* (1657), 15; see also 115 ("mais de voir que la mystique suive le tempérament"), and 351 ("La mystique a tellement cru").

132. Léon de Saint-Jean, *La France convertie* (1661), 315, and Surin, *Guide spirituel*, 179, 46; see Surin's letter of Feb. 1661: "quoi que ce soit qui marque l'extraordinaire ou la mystique" (*Correspondance*, 1054).

133. Bossuet, *Instruction sur les états d'oraison*, in *Oeuvres complètes*,

18:443. See also Bossuet, *Remarques sur la réponse á la relation,* in *Oeuvres complètes,* 20:229: "Attached the the Holy Fathers and to the principles of theology, of which *mystics* is a branch." See Jacques Le Brun, *La Spiritualité de Bossuet* (Paris: Klincksieck, 1972), 659–68. Fénelon, in the same vein, said: "You will bring upon yourself the derision (which is so easy in matters of spirituality and *mystics*) of the profane" (*Oeuvres,* 3:49).

134. See Jérôme Nadal, *Instructio brevis . . . ,* in *Monumenta paedagogica S. J.,* (Rome, 1901), 123–28, and Pierre Favre, *Mémorial,* ed. de Certeau (Paris: *DDB,* 1960), 335–36.

135. A rather apologetic report by Juan de la Peña, in J. I. Tellechea Idigoras, *El Arzobispo Carranza* (Madrid, 1968), 2:190–98.

136. Bossuet, letter of 24 Nov. 1698, *Correspondance,* ed. C. Urbain and E. Levesque, 15 vols. (Paris, 1909–12), 10:306, and Bossuet, *Ordonnance sur les états d'oraison,* in *Oeuvres complètes,* 18:365.

137. Bossuet, letters of 7 Dec. 1698 and 29 May 1695, *Correspondance,* 10:340 and 7:110. See his *Second traité,* ed. Levesque (1897), 201; *Instruction sur les états d'oraison, Oeuvres complètes,* 18:430–32, 484; and *Ordonnance sur les états d'oraison,* 18:351.

138. Quoted in G. Guitton, *Le P. de la Chaize* (1959), 2:181.

139. Bossuet, letter of 24 Nov. 1868, *Correspondance,* 10:266, where he also writes, "The refinements of devotion on the union with God began four hundred years ago," and *Instruction sur les états d'oraison,* 18:386.

140. See Henri Sanson, *Saint Jean de la Croix entre Bossuet et Fénelon. Contribution à l'étude de la querelle du pur amour* (Paris: PUF, 1953), 26–30, and Le Brun, *La Spiritualité de Bossuet,* 390, 591–93.

141. Bossuet, *Instruction sur les états d'oraison,* 18:384.

142. See Le Brun, *La Spiritualité de Bossuet,* 588.

143. Bossuet, *Instruction sur les états d'oraison,* 18:384.

144. Bossuet, letters of 10 and 26 Oct. 1694, *Correspondance,* 6:424, 426, and 443. See also 6:429 (16 Oct. 1694): the "madness of the mystics, that they have not yet defined," is set in opposition to "that of the Christians."

145. Bossuet, *Second traité,* 317.

146. Bossuet, letter of 12 Oct. 1695, *Correspondance,* 7:234–36. On these "refinements" of the mystics, one of Bossuet's favorite expressions, see *Correspondance,* 8:356; *Instruction sur les états d'oraison,* 18:647; and *Second traité,* 65, 201, 230, passim.

147. Bossuet, *Second traité,* 310.

148. Quoted by Orcibal, *RHEF* 43 (1957): 207.

149. Quoted by A. Mandouze, *Augustinus Magister* (1955), 3:104.

150. [Thus it is that sometimes an indolent mystic / A tranquil fanatic engulfed in sins . . . –Trans.] Bossuet agrees that certain mystics are no more than "pure fanatics" (*Épître 2, Oeuvres complètes,* 19:163; see *Correspondance,* 7:110).

151. *MS.,* BN, French coll., 9363, fol. 61.

152. In his "Mémoire" on the *Bibliothèque ecclésiastique de M. Dupin,* Bossuet remarks, in the entry about Fulgence: "He (Du Pin) adds this little

point of ridicule about Saint Fulgace 'that he had something of the mystic.' He doesn't want anything to escape his vigilence, nor any Father to slip through his fingers without getting scratched" (*Oeuvres complètes*, 20:530).

153. Madame de Sévigné, letter of 11 Sept. 1689, *Oeuvres*, coll. Les grands écrivains, 3:199.

154. D'Aguesseau, *Oeuvres* (1789), 13:169.

155. *Ms.*, Arch. nat., MN 621, 4, fol. 68.

156. This is what Fr. Baltus quotes and critiques in his *Défense des prophètes de la Religion chrétienne* (1737), 3:10 and 56ff.

157. *Dictionnaire de Trévoux* (1743), 4:1080. ["Mystiquerie" has the "-erie" suffix, which here, as generally, bears a pejorative connotation. Cf. "chinoiserie."–Trans.]

158. Pierre Bayle, *Dictionnaire historique et critique*, 16 vols. (1697; Paris: Desoer, 1820–23), 13:428 and [Pierre Jurieu], "Avis au curieux," *Traité historique contenant le jugement d'un protestant sur la théologie mystique*, 2d ed. (1699; n.p., 1700).

159. Jean de Saint-Simon, *Les Oeuvres spirituelles et mystiques* (Rennes, 1658), 144.

160. See J.-L. Goré, *La Notion d'indifférence chez Fénelon* (1956), 212–13, and Le Brun, *La Spiritualité de Bossuet*, 496.

161. Henri Gouhier, *Fénelon philosophe* (Paris: Vrin, 1977), 83.

162. Fénelon, *Mémoire sur l'état passif*, ed. Goré (1956), 212. See *Explication des articles d'Issy*, ed. Chérel (1915), 83.

163. Fénelon, *Mémoire sur l'état passif*, 222–23.

164. Fénelon, *Mémoire à l'évêque de Chartres*, *Oeuvres*, 2:224. See Fénelon, *Le Gnostique*, 166.

165. *Premières explications*, in *Revue Bossuet* 3 (1906): 207.

166. Fénelon, *Le Gnostique*, 166, 184, or *De l'autorité de Cassien*, ed. Goré (1956), 262, 268. On that "gnosis," see Raoul Mortley, *Connaissance religieuse et herméneutique chez Clément d'Alexandrie* (Leiden: Brill, 1973), 126–49.

167. Descartes, *Méditations*, II, 14, and Teresa of Avila, *Libro de la vida*, *Obras* (Madrid, Biblioteca de Autores Cristianos, 1951), 1:748.

## Chapter 4: Manners of Speaking

1. See Luis de la Puente, *Vida del P. B. Alvarez* (Madrid, 1615), all of chap. 33 (in the 1943 ed., 365–80). The theme is the struggle against the Spanish *alumbrados*. On the "lenguaje espiritual," see the "Memoriales" of Alonso de la Fuente (1575) in Alvaro Huerga, *Historia de los Alumbrados*, 2 vols. (Madrid: Fundación Universitaria Española, 1978), 1:426–33.

2. Constantin de Barbanson, *Les Secrets Sentiers* (1623), 1932 ed., 313. See also Barbanson, *Anatomie de l'âme* (1635), 1:95.

3. The 1632 edition of the *Opera* of Louis de Blois, 298. See Louis Chardon, *La Croix de Jésus* (1647), 1937 ed., 494: "It is what the mystics

call . . . "; Louis Lallemant, *Doctrine spirituelle*, 1985 ed., 356 ("a state the mystics call burning love"), 357 ("the fourth degree is named by the mystics the blazing of God"), 358 ("the second degree that the mystics call the state of divine obscurity"), and so on.

4. M. Sandaeus, *Pro Theologia mystica clavis*, (Cologne, 1640), dédicace and praeambula.

5. Jérôme de Saint-Joseph, "Introduction et Avis général," in *Oeuvres* of Saint John of the Cross (1641), 21.

6. Diego de Jesús, *Notes et remarques*, in *Oeuvres* of Saint John of the Cross, 19; see also 21, 27, passim.

7. Jean de Saint-Samson, *Oeuvres* (1658), 141.

8. Jean-Joseph Surin, *Guide spirituel*, VII, chap. 7; ed. Michel de Certeau (Paris: DDB, 1973), 303.

9. See P. Camus, *Théologie mystique* (1640), 336–42; Sandaeus, *Pro Theologia mystica clavis*, 3: "Theologia contemplativorum quae dicitur mystica"—the language of those who have the experience is termed "mystic." Honoré de Sainte-Marie speaks of "mystics who are only spirituals" to designate those who have the "experience" and not the "science" (*Tradition des Pères . . .* [1708], 2:601); he differentiates between "spirituality" or "experience" and rectitude in the "science" or "mystic" teaching (2:594–601).

10. Fénelon, *Le Gnostique du Saint Clement d'Alexandrie*, ed. Paul Dudon (Paris: G. Beauchesne, 1930), 254.

11. Lessius reveres in Dionysius a "plus quam humanum loquendi modum" (quoted in *DS*, 3:425). Thomas de Jésus analyzes the "modum loquendi mysticorum" (quoted in Jean Orcibal, *La Rencontre du Carmel thérésien avec les mystiques du Nord* [Paris: PUF, 1959], 234). In her famous letter of 8 March 1605, Anne de Jésus says, in reference to the French Carmelites, that she simply does not understand their (very Pseudo-Dionysian) procedures "any better than their way of speaking: you cannot even read it" (*Mémoires sur la fondation . . . des Carmélites Déchaussées* [1894], 2:23). Later, Sandaeus undertakes to define this *modum loquendi*; Nicolas de Jésus attempts to justify it; and so on. Fénelon speaks of "mystic language" (*Explication des articles d'Issy*, ed. Chérel [1915], 132) as do many others.

12. From *Li Livres dou tresor* (1260?) by Brunetto Latini, Dante's teacher, to Pierre Fabri's synthesis, *Le Grand et vray art de pleine rhétorique* (1521), an entire rhetorical and poetic tradition comments on "ways of speaking." See Warner F. Patterson, *Three Centuries of French Poetic Theory* (New York, 1966), 1:3–230.

13. See two old and beautiful books: O. Casel, *De philosophorum graecorum silentio mystico* (Giessen, 1919), esp. 111ff, and G. Mensching, *Das heilige Schweigen* (Giessen, 1926).

14. Christine Mohrmann, *Études sur le latin des chrétiens* (Rome: Storiae Letteratura, 1958–), vol. 136.

15. From the famous manifesto of Romolo Amaseo, *De linguae latinae usu retinendo* (Bologna, 1529), in his *Orationum volumen* (Bologna, 1563–64) (see W. Keith Percival, "The Grammatical Tradition and the Rise of the

Vernaculars," in *Historiography of Linguistics,* ed. Thomas Sebeok [The Hague: Mouton, 1975], 248ff) to the *Pro vetere genere dicendi contra novum* of François Vavasseur in his *Orationes* (Paris, 1646) (see Marc Fumaroli, *L'Age de l'éloquence. Rhétorique et "res literaria" de la Renaissance au seuil de l'époque classique.* [Geneva: Droz, 1980], 409–16).

16. Johannes Tauler, Serm. 51, 2, *Die predigten Taulers,* ed. Ferdinand Vetter (Berlin: Weidmann, 1910), no. 45, 196.

17. *Obras de Garcilaso de la Vega* (Seville, 1580), 121. See Arno Borst, *Der Turmbau von Babel. Geschichte der Meinungen über Ursprung und Vielfalt der Sprachen und Völker,* 4 vols. III/1 (Stuttgart: Hiersemann, 1957–63), 1154. The influence that the poetry of the Italianiser Garcilaso had on John of the Cross is well known.

18. For example, Pierre Favre, a traveler in France, Germany, the Netherlands, Spain, Portugal, Italy, and so on: the words whose pilgrim he becomes are the mystic events from which his theology is continually born. See Favre, *Mémorial,* ed. Michel de Certeau (Paris: DDB, 1960).

19. Bernard Boyl, "Prólogo," *Abad Isaac* (San Cucufate, 1489). See Meliquiades Andrés, *La Teología española en el siglo XVI* (Madrid: Editorial Católica, 1976–), 251–52. On the circulation of printed texts and their effects on languages, see L. Febvre and H.-J. Martin, *L'Apparition du livre,* 2d ed. (Paris: Albin Michel, 1971), 243–455, and Elizabeth L. Eisenstein, *The Printing Press as an Agent of Change: Communications and Cultural Transformations in Early Modern Europe* (Cambridge: Cambridge University Press, 1979), 520–74.

20. Henri de Herp, *Spieghel der Volcomenheit,* ed. L. Verschueren (Antwerp, 1931), 2 [prologue by Blomevenna].

21. See St. Axters, *La Spiritualité des Pays-Bas* (1945), 135–82, a French translation of Dutch authors; Helmut Hatzfeld, *Estudios literarios sobre mística española* (Madrid, 1955), 33–143; J. B. Da Silva Dias, *Correntes de sentimento religioso em Portugal (S. XVI a XVIII)* (Coimbra, 1960), 1:118ff; J. P. Van Schoote, "Les Traducteurs français des mystiques rhéno-flamands," *RAM* 39 (1963): 319–37; R. Ricard, "L'Influence des mystiques du Nord sur les spirituels portugais du XVIe et du XVIIe s.," *La Mystique rhénane* (1963): 219–33; Orcibal, "Les traductions du *Spieghel* de Henri Herp en italien, portugais et espagnol," in *Reypens-Album* (Antwerp, 1964), 257–68; and Orcibal, *Saint Jean de la Croix et les mystiques rhéno-flamands* (Paris: DDB, 1966), 21–56. The *Index* of Fernando de Valdés (1559), the *Index expurgatorius* of Paris (1598), and so on, in condemning and later in "expurgating" Herp, diminished the circulation of his work—in Spain much more than in Portugal or France.

22. Not that the translations (especially from Greek, Hebrew, and Arabic) were lacking in the Middle Ages! There was, specifically, a great tradition in Spain of Arabic translation, and in Sicily, and later in Venice, of translation from Greek. See Charles H. Haskins, *The Renaissance of the Twelfth Century* (Cambridge, Mass.: Harvard University Press, 1976), 278–302.

23. As A. Meillet already observed, whereas printers stabilize and histori-

cize texts, copyists "in part by choice, in part without thinking about it, modernized the texts as they reproduced them" (quoted in Febvre and Martin, *L'Apparition du livre*, 440).

24. Pierre Kuentz, "Le 'Rhétorique' ou la mise à l'écart," *Communications* 16 (1970): 145. See Charles Faulhaber, *Latin Rhetorical Theory in Thirteenth and Fourteenth Century Castille* (Berkeley and Los Angeles: University of California Press, 1972).

25. For Dante, the troubadours are the "dictatores illustres" (*De vulgari eloquentia* 2.6.5) and to Alcuin, God is the "dictator" to whom inspired men are the secretaries (*Poetae* 1.285.4 and 288.15). Hence the expressions: "dictante spiritu Sancto," "caritate dictante," "ipsa ratio dictat," and so on. See Ernst Robert Curtius, *European Literature and the Latin Middle Ages,* trans. Willard R. Trask (London: Routledge, 1979), 76, 314, passim, and G. Constable, *Letters and Letter-collections* (Turnhout: Brepols, 1976), 26–41.

26. J. L. Austin (*How to Do Things with Words* [Oxford: Clarendon Press, 1962]), by his analyses of the relationship between the performative, the illocutionary, the contractual, and the circumstantial, supplies an instrument with which to reopen the case of the *ars dicendi*. On that "art," see James J. Murphy, *Rhetoric in the Middle Ages: A History of Rhetorical Theory from Saint Augustine to the Renaissance* (Berkeley and Los Angeles: University of California Press, 1974), 194–268; *The Medieval Rhetorical Arts*, ed. Murphy (Berkeley and Los Angeles: University of California Press, (1971), 1–25; and *Medieval Eloquence*, ed. Murphy (Berkeley and Los Angeles: University of California Press, 1978), 85–111. Not to mention the classics: Curtius, *European Literature*; E. Faral, *Les Arts poétiques du XIIe et du XIIIe siècle* (Paris: Champion, 1958); J. de Ghellinck, *L'Essor de la littérature latine au XIIe siécle* (Brussels, 1946); and A. Giry, *Manuel de diplomatique* (Paris: Hachette, 1894), 488–92, passim.

27. Paul O. Kristeller, *Renaissance Thought: The Classic, Scholastic, and Humanistic Strains* (New York: Harper & Row, 1961), 12–13.

28. See Kuentz, "Le 'Rhétorique,'" 143–57.

29. John Webster, *Academiarum Examen* (London: 1654), 26–28.

30. See E. Pons, "Les langues imaginaires dans le langage utopique," *RLC* 10 (1930) and 11 (1932); Borst, *Der Turmbau von Babel*, 1048–1150; P. Rossi, *Clavis universalis* (Milan-Naples: Riccardo Ricciardi, 1960), 201–36; C.-G. Dubois, *Mythe et language au XVIe siècle* (Bordeaux: Ducros, 1970); L. Formigari, *Linguistica ed empirismo nel Seicento inglese* (Bari: Laterza, 1970), 29–139; and Russell Fraser, *The Language of Adam: On the Limits and Systems of Discourse* (New York: Columbia University Press, 1977), 114–52, etc.

31. See Dubois, *Mythe et language au XVIe siècle*, 24, 33, passim.

32. See Terence Cave, *The Cornucopian Text: Problems of Writing in the French Renaissance* (Oxford: Clarendon Press, 1979), 3–167.

33. See Formigari, *Linguistica ed empirismo*, 81–139.

34. See Percival, "The Grammatical Tradition," 233–38.

35. Ibid., 233.

36. See R.-H. Robins, *Brève histoire de la linguistique,* trans. M. Borel (Paris: Seuil, 1976), 98–103.

37. See Claude Imbert, "Théorie de la représentation et doctrine logique dans le stoïcisme ancien," in *Les Stoïciens et leur logique. Actes du collogue de Chantilly, 18–22 Septembre 1976* (Paris: Vrin, 1978), 223–49.

38. Investigating the mode of existence of the universal, Ockham makes a radical distinction between things (whose essence is individual) and concepts (endowed with universal meaning). Between the two, there are "proffered sounds" (*voces*): these belong to particular languages whereas *thought* terms do not. Between a metaphysics of the individual and an epistemology of mental "fictions" (*fictiones*) or "institutions," words represent a pluralist space of possible crossings. See P. Vignaux, "Nominalisme," *DTC,* vol. 11, no. 1, cols. 733–54.

39. As in the very famous *Minerva seu de causis linguae latinae* (Salamanco, 1587) by Francisco Sánchez de las Brozas (1523–1601). See Percival, "The Grammatical Tradition," 242ff.

40. Sánchez replaces the idea of the noun governed by the verb with that of a "concordia" between them.

41. See R. Howard Bloch, *Etymologies and Genealogies: A Literary Anthropology of the French Middle Ages* (Chicago: University of Chicago Press, 1983).

42. See Cave, *The Cornucopian Text,* 171–82, and François Secret, *Les Kabbalistes chrétiens de la Renaissance* (Paris: Dunod, 1964), etc.

43. G. L. Bursill-Hall, "The Middle Ages," in *Historiography of Linguistics,* 210ff. For J. Aurifaber (fourteenth century, Erfurt), the meaning of a word is nothing but the use made of it by the intellect. See Robins, *Brève histoire de la linguistique,* 118ff.

44. See Neal W. Gilbert, *Renaissance Concepts of Mind* (New York: Columbia University Press, 1963), who lists pedagogical works (from 1520 to 1631, from Erasmus to Comenius) with titles containing the word "methodus" (233–35).

45. Such as Pierre Gassendi (d. 1655), against that "generalem methodum qua scientiae omnes deinceps utantur," or, later, Daniel Georg Morhof (d. 1691), against methodologists without mathematical or physical competency who are incapable of making the necessary distinctions between various fields.

46. As is the case with Giacomo Aconcio, in his beautiful *De Methodo,* ed. Giorgio Radetti (Basel, 1558; Florence: Vallecchi, 1944), 80: "Equidem quibus constet vera methodus diu ac pertinaci quodam labore conatus sum intelligere, nec tantum libros volui consulere, sed multo etiam diligentius experientiam."

47. Albert the Great, "Proemium," *Liber I Topicum,* in *Opera omnia* (1890), 2:235–36.

48. So it is with Guigues II le Chartreux (*Scala Paradisi,* Cap. 1 and 2, PL 181, c. 475, 482). See Jean Leclerq, *Études sur le vocabulaire monastique du Moyen Age* (Rome, 1961), 138.

49. The theologians as well, for example in Salamanca (Pedro Martínez de Osma, Diego de Deza, and others), criticize the "verbosistae" and the "fumosistae," "novi doctores" (nominalists) who give priviledged status to the "nominum fictio." See Andrés, *La Teología española en el siglo XVI*, 261–73, 297–302. The mystic *modus loquendi* will also show its opposition to the *modus verbosista*. On rhetoric, see Eugenio Garin, *Moyen Age et Renaissance*, trans. (Paris: Gallimard, 1969), 101–19.

50. This was an essential feature of Erasmus's method. See Marjorie O'Rourke Boyle, *Erasmus on Language and Method in Theology* (Toronto: University of Toronto Press, 1977), 59–127.

51. Agostino Nifo, *Aristotelis Stagiritae Topicorum libri octo* (Venice, 1555) fol. 3r. Such texts are innumerable. See Gilbert, *Renaissance Concepts of Mind*, 59, 69, 71, 110, passim; or Fraser, *The Language of Adam*, 116ff.

52. Maps are an optical application of method: they allow for the plotting of shorter routes on the miniaturized projection of a field of knowledge.

53. See Albert Hyma, *The Brethren of the Common Life* (Grand Rapids, Mich.: 1950), and Gabriel Codina Mir, *Aux sources de la pédagogie des Jésuites. Le "modus parisiensis"* (Rome, 1968), 151–255.

54. See Orcibal, "Les Débuts de la spiritualité carmélite à Bordeaux," *BSBG* 89 (1969): 1–15.

55. There is an abundant literature. See especially Dom Chevallier, *Le Cantique spirituel de Saint Jean de la Croix* (1930); Jean Krynen, *Le Cantique spirituel de Saint Jean de la Croix* (1948); Eulogio de la Virgen del Carmen, *San Juan de la Cruz y sus escritos* (Madrid, 1969); and Roger Duvivier, *La Genèse du "Cantique spirituel" de Saint Jean de la Croix* (Paris: Belles Lettres, 1971).

56. See Orcibal, "La Montée du Carmel a-t-elle été interpolée?" *RHR* 162 (1964): 171–213.

57. See Duvivier, "L'Histoire des écrits de Saint Jean de la Croix," *Les Lettres romanes* 27 (1973): 323–80.

58. In Spanish: *Apuntamientos y advertencias en tres discursos para más fácil inteligencia de las frases místicas y doctrina de las obras espirituales de nuestro Padre*, in *Obras espirituales* (Alcalá, 1618), 615–82. The volume was introduced by a *Relación sumaria del autor deste libro y de su vita y virtudes*. The translations of these two texts by René Gaultier appeared in his edition of *Oeuvres spirituelles . . . du B. P. Jean de la Croix* (Paris, 1621); they were reedited in 1628. Only the first translation was retained ("revised and corrected") by Cyprian of the Nativity in his own translation of of John of the Cross, *Oeuvres spirituelles* (1642), pt. 2 [sep. pag.], 269–324. For the French text, I shall refer to that edition; for the Spanish, to *Obras* of John of the Cross, ed. Gerardo de San Juan de la Cruz (Toledo, 1914), 3:465–502, or ed. Silverio de Santa Teresa (Burgos, 1929), 1:347–95.

59. Thus Doria was able to authorize the publication of the Teresian doctrine, even going so far as to sign the dedication of the first edition (10 April 1588) and at the same time work toward the suppression of the doctrine of John of the Cross.

60. On Thomas de Jésus, who was known for his strong personality, see Krynen, *Le Cantique spirituel,* 229–308; Krynen, "Du nouveau sur Thomas de Jésus," in *Mélanges M. Bataillon* (Bordeaux, 1962), 113–35; and Siméon de la Sagrada Familia, "La Obra fundamental del P. T. de Jesús," *EC* 4 (1950): 431–518.

61. Diego de Jesús, *Notes,* trans. Gaultier (see above, note 58), with a few minor corrections. On that edition, see esp. Duvivier ("L'Histoire des écrits de Saint Jean de la Croix," 239–90, 489–501), who brings nuance to Krynen's interpretation (*Le Cantique spirituel,* 309–36).

62. Included in *Obras,* ed. Gerardo, vol. 3 and ed. Silverio, vol. 1.

63. In *Oeuvres spirituelles* (1642), 1–268; see above, note 58.

64. See Jacques Le Brun, *La Spiritualité de Bossuet* (Paris: Klincksieck, 1972), 540, 550; Bossuet, *Projet d'addition sur l'état passif* (1695), in *Revue Bossuet* (1906): 195.

65. I have made corrections, based on the Spanish, of Gaultier's French text. Gaultier distorts or omits many of Diego's expressions.

66. Teresa of Avila, *Moradas,* 6.5; *Cuenta de conciencia* no. 5 (1576, "Grados de la oración"), 3, 7, and 11. There are scores of other similar cases, and also cases in which the traditional language is rejected, for example: "They say [*dicen*] that the soul returns into itself . . . ; with this language [*lenguaje*] I will not be able to explain anything" (*Moradas,* 4.3).

67. John of the Cross, *Subida del Monte Carmelo,* 1.2. His text ("here" ["*aquí*"]) thus takes its distances from the expressions used by "the spirituals," from what "los espirituales llaman purgaciones o purificaciones" (ibid., 1.1).

68. Gen. 2:20 (Vulg.).

69. See *Elie le prophète,* 2 vols. (Bruges and Paris, 1956).

70. 1 Kings (Vulg., 3 Kings), 18 and 19.

71. Teresa de Jesús, *Moradas,* 4.3.2 and 6.2.3.

72. Juan de la Cruz, *Subida del Monte Carmelo*; see Michel Florisoone, *Esthétique de Mystique d'après Sainte Thérèse d'Avila et Saint Jean de la Croix* (Paris: Seuil, 1956), 113–27. The biblical account of the meeting with God on Mount Horeb is punctuated with the negation "*non* in spiritu Dominus," "*non* in commotione Dominus," "*non* in igne Dominus" (3 Kings 19:11–12 [Vulg.]). It is the rhythm of Saint John's drawing.

73. It is common knowledge that Teresa of Avila had an extraordinary "devotion" to Joseph, who was also a "very faithful coadjutor" (see *Estudios Josefinos* 7 [1953]: 9–54, and the special issue *San José y santa Teresa* 18 [1964]. She launched a contemplative Saint Joseph, who, by the way, bore a strong resemblance to John of the Cross.

74. In particular, since the *Expositio in Apocalipsim* of Joachim de Flore, chapter 12 (triumph of the Woman over the Dragon) seems to point towards a "crisis of the age of the Son" and permit the advent of an age of the Woman, which is associated with the reign of the Spirit and the return of Ely.

75. See Geneviève Javary, "La Sekina, aspect féminin de Dieu," *Recherches sur l'utilisation du thème de la Sekina dans l'apologétique chrétienne du XVe au XVIIIe siècle* (Lille: University of Lille III and Honoré Champion, 1978),

361–527. Of particular interest in that tradition are the relations between the Spirit and the Mother, which are more hidden but no less essential in the mystic tradition.

76. John of the Cross, *Oeuvres Spirituelles*, trans. Gaultier, 272, corrected according to the Spanish.

77. See Gen. 17.

78. Ex. 4:25–26.

79. That submission also implies a privileged, "homosexual" love between father and son (see Herman Nunberg, "Tentatives de rejet de la circoncision," *Nouvelle revue de psychanalyse* 7 [1973]: 205–28)a trait that reappears frequently in the Christian representation of the relations between the Father and the Son in the bosom of the Trinity.

80. The angels.

81. Diego de Jesús, *Apuntamientos*, 276–82. Diego begins by responding to the complaints made by "the moral philosopher" or "the scholastic theologian" against the mystic use of of terms such as "excess," "furor," "spot," and so on.

82. Sandaeus, *Pro Theologia mystica clavis*, 9. An expression that paraphrases one by Bernard de Clairvaux in his commentary on the Song of Songs: "Lingua amoris ei qui non amat barbara erit [To one who does not love, the language of love will be barbarous]."

83. See Jean Miles, *Style et pratique fondés et succinctement adaptés aux Ordonnances Royaux et Coutumes de France* (Lyons, 1549).

84. Lancelot de la Popelinière, for example, claims the right to "new forms of speech" in history (1581). See C. G. Dubois, *La Conception de l'histoire en France au XVIe siècle* (Paris: Nizet, 1977), 126–52.

85. Vallembert, in 1558, affirms that "to each condition and trade a certain way of speaking must be granted" (quoted in F. Brunot, *Histoire de la langue française* [1967], 2:164).

86. See Luther on the "manner of speaking" in his *De predicatione identica* (*Werke*, Weimar ed., 26:444; trans. "De la Cène du Christ," *Oeuvres*, 6:127).

87. This primacy of usage, already obvious in Ramus's *Grammaire française*, increased steadily until Glanvill (*An Essay Concerning Preaching*, 1678), Dalgarno (*Consonants*, 1680), Andry de Boisregard (*Réflexions sur l'usage présent de la langue française*, 1689), Callières (*Des mots à la mode et des nouvelles façons de parler*, 1692; *Du bon et du mauvais usage dans les manières de s'exprimer*, 1693), La Touche (*L'Art de bien parler français*, 1696), Renaud (*Manière de parler la langue française selon les différents styles*, 1697), and so on.

88. See *Triomphe du maniérisme européen*, exhibition catalogue, Amsterdam, 1955; M. Dvorak, "Ueber Greco und den Manierismus," *Kunstgeschichte als Geistesgeschichte* (Munich, 1924); and C. H. Smyth, *Mannerism and Maniera* (New York, 1963).

89. J. Baruzi, "Introduction à des recherches sur le langage mystique," *Recherches philosophiques* (1931–32): 75.

90. Teresa of Avila, *Moradas,* 1.1: "Mas habeis de entender que va mucho de estar a estar." See below, 117–19.

91. Sandaeus, *Pro Theologia mystica clavis,* preface and 6–9, and Sandaeus, *Grammaticus profanus* (Frankfurt: J. Volmar, 1621), comm. 12 and 15–18 (on *modi scribendi* and tropes). See also Sandaeus, *Theologia symbolica* (Mainz: J. T. Schönvvetter, 1627), on the origin of symbols and their production.

92. Du Marsais, *Traité des tropes* (1730; Paris: Nouveau commerce, 1977), 18–19.

93. J. Dubois et al., *Rhétorique générale* (Paris: Larousse, 1970), 120–21.

94. John of the Cross, *Vive flamme d'amour,* str. 2; *Cantique spirituel,* str. 14. On the other hand, in Marguerite Porete's *Miroir des simples âmes,* the name of the central and mysterious hero "Loingprès" (far-near) combines in his person many opposites.

95. An exception, therefore, to the "world" analyzed by Michel Foucault, *Les Mots et les choses* (Paris: Gallimard, 1966), 32–40. [See the English translation, *The Order of Things* (New York: Random House, 1970), 17–25. Trans.]

96. Dubois et al., *Rhétorique générale,* 124.

97. Jean de Léry, *Histoire d'un voyage fait en la terre du Brésil,* ed. Gaffarel, (1880), 1:157.

98. See above, 66–67.

99. Jan van Ruysbroeck, *L'Ornement des noces spirituelles,* trans. Maurice Maeterlinck (Brussels, 1910), 18.

100. See François Récanati, *La Transparence et l'énonciation* (Paris: Seuil, 1979), 31–47.

101. See above, 94–97.

102. "Non barbarismi confusionem devito . . . quia indignum vehementer existimo ut verba caelistis oraculi restinguam sub regula Donati" (Saint Grégoire le Grand, epistle to Leander, V, 53; MGH, *Epistolae,* I, 357).

103. Henri Plard, *La Mystique d'Angelus Silesius* (1943), 109–30, on the subject of "expression mystique."

104. Sandaeus, *Pro Theologia mystica clavis,* 2.

105. See Fumaroli, *L'Âge de l'éloquence,* 144–48.

106. See Erasmus, *De copia verborum,* in *Opera omnia* (Amsterdam, 1703), 1:3–74, esp. chap. 7 on the two "abundances" (one in the vocabulary and the other in the argumentation). Or, on Rabelais, see Cave, *The Cornucopian Text,* 183–222.

107. See Freud's analysis of the game played by his one-and-a-half-year-old grandson, who would throw a spool away from himself (substitute for his mother) with an "oh" of contentment (*fort,* far, "forth") and draw it back at the end of its thread with a joyful *da* (here, "returned"), in *The Interpretation of Dreams* and *Beyond the Pleasure Principle.* See also Sami-Ali, *L'Espace imaginaire* (1974), 42–64.

108. See Paul Zumthor, "L'Équivoque généralisée," *Le Masque et la lumière. La Poétique des grands rhetoriquers* (Paris: Seuil, 1978), esp. 267–81.

109. See Guilhelm Molinier et al., *Las Leys d'amors,* ed. M. Gatien-Arnoult (Toulouse: Privat, 1841), 2:18–25.

110. *La Hiérarchie céleste,* chap. 2. I quote from the trans. of Jean de Saint-François (Jean Goulu), *Les Oeuvres du divin Saint Denys Aréopagite* (Paris, 1608), 6–7. M. de Gandillac translates: "unreasonable and unresembling figures," "fiction," pushed "to the height of unlikeliness and absurdity" (in Dionysius the Aeropagite, *La Hiérarchie céleste* [n.p.: Sources chrétiennes, 1958], 77).

111. *Les Oeuvres du divin Saint Denys Aréopagite,* 4, 10.

112. Diego de Jesús, *Oeuvres spirituelles,* trans. Gaultier, 280–81. Goulu translated: "declaration . . . by fictions and applications of unresembling forms" (*Les Oeuvres du divin Saint Denys Aréopagite,* 7); Gandillac translated: "invisible beings reveal themselves by images bearing no resemblance to their objects" (*La Hiérarchie céleste,* 79).

113. See vol. 2 of the present work, forthcoming.

114. See René Roques, in Denys l'Aréopagite, *La Hiérarchie céleste,* xii–xxix, and Henri-Charles Puech, *En quête de la Gnose* (Paris: Gallimard, 1978), 1:122–29.

115. See sermo 28, 3: "In *propriety* we find ourselves ready for *impropriety,* and in *impropriety* we remain within *propriety.*" Tauler, a man of the fourteenth century, transposed that structure onto the affective register: "to find joy in suffering and sweetness in bitterness" (*Die predigten Taulers,* no. 28, 115). The same is true of Teresa of Avila (*Libro de la vida,* chap. 30) or John of the Cross (*Llama de amor viva,* str. 2).

116. Plato *Politicus* 273d, trans. A Diès (Paris: coll. Budé, 1935), 28. There is disagreement about the text: should one read "ocean" [*ponton*] or "region" [*topon*]? On the Christian posterity of that dissimilarity, see especially Etienne Gilson, "*Regio dissimilitudinis* de Platon à Saint Bernard de Clairvaux," *Mediaeval Studies* 9 (1947): 108–30, and P. Courcell, *Recherches sur les Confessions de Saint Augustin,* 2d ed. (1968), 405–40.

117. Quintilian, *Institutio oratoria* 8.6; ed. and trans. H. E. Butler (London: W. Heinemann, 1966), 3:322–23.

## Chapter 5: The "*Conversar*"

1. See J. G. A. Pocock, *The Machiavellian Moment: Florentine Political Thought and the Atlantic Republican Tradition* (Princeton, N.J.: Princeton University Press, 1975), and Henri Bremond, *L'invasion mystique (1590–1620),* vol. 2 of *Histoire littéraire du sentiment religieux en France,* which appeared in 1916, followed by the four volumes on *La Conquête mystique* (Paris: Bloud et Gay).

2. Donald Weinstein, *Savonarola and Florence: Prophecy and Patriotism in the Renaissance* (Princeton, N.J.: Princeton University Press, 1970), and Martin Davies, *The Earlier Italian Schools* (London: National Gallery Catalogues, 1951), 79–83.

3. Massimo Petrocchi, *L'Estasi nelle mistiche italiane della Riforma*

*cattolica* (Naples: Libreria Scientifica, 1958), and vol. 2 of *Storia della Spiritualità italiana* (Rome: Storia e Letteratura, 1978).

4. Pocock does not cover the French phenomenon, but Etienne Thuau confirms in advance and completes his thesis in *Raison d'État et pensée politique à l'époque de Richelieu* (Paris: A. Colin, 1966), 33–102, 166–409.

5. See Charles Webster, *The Great Instauration. Science, Medicine and Reform, 1626–1660* (London: Duckworth, 1975), 15–31.

6. See Keith Thomas, *Religion and the Decline of Magic,* 2d ed. (London: Penguin, 1973), 335–458.

7. See P. M. Rattansi, "The Social Interpretation of Science in the 17th Century," in *Science and Society, 1600–1900,* ed. P. Mathias (Cambridge: Cambridge University Press, 1972), 1–32.

8. See André Chastel and Robert Klein, *L'Age de l'humanisme* (Paris: Deux Mondes, 1963), 88–105.

9. At the same time the jurists were constructing the Merovingian myth of that alliance, which was the first article of a "fundamental law," the general population continued for a long while yet to associate the royal order with the stability of the stars. In connection with Charles V, Elizabeth I, and Charles IX, see Frances A. Yates, *Astraea: The Imperial Theme in the Sixteenth Century* (London: Routledge & Kegan Paul, 1975), and also the famous case studied by Elisabeth Labrousse, *L'Entrée de Saturne au Lion. L'Eclipse de Soleil du 12 août 1654* (The Hague: M. Nijhoff, 1974). The eclipse is a political upheaval, just as the English regicide (1649) is a cosmic event.

10. John Wallis, *Truth Tried* (1643), quoted in Webster, *The Great Instauration,* 30.

11. See Arno Borst, *Der Turmbau von Babel. Geschichte des Meinungen über Ursprung und Vielfalt der Sprachen und Völker,* 4 vols. (Stuttgart: Hiersemann, 1957–63), esp. III, 1, 1150–66, on the theme of Babel in the modern Spanish mystics. On the status of language, see Irène Behn, *Spanische Mystik. Darstellung und Deutung* (Düsseldorf, 1957).

12. See *Il Potere e lo spazio. La scena del principe* (Firenze e la Toscana dei Medici nell'Europa del Cinquecento), (Florence: Medicee, 1980).

13. Juan de la Cruz, "Prólogo," *Subida del Monte Carmelo,* in *Vida y obras de San Juan de la Cruz* (Madrid: Biblioteca de Autores Cristianos, 1955), 508. Countless mystic texts say the same thing.

14. Juan de la Cruz, *Cántico espiritual,* str. 6, in *Vida y obras,* 904. [*Complete Works of Saint John of the Cross, Doctor of the Cross,* trans. E. Allison Peers, 3 vols. (London: Burns, Oates & Washbourne, 1934–35), 2:51.–Trans.]

15. Joel 3:1–5, quoted in Acts 2:17, in Saint Peter's speech the day of Pentecost. See John 16:13.

16. Jer. 5:21; see Ezek. 12:2.

17. Yves Bonnefoy, "L'ordalie," *Hier régnant désert* (Paris: Mercure de France, 1958), 33.

18. Teresa of Avila, *Libro de la vida,* chaps. 2–5, 13, 28.

19. "No entenderse un alma ni hallar quien la entienda" (Juan de la Cruz, "Prólogo," *Subida del Monte Carmelo,* 509).

20. Jean-Joseph Surin, *La Science expérimentale,* II, chaps. 9 and 10; ed. Michel-Cavallera, *Lettres spirituelles* (Toulouse, 1928), 42–47.

21. John Calvin, quoted in P. Pidoux, *Le Psautier huguenot du seizième siècle* (Basel, 1962), 2:21.

22. Angelus Silesius, *Le Pèlerin chérubique,* 2.137, ed. Susini (Paris: PUF, 1964), 170.

23. On the *Proslogion,* see Paul Vignaux, *De saint Anselme à Luther* (Paris: Vrin, 1976), 76–130, and Claude Imbert, "Pour une structure de la croyance: l'argument d'Anselme," *Nouvelle revue de psychoanalyse* 18 (1978): 43–53.

24. "*Produced-producing* fiction," the organization of space as text, is the non-place of utopia; see Louis Marin, *Utopiques: jeux d'espaces* (Paris: Minuit, 1973), 15–50. Thus, in Alberti's *De re aedificatoria* (1485), the edification of discourse and of architectural space are inextricably linked; see Françoise Chouay, *La Règle et le modèle* (Paris: Seuil, 1980), 86–162.

25. See vol. 2 of the present work, forthcoming.

26. This term, used by J. L. Austin, can be replaced by "allocutionary" or "illocutory."

27. See, for example, Tzvetan Todorov, "Problèmes de l'énonciation," *Langages* 17 (1970): 3–11.

28. Emile Benveniste, *Problèmes de linguistique générale,* 2 vols. (Paris: Gallimard, 1974), 2:83.

29. Rabelais, *Le Quart Livre,* chap. 55.

30. Juan de la Cruz, *Cántico espiritual,* str. 1 [Trans. in *Complete Works of Saint John of the Cross,* 2:31. Trans.]

31. "Competence," according to Noam Chomsky, is to be understood as the manifold possibilities given the speaker by his or her language (O. Ducrot and Todorov, *Dictionnaire encyclopédique des sciences du langage* [Paris: Seuil, 1972], 158).

32. For Benveniste, discourse is "language in so far as it is taken over by the man who is speaking and within the condition of intersubjectivity, which alone makes linguistic communication possible." See Benveniste, *Problems in General Linguistics,* trans. Mary Elizabeth Meek (Coral Gables, Fla.: University of Miami Press, 1971), 230.

33. Ibid., 254, 263.

34. To analyze the performative (defined in its relation to "failure" or "success," not "error" or "truth") Austin refers very frequently to law (*How to Do Things with Words* [Oxford: Clarendon Press, 1962]). The connection between *mystics* and law is all the more readily established in view of the importance of the latter in the culture of the time under consideration.

35. See Eugenio Garin, "Reflexions sur la rhétorique," *Moyen Âge et Renaissance,* trans. (Paris: Gallimard, 1969), 101–19, and Garin, "Logica, retorica e poetica," *L'Umanesimo italiano* (Rome-Bari: Laterza, 1973), 171–92, etc.

36. Juan de la Cruz, "Prólogo," *Subida del Monte Carmelo.*

37. Malaval, *Pratique facile,* etc., 1670.

38. Meister Eckhart, *Les Traités,* trans. J. Ancelet-Hustache (Paris: Seuil,

1971), 1:53; see also "Instructions spirituelles," sect. 10, 53–56: "how the will can do all things, and how all the virtues reside in the will, provided it is upright."

39. *Guide spirituel*, ed. Michel de Certeau (Paris: DDB, 1963), 28–31.

40. Meister Eckhart, *Les Traités*, 1:42.

41. Surin, *Correspondance*, ed. de Certeau (Paris: DDB, 1966), 974.

42. Ibid. Henry Suso already made the distinction between the "prompt conversion" [*den geswinden Ker*], which is a break and a beginning, a first "breakthrough" [*Durchbruch*] characterized by its suddenness, and the progressive return to God, a slow "reversion" [*Widerfluz*]. See J. A. Bizet, *Henri Suso et le déclin de la scolastique* (Paris, 1946), 190–92.

43. Benveniste, *Problèmes de linguistique générale*, 2:187. On the modalities, see Alan R. White, *Modal Thinking* (Oxford: Basil Blackwell, 1975), and *Langages* 43 (Sept. 1976), issue on "the modalities." On willing, in this perspective, see also Jean-Claude Coquet, *Sémiotique littéraire* (n.p.: Mame, 1972), 184–97.

44. See Pierre Deghaye, "Psychologia sacra," in Jakob Böhme, *Cahiers de l'Hermétisme* (Paris: Albin Michel, 1977), 199–224.

45. Meister Eckhart, *Les Traités*, 1:57: "Nothing truly makes a man but the renunciation of his will."

46. See Reiner Schürmann, "Trois penseurs du délaissement: Maître Eckhart, Heidegger, Suzuki," *Journal of the History of Philosophy* 12 (Oct. 1974): 455–78, and Schürmann, *Maître Eckhart ou la joie errante* (Paris: Denoël, 1972), 207–27.

47. On the "sequences" of modalities, see the articles by Coquet and A. J. Greimas, in *Langages* 43 (Sept. 1976): 64–70, 90–107.

48. Meister Eckhart, *Les Traités*, 1:54.

49. M. Sandaeus, *Pro Theologia mystica clavis* (Cologne, 1640), 373–74.

50. Since Saint Augustine (see A. Maxsein, *Philosophia cordis* [Salzburg, 1966]) and Saint Thomas Aquinas (see V. Cathrein, "Gottesliebe und Verdienst nach der Lehre des hl. Thomas," *ZAM* 6 [1931]: 15–32), the spiritual literature on the subject of intention is immense. A few guideposts: Saint Thomas *Summa Theologica* IIa-IIae, quest. 1–12; J. Ruusbroec, *L'Ornement des Noces spirituelles* 2.64–65 (on the "simple" intention); J. Alvarez de Paz *De vita spirituali* 3.1.8; Sandaeus, "Intentio," *Pro Theologia mystica clavis*.

51. See Claude Filteau, "Le Pays de Tendre: l'enjeu d'une carte," *Littérature* 36 (Dec. 1979): 37–60.

52. Plotinus *Enneads* 6.8.5–8, ed. Emile Bréhier (Budé, 1963), 138–43.

53. Ibid., 6.8.4.

54. An indication of the permanence of this foundation: In the nineteenth century, Thérèse de Lisieux's spiritual itinerary begins with an absolute act of will ("I choose everything") and ends in the "night" that marks the end of her life with a faith reduced to "what I WANT TO BELIEVE." Thérèse de Lisieux, *Manuscrits autobiographiques* (Lisieux, 1957), 25, 254; capitals in original.

55. Austin, *How to Do Things with Words*, 159–60. And like the mystics,

Austin points out: "To declare one's intention is not the same as undertaking."

56. Ibid., 47–67.

57. Suso, *Livre de la vérité,* in *Oeuvres complètes,* trans. and ed. Jeanne Ancelet-Hustache (Paris: Seuil, 1977), 431–36.

58. See Benveniste, *Problems in General Linguistics,* 219.

59. See Coquet, *Sémiotique littéraire,* 197, 240.

60. 2 Cor. 1:19. The Greek "yes" [*nai*], opposed to the "no" [*ou*] becomes *Est* in the Vulgate: the changing of adherence to affirmation, or of will into judgment.

61. Angelus Silesius *Cherubinischer Wandersmann* 2.4. Hence his oath in the name of "Yes," *beim Ja* (ibid., 249).

62. Evagrius, *Centuries,* 1.1. See Irénée Hausherr, *Les Leçons d'un contemplatif. Le Traité de l'oraison d'Évagre le Pontique* (Paris: Beauchesne, 1960), 51.

63. See Jean-Louis Chrétien, "Le Langage des anges selon la scolastique," *Critique* 387–88 (1979): 674–89.

64. An overall thematic orientation, but one that for a long time is expressed in terms of an epistemology of the "truth" of propositions. Thus Tauler writes: "*All* that can be said of this mystery . . . resembles the *lie* rather than the truth" (*Die predigten Taulers,* ed. Ferdinand Vetter [Berlin: Weidmann, 1910], vol. 11, sermo 28, 1, 114; my emphasis). Hence the instability of mystic discourse: the act of "saying" it can invert it, suddenly and completely, into a lie. This explains the "confession" of Angèle de Foligno: "Omnia que dixi vobis sunt falsa . . . Omnia que locuta sum vobis fuerunt verba simulativa et diabolica" (*Le Livre de la bienheureuse Angèle de Foligno,* ed. P. Doncoeur [Toulouse, n.d.], 189–90).

65. In the sense that Emmanuel Levinas gives these categories, for example, in *Otherwise than Being: or, Beyond Essence,* trans. Alphonso Lingis (The Hague: M. Nijhoff, 1981), 23–59.

## Chapter 6: The Institution of Speech

1. See Exod. 3:14.

2. The Gospel According to Thomas, logion 42, in Henri-Charles Puech, *En quête de la Gnose* (Paris: Gallimard, 1978–), 2:17.

3. Paul Zumthor, *Langue, texte, énigme* (Paris: Seuil, 1975), 165–80. This poetic history of the "I" should be compared with the genesis of the *subjektive Erlebnisdichtung* in Germany. See Bernard Gorceix, *Flambée et Agonie. Mystiques du XVIIe siècle allemand* (Sisteron: Présence, 1977), 37, passim.

4. See already the Augustinian tradition analyzed by Jean Louis Schefer, *L'Invention du corps chrétien* (Paris: Galilée, 1975).

5. In the manuscript, the same hand wrote first "mystique," then crossed it out and wrote "future" after it.

6. These quotes from Saint John (1 John 1:1–2; John 3:11) show some differences from the Vulgate. See note 13 below.

7. The possession at Loudun (1632–40). See Michel de Certeau, *La Possession de Loudun*, 2d. ed. (Paris: Gallimard, 1980).

8. The word "felt" [*palpé*] has been corrected to "touched" [*touché*] by a different hand.

9. Quotation slightly modified from the Second Letter of Saint Peter (1:17; 1:19). Earlier in this sentence, in the phrase "he prefers," the "he" is but a pronoun repetition of the distant subject ("the apostle Saint Peter"), in keeping with a usage of French syntax during the first half of the seventeenth century.

10. BN, Fr. coll. 14596, fol. 2r-2v.

11. Jean-Joseph Surin, *La Science expérimentale*, incomplete version in Surin, *Lettres spirituelles*, ed. Michel-Cavallera, 2 vols. (Toulouse, 1926–28), 2:13.

12. See François Hartog, *Le Miroir d'Hérodote* (Paris: Gallimard, 1980), 243–49; the *thoma* (something extraordinary, a "marvel") is essential to a rhetoric of alterity (for example in the traveler's account of foreign lands).

13. That "structural" reading is equally discernable in Surin's selections from and modifications of the Vulgate text. In 1 John 1:1–2, he eliminates the rhythmic redundances (*quod perspeximus*), details (*oculis nostris*) and especially what concerns the manifestation of Christ (*quod fuit ab initio . . . vita manifestata est*, etc.). The form of experience becomes isolated from its content. On the other hand, John's text is translated in full in the letter of 21 June 1662 (Surin, *Correspondance*, ed. de Certeau [Paris: DDB, 1966], 1403). The same process is applied to Peter's epistle (2 Pet. 1:17–19): the quote retains an expression of which Surin is fond (*a magnifica gloria*, reinforced farther on by *lucernae lucenti in caliginoso loco*, preserved in the paraphrased form of "a torch that brings light to our shadows") but drops the content of what the voice heard on Mount Tabor says (*Hoc est Filius meus dilectus*, etc.).

14. On the Ignatian *discurso*, which designates a relationship between successive experiences and the orientation of the series, see de Certeau, "L'Espace du désir. Le fondement des *Exercices spirituels*," *Christus* 77 (1973): 118–28.

15. For the believing Christian, the certainty of being "awaited" grounds the endurance of desire while "waiting for [God] Godot."

16. Teresa de Jesús, *Moradas del castillo interior*, 6.5.9., in *Obras completas* (Madrid: Biblioteca de Autores Cristianos, 1954), 2:440.

17. Du Marsais defines the metaphor in this way in his *Traité des tropes* (Paris: Le Nouveau Commerce, 1977), 114.

18. Teresa de Jesús, *Moradas*, 2:339. The same expression recurs at the beginning of the prologue of *Libro de la vida* (*Obras completas*, 1:595) or its equivalent at the beginning of the prologue of *Libro de las Fundaciones* (*Obras completas*, 2:678).

19. Teresa de Jesús, *Moradas*, 2:440.

20. This term occurs frequently in the letters, together with the mention of a *letrado*.

21. See the reproduction of the autograph conserved in Seville, in Sta Teresa de Jesús, *El castillo interior* (Seville: Juan Moyano, 1882).

22. See Efrén de la Madre de Dios, in Teresa de Jesús, *Obras completas,* 2:311–12.

23. The original title was *Las Moradas* (the dwellings) to which *o Castillo interior* (or inner castle), was added. The first chapter of these *Primeras Moradas* was written on 2 June 1577, the Feast of the Holy Trinity, at the Carmel of Toledo.

24. *Aposento*: a lofty word, used in poetry as in the Aristotelian tradition to refer to the site, as one says "my abode." An Augustinian poem of the Renaissance gives the gradation from *aposento* [abode] to *casa* [house] to *morada* [dwelling]: "Pues tú eres mi aposento,/eres mi casa y morada" (quoted in Argimiro Ruano, *Lógica y mística* [Myagüez: Universidad de Puerto Rico en Myagüez, 1970], 400).

25. John 14:2.

26. Prov. 8:31.

27. Gen. 1:28.

28. Gen. 19:26.

29. My translation from the original, "Primeras Moradas," *Moradas,* 1.1–3, 5–7, 2:341–44.

30. Melquiades Andrés, *La Teología española en el siglo XVI* (Madrid: Editorial Católica, 1976), 1:166.

31. Robert Ricard, "Notes et matériaux pour l'étude du 'socratisme chrétien' chez sainte Thérèse et les spirituels espagnols," *Bulletin hispanique* 50 (1948).

32. Ricard, "Le Symbolisme du 'château intérieur' chez sainte Thérèse," *Bulletin hispanique* 67 (1965): 25–41.

33. Henri de Lubac, *Exégèse médiévale. Les quatre sens de l'Écriture,* 4 vols. (Paris: Aubier, 1959–64), 4:41–60.

34. Manuel Criado de Val, "Sta Teresa de Jesús en la gran polémica española: mística frente a picaresco," *Revista de espiritualidad* 22 (1963): 376–83. Francisco de Ribera, Teresa's first biographer, went so far as to claim that she wrote a book on chivalry with her brother Rodrigo.

35. See his recounting to Luis de León (4 Sept. 1588) of the account he claims Teresa gave him (in 1579) of a "vision" from God, in Teresa de Jesús, *Obras,* ed. Silverio de Santa Teresa, 6 vols. (Burgos, 1915–19), 2:490–505.

36. Neither vision nor dream, but something between the two, as Teresa says in *Libro de la vida*: "Parece que sueño lo que veo" (1:686). See Marcel Lépée's notes, *Sainte Thérèse mystique* (Paris: DDB, 1951), 174–77, on her experience, caught between two "dreams," now life, now her ecstasies appearing to her as "reverie and frivolity."

37. See Michèle Montrelay, "Aux frontières de l'inconscient freudien," *Confrontation* (1981): 23–43.

38. Yves Bonnefoy, *Hier régnant désert* (Paris: Mercure de France, 1964), 32.

39. That is the title given to *Las Moradas* in 1610: *Castillo encantado*.
40. See, for example, *Discurso del Señor Juan de Herrera, aposentador Mayor de S.M., sobre la figura cúbica*, ed. Edison Simons and Roberto Godoy (Madrid: Editora Nacional, 1976), a fascinating geometrical utopia contemporaneous with *Las Moradas*.
41. Teresa de Jesús, *Moradas*, 2:494.
42. In chapters 11–19 of *Libro de la vida*, the garden is the "comparison" [*comparación*] that plays the same role as the castle in the *Moradas*. On the garden in the sixteenth century as an erotic, monastic, and encyclopedic theme, see Terry Comito, *The Idea of the Garden in the Renaissance* (New Brunswick, N.J.: Rutgers University Press, 1978), esp. 89–148 on the "Garden of Love."
43. Teresa de Jesús, *Libro de la vida*, 1:683.
44. Louis Chardon, *La Croix de Jésus* (Paris: Antoine Bertier, 1657), 587.
45. Jean-Baptiste van Helmont, "Confessio authoris," *Ortus medicinae* (1648; Amsterdam, 1652), 12.
46. Robert Flud, *Integrum morborum mysterium, sive medicinae catholicae* (Frankfurt, 1631), 1.1. Flud's blueprint, with its towers, passageways, entrances, and exits, might well illustrate Teresa's castle. On this subject, see Allen G. Debus, *The Chemical Philosophy: Paracelsian Science and Medicine in the Sixteenth and Seventeenth Centuries*, 2 vols. (New York: Science History Publications, 1977), 1:205–93.
47. All that remains of the "mystic" question is the bare footprint on the shore of the island, and all the disarray ("fluttering thoughts") brought on by fear or hatred of the unknown other.

## Chapter 7: The Enlightened Illiterate

1. Timothy Husband, *The Wild Man: Medieval Myth and Symbolism* (New York: Metropolitan Museum of Art, 1980).
2. Jean-Joseph Surin, letter of 7 Oct. 1634 to Achille d'Attichy, *Correspondance*, ed. Michel de Certeau (Paris: DDB, 1966), 235. This edition will be referred to hereafter as *Correspondance*.
3. Preface to the 4th Mons ed. (1648), reprinted in P. Poiret, *La Théologie de coeur* (Cologne, 1690), 1:3.
4. Surin, *Correspondance*, 140–43.
5. *Lettres spirituelles* by *** (Nantes: J. Mareschal, 1695), 1:1–16. This edition is designated by the symbol c (Champion ed.)
6. BN, Fr. coll. 24809, fols. 1–27, designated by the symbol N.
7. N places toward the end of the letter (fols. 19–23) a block of text that in c is at the beginning (c 1:3–5): "I got him talking on all points of spiritual life . . . " to "[the young man's practice] at present is to refer them [gifts] to him [God] and to give them back to him and to. . . ." See m 1:4 n. 7, 1:5 n. 9, 1:9 n. 25 (m = *Lettres spirituelles*, ed. Michel-Cavallera, 2 vols. [Toulouse, 1926–28]. Champion's order is confirmed by the rest of the manuscripts; so that of N can only be the result of an error, for which there is further evidence

in the artificial manner in which the two passages are fitted together in N, fol. 4.

8. See the stamp of the Foreign Missions in N, fol. 1.

9. See the letters of Anne Buignon to Henri-Marie Boudon, 15 Aug. and 18 Dec. 1671, *Correspondance*, 74–77.

10. See *Correspondance*, 1672–73 and 1547–48.

11. Letter to Anne Buignon, 31 Mar. 1661, *Correspondance*, 1096.

12. Letter to Anne Buignon, 14 Apr. 1661; *Correspondance*, 1106.

13. Letter to Boudon, *Correspondance*, 76.

14. A secret pious association that drew its membership from the *bourgeoisie* in the seventeenth century. (The "A" stands for "Association," and the second "a" indicates plurality; there were branches of this association in many cities.)–Trans.

15. *Correspondance*, 812, 613.

16. Municipal Library, Carpentras, *MS*. 1816, fols. 497r–98v; hereafter designated by the symbol Ca.

17. Thus the impossibility of praying for a special intention without special divine impulse is *justified*, in N, by Saint Catherine of Genoa (N 1:7; m 1:5–6); the union with God in sickness is *illustrated*, in N, by the life of Saint Louis de Gonzague (N 1:12; m 1:7–8); and so on.

18. See the two long passages in N (1:13–17, 18–19, 23) and c (1:10–12, 13–14), which alone make up a quarter of the text in the long version.

19. "A soul that is detached from its own interests can keep watch over itself continually *without harming the body's health*" (N 1:19). That sentence does not exist in Ca and modifies considerably the passage a few lines earlier in N and Ca: "He told me . . . that one of our great misfortunes is not to make good use of our physical ills, in which God has great designs for us, *uniting himself to our souls far more perfectly through pain and suffering than through great consolations*" (N 1:22).

20. See the letter from M. R. Caillet, librarian at the Bibliothèque de Carpentras, to Fr. Cavallera, 14 Sept. 1924 (SJ Archives of Toulouse).

21. This date, given by Champion, is confirmed by another manuscript. See below, 220–21.

22. Municipal Library, Carpentras, *MS*. 1820, fol. 314.

23. Ibid., fols. 326, 319.

24. Fr. Marin Mersenne, *Correspondance*, ed. Paul Tannery and Cornelis de Waard, 17 vols. (Paris: Beau-Chesne, 1932–88), 5:271, 320.

25. *Correspondance*, 950 n. 1.

26. Nicolas-Claude Fabri de Peiresc, *Correspondance*, ed. P. Tamizey de Larroque, 3:347.

27. See *Correspondance*, 270–71.

28. The significance of this last observation should not be overrated. Caillet remarks, in the above-quoted letter, that "in Peiresc's collections or files of manuscript documents, which contain a very great number of copies of letters, it is frequent for the mere formalities to be left out, that is, the beginnings and the endings of letters." Still, in other letters, the receiver is specified.

Moreover, in this case the story is told to the very end, with the exception of the "my Reverend Father." It should be observed that after the death of Peiresc, his "collections" were passed on to his brother, Palami de Fabry de Valavez. From there they were taken to Paris, then brought back to Aix in 1660. They were collected by the councillor of Mazauges (1647–1712), whose name appears at the top of the manuscript letter ("For M. de Masaugues"), and finally, after many losses, gathered together in 1747 by Malachie d'Inguimbert, the bishop of Carpentras. See J. Delisle, *Le Cabinet des manuscrits*, 1:283–84.

29. Pierre Poiret, *La Théologie du coeur* (Cologne: chez Jean de la Pierre, 1690), 1:1–72.

30. On this Mons edition, 1648, *Le Berger illuminé, ou colloque spirituel d'un dévot ecclésiastique et d'un berger,* chez de la Bruyère's, see Bibl. Catholica Neerlandica, nos. 10260 and 10261.

31. Ibid., préface, [18], IV, 2.

32. Ibid., [18–19].

33. See Marjolaine Chevallier, *Pierre Poiret (1646–1719)*, unpub. thesis Strasbourg, 1972, on *Cogitationes rationales* (1677), and Geneviève Lewis, *Le Problème de l'inconscient et le cartésianisme* (Paris, 1950), 190–200. There is a brief and vigorous exposition of Poiret's mystic theology in Erich Seeberg, *Gottfried Arnold, die Wissenschaft und die Mystik seiner Zeit: Studien zur Historiographie und zur Mystik* (Darmstadt: Wissenschaftliche Buchgesellschaft, 1964), 347–51.

34. See M. Wieser, *Peter Poiret, der Vater der romanischen Mystik in Deutschland* (Munich, 1932), 54–58.

35. See below, 277–78.

36. The approbation was reproduced by Poiret at the beginning of his edition.

37. Matthias de Nave, or "Naveus," whose approbation Poiret reproduced (Poiret, *La Théologie du coeur,* 1:72) was a doctor of the Faculty of Theology of Douai: after a short stay in Arras, he moved to Tournai (1633), where he resided until his death (1660 or 1661). See J. F. Foppens, *Bibliotheca belgica* (Brussels, 1739), 2:877–78; *Biographie nationale* (Brussels, 1899), 15:491.

38. Mention of the city of Rouen is absent from the Mons and Cologne editions.

39. Poiret, *La Théologie du coeur,* 1:6. That *sole* mention of the "shepherd" in the "first" lecture is in the French editions up until (but not including) that of 1695, which marks the triumph of the "southern" tradition.

40. See *Les Bergeries de Vesper ou les amours d'A. Florette et autres bergers et bergères* by Coste (1618); *L'Heureuse Bergère* (1614), *Le Berger inconnu* (1621), *La Bergère de la Palestine* by the Normand Bazire d'Amblainville; *La Bergère amoureuse* (1621) by Du Verdier; *Bergeries* by Racan (1625); *L'Orphyse de Chrysante* (1626) by Sorel, who went on to deride pastorals in *Le Berger extravagant* (1627) and in *Anti-roman ou l'histoire du berger Lysis* (1633–34). *Le Berger extravagant* by Thomas Corneille, in 1653, or *Berger*

*gentihomme* by Chavigny prove the persistance of that literary fashion. In the popular literature of the seventeenth and eighteenth centuries, there were also two types of shepherds: the one who knew the secrets of the sky, the astrologer (see *Le Grand Calendrier et Compost des Bergers*, etc.), and the one who opposed luxury and depravation, saying: "Fi, de richesse et de soucy [Fie on riches and care]." See Robert Mandrou, *De la culture populaire en France aux XVIIe et XVIIIe siècles* (Paris: Stock, 1964), 56–80, and M.-T. Kaiser-Guyot, *Le Berger en France aux XIVe et XVe siècles* (Paris: Klincksieck, 1974).

41. Poiret, *La Théologie du coeur*, 1:13.

42. Ibid.

43. M. Viller, "La première Lettre de Surin," *RAM* 22 (1946): 276–99 and *RAM* 23 (1947): 68–81.

44. Poiret, *La Théologie du coeur*, preface to vol. 1.

45. In 1683, Boudon published in Chartres *L'Homme de Dieu en la personne du R. P. Jean-Joseph Seurin*. From 1679 to 1685, he often speaks of that work of Surin's in his correspondence. See de Certeau, "Les oeuvres de J.-J. Surin," *RAM* 40 (1964): 449–53.

46. Boudon himself described this trip to M. Bosguérard: "In Valenciennes, Lille, Tournai, Mons, Brussels, Angers, Namur, and wherever it [divine providence] led us, it made the truths of the Gospel manifest to us, particularly in Mons for a month" (letter 142, *Oeuvres complètes de Boudon*, ed. Migne [1856], vol. 3, col. 967.) The author (R. de Rocquemont?) of *La Vie et les vertus de feu Mr. Henry Marie Boudon* (Antwerp, 1705), 64, cites a letter written from Mons (missing from the *Oeuvres complètes*) in which Boudon speaks enthusiastically of his stay in that city, before his departure for Antwerp. His *Dieu seul* was translated into Flemish at the very moment when Boudon went to Flanders and *Le Triomphe de la Croix* appeared in Brussels just before that trip, in 1686.

47. SJ Archives, Chantilly, Rybeyrete coll., doc. 190, 2 fols. The title is followed by the comment, in a different handwriting: "Extraordinary adventure."

48. See Sommervogel, vol. 7, col. 341.

49. M I, XL.

50. As is proved by a comparison of the handwriting with that of a text in the same collection (doc. 99, *Notata pro congregatione provinciali* [1628], written and signed by Fr. René Ayrault, then rector of the college of Sens).

51. SJ Archives, Chantilly, Rybeyrete coll., doc. 190, fol. 2v. The document still shows the fold marks.

52. See Carrez, *Catalogi sociorum et officiorum provinciae Campaniae SJ*, vols. 3 and 4.

53. "Au sortir de mon pays" ["In leaving my region"] (Rybeyrete, fol. 1r) and "à la sortie de mon pays" [same trans.] (Cologne ed., 1.5) whereas N and c have: "au sortir de Rouen."

54. BN, Fr. coll. 19231, fols. 131r–32v; hereafter designated by the symbol $P^1$.

55. Ibid., fols. 132v, 133r–44v, 144v.

56. On Jean de Launoy, s.v. "Launoi" in Moreri, *Le Grand Dictionnaire historique* (Paris, 1759), 6:197–98; P. Féret, *La Faculté de théologie de Paris, époque moderne* (Paris, 1907), 5:5–30; and Bruno Neveu, "La vie érudite à Paris à la fin du XVIIe siècle," *Bibliothèque de l'Ecole des Chartes* 124 (1966): 496–97.

57. Epitaphe de Launoy, quoted in Féret, *La Faculté de théologie de Paris,* 5:29 n. 1.

58. See ibid., 5:9.

59. See René Pintard, *Le Libertinage érudit dans le première moitié du XVII siècle* (Paris: Boivin, 1943), 409.

60. This bears on the problem of the coexistence of historical criticism and religious conviction. It would be simplistic to say, as has been said of Launoy, "that he drops a saint from heaven every year, and there is the danger that he may end up dropping God himself" (Guy Patin). Even if the criticism of scholars has often been a sign or harbinger of their unbelief, that was not the experience of many of them, whose convictions sunk down into the "innerness" of *devotion,* divorced from their *methods of investigation.* See *Religion, érudition et critique à la fin du XVIIe siècle et au début du XVIIIe* (Paris: PUF, 1968).

61. *Les Secrets* (1649), 123.

62. Sommervogel, s.v. "Febvre (Turrien Le)," vol. 3, col. 581, no. 5.

63. Having belonged to the personal library of Louis Cognet, the volume bears the date M.DC.XLIV (1644). It is a typographical error (IV instead of IX): the approbation is by Launoy and Le Fevre (20 Dec. 1647). The pagination, the contents, the texts published and even the arrangement of the lines are strictly identical to the Paris (1649) edition, except for the mention of *Seurin.*

64. SJ Library, Chantilly, E 92.5.

65. BN, D 40063 and D 51848; SJ Library, Chantilly, E 92.5.

66. SJ Library, Chantilly, W 115. With the approbation of Launoy and Le Fevre, like the others.

67. That can be induced from the approbation of the King's Attorney in the Lyon editions of 1665 and 1668: "Given the approbations of the Doctors [Launoy and Le Fevre] and of the Vicar-General [the abbot of Saint-Just], I do not impeach on the King's behalf that the impression of the present book entitled *Les Secrets. . . .* be given to the public by Nicolas Vetet . . . At Lyon, this eighteenth day of November, 1658. Vidaud." The confirmation, by the abbot of Saint-Just, of the approbation of the Parisian doctors is dated 5 July 1658.

68. SJ Library, Lyon, Fourvière, 236786.

69. Municipal Library, Lyon, 805615.

70. *Colloque spirituel d'un dévot ecclésiastique . . .* (Tournai: Luik, 1657). See *Bibl. Catholica Neerlandica,* n. 11379.

71. "Extraicts d'une Lettre du R. P. Seurin de la Compagnie de Iesus," 123.

72. "Sevrin" in the Brussels edition.

73. "Avis aux bonnes âmes," *Les Secrets* (Paris, 1649), n.p.

74. Mechelen [Malines], Veuve Jaye, 1648; Bibliotheek van het Ruusbroec-Genootschap (Antwerp). The first conversation begins on page 1.

75. See L. Verschueren, "De Boeken eener Geestelijke Dochter," *OGE* (1939): 185–209. A great reader of *mystics* (Ruysbroeck, Herp, Canfield, etc.) Joanna Van Randenraedt titled the text *Geestelijcke tsamenspreekinge tussen eenen devoetten persoen en eenen schaepherder* (ibid., 195 n. 3).

76. "Gheestelyck Discours van den Eerw. P. Surin van de Societeyt Iesu [de la province de Paris] met een ionghman oudt tusschen achtien ende negentien iaren," Bibliothèque Royale, Brussels; *MS.* 2459 (49 fols.), fols. 1–11.

77. See above, 211.

78. The translation from French into "Neder-duytsche" was approved on 1 Sept. 1648 by "Alexander van der Laen, Aerdts-Priester, ende Canoninck van Mechelen, visitateur der Boecken" (Mechelen ed., [136]).

79. See ibid., 2,1.

80. See ibid., 9. All that remains in Flemish of the comparisons between Saint Joseph and the Virgin or the apostles is what is said about Joseph himself, "one of the greatest saints" with "the fullness of the Holy Ghost."

81. See ibid., 1.

82. The *manuscript* of Brussels (and not the French *edition* of Brussels, 1661, which is connected with Paris) seems, though Flemish, to be a point of contact between that northern constellation and the subgroup Mechelen-Ruremonde-Antwerp.

83. "Angély" was written by a different hand, correcting "Angélique."

84. BN, Fr. coll. 19231, fol. 132v.

85. BN, Fr. coll. 24809, fol. 1.

86. Only the second edition of Champion (Paris 1700) gives the place of writing: "Bordeaux."

87. SJ Archives, Chantilly, microfilm of the "Catalogus anni 1630 exeuntis."

88. See A. Mesnard, "Le retour des Bénédictins à Saint-Jean-d'Angély (27 Octobre 1623)," *Rev. Saint. et Aunis* 41 (1925): 177–82. The role of the Maurists of Saint-Jean-d'Angély in safeguarding the Pascal files entrusted to them by the Périer family is well known; see Blaise Pascal, *Oeuvres complètes,* ed. J. Mesnard (Paris: DDB, 1964), 1:117–31, 1:279–92.

89. The Maurists did not take up residence at Saint-Nicolas until 1639, but there were already Benedictines at Saint-Pierre-le-Haut. See H. Cottineau, *Répertoire topo-bibliographique des Abbayes et prieurés,* 2:2434ff.

90. See chapter 8. The proximity would lead one to assume that the manuscript copy of Semoine (near Arcis-sur-Aube) was done by this group from Reims. In fact, it is the text published by Poiret at Mons (attributed to "Buzin," which had become "Burin" at Semoine), and probably copied long before 1718, when that copy was used as a cover for a volume of the parish records of Fr. Gilles Guillaume.

91. Carrez, *Catalogi sociorum,* 3:23, 43, 63, 64.

92. Ibid., 79, 82.

93. The word is *pays* (here "region") instead of "Rouen" in the Mons edition, as in the *MS*. BN, Fr. coll. 19231. A slight modification in the Mons edition indirectly proves respect for the original: "for perfection, one had to do violence to oneself," is all that the young man said in the Rybeyrete and Paris 19231 (fol. 131v) manuscripts; the Mons edition adds, but *in italics,* a rectification that nothing designated as such in the later in the Paris editions: it was necessary to "*know oneself and correct oneself,*" and "do violence to oneself" (Poiret, *La Théologie du coeur,* 1:8).

94. The exceptional mention of *Seurin* in the 1649 Rouen edition (which will not occur again in the editions until 1661), suggests a local tradition linked to the event. Or could it be that the name (given in the manuscript) was erased in Paris, and replaced with "that religious known in France for his virtue and great capacity" (Paris ed. [1649], "Advis")?

95. Viller ("La Première lettre de Surin") notwithstanding.

96. For example, "Rouen."

97. See Sommervogel, vol. 3, col. 581. "Sister" Joanna Van Randenraedt, read, at Ruremonde, the Flemish 1653 edition of this work, which was based on the text published in Douai in 1647. See Verschueren, "De Boeken eener Geestelijke Dochter," 202.

98. Carrez, *Catalogi sociorum,* 3:161.

99. See Catalogue de la Province de France, microfilm, SJ Archives, Chantilly.

100. See *Correspondance,* 433–60, and de Certeau, "Réponse à l'Examinateur de la théologie mystique," in Surin, *Guide spirituel,* ed. de Certeau (Paris: DDB, 1963), 39–50.

101. See *Correspondance,* 467–70.

102. See above, 212–13.

103. See above, 212.

104. See de Certeau, "Résponse à l'Examinateur de la thélogie mystique," 53–54.

105. Surin, *Guide spirituel* 4, 185.

106. His repudiation, which future editors insisted upon, was of additions. Champion, in his 1695 edition, wrote: "That letter has already been published often in various places, but none of the editions is true. The author would disown all of them, because of the additions that have been made to them, contrary to the historical truth" (*Lettres spirituelles* [Nantes, 1695], 1:1). The texts in question are the five "lectures" following the letter. Boudon echoes the same protest, but he speaks of a "shepherd" and cites the sixth lecture of the *Secrets* as being Surin's. See Henri-Marie Boudon, *L'Homme de Dieu en la personne du Révérend Père Jean-Joseph Seürin* (Chartres, 1683), 30, 51–52.

107. See below, 269–70.

108. Boudon, *L'Homme de Dieu,* 30.

109. "I remain quite persuaded that he [Lallemant] has never seen these pages filled with unlikely tales" (A. Hamon, *RAM* 5 [1924]: 264). See also

Hamon, *Revue apologétique* 44 (1927): 462: "Father Lallemant was, in my opinion, never aware of the existence of that [letter] that was addressed to him."

110. *Correspondance,* 140.

111. See below, 260ff.

112. *Lettres spirituelles* 1:1.

113. From this point on we follow the edition given above, 207ff. The long version depicts the neighboring woman who carried on "some mean discourse" and "a gentleman with a scarlet coat" (N 1:14–15; m 1:8).

114. Letter of 30 June 1659. See above, 212.

115. The word will recur often to designate the world. See the letter of 16 June 1631 to d'Attichy, *Correspondance,* 152.

116. In adopting the variant "upon leaving my region" (rather than "upon leaving Rouen"), I have corrected the edition in the *Correspondance* (140) because that variant is given by the best witnesses (Rybeyrete, P$^1$; Mons ed., 1648; Mechelen ed., 1648, etc.).

117. Gen. 12:1.

118. In a few of the versions that retain it, this expression seemed to be an indication of the origin of the author: "a Jesuit from the province of France" (Mons and Cologne eds., preface; see B$^1$), "a Jesuit from the province of Paris" (*MS* Carpentras, fol. 497r).

119. *Retarder* [Surin's term] has the meaning [in modern French] of *empêcher, faire obstacle.*

120. *La Vie et la Doctrine spirituelle du P. Lallemant,* ed. Courel (Paris, 1960), 90.

121. "Voluntary" was added later by the Carpentras *MS*—a typical attenuating qualifier.

122. *La Vie du P. Surin* (*MS* at SJ Library, Chantilly), 9; see Boudon, *L'Homme de Dieu,* 29, who changes the beginning to: "since he had a cultivated mind [*un bel esprit*]." On Surin's education, see *Correspondance,* 103–7.

123. Letter of 7 Oct. 1634 to d'Attichy, *Correspondance,* 231.

124. D'Attichy was with Surin in theology class, at the college of Clermont in Paris during the 1623–24 academic year.

125. A "crisis" to which seventeen letters are related (*Correspondance,* 107–36).

126. Letters 9, 11, and 13 (*Correspondance,* 124, 127, 130–31).

127. *La Vie du P. Surin,* 9; see also Boudon, *L'Homme de Dieu,* 29; my emphasis.

128. "Mixture" [*mélange*] is one of the characteristic words in Surin's vocabulary.

129. *La Vie du P. Surin,* 9–10; see Boudon, *L'Homme de Dieu,* 29–30.

130. For the provinces, if the letter of May 8 was written from Bordeaux. But mention of this place of composition does not appear prior to 1700 (Champion, 2d ed.), that is, seventy years after the letter was written. Moreover, the supplement to the catalogue of the province of France notes, for the year 1630: "*In August,* Fr. Jean Seurin and Fr. Jean Simon returned to their

province of Aquitaine" (ARSJ, *Franc.* 22, fol. 257). Simon was finishing his second year of theology in Paris at the time, at the college of Clermont. It is probable that Surin remained in Paris until August. Later, in 1683, Boudon wrote that the meeting with the young man took place "when he [Surin] was on his way back to his province" (Boudon, *L'Homme de Dieu,* 30). He was doubtless lumping together the two legs of the return journey. On the strength of that simplification, Champion or his editor must have concluded, in 1700, that the letter had been addressed to Bordeaux.

131. Tobit 5:4.

132. Tobit 5:10.

133. Walter Benjamin, "Agesilaus Santander" (1933), in *Zur Aktualität Walter Benjamin* (Frankfurt am Main: Suhrkamp, 1972), 94–102.

134. Repetition of a primal scene. On Surin's relationship with his mother, see the introduction to *Correspondance.*

135. Louis Chardon, *La Croix de Jésus,* 3.27, ed. Florand (1937), 526–27.

136. There is only a late copy of this text extant (end of the seventeenth century?) in the SJ Archives, Chantilly. But it appears to antedate Boudon's book, *L'Homme de Dieu* (1683). The two texts are nearly identical, except that the former does not contain Boudon's long considerations and elevations, but, on the other hand, does provide a certain number of details, the absence of which, in Boudon, can in every instance be explained by doctrinal precautions or consideration for surviving contemporaries or family members involved. That biography could be "la Vie du Père" that Anne Buignon asked (in 1679) M. Bézard (Foreign Missions) to send to Boudon (*Correspondance,* 77). Boudon may then have enveloped the text of the biography in his devout prose. On this hypothesis, the date of *La Vie du P. Surin* would be prior to 1679, that is, during the decade following Surin's death.

137. *La Vie du P. Surin,* 10; see Boudon, *L'Homme de Dieu,* 30. 138. See Cottineau, *Répertoire topo-bibliographique,* 2: 2550.

139. See above, 212.

140. "These are his very words"; "I use his own terms"; and so on.

141. See chapter 3.

142. *Correspondance,* 150.

143. See *Correspondance,* préface, 56–66.

144. "Avis aux bonnes âmes," n.p.

145. Letter to d'Attichy, 7 June 1631, *Correspondance,* 154.

146. *Récit du pèlerin,* no. 29.

147. See A. Chiquot, *Histoire ou légende? Jean Tauler et le "Meisters Buoch"* (1922), 6–13.

148. This is the thesis Chiquot takes over from Fr. Denifle, nuancing it with Nicolas de Louvain's modifications. See ibid., 117–41.

149. See I. Weilder, *Johannes Taulers Bekehrungsweg* (1961), 232, and the overall problem Louis Cognet brings up with that suggestion, in *Introduction aux mystiques rhéno-flamands* (1968), 121–23.

150. See Chiquot, *Histoire ou légende?* 179–90, in which the strict argumentation needs further refinement.

151. See Chiquot, "Amis de Dieu," *DS* vol. 1, cols. 493–500.

152. *Les Institutions divines et salutaires. Enseignemens* [sic] *du R. P. F. Thaulère* . . . (Arras, 1595), title.

153. See chapter 1.

154. See Jules Lebreton, "Le Désaccord de la foi populaire et de la théologie savante dans l'Église chrétienne du IIIe siècle," *RHE* 19:481–505, and *RHE* 20:5–37.

155. See F. P. Pickering, "A German Mystic Miscellany of the late Fifteenth Century in the John Rylands Library," *Bulletin of the John Rylands Library* 22 (1938): 455–92, and G. Constable, "The Popularity of the Twelfth Century Spiritual Writers in the late Middle Ages," in *Renaissance Studies in Honor of Hans Baron,* ed. A. Molho and J. A. Tedeschi (Dekalb, Ill., 1971), 3–28.

156. Nicholas of Cusa, *Idiota De Sapientia,* in *Philosophische Schriften,* ed. A. Petzelt (Stuttgart: W. Kohlhammer, 1949), 300–369, where, as in Surin, "idiota" ("pauper quidam idiota") is the interlocutor of "orator" in a square in Rome (a place of circulation), within the space of exchanges organized by the "auctor," that is, by the text.

157. See Robert Muchembled, *Culture populaire et culture des élites dans la France moderne* (Paris: Stock, 1978).

158. See Mauricio Mohlo, "Raíz folklórica de Sancho Panza," *Cervantes: Raíces folklóricas* (Madrid: Gredis, 1976), 217–336.

159. See *La Vie de la Mère de Ponçonas (1602–1657)* . . . (Lyon, 1675), 26–27, quoted in Henri Bremond, *Histoire littéraire du sentiment religieux en France depuis la fin des guerres de religion jusqu'à nos jours,* 11 vols. (Paris, 1916–33), 2:66. [Available in English: Henri Bremond, *A Literary History of Religious Thought in France* (New York: Macmillan, 1928–38), Vol. 2 ("The Coming of Mysticism: 1590–1620").–Trans.]

160. Louis de La Rivière, *Histoire de la vie de moeurs de Marie Tessonnier* . . . (Lyon, 1650), 120–24, quoted in ibid., 2:65.

161. Quoted in ibid., 2:66.

162. *Eloges de plusieurs personnes illustres en piété de l'Ordre de Saint-Benoît* (Paris, 1679), 132–33, quoted in ibid., 2:66.

163. Amelote, *La Vie du Père Charles de Condren* (Paris, 1643), 264–65.

164. P. J. d'Orléans, *La Vie du Père Pierre Coton* (Paris, 1688), 276.

165. L. Abelly, *L'Idée d'un véritable prestre . . . exprimés en la vie de M. Renar* (Paris, 1659), 61. The words of the carpenter on Saint Joseph are quoted at length on 62–63.

166. *L'Ouverture intérieure du Royaume de l'Agneua occis dans nos coeurs* . . . (Paris, 1660), with the approbation of Grandin and Le Bail. The edition of the *Abbrégé de l'Agneau occis* (Rennes, 1669) bears the authorization of two "approbators" of Surin, M. Grandin and Gilles de Gain (see de Certeau, "Les Oeuvres de J.-J. Surin," *RAM* 40 [1964]: 475–76).

167. "Avis au lecteur chrétien," *Abbrégé de l'Agneau occis.*
168. *Le Compost des Bergers,* quoted in Mandrou, *De la culture populaire,* 160.
169. Mandrou, *De la culture populaire,* 84. But the "child" already makes social claims. The future prospects of the merchants, he says, will be dim, "for they get by fraud or deceit." The workers in the fields, on the other hand, will have their eternal recompense: "The majority of them will be saved, for they live by their simple earnings and the people of God live from their work" (quoted in ibid., 85–86); the rural yield is a value upon which the eternal may be judged.
170. Chiquot, *Histoire ou légende?* 15–34 (30–31 for seventeenth-century France).
171. *Les Institutions divines . . .* [Tauler] (Paris, 1587), fol. 18. Louis Chardon's 1650 translation takes it even further: "I am nothing but an insignificant little layman, without study or substance, and you are a qualified doctor and famous doctor of theology" (*Institutions . . .* [1650], 531).
172. See Louis Cognet, *La Spiritualité moderne,* vol. 3 of *Histoire de la spiritualité chrétienne* (Paris: Aubier, 1966), 452. On Du Sault, see *Correspondance,* 1422–23.
173. *Traité de la Confiance en Dieu,* 1.1, in Nicolas Du Sault, *Oeuvres spirituelles* (Paris, 1651) 1:361–64. The "beggar" is happy, and he has this marvelous phrase, in speaking of God: "He does what I like when he does what he likes" (ibid., 1:362).
174. A. de Rojas, "Rencontre merveilleuse et très digne de remarque rapportée par Taulère . . . ", *La Vie de l'esprit,* trans. Cyprien de la Nativité (Paris, 1652), 186–203.
175. H.-M. Boudon, letter 184, *Oeuvres complètes* (Migne, 1856) vol. 3, c. 1024.
176. Boudon, letter 181, ibid., c. 1019.
177. Madame Guyon, *La Vie de Mme J. M. B. de la Motte-Guyon, écrite par elle-même* (Cologne, 1720), 131–32. Thus Madame Guyon's call for prayer, that echoes that meeting: "Oh poor people, slow-witted and idiots, children devoid of reason and knowledge, obdurate minds that can retain nothing, come and pray and you will become learned" (42).

## Chapter 8: The "Little Saints" of Aquitaine

1. Nicolas Du Sault, *Caractères du vice et de la vertu* (Paris, 1655), 247–48. It should be recalled that the term "saint" referred to what we would today call a "mystic."
2. A situation that has some bearing on the problem posed by Leszek Kolakowski (*Chrétiens sans Eglise. La conscience religeuse et le lien confessionel au XVIIe siècle,* trans. Anna Posner [Paris: Gallimard, 1969]) in terms of his past personal experience in the Polish Communist Party. See Introduction.
3. See Michel de Certeau, *L'Invention du quotidien. I. Arts de faire* (Paris: Union General d'Éditions 10/18, 1980), 58.

4. On this too-little-studied man, see J. de Guibert, *La Spiritualité de la Compagnie de Jésus* (Rome, 1953), 219–37, and esp. Mario Rosa, "Acquaviva (Claudio)," in *Dizionario biografico degli Italiani* (Rome, 1960), 1:168–78.

5. Given the privileged role of these "professed," called "of the four vows," in the internal organization of the Society, this is a significant fact. In 1574, out of 273 members, the French provinces themselves had ten, of whom two were Spanish, five French, two Scottish (exiles), and one Italian (see the catalogues of 1574, ARSJ, *Hist. Soc.* 41, fols. 190–96). On the problems connected with the selection of these "professed" and with the intellectual (more than spiritual) criteria that governed it (university titles were required), see A. Demoustier, "Difficultés autour de la profession en France sous Borgio et Mercurian, 1565–1580," AHSJ 37 (1968): 317–34. The Spanish ascendancy was, moreover, also maintained by the fact that, for a time, French Jesuit students were sent to Spain for their preparation.

6. On the Spanish side, in 1595, the attempt was made to have Acquaviva chosen for the Capua seat, thus eliminating a man adjudged too independent. See Rosa, "Acquaviva (Claudio)," 1:170.

7. For example, on 3 Dec. 1593, periodic general congregations were considered.

8. On 21 Dec. 1593, the general congregation condemned the compromising political involvement of members of the Society.

9. Sommervogel, vol. 5, col. 898, gives 1615 as the date (without place of publication). The printed text we found in Paris (BN, Fr. coll., 15781, fols. 365–384v) bears the handwritten date 1609. Mendoça left the Society in 1608 and became the archbishop of Cuzco (Peru) in 1611.

10. BN, Fr. coll., 15781, fol. 366 (p. 3 of the printed text).

11. Ibid., fol. 366v (p. 4 of the printed text): "Let there be someone like a General in Spain, for all of its affairs."

12. Ibid., fol. 367 (p. 5 of the printed text): "If one General is a foreigner, let the following one be Spanish."

13. Ibid., fol. 370 (p. 11 of the printed text).

14. The text, dated 1625, had, according to some, already been published in 1624. See Sommervogel, vol. 5, cols. 563–64. One hundred years later, the *Mémoires de Trévoux* (year 1765, p. 1895) claimed that the printed text was the work of a Dominican.

15. The memorandum still exists: ARSJ, *Inst.* 107, fols. 1–38. Five years later, Maggio, having become vice-superior of the profess house in Rome, again asked the Fathers of his house to allot more time to prayer and penitence. See B. Schneider, "Der Konflikt zwischen Claudius Acquaviva and Paul Hoffaeus," AHSJ 26 (1957): 20 n. 66a. He soon came under suspicion of encouraging "new things" and spreading a spirit "alien" to the Society (see ibid., n. 80). It was under the direction of this defender of Gagliardi that Bérulle, in 1602, went on his retreat at Verdun; on the importance of that meeting for the future founder of the Congregation of the French Oratory, see Jean Orcibal, *Le Cardinal de Bérulle* (Paris: Cerf, 1965), 25–41.

16. In 1611, Acquaviva undertook another large-scale survey of the entire

Society, this time of its theologians: *Pro soliditate atque uniformitate doctinae per universam Societatem.* The responses have been preserved in ARSJ, *Inst.* 213, arranged by province.

17. ARSJ, *Hist. Soc.* 137.

18. ARSJ, *Hist. Soc.* 137, fol. 152. The spiritual renewal was often connected with a better choice of superiors. All depended upon the quality of the superiors. See also *Brevis tractatus De adhibendo remedio iis malis quae aut jam in Societate irrepiere aut in eandem irrepere in posterum possent* (ARSJ, *Inst.* 186d, fol. 42–52).

19. ARSJ, *Hist. Soc.* 137, fol. 161r–v. This deficit was mentioned even in the province of Lyon, which, under the chapter headings projected by Acquaviva in his survey format, failed to respond to anything about *interna cultura, studium orationis,* and so on. Richeome notes: "Passim maximus invaluit languor et negligentia in oratione, meditatione, exercitiis spiritualibus" (ibid, fol. 177).

20. The province of France points out: "Nimia attentio ad studium et desiderium excellentiae in talentis externis, ad satisfactionem hominum et pompae" (ibid., fol 130). Aquitaine: "Major affectus ac diligentia ad literas et doctrinam quam ad virtutes et sanctimonium" (ibid., fol. 161v). Fifteen years later, Pierre Coton, rector of the college of Bordeaux, noted the regularity of religious life, but found that it remained too external, that the Jesuit students were too taken up with worry over exams, and that excessive study was hindering prayer and preaching (letter to Vitelleschi, 31 Jan. 1621, ARSJ, *Aquit.* 18, fols. 233–35v).

21. ARSJ, *Hist. Soc.* 137, fol. 152. In 1625, Vitelleschi authorized that Etienne Binet keep the watch that had been given to him, but only during his provincialate (letter of 26 May 1625, ARSJ, *Camp.* 7, fol. 159).

22. See *Informationes* of the province of France, ARSJ, *Hist. Soc.* 137, fol. 129v, and *Informationes* of Aquitaine, ibid., fol. 161v.

23. There are two copies of it, both autograph, in the Roman Archives; ARSJ, *Hist. Soc.* 137, fols. 132–39, 140–49. The second appears to be a final version of the first.

24. Ibid., fol. 132.

25. Ibid. The original Latin texts and their variants are published in de Certeau, "Crise sociale et réformisme spirituel au début du XVIIe siècle," *RAM* 41 (1965): 347ff.

26. Quoted in Demoustier, "Difficultés autour de la profession en France," 326.

27. ARSJ, *Hist. Soc.* 137, fols. 132, 140; complete Latin text in de Certeau, "Crise sociale et réformisme spirituel," 347–48.

28. ARSJ, *Hist. Soc.* 137, fol. 142v.

29. Ibid., fol 143v. See de Certeau, "Crise sociale et réformisme spirituel," 349.

30. ARSJ, *Hist. Soc.* 137, fols. 143v–45. See de Certeau, "Crise sociale et réformisme spirituel," 349–51.

31. On several occasions Acquaviva, and his successor Vitelleschi after

him, condemned the thesis on the "lightness of matter" in luxury. See A. Astrain, *Historia de la Compañía de Jesús en la Asistencia de España* (Madrid, 1920), 6:144, and Massimo Petrocchi, *Il problema del lassismo nel secolo XVII* (Rome, 1953), 55.

32. On Achille Gagliardi, see Mario Bendiscioli's edition of *Breve compendio di perfezione cristiana* (Florence: Libreria editrice fiorentina, 1952) (with a "Vita di Isabella Bellinzaga," 155–203), and the documents published by Pirri (AHSJ 20 [1951]: 231–52), concerning the judgments brought in Milan in 1590 (by J. B. Vanino, the harshest) and then in Rome (by E. Tucci, more moderate) against the manuscript of Gagliardi. Gagliardi's papers (full of the author's corrections) and the censures of which they were the object constitute the documentation of a Milanese "affair" analogous and prior to that of the "little prophets" of Aquitaine: ARSJ, *Opp. NN.* 304; Fdo Gesuitico, *Ep. Select.*, 646 and 653; and Pont. Univ. Gregor., *MS.* 973 and 1463, etc.

33. P. Roverus, *De vita Patris Cotonis libri III* (Lyon, 1660), 20.

34. On Balthasar Alvarez, who was reproved for his "strange manner of praying" ["modo peregrino de orar"], and the measures taken against him by Everard Mercurian, a rather inflexible Fleming (general from 1573 to 1581), see *DS* vol. 2, cols. 2314–19.

35. From the first years of Acquaviva's generalship on, the *propre* (that which is distinctively "our own") was a slogan of the Roman authorities. See F. Londoño, *Espiritu proprio e improprio de la Compañía de Jesús (1590)* (Bogotá, 1963).

36. On that "spiritual administration," see Pedro de Leturia, *Estudios ignacianos* (Rome, 1957) 2:189–378, and also the general remarks of Mabel Lundberg, *Jesuitische Anthropologie und Erziehungslehre in der Frühzeit des Ordens (ca. 1540–ca. 1650)* (Uppsala, 1966), 219–29.

37. See *Directoria Exercitiorum* (Rome, 1955), 301ff. The problem arises particularly with respect to the "application of the senses," which can be interpreted either as an exercise of the imagination or in terms of the mystic tradition of the "spiritual senses." Gonzalez Dávila, in 1585–88, criticized the the "subtleties" of the latter point of view. In the end there was a "depreciation" of the application of the senses, in favor of discursive meditation. See Joseph Maréchal, in *DS*, vol. 1, cols. 813–16.

38. See F. de Dainville, "Pour l'histoire de l'Index . . . ," *RSR* 42 (1954): 86–98, and Leturia, *Estudios ignacianos*, 2:269–378.

39. See Pedro de Ribadeneyra, *Vita Ignatii Loyolae*, ed. C. de Dalmases (Rome, 1965), esp. the "Prolegomena," 1–54, and the text of the "censures" of the work, from 1572 to 1609, 933–98, and an interesting "apology" for the text, Jakob Gretser's *Libri quinque apologetici pro Via Ignatii Loiolae . . . edita a Petro Ribadeneira* (Ingolstadt, 1599).

40. See P. Tacchi Venturi, *S. Ignazio nell'arte dei secoli XVII e XVIII* (Rome, 1929), and the illustrated lives of Ignatius, like those of N. Lancicius and Ph. Rinaldi (Rome, 1609) or the *Vita . . . ad vivum expressa* inspired by Ribadeneyra (Antwerp, 1910).

41. SJ Archives, Chantilly, Rybeyrete coll., no. 220, original. See the version (not absolutely faithful) in François Garasse, *Histoire des Jésuites de Paris pendant trois années (1624–1626)*, ed. Auguste Carayon (Paris: L'Ecureux, 1864), 232.

42. See a 1645 *memoriale* on Vitelleschi, ARSJ, *Vitae* 127, fol. 214.

43. He entrusts it to Le Moyne on 15 Jan. 1636; ARSJ, *Camp.* 7, fol. 333v.

44. Letter of 12 March 1624, ARSJ, *Gall.* 41, fol. 148.

45. See the explanations and justifications given in the file on Vitelleschi in ARSJ, *Vitae* 127.

46. See Schneider, "Der Konflikt Zwischen Claudius Acquaviva and Paul Hoffaeus," 3–56.

47. Letter of 12 Sept. 1623, ARSJ, *Gall.* 41, fol. 125v.

48. Letter to Nicolas Villiers, provincial of Aquitaine, 6 April 1626, ARSJ, *Aquit.* 2, fol. 281.

49. Letters of 30 June and 12 Dec. 1626, to Villiers; ARSJ, *Aquit.* 2, fols. 284v, 291v.

50. Letter to Malescot, rector of the college of Bordeaux, 23 Mar. 1627, ARSJ, *Aquit.* 2, fol. 295v.

51. Letters to Bosquet and Villiers, 22 Feb. and 24 Aug. 1627, ARSJ, *Gall.* 41, fol. 162, and *Aquit.* 2, fol. 302v.

52. Letter to Charlet, 7 Aug. 1627, ARSJ, *Gall.* 41, fol. 40.

53. Letters to Villiers, 23 Mar. and 1 Dec. 1627, ARSJ, *Aquit.* 2, fols. 295, 306.

54. See ibid., and also the letters to Villiers, 29 Feb. 1628, and Bosquet, 21 Mar. 1628, ARSJ, *Aquit.* 2, fols. 309, 311. See, again in 1639, the letters to Barthélemy Jacquinot on that "alien spirit," on 15 June, 16 Aug., 1 Nov., 25 Dec., etc. (ARSJ, *Gall.* 40, fol. 38v; *Aquit.* 2, fols. 525, 528v, 533, 535v, etc.).

55. Letter to Jean Filleau, provincial of Paris, 5 Apr. 1629, ARSJ, *Franc.* 5, fol. 291.

56. See a very characteristic letter to François Poiré, 26 May 1625, ARSJ, *Camp.* 7, fol. 158, and a whole series of letters to Bernard Dangles and Nicolas Javelle, 1626 to 1636; or yet again, a report from Gérard Bouvier to General Carafa on 14 July 1646, on the "extraordinary" and "mystic" devotions in Nancy (ARSJ, *Camp.* 36, fols. 231–32).

57. Letter to Henri Adam, 15 Dec. 1626, on "revelations" and "apparitions," ARSJ, *Camp.* 7, fol. 187v.

58. Letter to Filleau, 5 Apr. 1629, ARSJ, *Franc.* 5, fol. 291.

59. Surin, letter of 20 Dec. 1632, *Correspondance,* ed. de Certeau (Paris: DDB, 1966), 177.

60. Letter to Binet, provincial of Paris, 2 Dec. 1636, ARSJ, *Franc.* 5, fol. 515.

61. See A. Dodin, "Saint Vincent de Paul et les illuminés," *RAM* 25 (1949): 445–56.

62. Such as, among countless others, Jan Van Crombeeck (or Com-

becius), in his *De studio perfectionis* (Antwerp, 1613), chap. 30 (the book is immediately translated by Chesneau, *De l'estude de la perfection* [Saint-Omer, 1615]). The controversy becomes more entangled as a result of an equivocation in the use of the term "inaction," which for some meant "absence of action" and for the spirituals meant "interior action" of God.

63. Jean-Louis Guez de Balzac, letter of 25 Feb. 1624 to Boisrobert, *Les Premières Lettres de Guez de Balzac, 1615–1627,* ed. H. Bibas and K. T. Butler, 2 vols. (Paris: Droz, 1933), 1:153.

64. See Jean Rousset, *La Littérature de l'âge baroque en France* (1953), 219–28, and Jean-François Maillard, *Essai sur l'esprit du héros baroque (1580–1640)* (1973), 91–116.

65. ARSJ, *Franc.* 33, fol. 87v.

66. Surin, *Correspondance,* 46–49.

67. See letter from Vitelleschi to Poiré, 26 May 1625, ARSJ, *Camp.* 7, fol 158.

68. Guillaume du Vair, *La Sainte Philosophie,* ed. Michaut (1946), 55.

69. See Petrocchi, *Il Quietismo italiano del seicento* (Rome, 1948), 17 n. 12.

70. See de Certeau, "Bordeaux," in Surin, *Correspondance,* 30ff.

71. SJ Archives, Toulouse, Carrière coll., *MS.* Cros, *Documents . . . ,* vol. 1, 1630.

72. See above, 22–23.

73. A typical case of family connections: one brother, Pierre, is a professor at the Faculty of Medicine in Bordeaux; another, François, a medical doctor on the Faculty in Paris; a third, Antoine, owner of a barony in Flanders; a fourth, Jean (who answers to the name Jacob Francès), is to become the father of the famous Francisco Lopès de Lis at The Hague; a sister marries Abraham da Veiga, well known among Amsterdam's Portuguese Jews; and so on. See Callen, "Vie de Jérôme Lopez," in J. Lopez, *L'Eglise métropolitaine et primatiale Saint-André . . .* (Bordeaux, 1882), 1:1–94; *AHG* 58 (1929–32): 31; and E. V. Teixera de Mattos, "Les Frères et soeurs du chanoine théologal J. Lopès," *RHB* 25 (1932): 135–36. See also the unpublished courses of J. Lopès on grace (Municipal Library, Bordeaux, *MS.* 258), inspired by the spiritual theology of Augustine and Bernard de Clairvaux. On the Jews of Bordeaux in the seventeenth century, see Théophile Malvezin, *Histoire des Juifs à Bordeaux* (Boredaux, 1800); G. Cirot, "Les Juifs à Bordeaux," *RHB* 29 (1936); and Frances Malino, *The Sephardic Jews of Bordeaux: Assimilation and Emancipation in Revolutionary and Napoleonic France* (University: University of Alabama Press, 1978), chap. 1. In the eighteenth century, Jewish writers noted the unprecedented nature of Bordeaux's Sephardic community; see Isaac Pinto, *Réflexions critiques,* in abbé Guénée, *Lettres de quelques Juifs* (1821), 1:12ff.

74. I publish the copy made by Cros, *Documents . . . ,* vol. 1 (1627); SJ Archives, Toulouse, Carrère coll. Cros notes that on the original "the name of the priest has been eaten away by time." I have not been able to locate the document in the archives of the *département de la Gironde.*

75. It was 16 May 1627, the Sunday after the Ascension. After the *Oremus* ["Let us pray"], the celebrant was to read the prayer of the day instead of letting himself be carried away by a hymn to the Holy Ghost: "Send your Spirit, and all will be created."

76. The celebrant was therefore seated while the assisting priests, functioning as deacon and subdeacon, remained standing.

77. Unknown.

78. See de Certeau, "The Formality of Practices," *The Writing of History,* trans. Tom Conley (Berkeley and Los Angeles: University of California Press, 1988), 147–205.

79. "Deum ipsum in se (ut ita dicam) propter Deum in priximis aliquando relinquat" (*Vita Ignatii Loyolae* [1556], 5.10, *Fontes narrativi SJ* [Rome, 1965], 4:870–72).

80. Gen. 12:1, the words of Yahweh to Abraham.

81. "Privarsi di Dio per amore dello stesso Dio" (*Essercitii spirituali del R. P. Ignatio* [Milan, 1587], 55). Bérulle said the same thing: "We must leave God for God himself" (quoted in Orcibal, *Le Cardinal de Bérulle,* 28).

82. Surin, letter of 12 Oct. 1664, *Correspondance,* 1575.

83. Du Sault, *Caractères du vice et de la vertu,* 247–48, 190–201. One can already hear Bossuet, when Du Sault, speaking of these "new mystics," adds: "In refining piety overmuch, one loses it" (194, 200). See above, 109–10.

84. Henri Bremond, *Histoire littéraire du sentiment religieux en France depuis la fin des guerres de religion jusqu'à nos jours,* 11 vols. (Paris, 1916–33), 11:182.

85. See chapters 6, 7, 9, and vol. 2, forthcoming.

86. "Relatio fratris nostri Petri Cluniac de iis quae sibi extraordinarie contingunt, sive inoratione, sive extra illam. Scripta ipsius manu et subscripta," ARSJ, *Franc.* 45, fols. 310–11v. It is the title given to the Roman administration. "Brother" designates a religious who is not a priest. For the original Latin of the fragments quoted below in original translation, see de Certeau, "Crise sociale et réformisme spirituel," 364–69.

87. S. N. Ni. T. [?] J. (ARSJ, *Franc.* 45, fol. 311v), initials designating, respectively, Stephanus Charletus (French assistant from 1627 to 1646), Nunius Mascaregnas (Portuguese assistant from 1615 to 1637), Nicolaus Almazan (Spanish assistant from 1619 to 1631), Theodorus Busaeus (German assistant from 1615 to 1636), and Jacobus Croce (Italian assistant from 1618 to 1638).

88. Letters to Villiers, 25 and 29 Feb. 1628, ARSJ, *Aquit.* 2, fols. 308–9.

89. See ARSJ, *Aquit.* 6, fols. 172, 175, catalogue of the college of Périgueux (that year, five students from the college entered the novitiate at Bordeaux), and ARSJ, *Aquit.* 9, fol. 452v.

90. ARSJ, *Aquit.* 6, fols. 198, 203, 208v, 213v, 228, 235. In 1633, Cluniac was professor of philosophy at the college of Bordeaux, where Jérôme Lopès was one of his students (see Callen, "Vie de Jérôme Lopez," 7, and above, 255).

91. Letters of 23 Mar. 1627 to Villiers and Malescot, ARSJ, *Aquit.* 2, fol. 295.

92. Letter to Malescot, 1 Dec. 1627, ARSJ, *Aquit.* 2, fol. 305v.

93. Petrocchi, *Il Quietismo italiano,* 18.

94. SJ Archives, Chantilly, Rybeyrete coll., doc. 20, 2 fols. The document was originally intended to be circulated; it was sent from Tournon to the novitiate at Nancy, thence to the college of Sens, and so on.

95. ARSJ, *Franc.* 45, fol. 310. Apropos of that "innate" inclination, Surin spoke of an "instinct": the problem of a nature oriented toward God.

96. Surin, *Catéchisme spirituel* (Rennes, 1657), 71.

97. ARSJ, *Franc.* 45, fol. 310v.

98. Ibid., fols. 310–11.

99. Ibid, fol. 311.

100. Letter to Vitelleschi, 10 Nov. 1633, ARSJ, *Aquit.* 19, fols. 22–23.

101. ARSJ, *Aquit.* 6, fols. 249, 252, 258, 266, 277, 287, 293, and *Aquit.* 2, fol. 554v.

102. Letter to Jean Ricard, provincial of Aquitaine, 1 July 1644, ARSJ, *Aquit.* 3, fol. 39v.

103. On 28 Mar. 1620, du Tertre, "scholar in theology" (novice) and therefore also teacher in the lower classes, along with several other Fathers of the college of Bordeaux, lodged a complaint against the uprisings of their students, particularly against a certain Jovit, "who attempted to knock over and jostle several of the said Fathers" (Toulouse, ARSJ, *MS.* Cros, *Documents . . . ,* vol. 1, doc. 388).

104. This memoir, kept in the Roman Archives (ARSJ, *Aquit.* 18, fols. 292–93), has been published by Alfons Kleiser, "Das Selbstzeugnis P. du Tertres über seine inneren mystischen Erfahrungen," *ZAM* 1 (1926): 187–92. See also Kleiser, "P. Jakob du Tertre. Ein Beitrag zur Geschichte der Mystik in Frankreich im Anfang des 17. Jahrhunderts," *ZAM* 1 (1926): 183–86.

105. P. Pourrat, *La Spiritualité chrétienne* (1930), 4:103.

106. Henri Busson, *Littérature et théologie* (Paris, 1962), 13.

107. Pierre de Lancre, *L'Incrédulité et mescréance du sortilège plainement convaincue* (Paris: N. Buon, 1622), 20–22.

108. Letter to du Tertre, 4 Nov. 1624, ARSJ, *Aquit.* 2, fol. 261. Eight months earlier, Vitelleschi had asked Coton, the provincial of Paris, to set du Tertre's "solemn profession" back a year (letter of 9 Apr. 1624, ARSJ, *Gall.* 40, fol. 22v).

109. Letter to Villiers, provincial of Aquitaine, 28 July 1626, ARSJ, *Aquit.* 2, fol. 285v.

110. Letter to Vitelleschi, 4 Nov. 1627, ARSJ, *Aquit.* 18, fol. 291.

111. Vitelleschi to Villiers, 1 Dec. 1627, ARSJ, *Aquit.* 2, fol. 306.

112. Du Tertre to Vitelleschi, 24 Jan. 1628, ARSJ, *Aquit.* 18, fol. 294.

113. "Aestus animi," "ardor animi," "flammae," "excessus," "conjungere se Deo ardentius," "cordis motus," "stimuli acutiores," and so on.

114. "Ebullire": a memory of Eckhart? In Eckhart, an internal "efferves-cence" [*bullitio*] of the divinity precedes and produces an external "efferves-cence" [*ebullitio*]. The former is "self-parturition" [*parturitio sui*]. The latter is creation: when the divinity creates, it "bulliat extra" (*Die lateinische Werke*, vol. 2, *Expositio libri Exodi*, 1 (Stuttgart: W. Kohlhammer, 1954), 21–22.

115. Letter to du Tertre, 20 Mar. 1628, ARSJ, *Gall*. 41, fol. 163. See his letter to Antoine Bosquet, who had denounced du Tertre, 21 Mar. 1628, ARSJ, *Aquit*. 2, fol. 311.

116. Vitelleschi already alluded to it on 28 July 1626, ARSJ, *Aquit*. 2, fol. 285v.

117. Letter of 24 Feb. 1629, ARSJ, *Aquit*. fol. 327.

118. At Saintes, the masses and the chapels founded on the occasion of his death indicate the breadth of his influence. See "L'obituaire du collège de Saintes," *Archives historiques de la Saintonge et de l'Aunis* 25 (1896): 372.

119. Letter to Villiers, 1 Dec. 1627, ARSJ, *Aquit*. 2, fol. 306.

120. See Surin, *Correspondance*, 101–5.

121. See Kleiser, "Claude Bernier SJ (1601–1654). Ein französischer Mystiker aus dem 17. Jahrhundert," *ZAM* 2 (1927): 155–64, and *ZAM* 5 (1930): 366–68; Michel Olphe-Galliard, "Bernier (Claude)," *DS*, vol. 1, cols. 1521–22.

122. See Vitelleschi's answer to Ragueneau, 24 Jan. 1629, ARSJ, *Franc*. 5, fol. 283.

123. ARSJ, *Franc*. 33, fols. 92, 103.

124. Ibid., fols. 96v, 98, 100v.

125. Ibid., fols. 96v, 98v.

126. Letters from Vitelleschi to Bernier, 18 May 1626 and 18 Aug. 1632, ARSJ, *Gall*. 41, fol. 110, and *Franc*. 5, fol. 381v.

127. This was the prevailing situation throughout Europe. See above, 25–26, on "the humbled tradition."

128. In 1631, Vitelleschi was surprised that Bernier had been specially authorized to take the final-year courses despite the insufficiency of his exam results; see ARSJ, *Franc*. 5, fol. 290.

129. See his "very great anger" at Chauveau's friendly indiscretion; ARSJ, *Franc*. 33, fol. 96v.

130. Ibid., fols. 84v, 87v.

131. Ibid., fols. 102, 104.

132. Ibid., fols. 91v, 90v.

133. Ibid., fol 92v. The last words ("who professed to be learned") and others following them (illegible) were carefully crossed out in the manuscript. A prudent reaction on Chauveau's part, perhaps, who was copying this text and sending it on to the authorities?

134. Among the lives of Saint Ignatius published before 1631, the "four" are probably: P. de Ribadeneyra, *Vita Ignatii Loiolae* (Naples, 1572); G. P. Maffei, *De vita et moribus Ignatii Loiolae* (Rome, 1585); P. Bombino, *Vita di Sant'Ignazio Lojola* (Naples, 1615); and P. Morin, *La Vie du glorieux S. Ig-nace de Loyola* (Paris, 1622).

135. ARSJ, *Franc.* 33, fol. 104.

136. See above, 251ff, and de Certeau, "L'épreuve du temps," *Christus* 13 (1966): 311–31.

137. ARSJ, *Franc.* 33, fol. 104v. "L'*In principio* de saint Jean," refers to the prologue to the Gospel According to Saint John, the apostle represented by the eagle.

138. ["Symbolize" here has its seventeenth-century meaning of agreeing or harmonizing.–Trans.]

139. ARSJ, *Franc.* 33, fol. 106v.

140. Letter from L. Lallemant to M. Boutard, residing at the college of Clermont, 5 Dec. 1630; reprinted in *RAM* 16 (1935): 228–29.

141. P. J. d'Orléans, *La Vie du Père Pierre Coton* (Paris, 1688), 305. Lallemant was then rector and master of the novices at Rouen.

142. *Summa vitae R. P. Lud. L'Allemant,* SJ Archives, Chantilly, Rybeyrete coll., doc. 25, fol. 3.

143. Letter of 5 April 1629 to Filleau, reprinted by Kleiser in *ZAM* 2 (1927): 162.

144. Alfred Loisy, *Mémoires* (Paris, 1931), 3:252.

145. [Louis Jobert], *La Vie du R.P. P. Champion, MS.* (SJ Archives, Chantilly,) fol. 114v.

146. On the history of the text of this book, which is the subject of much debate, and in anticipation of a study on the subject in progress, see A. Hamon, "Qui a écrit la *Doctrine spirituelle* du Père Lallemant?" *RAM* 5 (1924): 233–68; A. Pottier, "Rigoleuc ou Lallemant?" *RAM* 16 (1935): 329–50; B. Julio Jiménez, "En torno a la formación de la *Doctrine spirituelle* del P. Lallemant," *AHSJ* 32 (1963): 225–92; and de Certeau, in Surin, *Correspondance,* 71–84.

147. Too rapid a summary, of course. There are also numerous manuscript documents on other spiritual "disturbances" (impossible to present here), in particular at Nancy and Pont-à-Mousson, from 1620 to 1648. The movement becomes marginalized but does not stop.

## Chapter 9: Labadie the Nomad

1. This is the title given to the mystical poems of Angelus Silesius. See above, 13–14.

2. See above, 31.

3. [An oblique, passing allusion to Sartre's play, *Les sequestrés d'Altona,* which has been translated as *The Condemned of Altona.*–Trans.]

4. J. M. Maillard, *Essai sur l'esprit du héros baroque* (Paris: A. Nizet, 1973), 162–63.

5. Eugène and Émile Haag, *La France protestante,* 10 vols. (Paris and Geneva: J. Cherbuliez, 1846–59), 6:140–47. As early as 1786, Sénébier, in the *Bibliothèque littéraire de Genève* (2:208ff) had expressed reservations about Labadie, alluding to the "immorality" of this "proud, ambitious, fanatic" figure.

6. A few general studies: H. Van Berkum, *De Labadie en de Labadisten,* 2 vols. (Sneek, 1851) (very fictionalized, but crammed with accurate information and raided by all the following); Heinrich Heppe, *Geschichte des Pietismus und der Mystik in der reformierten Kirche, namentlich der Niederlande* (Leiden, 1874), 240–374 (chapter 4 on Labadie's mystic theology); C. B. Hylkema, *Reformateurs. Geschiedkundige Stüdien over de godsdienstige bewegingen uit de nadagen onzer gouden eeuw,* 2 vols. (Haarlem, 1900–1902) (thesis: individual freedom opposed to institutions); William Lindeboom, *Stiefkinderen van het christendom* (The Hague, 1929), 369–76 (Labadie's socialist individualism); Leszek Kolakowski, *Chrétiens sans Eglise. La conscience religieuse et le lien confessionel au XVIIe siècle,* trans. Anna Posner (Paris: Gallimard, 1969), 719–97 (a reworking of Van Berkum and Hylkema for the Marxist presentation of a psychological case).

7. See preceding note.

8. "Au lecteur," *Lettre de Jean de Labadie à ses amis de la communion romaine touchant sa Déclaration . . .* (Montauban: P. Braconier, 1651).

9. See above, 262.

10. *Déclaration de Jean de Labadie . . . contenant les raisons qui l'ont obligé à quitter . . . l'Église romaine* (Montauban: P. Braconier, 1650), 41–42. There was a second edition of Labadie's *Déclaration* (Geneva: J. A. et S. de Tournes, 1666).

11. A. Arnauld and P. Nicole, *La Logique ou l'Art de penser,* ed. P. Clair and F. Girbal (1662; Paris: PUF, 1965), 76.

12. ARSJ, *Aquit.* 9, fol. 422.

13. ARSJ, *Aquit.* 6, fol. 211.

14. See above, 260ff.

15. ARSJ, *Aquit.* 6, fol. 272.

16. From Rome to Father Jacquinot, 20 Mar. 1637, ARSJ, *Aquit.* 2, fol. 471.

17. ARSJ, *Aquit.* 6, fol. 154.

18. ARSJ, *Gall.* 46, fol. 238.

19. BN, *MS.* fds fr. 15722, fol. 173.

20. Bibliothèque Ste-Geneviève, Paris, *MS.* 1480, fol. 64.

21. J.-P. Nicéron, *Mémoires pour servir à l'histoire des hommes illustres* (Paris, 1732), 20:143–44.

22. *Déclaration de Jean de Labadie* [1650 ed.], 91.

23. Just among the Jesuit authors, there is M. Bettini, *Apiaria universae philosophiae mathematicae* (Bologna, 1642); A. Kircher, *Ars magna lucis et umbrae* (Rome, 1646); the *Tabula scalata* of Fr. du Breuil (1649); and so on. But others preceded them: J. Leurechon (1624), Cl. Mydorge (1630), J.-P. Nicéron (1638), and others. See Jurgis Baltrušaitis, *Le Miroir. Essai sur une légende scientifique. Révélations science-fiction et fallacies* (Paris: Elmayan, 1978), 67–94.

24. Baltrušaitis, *Le Miroir,* 83.

25. *Déclaration de Jean de Labadie,* 91, 102.

26. On the movement that, beginning in the thirteenth century, favors vision, see above, 85–90.

27. See Michel de Certeau, *La Possession de Loudun,* 2d ed. (Paris: Julliard-Gallimard, 1980), and Surin, *Correspondance,* ed. de Certeau (Paris: DDB, 1966), 241–464.

28. Surin, *La Science expérimentale,* in *Correspondance,* 436–38. Surin makes frequent allusions to this controversy: see *Guide spirituel,* 1.7, 6.6; *Fondements de la vie spirituelle,* 5.7, etc.

29. Letter to Labadie, 8 Dec. 1638, ARSJ, *Aquit.* 2, fol. 511.

30. Letter of 25 Feb. 1639, ARSJ, *Aquit.* 2, fol. 520. Labadie was to become a "type," an exemplum, according to a model comprising three stages, already present in Surin: (1) "marvelous beginnings"; (2) loss of "deference" toward others; (3) deplorable "outcomes." See, for example, Nicolas Du Sault, *Caractères du vice et de la vertu* (Paris, 1655), 233, and Paul Lejeune, *Epîtres spirituelles* (1665), 537; etc. In this way, the praise he received from the Jesuits was justified, the virtue of obedience exalted, and his departure "explained."

31. BN, *MS.,* Dupuy 641, fol. 130.

32. *Déclaration de Jean de Labadie,* 435.

33. Ibid., preliminary "Avis."

34. *Récit véritable du procédé tenu par Mgr l'Illustr. évêque d'Amiens . . . pour servir de défenses aux sieurs de Labadie . . . et Me Dabillon . . .* (n.p., n.d. [1644]), 10–11; BN, *MS.,* Dupuy 641, fols. 123–30. Labadie was attacked in the sermons of "Father Le Juge, Jesuit."

35. See above, 144ff.

36. See *Le Grand chemin du jansénisme au calvinisme enseigné par . . . Labadie,* 2d. ed. (Paris, 1651); *Lettre d'un docteur en théologie [Antoine Arnauld] . . . sur . . . l'apostasie . . . de Labadie* (n.p., 1651); and le sieur de Saint-Julien [Godefroy Hermant], *Défense de la piété et de la foi . . . contre les mensonges . . . de J. de Labadie, apostat* (Paris, 1651). Hermant is responding in the name of the Jesuits to the accusation of having led Labadie into heresy.

37. For example, according to the memoirs of two Protestants, Pascal was later instructed by Labadie in the reformed religion and "used him to get his *Lettres provinciales* to his friends" (see Charles Augustin Sainte-Beuve, *Port-Royal,* 2.13, ed. Maxime Leroy, 3 vols. [Paris: Gallimard, 1953–55], 1:659, and Kolakowski, *Chrétiens sans Eglise,* 787); or *L'Impiété convaincue* (1681), a treatise written by Yvon, Labadie's most faithful disciple, against the atheism of Spinoza, may have been the source of Pascal's "religion of the heart" (see Paul Vernière, *Spinoza et la pensée française avant la Révolution* [1954], 1:43–47). These are pieces of an unsolved puzzle.

38. BN, *MS.,* Fr. coll., new acq. 4333, fols. 113–14. Comments on the Socinians by a "M. Labadie" (who indeed appears to be the same one): "The Calvinists have answered the Socinians better than the Catholics have. The Dutch were wrong to allow the books of the Socinians to be translated into

the common tongue. Almost all of the bishops of England are Socinian." Given Labadie's altercations with the Socinians and his connections in England and Holland, there is scarcely any hesitation on the identity of this person.

39. See note 36.

40. See Hermant, *Mémoires,* ed. A. Gazier (1905), 1:293; René Rapin, *Mémoires,* ed. L. Aubineau (1865), 1:52; Van Berkum, *De Labadie en de Labadisten,* 1:176; and Bonnault d'Houet, "Les Débuts du jansénisme dans le diocèse d'Amiens," *Mémoires de l'Académie des sciences, lettres et arts d'Amiens* 63 (1920): 1–59.

41. See G. Doublet, *Jean du Ferrier* (1906), 112. Moreover, that "dance before the Ark" is not inconceivable: Labadie introduced and practiced it in his communities at Hervord and Altona at the end of his life. It was to become a favorite target for pamphleteers. See Door Jacobus Koelman, *Der Labad. dwalingen ontdekt* [The Errors of Labadie Exposed], 152–58, 217. But already at the beginning of the thirteenth century, French "devouts" were scandalized to see the Spanish Carmelites dancing before the Holy Sacrament.

42. See [Rivet], *Supplément au nécrologe* (of Port-Royal), 67ff (the disputes between Labadie and the bishop of Bazas, Henri Litolfi-Maroni in 1645); Le Fougeray, Arch. de la Visitation, *MS.* "Lettres spirituelles de Loudun," vol. 2, fol. 988ff (the judgment of the new bishop, Samuel Martineau, in 1652, on the convent, "spoiled" by Labadie). See the curious *Lettre du R. P. Antoine Sabré, prêtre et religieux solitaire, écrite au Sr Labadie . . .* (Bazas, 1651) (Sabré, the superior at the Hermitage d'Agen, is among the "seduced"); and some not very crucial details in A. de Lantenay [M. Bertrand], *Labadie et le carmel de Gravelle* (Bordeaux, 1886).

43. Labadie, *La Solitude chrestienne, ou la vie retirée du siècle* (Paris: S. Piquet, 1645), 79, 142.

44. See above, 20–21.

45. Luke 12:51; see Matt. 10:34.

46. See Labadie, *Le bon usage de l'Eucharistie* (Montauban: P. Bertié, 1656), a long thesis, notable for its mystic radicalism.

47. See *Déclaration de Jean de Labadie,* and *Lettre de Jean de Labadie à ses amis de la communion romaine touchant sa déclaration, divisée en deux parties dont la première leur fournit douze advis et motifs à ce qu'ils ne jugent pas son action injuste ou mauvaise; la seconde leur fournit douze autres advis ou moyens de se désabuser de l'erreur et de rencontrer la vérité* (Montauban: P. Braconier, 1651).

48. *Lettre de Jean de Labadie,* 36.

49. *Le grand chemin du jansénisme au calvinisme.*

50. Ibid., 15–16.

51. See Louis Marin, "Sémiotique du traître," *Sémiotique de la Passion. Topiques et figures* (Paris: DDB-Aubier, 1971), 97–186.

52. See Archivio Segreto Vaticano, Rome, Segreteria di Stato, Legazioni, Avignone, nos. 56, 173.

53. Description of "l'Abadie": "first Jesuit in the province of Vienne, then

Carmelite and hermit, finally Calvinist apostate and minister of that sect" (ibid., no. 56, p. 92).

54. "La corrotione del buono è pessima"; letter from G. N. Conti to the Vatican Secretary, 20 Nov. 1658, ibid., no. 56, p. 60.

55. Dated from London, 24 Oct. 1658; ibid., no. 56, p. 72.

56. State Archives, Geneva, Department of the National Protestant Church, Cp. Past., R. no. 11 (1658–65), "Registre de la Cie des pasteurs et professeurs de l'Eglise et Académie de Genève," fols. 75–76, 77; hereafter called "Registre de la Cie."

57. Ibid., fol. 78.

58. Ibid., fols. 78–80.

59. Ibid., fol. 81.

60. Ibid., fols. 85–86, 100.

61. Ibid., 30 Dec. 1659, fols. 105–6.

62. [François Mauduit], *Advis charitable à Messieurs de Genève touchant la vie du Sieur Jean Delabadie* (Lyon, 1662), republished in H. H. Bolsec, *La Vie, mort et doctrine de Jean Calvin* (Lyon: A. Offray, 1664). According to "Registre de la Cie," fol. 269 (30 Jan. 1663), Mauduit's second book, printed in Grenoble, is entitled: *Second Advis à Messieurs de Genève touchant le Sr Jean Delabadie.* I have not been able to find it.

63. "Registre de la Cie," fol. 274, 309, etc.

64. See M. Queckbörner, *Ph. J. Speners Reformtätigkeit in Frankfurt/M. unter bes. Berücksichtigung seines Verhältnisses zu Jean de Labadie,* theology thesis (Mainz, 1960).

65. For example, he holds "assemblies" evenings at home: Why, he is asked, after "a certain hour" does he close the door? Some pastors denounce him for folding his hands when saying the Lord's prayer (an evangelical text) and unfolding them when saying the "symbol of the apostles" (an ecclesiastical text). He therefore reproaches them with "having a passion against him." See "Registre de la Cie," fols. 243–51 (July–Sept. 1662).

66. Labadie, *La Puissance ecclésiastique bornée à l'Ecriture et par elle* (Amsterdam: J. Van Elsen, n.d.), 140.

67. "Épître dédicatoire," *La Puissance ecclésiastique,* quoted in Kolakowski, *Chrétiens sans Eglise,* 794.

68. See Elisabeth Labrousse, *L'Entrée de Saturne au Lion. L'éclipse de soleil du 12 août 1654* (The Hague: Nijhoff, 1974).

69. Van Berkum, *De Labadie en de Labadisten* (2:204) shows that Labadie died without having been married, despite claims he was married to a Miss Van der Haer, or a Miss Sommelsdijk, or Anna Maria Van Schurman.

70. A. M. Van Schurman, *Eukleria seu Melioris partis electio. Tractatus brevem vitae ejus delineationem exhibens* (Altona, 1673).

71. Ibid., 60–65, 108ff. One finds, in other writers of the period, the *vision* of a primal "hatred" in God, but in Van Schurman that experience seems to have been *auditory.*

72. See Jakob Böhme, *Mysterium Magnum,* chaps. 3, 11, etc.

73. See Labadie, *L'arrivée apostolique aux Eglises, représentée par celle de*

*l'apostre saint Paul aux Eglises de Rome et de Corinthe* (Middelburg: J. Misson, 1667), and the sermon delivered in Amsterdam on 15 May 1667: *L'Idée d'un bon pasteur et d'une bonne Église* (Amsterdam: A. Wolfgang, 1667).

74. Labadie, *Extrait de quelques propositions erronées et scandaleuses couchées dans le livre du Sr. Louys Wolzogen, ministre de l'église walone d'Utrecht* (n.p., n.d. [1668]).

75. Ibid., 7–13, 31. See also Kolakowski, *Chrétiens sans Église,* 750–55.

76. Labadie, *Quatorze remarques importantes sur le jugement prononcé par le synode walon tenu à Naerden le 5 de Sept. 1668* (n.p., n.d.). It was during this trial that Samuel Des Marets (who was, along with his brother, a member of the synod that ousted Labadie) anonymously published *Histoire curieuse de la vie, de la conduite et des vrais sentiments du Sr Jean de Labadie dont le nom et la réputation font tant de bruit parmi les gens de bien* (The Hague: Th. Duurcant, 1670), 375 pages of accusations.

77. See soon, among countless other examples, Fénelon himself in his letter "Sur la lecture de l'Ecriture sainte en langue vulgaire [On the Reading of the Holy Writ in the Vulgar Tongue]," *Oeuvres complètes* (1848), 2:190–201: "Listening to the pastors who explain the Scriptures is the same thing as reading them," for, "the pastors are the living Scriptures."

78. See Herman Witsius and Johannes Van der Waeijen, *Ernstige betuiginge der Gereformeerde Kercke aen hare afdwalende Kinderen* (Amsterdam, 1670), a "Pietist" refutation of Labadie, and James Tanis, *Dutch Calvinistic Pietism in the Middle Colonies* (The Hague: Nijhoff, 1967), 135–62.

79. Especially, of course, Van Berkum, *De Labadie en de Labadisten* (2:1–174), exploited by all the historians.

80. Jacob Dittelbach, *Verval en Val der Labadisten* (Amsterdam, 1692). It is a second edition, a success.

81. Quoted in Marthe Van der Does, *Antoinette Bourignon. Sa vie (1616–1680). Son oeuvre* (Groningen, 1974), 132.

82. See Max Wieser, *Peter Poiret, der Vater der romanischen Mystik in Deutschland* (Munich: G. Müller, 1932), 52–53. On Poiret, see also above, 215–16, and Marjolaine Chevallier, *Pierre Poiret (1646–1719). Métaphysique cartésienne et spiritualité* . . . (The Hague: Nijhoff, 1975).

83. *Veritas sui vindex, seu solemnis fidei Declaratio Joh. de Labadie, Petri Yvon, Petri du Lignon, Pastorum* (Hervord, 1672). The work also includes a "tractatus" on "the essential and multiple difference between Us and those called Quaker"a pamphlet against the "sect," which public opinion associates with Labadie's "Us."

84. See *Journal of Jasper Danckaerts, 1679–1680,* ed. B. B. James and F. Jameson (New York: Barnes & Noble, 1959), a rather remarkable travel journal, and also James, *The Labadist Colony in Maryland* (Baltimore: Johns Hopkins University Press, 1899).

85. Labadie, *Saintes Décades de quatrains de piété chrestienne par M. D. L.* (Amsterdam: Vve J. Bruyning, 1680).

86. Labadie, *Le Triomphe de l'Eucharistie* (Amsterdam: A. Wolfgang, 1667), 17. Kolakowski considers these poems without "the slightest poetic

authenticity" amd "terribly pedantic" (*Chrétiens sans Eglise,* 795–96). There are less severe judges: see Jean Rousset, "Un Brelan d'oubliés," *L'Esprit créateur* (Minneapolis, 1961), 1:91–100, or already A. Cherel, in *RHLF* (1911): 823.

87. See the panorama of this historiography, "Jean de Labadie et la conscience religieuse au XVIIe siècle, État de la question," presented by Fabrizio Frigerio at the Colloque de L'Institut d'histoire de la Réforme, Geneva, 17 May 1976, photocopy, 32 pp.

88. G.W. Leibniz, reading notes of 1695, *Textes inédits,* ed. Grua (Paris: PUF, 1948), 1:93. See also Leibniz's letter to Morell, 10 Dec. 1696, ibid., 1:105.

89. René Descartes, *Les Principes de la philosophie,* 2.21, in *Oeuvres et lettres,* ed. A. Bridoux (Paris: Pléiade, 1953), 623.

90. *Déclaration de Jean de Labadie,* 1666, 64, 86.

91. Ibid., 68.

92. Descartes, *Discours de la méthode,* in *Oeuvres et lettres,* 136.

93. See chapter 4.

94. See Bernard Gorceix, *Flambée et agonie. Mystiques du XVIIe siècle à Memand* (Sisteron: Présence, 1977), 157–228.

95. See the report, unfortunately unpublished, by M. J. Shatzmiller at the Colloque de Toronto on Marranism, 30 April–1 May 1979.

96. See above, 80ff.

97. See above, 142.

98. Yves Bonnefoy, *Hier régnant désert* (Paris: Mercure de France, 1964), 14.

99. See vol. 2 of the present work, forthcoming.

100. See the remarks of Rosario Assunto, *Infinita contemplazione. Gusto e filosofia dell'Europa barocca* (Naples, 1979), 89–113.

### Overture to a Poetics of the Body

1. Catherine Pozzi, *Poèmes* (Paris: Gallimard, 1959), 15–16.

2. Hadewijch d'Anvers, *Écrits mystiques,* trans. (Paris: Seuil, 1954), 134.

3. Ibid., 141.

4. [Oblique allusion to A. Rimbaud's poem "The Drunken Boat." – Trans.]

# Index

Made in the USA
Middletown, DE
10 January 2016